LANGUAGE, HERMENEUTIC & HISTORY

LANGUAGE, HERMENEUTIC & HISTORY

Theology after Barth and Bultmann

James M. Robinson

CASCADE *Books* • Eugene, Oregon

LANGUAGE, HERMENEUTIC, AND HISTORY
Theology after Barth and Bultmann

Copyright © 2008 James M. Robinson. All rights reserved. Except for brief quotations in critical publications or reviews, no part of this book may be reproduced in any manner without prior written permission from the publisher. Write: Permissions, Wipf and Stock, 199 W. 8th Ave., Suite 3, Eugene, OR 97401.

Cascade Books
A Division of Wipf and Stock Publishers
199 W. 8th Ave., Suite 3
Eugene, OR 97401

ISBN 13: 978-1-59752-881-8

Cataloging-in-Publication data:

Robinson, James McConkey, 1924–

    Language, hermeneutic, and history : theology after Barth and Bultmann / James M. Robinson.

    x + 250 p. ; 23 cm. Includes bibliographic references

    ISBN 13: 978-1-59752-881-8

    1. Hermeneutics. 2. Bible—Hermeneutics. 3. Theology, Doctrinal—History—20th century. 4. Theology—Methodology. 5. Barth, Karl, 1886–1968. 6. Bultmann, Rudolf, 1884–1976. 7. Ebeling, Gerhard, 1912–. 8. Fuchs, Ernst, 1903–. 9. Heidegger, Martin, 1889–1976. 10. Ott, Heinrich, 1929–. 11. Pannenberg, Wolfhart, 1928–. I. Title.

BT15 R63 2008

Manufactured in the U.S.A.

Contents

Abbreviations vii

Introduction ix

1 The German Discussion of the Later Heidegger 1

  Bibliography 1 64

2 Hermeneutic since Barth 69

  Bibliography 2 138

3 Revelation as Word and as History 147

  Bibliography 3 232

  Index of Names 241

  Index of Scripture 245

  Index of Key Foreign Words and Phrases 247

Abbreviations

AHAW	Abhandlungen der Heidelberger Akademie der Wissenschaften, Philosophisch-historische Klasse
ANQ	*Andover Newton Quarterly*
ATANT	Abhandlungen zur Theologie des Alten und Neuen Testament
BHTh	Beiträge zur historischen Theologie
CBQ	*Catholic Biblical Quarterly*
ChrW	*Christliche Welt*
EvTh	*Evangelische Theologie*
FKDG	Forschungen zur Kirchen- und Dogmengeschichte
FRLANT	Forschungen zur Religion und Literatur des Alten und Neuen Testaments
IB	*Interpreter's Bible*. 12 vols. Edited by George A. Buttrick. Nashville: Abingdon, 1951–57
IDB	*Interpreter's Dictionary of the Bible*. 4 vols. Edited by George A. Buttrick. Nashville: Abingdon, 1962
Int	*Interpretation*
JBL	*Journal of Biblical Literature*
JBR	*Journal of Bible and Religion*
JTC	*Journal for Theology and the Church*
KRS	*Kirchenblatt für die reformierte Schweiz*
KD	*Kerygma und Dogma*
McCQ	*McCormick Quarterly*
MPT	*Monatschrift für Pastoraltheologie*
NKZ	*Neue kirchliche Zeitschrift*
NZZ	*Neue Zürcher Zeitung*

PG	*Patrologiae cursus completus, Series graeca.* 162 vols. Edited by J.-B. Migne. Paris: Frères, 1857–1886
PhR	*Philosophische Rundschau*
PRE	*Realencyklopädie für protestanische Theologie und Kirche.* Edited by Albert Hauck. Leipzig: Hinrichs, 1899
RGG²	*Die Religion in Geschichte und Gegenwart.* 2nd ed. 5 vols. Edited by Herman Gunkel and Leopold Zscharnack. Tübingen: Mohr/Siebeck, 1927
RGG³	*Die Religion in Geschichte und Gegenwart.* 3rd ed. 7 vols. Edited by Kurt Galling. Tübingen: Mohr/Siebeck, 1957–65
SHAW	Sitzungsberichte der Heidelberger Akademie der Wissenschaften, Philosophisch-historische Klasse
TDNT	*Theological Dictionary of the New Testament.* 10 vols. Edited by Gerhard Kittel and Gerhard Friedrich. Translated by Geoffrey Bromiley. Grand Rapids: Eerdmans, 1964–76
TB	*Theologische Bücherei*
TF	*Theologische Forschung*
ThSt	*Theologische Studien*
ThZ	*Theologische Zeitschrift*
TLZ	*Theologische Literaturzeitung*
TTo	*Theology Today*
TWNT	*Theologisches Wörterbuch zum Neuen Testament.* 10 vols. Edited by Gerhard Kittel and Gerhard Friedrich. Stuttgart, 1932–79
ZKT	*Zeitschrift für katholische Theologie*
ZST	*Zeitschrift für systematische Theologie*
ZTK	*Zeitschrift für Theologie und Kirche*
ZTKB	*Zeitschrift für Theologie und Kirche Beihefte*

Introduction

MY FATHER, A PRESBYTERIAN CHURCH HISTORIAN BY TRADE, SPENT A sabbatic semester just before World War II studying under Karl Barth at the University of Basel, Switzerland. Barth had, after all, written the Barmen Declaration on which the Confessing Church was built in Germany, which cost him his German professorship, leading to his return to his native Switzerland.

The issue of the day back then had been between Barth and the other leading (though now forgotten) Swiss theologian, Emil Brunner of Zürich (who had once been a visiting professor at Princeton Theological Seminary). The debate was over Brunner's argument that humans have an innate capacity to hear God's word, which Barth had repudiated as "works righteousness," in his famous pamphlet entitled simply *Nein!*[1] Obviously my father took Barth's side of the argument with Brunner. So, in 1947, right after the war, he sent my brother and myself to Basel to pick up where he had left off.

But things had changed somehow over the war years! Now German students studying in Basel were not even allowed to live in Switzerland. They could only live in the nearby German town of Lörrach and commute daily by streetcar to attend classes in Basel, so long as they went back over the border every evening. But, in addition to whatever other smuggling might have been involved, they smuggled into Basel the New Testament theology of Rudolf Bultmann: existentialistic interpretation

---

1. Barth, *Nein: Antwort an Emil Brunner* (Munich: Kaiser, 1934).

and demythologizing![2] As a result, I managed to slip away from Basel for the winter semester of 1950–51 to hear Bultmann in Marburg just before he retired. I oriented my 1952 dissertation to the bifurcation of dialectic theology into Barthian and Bultmannian alternatives.[3]

When I returned to Germany as a Visiting Professor at the University of Göttingen in the Summer Semester of 1959, I discovered that post-war theology had again already taken exciting new turns. So when I returned to America, I persuaded John B. Cobb Jr., my colleague at the then-new Claremont School of Theology in California, to join me in introducing these newest trends to America by means of a series of symposia: I would write an extensive introduction to each volume detailing one such new theology, and then American theologians would evaluate that European trend, and Cobb, along with the European theologian being discussed, would provide concluding assessments. The series was entitled New Frontiers in Theology: Discussions among Continental and American Theologians. We published three volumes in all: *The Later Heidegger and Theology* (1963), *The New Hermeneutic* (1964), and *Theology as History* (1967), featuring, respectively, Heinrich Ott, Ernst Fuchs and Gerhard Ebeling, and Wolfhart Pannenberg.

Since then, a good number of American colleagues have expressed appreciation for the series. It had appeared when they were first studying theology, and my lengthy introductions provided them with their first entry into the unknown dimensions of continental theology. Hence it has seemed useful to lift these introductions out of the three volumes and reprint them together, as a kind of survey of the roots of modern German-language theology. They did indeed provide a detailed documentation of that younger generation of theologians, as they emerged on the continent after World War II and shaped theology's course for the last half of the twentieth century.

2. Bultmann, *Theologie des Neuen Testaments*, Neue theologische Grundrisse (Tübingen: Mohr/Siebeck, 1948–53) = *Theology of the New Testament*, 2 vols., trans. Kendrick Grobel (New York: Scribner, 1951–55).

3. Robinson, *Das Problem des Heiligen Geistes bei Wilhelm Herrmann* (Marburg: Gleiser, 1952).

CHAPTER 1 | *The German Discussion of the Later Heidegger*

IMMEDIATELY AFTER THE SECOND WORLD WAR, JEAN-PAUL SARTRE PUB-lished a manifesto entitled "Existentialism Is a Humanism."[1] Thereupon Jean Beaufret of Paris wrote Martin Heidegger inquiring as to his position, to which Heidegger replied in the autumn of 1946 with an open "Letter on Humanism."[2] Here Heidegger explicitly repudiates the existentialism of Sartre, who only three years before, with the appearance of *Being and Nothingness,* had been hailed as Heidegger's French equivalent.

> Sartre on the contrary expresses the basic statement of existentialism thus: existence precedes essence. Here he takes *existentia* ("existence") and *essentia* ("essence") in the meaning current in metaphysics, which since the time of Plato has said that *essentia* precedes *existentia*. Sartre turns this sentence around. But the reversal of a metaphysical sentence remains a metaphysical sentence. As such it remains with metaphysics in the forgetfulness of being.[3]

Heidegger explains Sartre's failure to attain to the kind of thinking he himself intended as follows:

> The adequate reproduction of and participation in this other thinking that leaves subjectivity behind is indeed rendered dif-

---

1. Sartre, *L'Existentialisme est un Humanisme* (1946); *Existentialism* (1947).
2. Heidegger, "Brief über den Humanismus"; republished separately as *Über den Humanismus.*
3. Heidegger, *Über den Humanismus,* 17.

ficult by the fact that when *Being and Time* was published, the third Division of the first Part, entitled "Time and Being," was held back.⁴ In "Time and Being" everything is turned around. The Division in question was held back because thinking failed in adequately articulating this turn, and did not achieve its goal by means of the language of metaphysics.⁵

Although this comment seems to turn away from *Being and Time* as well as from Sartre, Heidegger also emphasizes the continuity in the turn from *Being and Time* to "Time and Being."

This turn is not an alteration of the standpoint of *Being and Time*. Rather it is only in the turn that the thought which was attempted arrives into the proximity of the dimension out of which *Being and Time* was experienced, though experienced out of the basic experience of the forgetfulness of being.⁶

Various kinds of ambiguous allusions to this turn have occurred in the writings of Heidegger ever since. In reply to a question as to whether he had changed his position, Heidegger answered:

I have forsaken an earlier position, not to exchange it for another, but because even the former position was only a pause on the way. What lasts in thinking is the way. And ways of thought conceal within them the mysterious factor that we can walk on them forwards and backwards; even the way back first leads us forward.⁷

The relevance for theology of this turn or change of position is made explicit by Heidegger himself. "As long as anthropological-sociological conceptualizing and the conceptualizing of existentialism are not over-

---

4. Heidegger, *Sein und Zeit*, First Half, appeared in *Jahrbuch für Philosophie und phänomenologische Forschung*. It has been republished separately. The English translation by John Macquarrie and Edward Robinson, *Being and Time* (1962) is based on the 8th German edition (1957), which contains minor alterations introduced in the 7th ed. of 1953. Cf. the outline of the total work as originally proposed, in *Sein und Zeit*, 39 = *Being and Time*, 64. Heidegger's address on "Time and Being" at the meeting of Old Marburgers in October 1962, held at Marburg, was apparently derived from the unpublished third Division of the first Part.

5. Heidegger, *Über den Humanismus*, 17.

6. Ibid.

7. Heidegger, *Unterwegs zur Sprache*, 98–99.

come and pushed to the side, theology will never enter into the freedom of saying what is entrusted to it."[8]

Although the turn in Heidegger's thought began to be debated in philosophical publications as early as 1953,[9] the relevance of this turn for theology was not immediately seen. Rather, Heidegger's thought continued to be treated by theologians generally as a single position that had already been classified.[10] Only in 1959 did the explosive potentialities of "the later Heidegger" for theology become evident, when a young Privat-Dozent at Basel, Heinrich Ott, presented a monograph[11] arguing that the later Heidegger shows us that the philosophy of Heidegger as a whole is more compatible with Barthian theology than with Bultmannian theology. The significance of this monograph was enhanced by Heidegger's positive appraisal of it.

The annual meeting of Bultmann's former pupils, the Old Marburgers,[12] chose as its topic the same year the relation of Heidegger to theology. This meeting was climaxed by a day-long seminar conducted by Heidegger on "Christian Faith and Thinking." He concluded by remarking that the door remains open for a nonmetaphysical God, and he proposed that the next year's meeting should continue the discussion under the theme, "New Testament Exegesis and Systematic Theology." This topic arose from the sentiment that if there is to be any theology at all it must be a nonspeculative clarification of faith from within faith, so that the need for systematic theology in addition to exegetical theology was put in question. The meeting of 1960[13] followed this proposal with a

---

8. From a letter to Heinrich Ott on the appearance of the latter's *Denken und Sein* (1959). Ott quotes the sentence in his essay, "What is Systematic Theology?"

9. Löwith, *Heidegger* (1953; 2nd ed. 1960). Citation is from the 2nd ed. See also Schulz, "Über den philosophiegeschichtlichen Ort Martin Heideggers."

10. Diem, *Gott und die Metaphysik* (1956), continued the traditional Barthian rejection of Heidegger, whereas the use of the later Heidegger by Friedrich Gogarten and Ernst Fuchs seemed to be merely a continuation of the traditional Bultmannian use of Heidegger. Cf. Gogarten, *Demythologizing and History* (1955; German ed. 1953); *The Reality of Faith: The Problem of Subjectivism in Theology* (1959; German ed. 1957). Fuchs, *Hermeneutik* (1954; 2nd ed. 1958), 62–72.

11. Ott, *Denken und Sein*.

12. This meeting of Old Marburgers was held at Höchst in Germany's Odenwald in October, 1959.

13. This meeting was held in the Kirchliche Hochschule in Bethel bei Bielefeld, Germany, in October, 1960.

paper on the New Testament by Herbert Braun[14] and one on systematic theology by Heinrich Ott.[15] Wilhelm Anz replied to this paper by Ott from a Bultmannian perspective.[16]

The debate begun at the 1960 meeting of Old Marburgers has been continued by Ernst Fuchs and Gerhard Ebeling. Fuchs published a highly critical review of Ott's book,[17] and this has been supplemented by contributions of his pupils.[18] In the semester following the meeting, Ebeling conducted a seminar on "The Philosophy of M. Heidegger and Theology" in which Heidegger himself participated. The theses presented by Ebeling have been published,[19] together with most of the papers just mentioned, in a special issue of the leading Bultmannian periodical, edited by Ebeling, *Zeitschrift für Theologie und Kirche*.

It is this debate about the later Heidegger in the German discussion that the present essay proposes to analyze.

I. THE LATER HEIDEGGER

The very fact that one speaks of the "later" Heidegger presupposes some turn in his career in terms of which the distinction of "early" and "late" is to be understood. This turn is both a movement within Heidegger's own thought and a movement within the understanding of Heidegger by his contemporaries. Walter Schulz opens his interpretation of the later Heidegger with a summary of the course of Heidegger's career in both these respects. The role of *Being and Time* is described as follows:

> The appearance of Heidegger's first larger work, *Being and Time* (1927), drew the attention of the philosophical world to this thinker. In contrast to the "existential misunderstanding," to the effect that Heidegger wished to describe or even proclaim the nihilistic, heroic man of the time just after the First World War, those who penetrated more deeply into this work recognized that here a new

---

14. Braun, "Die Problematik einer Theologie des Neuen Testaments."
15. Ott, "Was ist systematische Theologie?" = "What is Systematic Theology?"
16. Anz, "Verkündigung und theologische Reflexion."
17. Fuchs, "Denken und Sein?"
18. Jüngel, "Der Schritt züruck": 104–22. Jüngel was an assistant at the Kirchliche Hochschule in Berlin-Zehlendorf and then became instructor in New Testament in the theological house in the Russian Sector of Berlin. Helmut Franz, "Das Denken Heideggers und die Theologie." Franz had already published a small volume *kerygma und kunst*, which was a highly original attempt to theologize in the style of the later Heidegger.
19. Ebeling, "Verantworten des Glaubens."

beginning in philosophy was being attempted. Heidegger sought to overcome traditional ontology which defined man in terms of the way *things* are. He sought to do this by showing that man is a being of quite his own kind, namely *Dasein,* which in its being is concerned with its being and is this being. The so-called "existentialist analysis" of the first and only part of this work to appear sought to reveal the characteristics of this *Dasein,* the "existentials" in their inner connection. Yet it was at first less noticed that Heidegger had not carried through the existentialist analysis for its own sake, but rather in order to awaken anew the question as to the meaning of being. The phenomenological descriptions which in fact comprised the concrete content of the work were convincing even without this "background."[20]

When, two years later, two smaller works, *What is Metaphysics?*[21] and *Vom Wesen des Grundes,*[22] appeared, they hardly seemed to alter the current view of *Being and Time.* They merely seemed to be intended to clarify the metaphysics implicit in the existentialist analysis. *What is Metaphysics?,* which was built upon the analysis of anxiety in *Being and Time,* seemed merely to lay hold of the finitude of *Dasein,* which as "thrown projection" rests only upon itself. *Vom Wesen des Grundes* traced *Dasein* back to freedom as the inner source of its possibility. Hence both pamphlets seemed merely to be supporting the existentialist analysis of *Being and Time* by showing *Dasein* grounding itself transcendentally in itself. Though Heidegger[23] has suggested that his lecture of 1930 "On the Essence of Truth" gave some insight into the turn in his thought, this

---

20. Schulz, "Über den philosophiegeschichtlichen Ort Martin Heideggers," 65–66.

21. Heidegger, *Was ist Metaphysik?* (1929; 8th ed., 1960). A Postscript was added in 1943, an Introduction in 1949. The English translation by R. F. C. Hull and Alan Crick in *Existence and Being* (1949) contains the lecture (353–80) and the Postscript (380–92). *Existence and Being* is also published as a Gateway Paperback Edition (1960). The lecture appears on 325–49 and the Postscript on 349–61 in this edition. The Introduction is translated by Walter Kaufmann, "The Way Back into the Ground of Metaphysics," in *Existentialism from Dostoevsky to Sartre,* 206–21.

22. Heidegger, *Vom Wesen des Grundes* appeared in 1929 in the *Festschrift* for E. Husserl and also as a separate pamphlet. The 2nd ed. was published in 1931; the 4th ed. was published in 1955. There also appeared in 1929 *Kant und das Problem der Metaphysik* (1929; 2nd ed. 1951). This book has been subjected to wide criticism by Kant scholars—criticism which Heidegger accepts in the preface to the 2nd ed.

23. Heidegger, *Über den Humanismus,* 17.

lecture was published only in 1943,[24] and, as Schulz has shown,[25] the published form makes the turn more explicit than did the original lecture.

Heidegger's notorious address as Rector of the University of Freiburg in 1933 on "The Self-Assertion of the German University"[26] was still prior to the turn. But the lecture on "The Origin of the Work of Art" in 1935[27] and the lecture at Rome in 1936 on "Hölderlin and the Essence of Poetry"[28] reflected the turn taking place. The way in which this turn was experienced is reported by Schulz:[29]

> In connection with the commentaries on Hölderlin and the corresponding discussions of art, Heidegger took his departure from the tradition with a radicality that left far behind it the overcoming of the traditional approaches that the existentialist analysis of *Being and Time* had in certain respects carried through. Now the epoch of metaphysics, lasting from Plato to Nietzsche, is held to be an "error." To be sure, it is not an error to be condemned, or that could in principle have been avoided. Rather it is an error in which thinking was "led astray" by being. Being—this was now the center of Heidegger's thought. It was clear that Heidegger placed this concept of being—and the concept of the "holy," which was apparently somehow equivalent to it—at the center of his works, and that it was from this center that he dismantled[30] the tradi-

---

24. 3rd ed. Frankfurt: Klostermann, 1954. English translation, *Existence and Being*, 319–51; paperback ed., 292–324.

25. Schulz, "Über den philosophiegeschichtlichen Ort Martin Heideggers," 88–90.

26. Heidegger, *Die Selbstbehauptung der deutschen Universität* (1933). This lecture has not been reprinted. One importance of this lecture for the analysis of the turn in Heidegger's thought is that it reveals the extent to which the turn, which at some points seems so abstract, is related to the down-to-earth course of political reality. The renunciation of self-assertion in the later Heidegger is materially a repudiation of this lecture.

27. Heidegger, "Der Ursprung des Kunstwerkes."

28. Heidegger, *Hölderlin und das Wesen der Dichtung* (1937); reprinted in *Erläuterungen zu Hölderlins Dichtung*, 31–43. English translation by Douglas Scott in *Existence and Being*, 291–315; paperback ed. 270–91.

29. Schulz, "Über den philosophiegeschichtlichen Ort Martin Heideggers," 66.

30. The German verb *destruieren* and the noun *Destruktion* used by Heidegger in this connection are not fully equivalent to the English "destroy" and "destruction," for which one has as German equivalents *zerstören* and *Zerstörung*. Rather they suggest dismantling the history of metaphysics so as to learn from its inevitable defects and to lay bare its foundation. Löwith in *Heidegger*, 17, circumscribes the term *Destruktion* with the following: "dismantling to the point of exposing the foundations, and beyond that, undermining metaphysics as such."

tion so radically. But it was less clear exactly what he really meant with this term "being." The following publications and lectures,[31] which came one behind the other, each more extraordinary than the preceding, did not give any directly illuminating information, but increased the odd helplessness in which the scholarly world found itself with regard to Heidegger.[32]

Schulz brought order into this confusion by interpreting the turn in Heidegger's thought as the consistent, even necessary result of his having brought Western metaphysics to its ultimate outcome. German idealism had eliminated substance as an unalterable substratum in which selfhood

---

31. The postwar publications of Heidegger are as follows: *Platons Lehre von der Wahrheit: Mit einem Brief über den "Humanismus"* (1947; 2nd ed., 1954). The letter on humanism appeared separately as *Über den Humanismus* (1949). *Aus der Erfahrung des Denkens*, written in 1947 and published in 1954. *Der Feldweg* (1949; 2nd ed. 1956). *Vorträge und Aufsätze* (1954; 2nd ed. 1959).The pamphlet *Die Frage nach der Technik* (1962) is a reprint of the first essay in this volume. *Was heisst Denken?* (1954). "Ein Briefwechsel mit Martin Heidegger," in Emil Staiger, *Die Kunst der Interpretation* (1955; 2nd ed. 1957) 34-49. *Zur Seinsfrage* (1956; 2nd ed. 1959); English translation, *The Question of Being* (1958). *Was ist das—die Philosophie?* (1956); English translation, *What Is Philosophy?* (1958). *Gespräch mit Hebel* (1956). *Hebel—Der Hausfreund* (1957). *Identität und Differenz* (1957); English translation, *Essays in Metaphysics: Identity and Difference* (1960). *Der Satz vom Grund* (1957; 2nd ed. 1958). *Einführung in die Metaphysik* (1957; 2nd ed. 1958). English translation, *An Introduction to Metaphysics* (1959). *Gelassenheit* (1959; 2nd ed. 1960). *Unterwegs zur Sprache* (1959; 2nd ed. 1960). "Der Weg zur Sprache," in *Die Sprache*, reprinted in *Unterwegs zur Sprache*, 239-68. "Aufzeichnungen aus der Werkstatt," (1959). *Nietzsche*, 2 vols. (1961). "Aus einer Erörterung der Wahrheitsfrage" (1962). *Die Frage nach dem Ding* (1962).

32. Heidegger's bibliography does not facilitate clarity in tracing the course of his thought. There are two sources of difficulty. First, several volumes contain collected essays, many of which antedate by several years their publication in the collection (*Holzwege; Vorträge und Aufsätze; Identität und Differenz; Unterwegs zur Sprache*). Secondly, other volumes contain lectures and university courses given in the past but only recently published. These have been reworked before publication in such a way that the original version and the later revisions can hardly be distinguished (*Vom Wesen der Wahrheit; Einführung in die Metaphysik; Nietzsche*). Bibliographical remarks at the end of most volumes clarify these matters to some extent. The English reader suffers the additional handicap that most of the later writings remain untranslated, and he may be confused by the fact that the translation of the earlier Heidegger's major work, *Being and Time*, has much later been published. Furthermore, Heidegger's later concern for overcoming metaphysics has been obscured by the positive use of metaphysics in the titles of two recent English translations. One title, *Introduction to Metaphysics*, is the literal translation of the German title, but this title dates from 1935, when the first draft of this book was written. The second title, *Essays in Metaphysics: Identity and Difference*, is an expansion of the German title *Identität und Differenz*. The expansion is peculiarly misleading since the essays included are intended as the overcoming of metaphysics.

can be grounded and had instead viewed the mind as mediating itself in a dialectic movement. However, the later Schelling failed in his attempt to establish a ground in which this dialectic movement of the mind *is* itself grounded. As a result, there emerged the irreducible facticity of man's selfhood. Whereas Schelling and Kierkegaard attempted to ground this facticity of man in God, Heidegger accepted the irreducibility of that facticity as such, that is to say, he sought to interpret *Dasein* only in terms of its own structure. This problem of analyzing the whole of *Dasein* in terms of its own structure is resolved by the successive analyses of the existentials. "Being-in-the-world" is meaningful in terms of "care," and this in turn can be grounded in "temporality." But rather than providing a ground outside *Dasein*, temporality has been recognized as itself an existential. Put otherwise: To understand *Dasein* as "thrown" does not relate it to a "thrower" outside *Dasein*, but rather relates it to *Dasein's* own projection of itself. *Dasein* is grounded in *nothing* outside itself.

It is this "nothing" upon which *What is Metaphysics?* focuses attention, in answering the question of metaphysics as to what is beyond *Dasein*. *Dasein*, held out into nothing, is beyond all beings, and has in this sense attained ultimate transcendence, the goal of metaphysics. Transcendence beyond all beings leads neither to God, nor to the cosmos as the sum total of all beings, nor to an established Cartesian subject upon which a world of objects can be built, but rather to nothing. Thus the metaphysical question is answered in "nothing," and this answer to the metaphysical question is at the same time the end of metaphysics. For the outcome of the metaphysical question demonstrates the futility of the question, which consisted in seeking the "something" in which *Dasein* is grounded, whereas *Dasein* is in fact grounded in nothing. Heidegger's completion of metaphysics is the end of metaphysics.

The end of metaphysics is the experience of the ultimate impotence of *Dasein*. For the recognition that *Dasein* cannot transcend to a ground outside itself, but only to nothing, does not ground man in a Cartesian sense in himself, in self-reliance or Nietzsche's "will to power." Rather it involves the ultimate renunciation of one's role as the grounded subject that has both grasped its own ground and provided the ground for all other beings as its objects. For the nothing to which *Dasein* transcends is not at *Dasein's* disposal, but comes upon *Dasein* in anxiety, which is not fear of something specific, but rather a vague dread, simply being afraid—of *nothing*.

This ultimate impotence or facticity of *Dasein* leads Heidegger to give up the whole metaphysical attempt to ground *Dasein* outside itself, a renunciation that Heidegger calls "overcoming" metaphysics. This renunciation replaces a heroic self-assertion over against nothing. This is the turn in Heidegger's thought, necessitated by the course of that thought itself. Once this turn is made, the nothing that emerged when metaphysics sought to ground *Dasein* in something outside itself ceases to emerge as nothing, and, instead, *being* dawns. If it was metaphysics' engrossment with analyzing beings that prevented it from catching sight of being, then the arrival at nothing, by ending the engrossment with beings, corresponds to the unveiling of being.

This turn in direction brings with it a reversal of the basic mood of Heidegger's philosophy. Rather than calling man "the one who stands in nothing's place," Heidegger now speaks of him as the "shepherd of being." Instead of anxiety, there emerges gratitude for being's "favor." Once the Promethean direction of metaphysics is renounced, the positive emerges. "Renunciation does not take away, it gives."[33]

If Schulz interprets the turn in Heidegger's thought as the logically necessary outcome of Western metaphysics, with the implication that the follower of Heidegger, and indeed Western philosophy as a whole, must go along with Heidegger in this turn, Karl Löwith interprets the turn in Heidegger's thought as less the "consequence of his point of departure" than "the result of an about-face" equivalent to a conversion,[34] a move in which the consistent Heideggerian would hardly participate. For what is at stake is whether *Dasein* is to be grounded "in its own, 'authentic' being, or in the wholly other 'being,' which on its own initiative brings mankind's *Dasein* into its own."[35] There has been a decisive "shift of emphasis from *Dasein* which is resolved for itself and asserts itself in confrontation with 'nothing,' to being, which gives itself, and for whose understanding one's own *Dasein* was originally the 'foundation,' whereas, later, *Dasein*

---

33. Heidegger, *Der Feldweg*, 7.

34. Löwith, *Heidegger* (2nd ed.) 7. Whereas Schulz speaks of a *Kehre* ("turn"), Löwith speaks here of *Umkehr*, a term that uses the same root but implies more a reversal of direction with religious overtones, since it is the term also used to mean "repentance" (cf. "return" as the biblical term for repentance). On 21, Löwith describes the turn *in malam partem* as a religious "conversion" and "regeneration." Schulz, *Der Gott der neuzeitlicher Metaphysik* (2nd ed.) 54, also suggests that we have to do with "the secularized form of Christian conversion." Similarly, Diem, *Gott und die Metaphysik*, 18.

35. Löwith, *Heidegger* (2nd ed.), 7.

has merely to correspond to the claim of being and hence is no longer fundamental."[36] Löwith's interpretation amounts to saying the "existential misunderstanding" of *Being and Time* was the correct understanding of it, and that Heidegger has in old age given up that "heroic nihilism" and turned to religion as a "return to his theological beginning."[37]

The subtitle of Löwith's book, "thinker in a needy time," derived from Heidegger's characterization of Hölderlin as the poet who stands "in the no-more of the departed gods and the not-yet of the coming (God),"[38] is intended to suggest the later Heidegger's understanding of himself as the prophet of a new age marked by the imminent advent of being.[39] Such an eschatological hope is for Löwith no more than "wishful thinking";[40] and Heidegger's philosophizing in terms of an understanding of his time is for Löwith little better than keeping in step with the fads, far beneath the timeless "primal wisdom of the Greeks."[41]

If authentic existence had meant anticipating one's own death, the urgent need for our times is now seen to consist in recovering the dimension of the whole and the holy. The original claim to be initiating a "universal phenomenological ontology" as a scientific philosophy has given way; that is to say, Heidegger has given up the attempt to provide a phenomenological basis for his view, and positions are merely asserted, when not simply veiled in silence. Heidegger's thinking has become a meditation, and even a thanking of being for its favor in unveiling itself. Language is no longer understood as the articulation of the intelligibility of our "being-in-the-world," but is rather the "house of being." Resolve is no longer the determination to be oneself rather than being an imper-

---

36. Ibid., 17–18 n. 2.

37. Ibid., 21. On 20, when Löwith remarks that no one can honestly claim to understand what Heidegger means by "being," he adds: "Those who will come nearest to understanding it are believers, who think they find in Heidegger's ontological talk of 'revelation' and 'unveiling' an access to the Christian revelation of a God who too is not a being—believers who as such do not pretend to comprehend with the reason the God of revelation." In a footnote he indicates how Heidegger's *Habilitationsschrift* of 1916, *Die Kategorien- und Bedeutungslehre des Duns Scotus*, says in theological language what the later Heidegger is saying in terms of "being."

38. Heidegger, *Erläuterungen zu Hölderlins Dichtung* (2nd ed.), 44.

39. Löwith, *Heidegger* (2nd ed.), 12.

40. Ibid., 17.

41. Ibid., 12. One may recall Löwith's volume, *Meaning in History*, in which the philosophical concern for history is traced back to primitive Christian eschatology.

sonal "one," but, by an etymological play on words, means one's openness to being.[42] Freedom is no longer understood as one's ability to be, but rather as one's letting being be. The meaning of being has been replaced by the "truth" or unveiling of being.[43]

Löwith's basic protest is that Heidegger has not adequately conceded this reversal of position, but has in later years reinterpreted his earlier position to make it conform to his later position.[44] Löwith quotes *Being and Time* to the effect that it attempts a hermeneutic of *Dasein* because existence is the point from which philosophical inquiry arises and to which it returns. Having thus quoted *Being and Time* as intending existentialism, Löwith proceeds to contrast this original meaning of the basic categories of *Being and Time* with the meaning the later Heidegger has found in them, especially in his "Letter on Humanism" of 1946. In *Being and Time* man is defined as *Dasein* because his essence is "there-ness," the fact that he is and has to be himself; in the "Letter on Humanism" man is *Da-sein* because he is where being becomes clear, where its "there-ness" emerges. "Care" is no longer primarily *Dasein*'s concern for its own being, but rather has become care for being in and of itself. *Dasein*'s burden, in that it rests upon itself, has been replaced by gratitude for being's favor. "Existence" is no longer transcending oneself in projecting one's world, but, as "ek-sistence," means "ec-statically" standing-out into the truth of being. Man's thrown-ness is no longer the brute facticity of his being there, in terms of which he must in resolve project his existence, but is a throw of being, suggesting man's nearness to being. Hence the correlative term "projection" no longer refers to man's resolute laying hold of the existence that lies before him, but refers rather to being's act of sending man into ek-sistence, into openness to being, as his true nature. Anxiety in confrontation with nothing turns into shyness in the presence of being. The self-assertion of a *Dasein* responsible for itself gives way to "sacrifice" for the sake of preserving the truth of being.

---

42. By emphasizing the prefix in *Ent-schlossenheit*, Heidegger suggests the negation of *Verschlossenheit*, which means being closed or shut up in oneself.

43. Löwith, *Heidegger* (2nd ed.), 8–18. In this last instance Löwith concedes that already in *Being and Time* the concept "meaning" had been divorced from existential meaning when it was defined as the "horizon of projection."

44. Löwith, *Heidegger* (2nd ed.), 18 n. 2.

If *Being and Time* could say that "only so long as there is *Dasein*, is there being," the "Letter on Humanism" interprets this sentence to mean that only so long as being gives itself is there *Dasein*.[45]

Löwith, one of Heidegger's outstanding pupils of the twenties, returned to Germany in 1952 after teaching *Being and Time* as existentialism for eighteen years in Rome, Japan, and the United States, and indeed in Heidegger's own Marburg from 1928 to 1934.[46] It is understandable that he should take offense at Heidegger for having changed the official interpretation of the work that is at the basis of Löwith's own position. This relation of Löwith to the turn in Heidegger's thought is in interesting contrast to that of Heinrich Ott. If the "Letter on Humanism" was for the mature Löwith Heidegger's postwar repudiation of Heideggerianism, it was for the youthful Ott, then in his last year of studies at the *Gymnasium* in Basel, a first introduction to Heidegger. What was for Löwith an unfortunate reinterpretation was for Ott simply Heidegger's authoritative statement, a solid basis on which to enter into a valid understanding of his thought. And this basis seemed to suggest a more obvious correlation with Barthian theology, which Ott was already reading, than with Bultmannian theology, which had laid claim on Heidegger. It is thus as a spokesman for the later Heidegger and Barthian theology that Heinrich Ott subsequently emerged. For him "the later Heidegger" includes both the concept of a turn in Heidegger's career and the validity of the reinterpretation of *Being and Time* that brings it into a more direct relation to the position after the turn.

Ott summarizes the main lines or the movements in Heidegger's thought as follows: "The point of departure for the question of being is in the existentialist analysis of *Being and Time*; then comes the turn, that shift which becomes perceptible in Heidegger's postwar publications and which is characterized by a far-reaching change in point of view as well as in the methods of thought and in terminology, yet with an unaltered

---

45. The original German sentence was "Nur solange Dasein ist, gibt es Sein." The German idiom "es gibt," literally "it gives," means "there is." This indefinite "there" or "it" is identified with being, in the sense that being gives or unveils itself. Thus Heidegger's interpretation of what the sentence means is technically a meaning that could be associated with the sentence, but is hardly what Heidegger meant when he wrote the sentence in *Being and Time*. Cf. Löwith, *Heidegger* (2nd ed.), 22–28.

46. On 21, Löwith comments bluntly: "After all it was no mere misunderstanding, when so many hearers of Heidegger's lectures and readers of *Being and Time* understood the author then differently from the way he understands himself today."

theme."[47] Ott's first objective in his presentation of Heidegger is to interpret *Being and Time* as an analysis of *Dasein* whose only purpose is to provide a point of departure for the question of being, the unaltered theme of Heidegger's whole career. Put negatively, Ott's objective is to show that the direction even of *Being and Time* is misunderstood when its analysis of *Dasein* is seen as an end in itself, as might be the case in existentialism. Put polemically, his objective is to show that the Bultmannian use even of *Being and Time* is only to a certain degree legitimate, in that Bultmann used *Being and Time* in terms of a concern and a purpose different from that of Heidegger. Thus, although Ott emphasizes the turn in Heidegger's thought and builds primarily upon the later Heidegger, he would, at least by implication, maintain that a position built upon the later Heidegger could lay claim to the early Heidegger with more appropriateness than can Bultmannian theology. In substance this amounts to a preference for the interpretations of *Being and Time* by Walter Schulz and the later Heidegger himself rather than for those by Karl Löwith and the handbooks on existentialism.

Ott traces the turn through three interrelated dimensions of Heidegger's thought: the turn from nothing to being, the overcoming of metaphysics, and the "step backwards."

The stages in the turn with regard to the first of these dimensions may be summarized as follows. Still within the earlier period, in his inaugural address at the University of Freiburg in 1929 on *What is Metaphysics?*, Heidegger introduced the concept of "nothing." This theme was foreign to *Being and Time*; yet *What is Metaphysics?* carried it through in the method characteristic of *Being and Time*, namely, in an analysis of the situation of *Dasein*. Then in the Postscript to that address, written in 1943, and in the Introduction to it, written in 1949, nothing is brought increasingly into relation to being. Thus the history of being—the forgetfulness of being in metaphysics, the end of metaphysics in nothing, the replacement of nothing with being once metaphysics is renounced—gradually emerges as the central theme of the later Heidegger.

The address of 1929 analyzes the situation of the *Dasein* of the university audience, i.e., of science itself. Science is concerned with establishing what is, and nothing else. Thus science inevitably has to do with the concept of "nothing." However, this inevitable emergence of the concept

---

47. Ott, *Denken und Sein*, 26–27.

within science does not mean that nothing is merely negation by reason. Nothing is not first constituted by a logical inference of nonexistence. Rather, nothing is rooted in a region prior to logical inference, in *Dasein* itself. *Dasein* is inevitably characterized by anxiety, which is not fear of a specific danger but rather a vague dread in which the very givenness of beings ceases to be a matter of course, and their contingency, the oddity that they are at all, is sensed. *Dasein*'s anxiety brings home the question, "Why are there beings at all, and not, rather, nothing?" Anxiety is not fear of something, but of nothing. Thus anxiety reveals nothing, and in so doing reveals beings as beings, that is, draws attention to the really rather surprising fact that there are things at all—which is thus seen to be anything but a matter of course. Thus anxiety, by revealing beings as beings (via the concept "nothing"), makes science possible. Nothing, given in *Dasein* prior to all logical operations, is the condition of the possibility of the form of *Dasein* called science.

In the Postscript of 1943 Heidegger raises the question whether this nothing, which is by its very nature not a being, is not actually being itself. For the being of beings is by *its* very nature not a being. "This which is wholly other than all beings is that-which-is-not. But this nothing functions as being." Somewhat more carefully formulated, "nothing, as that which is other than the beings, is the veil of being."[48] Nothing, by pointing to the contingency of the beings, draws our attention to their being, so that the possibility of their not being functions as a veil through which we catch sight of the surprising fact that they are. Being dawns upon us first as a question to ponder, that is, in the form of nothing. Yet this unveiling of being is increasingly described positively as the occurrence of being itself, as the voice of being calls upon us, revealing the beings as being, that is, unveiling being as "the marvel of all marvels, that beings are."[49] Here one observes the turn taking place, as the emergence of being in the move from nothing to being.

The condition of the possibility of *Dasein* confronting the being of beings had been located simply in the fact that *Dasein* is suspended in nothing. But when thus confronted by nothing, the prior condition of the possibility of *Dasein* actually confronting the being of beings is now seen to be that being gives itself to *Dasein* even more basically than *Dasein* is

---

48. Heidegger, *Was ist Metaphysik?* (8th ed.), 45, 51 = *Existence and Being*, 384, 392; paperback ed., 353, 360.

49. Ibid., 45–46 = *Existence and Being*, 386; paperback ed., 355.

held out into nothing.⁵⁰ Thus the flow of Heidegger's thinking has turned: rather than thought moving via *Dasein* to being, being moves to *Dasein* and thus into thought. Prior to the turn, thinking is conceived as basically derived from *Dasein*'s initiative; after the turn, thinking is envisaged as given to *Dasein* by the initiative of being.

The turn in Heidegger's thought in terms of overcoming metaphysics is externally documented by the observation that up through the address of 1929 on *What is Metaphysics?* and the lecture course, *An Introduction to Metaphysics*, given in 1935, the term metaphysics was used in a positive sense. This suggests that Heidegger initially proposed to purify and thus revitalize metaphysics. But in his subsequent writings the term tends increasingly to be used in a pejorative sense. Heidegger now conceives of his task as that of "overcoming metaphysics," which is the title he chose when publishing his notes on the topic dating from 1936-1946.⁵¹ Heidegger in retrospect even defines his essay *What is Metaphysics?* as moving beyond metaphysics, and actually as involved in overcoming metaphysics. He explains the ambiguity: "It belongs to the nature of such transitions that they to a certain extent must still speak the language of what they are helping to overcome."⁵²

Heidegger's criticism of metaphysics can be summarized as follows: Metaphysics is *Dasein*'s effort to ground itself, so that all beings are ultimately grounded in some supreme being, itself an uncaused cause (*causa sui*). The investigation of this problem has been the traditional task of ontology. Since this supreme being was often conceived of by metaphysics as God, Heidegger speaks of "the onto-theo-logical nature of metaphysics."⁵³ Furthermore, metaphysics, especially since Descartes, is an objectifying kind of thought in which the subject establishes itself as the basis of reality and builds the world of reality upon itself. The subject forms propositions (*Vorstellungen*) by placing the object before it (*vor-stellen*), the result of which is that reality becomes only the subject's picture, his world view. It is in this context that Heidegger understands modern science and technology as the outcome of metaphysics. Here man's relation

---

50. Ott, *Denken und Sein*, 82-83.

51. "Überwindung der Metaphysik," in *Vorträge und Aufsätze* (1954), 71-99.

52. Heidegger, *Was ist Metaphysik?* (8th ed.), "Nachwort," 43 = *Existence and Being*, "Postscript," 380-81; paperback ed., 350.

53. Cf. "Die onto-theo-logische Verfassung der Metaphysik," in *Identität und Differenz*, 35-73 = *Essays in Metaphysics*, 33-67.

to nature is no longer that of finding a *modus vivendi* in conformity to nature, but rather that of obliging nature to assume a shape assigned to it by man. Western metaphysics has on the one hand produced a concept of God that the modern world has rejected, so that "God is dead," and on the other hand has produced a technological scientific progress that has become the world's fate.

The positive achievement of *Being and Time* consists in having posed once and for all the question of the meaning of being, and in having taken the first step in limiting the pervasive subjectivity of objectifying conceptualization by rooting objective thought in something more primal than a metaphysically understood subject. Instead, thought is rooted in the structure of *Dasein,* as when science is rooted in the existentialist category "being-in-the-world." Thus, when the turn in Heidegger's thought is defined as the overcoming of metaphysics, *Being and Time* can itself be defined as already beginning this turn, although it is clearly not yet around the turn. Rather the defect of *Being and Time* lies in its "failure to recognize that there is thought that is more rigorous than conceptual thought."[54] To force being into a concept is precisely not to understand the truth of being. It was in fact such conceptualizing thinking that had led the West into forgetting being.

Heidegger concedes to metaphysics that it is an effort at thinking "beyond" *(meta-)* beings in order to conceptualize them as such, i.e., as beings. To the extent that metaphysics is aware of beings as beings, it senses them as being. It investigates beings in the light of their being. But it does not directly face the light itself, it does not direct itself to the problem of being as such. Or, to change the figure, if philosophy is a tree whose roots are metaphysics (Leibniz), Heidegger would direct attention to the soil in which the roots grow. This light or this soil is the condition of the possibility of metaphysics. At the same time it constitutes the limitation of metaphysics, in that metaphysics does not concern itself with this presupposition of its own occurrence.

This light or soil is, of course, being itself. Metaphysics, in its concern with beings, does recognize them as being, and to this extent senses the being of beings. But here "being" is a static concept, expressed by the German abstract noun, *Seiendheit,* which one might better translate "being-ness." Metaphysics does not really understand the true nature of

---

54. Heidegger, *Über den Humanismus,* 41.

being, and hence can be spoken of as "forgetting being." For being in its true sense Heidegger uses the verbal noun, *Sein*.

Now the "essence" of being is its happening. The German word here translated "essence" is *Wesen*, a Middle High German infinitive meaning "to be" (compare the Old High German and Anglo-Saxon, *wesan*). This term survives today only as the German past participle, *gewesen* ("been") and as the English past tense "was." The original Indo-Germanic meaning is reflected in the Indian root *vas*, meaning "remain," "abide," "reside," "camp." Heidegger uses the term in this verbal sense of coming to reside, arriving, taking place. Thus being essentially takes place—and this is what metaphysics had ignored. In Heidegger's more recent writings the verbal noun *Anwesen*, where the prefix accentuates the temporal meaning of arriving, tends to replace the verbal noun *Sein*. The "being of beings" is formulated "the arriving of what arrives" (*das Anwesen des Anwesenden*).[55]

The same point is made by another etymological reflection, which is involved in the statement that metaphysics does not reach the truth of being. For metaphysics conceives of truth as the correspondence of the subject's concept and the object's reality (*adaequatio rei ad intellectum*).[56] But originally truth is un-hiddenness, un-veiling. The Greek term for truth is *alētheia*, composed of the negating *alpha* privative and the root of the verb *letho* or *lanthano*, which means to escape notice, to be hidden, or, in the middle and passive, to forget. Thus being's truth is its no longer escaping notice, its unveiling, the act of its making itself known.

The essence of being and the truth of being tend to converge in Heidegger's focal understanding of being as an event of unveiling or revealing. This event of being has to do both with beings and with thought. It is this understanding of being that is involved in overcoming metaphysics and arriving at non-conceptual thought.

Non-conceptual thinking may seem at first sight to be a contradiction in terms, in that words are after all inseparable from concepts. Yet Heidegger's later thinking is non-conceptual in that it does not think of

---

55. Cf., for example, Heidegger, *Unterwegs zur Sprache*, 122.

56. In *Vom Wesen der Wahrheit* (3rd ed., 1954) 8, Heidegger points out that this concept of truth originally meant the correspondence of created beings to the divine intellect, which provided the basis for assuming the correspondence of the human intellect to created beings. Only in the period of Cartesian subjectivism has the metaphysical concept to truth meant simply the correspondence of the objective world to man's intellect.

language as composed of or seeking after clearly defined and rationally fixed concepts, whose static and compartmentalized nature would insure their clarity. Rather Heidegger asks how it is that certain subject matters have come to be articulated with certain concepts. Rather than thinking of this as a somewhat arbitrary choice on the part of the thinker, who largely for convention's sake uses certain terms, Heidegger holds that the initiative resides in language—more exactly, in being as it calls forth language. By means of this primal call of being something happens to us, the subject matter of thought clarifies or obscures itself for us. Thought is not primarily our action, but something that comes upon us when being clears itself to our thought. A concept is the occurrence of the clearing or veiling of the subject matter. Thus each concept has its history—not just in retrospect as the history of ideas, but in itself, as the very nature of what a concept is. "Being" is not a fixed concept, but an occurrence that happens to us, something that dawns on us, and the various views about being that have been held over the centuries are the necessary result of the way in which being has on various occasions shown itself. This is a more primal grasp of the nature of thinking than that characteristic of the subject-object approach.

The overcoming of metaphysics is sometimes referred to by Heidegger as a "step backwards," the renunciation of the desire to produce a system of concepts and thus have a viewpoint. This step backwards refers neither to a return to an earlier position in the history of philosophy nor to some logical inference still to be drawn within conceptual thinking. Rather it has to do with the kind of movement involved in thinking. It involves thinking back behind opinions and viewpoints into the dimension out of which the subject matter of thought comes to encounter us. It is the return to the soil out of which metaphysics grew.

To be sure, such a step backwards is extremely difficult. Heidegger's effort to take this step makes use of the combination of two paths. The one consists in including the background of the concepts, their history, even their sound, within concepts, so that they themselves are understood as historic. His frequent etymological play on words is not play, but is a serious effort at understanding. The other approach consists in a rapprochement of his thought to poetry. Heidegger holds that many poets, especially Hölderlin, Trakl, and Hebel, thought the subject matter of thought much more primally than did the metaphysical philosophers. Composing poetry and thinking being are two forms of language rooted in the same truth of being. Thus the poetic, hauntingly suggestive rather than conceptually explicit style of the later Heidegger is not to be seen as a weakening of his intellectual rigor, but rather as a serious experiment in a new mode of thought.

If the position of the early Heidegger could be focused by the Bultmannians upon the historicness of *Dasein*, Ott proposes to approach the position of the later Heidegger by focusing upon the history of being. Already in *Being and Time* Heidegger had argued that the question of being was to be pursued in terms of the history of ontology. Heidegger is "the thinker about thinking," as Ott puts it. In his seminar of 1959 on "Christian Faith and Thinking," Heidegger said that in his seminars and lectures he never thinks of matters in and of themselves, but only in their relatedness to specific historic events.[57] Insisting that one must think historically, he investigated the question as to what thinking is by inquiring what a specific thinker thought it to be.

Since in some respects Heidegger's emphasis upon thought as historic and upon his own role as a thinker about thought calls Hegel to mind, Heidegger's position gains sharper profile through his comparison of his own procedure with that of Hegel.[58] The subject matter of both Hegel's and Heidegger's thought is thought itself; but for Hegel this means the absolute concept, whereas for Heidegger the subject matter is the ontological difference between being and the beings. The nature of Hegel's treatment of the history of thought is "to take it up and resolve it" (*aufheben*) into the absolute truth, whereas Heidegger's stance toward the history of thought is characterized by the step backwards into the sphere overlooked by metaphysics. Thus, if Hegel focused his attention upon the thoughts of earlier thinkers, Heidegger proposes to penetrate through their thoughts to their subject matter, which Heidegger distinguishes from the thoughts themselves by referring to it as "what is not thought" (*das Ungedachte*). What is not thought is not simply nothing, but is rather the hidden power of thought, the subject matter that is never fully grasped in any thought. This subject matter of thought is both back of and ahead of thought. It is the origin and the goal of thought, the condition of the possibility of thought and the theme of thought. Thus

---

57. Cf. Heidegger's call for "perseverance in authentically historic thinking" and his criticism of "the increasing flight from the historic tradition"; *Der Satz vom Grund*, 138.

58. "Die Onto-theo-logische Verfassung der Metaphysik," in *Identität und Differenz*, 35–73 = *Essays in Metaphysics*, 33–67.

thought is encompassed, closed in on both sides, by its subject matter—a pattern that for Heidegger replaces the subject-object schema.

The basic experience out of which Heidegger philosophizes is amazement that thinking happens. Hence his concern with what is not thought is that it is "what is to be thought" (*das Zu-Denkende*), that which brings thought into motion. Hence what is not thought cannot simply be the various beings, since the existence of various entities does not in itself necessitate thought. Rather what is to be thought is being itself, in its distinctness from the beings, that is, in its ontological difference. This difference is not a separation, as if being were some entity alongside the beings. It is rather their being, seen in itself. Being speaks to us through the beings, by unveiling to us that they are. It is because of their being that beings become the theme of thought. It is this unveiling of the being of beings that sets thought in motion. Modern science, in that it has focused exclusively upon beings and has forgotten being, has, in the pregnant sense intended by Heidegger, ceased to think. For being and what is to be thought tend to converge.

Since the basic subject matter of thought is being, the history of thought is rooted in the history of being. Thinking takes place in the way being gives itself to be thought. Being, as the condition of the possibility of the history of thought, must itself have a history, must itself be historic. The epochs in the history of thought are basically epochs in the history of being. For being is not a static entity but an event. Hence Heidegger speaks of being in terms of *Lichtungsgeschichte*, "clearing history." Being, again and again, in different times and ways, clears out the underbrush of thinking so as to make itself clear to thought. If the truth of being is its unveiling of itself to thought, the history of being is the history of these clearings.

Since whether this happens or how it happens is not at the disposal of the thinker, thinking about being has a fate-like character. Heidegger speaks of the *Geschick* of being. This term, not to be confused with *Geschichte* (history), derives from the verb *schicken*, which means to send, ordain. (Compare the obsolete usage of the cognate English verb, "shift," meaning to distribute or apportion.) Thinking's lot is cast by being. Being speaks to thought, and what it speaks is thought's lot. Thus the noun *Geschick* is quite comparable to the English noun "fate," derived from the Latin *fatum*, meaning "what is spoken." Thus the historicness of thinking is often referred to with the adjective *geschicklich*, "fateful" (not to be confused with *geschichtlich*, "historic"). This adjective, though difficult to translate, refers to this fateful nature of thought, the dependence of thought upon what is sent into it. This may sound as if being were here hypostasized, but, since being is not itself a being, such an inference would be incorrect. Instead, the emphasis upon the activity of being rather than of thought is to be understood in terms of Heidegger's consistent effort to overcome the subjectivity of thought.

There is then a fate-laden movement in the course of Western thought. Being gave itself at different times differently to thought. It is the fate of thinking that being has been described in different periods with different terms, such as nature, truth, *logos*; just as the movement from the Greek meaning of *physis* to the Latin meaning of *natura* and to the modern scientific concept of "nature" is not simply a matter of philology but also and more basically a matter of clearing history.

The general course of this history is sketched by Heidegger in terms of the concepts used successively for being: "There is being only from occasion to occasion in this and that fate-laden contour: *physis, logos, hen, idea, energeia*, substantiality, objectivity, subjectivity, will, will to power, will to will."[59] This series of interpretations of being reflects the occurrence of being from early Greek thought via Plato and Aristotle to the Middle Ages, Descartes, German idealism, Nietzsche, and, finally, modern technology.

Why this clearing history is at the same time referred to by Heidegger as "forgetting being" can be made clear from his presentation of the beginning of this path with Plato and its end with technology. Whereas the Greek word for truth, *a-lētheia*, implies that truth is self-disclosure, Plato's parable of the cave treats truth as a function of the subject's point of view, that is, the question of truth becomes that of the correctness of one's view. This shifts the location of truth. It ceases to be a trait of the beings as they unveil themselves, and becomes a matter of the subject's approach to the beings.[60] Truth is subjugated to idea, which is etymologically related

---

59. Heidegger, *Identität und Differenz*, 64 = *Essays in Metaphysics*, 59.

60. Here we have a striking instance of the antithesis between what the term "Heidegger" symbolizes down to the present and what the later Heidegger himself maintains. Ernst Heitsch, the most theologically interested classical philologian of German today, has presented in the journal for classical philology, *Hermes*, a detailed refutation of the "subjectivistic" interpretation of *alētheia*, for whose popularity he holds "Heidegger" as popularly understood responsible, although he concedes this "subjectivistic" view

to the Greek infinitive *idein,* to see or view. Thus Heidegger identifies in Plato the origin of the secondary concept of truth as *adaequatio rei ad intellectum.* This is the same as the beginning of metaphysics, of subjectivism, or, as Heidegger also puts it, of humanism: the primacy of man over all beings. Thus something happened in Plato's thinking, something of which Plato himself was not aware. Through Plato's thoughts one reaches what was not thought, the fate-laden ordinance of being in which it veiled itself for the West, an occurrence which only made itself known via the long history of thought.

The other end of this metaphysical tunnel is modern technology. Subjectivity reached its last philosophical stage in Nietzsche's will to power, where being is only the value posited by the will. Ultimately the will wills nothing external to itself; the will wills itself. This first became fully clear after Nietzsche in technology, which Heidegger characterizes as the will to will. Here man actualizes his will by constructing the world to conform to it. In this sense the will to will is the last stage in the process whereby metaphysics has altered the world by placing man as the subject in the center of it. Thus the completion of metaphysics eventuates in technology, which according to Heidegger does not itself think.

---

had the support of classical philologians through Friedländer, whose *Platon* I (2nd ed., 1954) 242 is cited: "There is no such thing as hiddenness and unhiddenness in and of themselves. (Un)hiddenness does not exist unless it is (un)hidden for someone." On the basis of a study of "Die nicht-philosophische *Aletheia*" ("the non-philosophical *alētheia*") as Heitsch's essay is entitled, he confirms the philological presupposition of Heidegger's discussion of *alētheia,* to the effect that the alpha privative was "heard" by the Greek ear, but uses the evidence to repudiate the "subjectivism" of "Heidegger" and to favor "the opposite of Heidegger, Nikolai Hartmann" (25 n. 2). The counter-thesis of Heitsch to Friedländer is as follows: "It is an easy suggestion that (un)hiddenness presupposes an observer and consequently that the understanding of *alētheia* oriented etymologically to the fact that it is a composite subjectivizes the concept of truth. But this view does not get beyond externals and obscures the decisive distinction between *alētheia* and the German word 'truth.' What is decisive is that *alētheia* as unhiddenness pertains to the object, but 'truth' pertains to the statement (made by the subject). *Alētheia* is primarily a quality of the world, i.e. of the sum total of objects, whereas the German word is a quality of the judgment about the objects" (31). Thus Heitsch arrives at the same material position as that of the later Heidegger. However, lest one assume that this leaves Bultmann with the "subjectivism" attributed to Heidegger, it should be noted that Heitsch defends his own "objective" interpretation of *alētheia* by reference (31 n. 1) to Bultmann ("Untersuchungen zum Johannesevangelium," 134).

Under technology[61] Heidegger understands not simply the machines of production, but also objectified nature, an engineered culture, professional politics, superimposed ideals—the whole artificial stance of modern man toward beings as a whole. He characterizes technology as follows: Man's relation to beings is reduced to mathematical calculation; what cannot become a statistic is no longer said to be, and the mathematical solution is held to be an explanation of being. The will to will thus achieves security by putting all beings at its disposal. Man's reduction of reality to his object reaches in technology the acute stage of a revolt against or attack upon reality. Man "challenges" reality. (*Stellen,* the verb normally meaning "to place," can mean "to challenge," "to stand someone down.") The subject places its object before it, first as its propositions (*Vor-stellungen*), then in technology as the product (*her-stellen,* i.e., "to produce") it has ordered (*be-stellen*), Reality thus becomes what man has posited or placed, which leads Heidegger to name reality from this point of view *Ge-stell,* a thing that is placed somewhere or that is stood up or erected, a "stand." Reality as the sum of such stands is for technology stock or inventory. Even the picturesque and scenic is merely tourism's stock, and man himself becomes only manpower, part of the cold war's arsenal.

This characterization of technology means that the will to will has eliminated the fate-ladenness of existence, the initiative of being pressing in upon thought. Thus technology is unhistoric. Yet technology itself has come upon thought as an action of being, and is itself an epoch in the history of being. When one recognizes that the essence of technology is rooted in the history of being, one is freed from a romantic, nostalgic flight from technology, and on the other hand one has historically relativized technology so as to transcend it and be free from it. Man cannot overcome technology with a technological understanding of technology, but only by hearing in it a claim of being upon us. Thus, even as forgetfulness of being, the history of being bears in upon us determining world history.

Man does not create history by initiating a causal chain that produces the connection of history; rather it is the sharing of a common fate in the history of being that produces a common history under which a whole culture or epoch stands. One does not have freedom of choice

---

61. Cf. Heidegger, "Die Frage nach der Technik."

merely to take or leave the situation in which one is placed and finds oneself. Yet the very fact that Heidegger has uncovered the forgetfulness of being is a return to a more primal thinking. This fact sometimes leads Heidegger to prophetic utterances about a return by the West to more contemplative thinking, which cherishes being.

THE LATER HEIDEGGER AND THE THEOLOGY OF HEINRICH OTT

The question of the relation between the thought of the later Heidegger and theological thought is obviously much broader than the question of the theological implications that Heinrich Ott finds in the later Heidegger. Ott is not the only theologian to have concerned himself thus far with the thought of the later Heidegger, nor even the first. The Bultmannians have remained in close contact with Heidegger down through the years, and especially Friedrich Gogarten and Ernst Fuchs have made use of his more recent writings. Yet Ott is the first theologian to have attempted in a programmatic and concentrated way a statement of the theological implications specifically of the later Heidegger. Hence his position has presented the concrete point of departure for the theological discussion of the later Heidegger.

Heinrich Ott was born at Basel in 1929 and began to read Barth as well as Heidegger while still a pupil in the *Gymnasium*. He remained in Basel for the study of theology and made so favorable an impression on Barth that Barth accepted him as a doctoral candidate and assigned him a choice topic: a critique of the theology of Rudolf Bultmann. For two semesters Ott studied in Marburg under Bultmann and during that time lived in the Bultmann home. The result of his intensive study was a dissertation on "History and *Heilsgeschichte* in the Theology of Rudolf Bultmann."[62] This book closes with a call for a positive, constructive criticism of Bultmann, which would make use of what he then termed the "newer Heidegger." Four years later, when Ott published his Heidegger volume on "Thinking and Being,"[63] he began by quoting this passage from the earlier book to indicate his own approach to the later Heidegger:

> Our investigation sought to clear the ground for a productive criticism of Bultmann. Perhaps the course of the immanent criticism carried through thus far has already indicated the lines

62. Ott, *Geschichte und Heilsgeschichte in der Theologie Rudolf Bultmanns.*
63. Ott, *Denken und Sein.*

along which one should think further. One must seek in connection with Bultmann (1) a concept of reality of a historic type that overcomes the Bultmannian cleavage with a synthesis embracing both "significance" and "corporeality," "history" and "nature"; (2) a comprehensive interpretation of understanding as the actualizing of historic being that goes beyond the limits of Bultmann's hermeneutic; (3) a synthetic concept of time that takes into account both the eminent significance of the historic Now and the reality of past and future as such; (4) the primal essence of language. The fourth point also indicates that such ontological reflection does not stand apart from but rather very close to practical church life. For what is involved is language as it occurs in scripture and confession, in exegesis and dogmatics, in preaching and prayer, i.e., language as the medium of all the church's and theology's activity. Further thinking along these four lines could perhaps use as its concrete point of departure the work especially of the newer Heidegger, a thinker who has inspired Bultmann in his theological thought but who speaks up from time to time just where Bultmann's limits are met, as we could observe again and again. His work may contain a flood of perspectives important for theology that have probably never been correctly exploited.[64]

This program had undergone some modification by the time of *Denken und Sein* in 1959. The intervening four years and the general rejection by the Bultmannians of his criticism of Bultmann had convinced Ott that

> Bultmann's most personal position is not reached by such a formal ontological criticism, since that position rests upon an ultimate basic religious decision, which transcends all purely formal considerations. This decision can be defined as "eschatological paradoxical dualism" and doubtless has its ultimate basis in the dualism of law and gospel.[65]

---

64. *Geschichte und Heilsgeschichte*, 210-11; *Denken und Sein*, 7.

65. Ott, *Denken und Sein*, 8. From note 8 of "What is Systematic Theology?" 95, one observes that we have to do with a basic distinction between the Reformed tradition in which Ott stands and the Lutheran tradition in which Bultmann stands. The potentiality for a positive use of the law-and-gospel pattern for approaching the later Heidegger has been developed by the Lutheran theologian Gerhard Ebeling, in his "Verantworten des Glaubens," 122. In his pamphlet devoted to overcoming Bultmann's supposedly "dualistic" view of history, *Die Frage nach dem historischen Jesus und die Ontologie der Geschichte* (1960), Ott advocates the "single reality of history" and yet concedes (33): "One can speak of a genuine duality at most when one confronts the *old and new aeon*."

Rather than assuming his proposals will be accepted by Bultmann into an improved Bultmannian theology, Ott now proposes to present a theology that can claim to be more truly Heideggerian. To be sure, this would not "disprove Bultmann," but it would break down one of Bultmannianism's major elements of strength at the time.[66] Hence Ott proposes to "prove that Bultmann may legitimately appeal to Heidegger only to a very limited extent."[67] Of course the outcome of such an argument may very well be that the Bultmannians, like the Barthians, will turn away from Heidegger altogether, rather than join Ott in a theology corresponding to the later Heidegger.

The theological position in terms of which Ott approaches a correlation between the later Heidegger and theology is more nearly that of Barth. To be sure Barth had disassociated himself from any correlation with existentialism and Kierkegaard just at the time when Heidegger was introducing Kierkegaardian motifs into philosophy, as if Barth wished intentionally to avoid a correlation with Heidegger. Barth's rare references to Heidegger have been consistently critical,[68] so that Ott's project could hardly count on support from Barth. In fact, the Barthian rejection of the interpretation of the later Heidegger as presented by Walter Schulz[69] had already been supplied by Hermann Diem.[70] Hence Ott's attempt to achieve a positive relation between the later Heidegger and Barthian theology indicates a new alternative within the Barthian movement.

Since the publication of Ott's book there has appeared an essay by Karl Barth on the relation of philosophy and theology that well illustrates the ambiguous relation of Ott's undertaking to Barthianism.[71] Here Barth

---

66. Cf. Robinson, "Basic Shifts in German Theology," esp. 96–97.

67. Ott, *Denken und Sein*, 8.

68. Jüngel, "Der Schritt zurück," 122, speaks of the "irony" of Barth's misunderstanding of the statements of the later Heidegger that involve "a hidden kinship" between Barth and Heidegger.

69. Walter Schulz's address, "Der 'Gott der Philosophen' in der neuzeitlichen Metaphysik," (1956) was published in his volume *Der Gott der neuzeitlichen Metaphysik* (1957; 2nd ed. 1959).

70. Diem's address in reply to Schulz, *Gott und die Metaphysik*, appeared in the series Theologische Studien, edited by Karl Barth (1956). See also the dissertations of Diem's pupils: Lothar Steiger, *Die Hermeneutik als dogmatisches Problem* (1961), and Gerhard Noller, *Sein und Existenz* (1962); and Eduard Thurneysen's association of Ott with "Heidegger's existialistic philosophy" in his article "Warum nicht Gollwitzer?"

71. Barth, "Philosophie und Theologie" (1960).

concedes that philosophy and theology may be concerned with the same problem. The theologian describes this problem as the relation of Creator and creature, while philosophers have treated it under a variety of terms. In this connection Barth speaks specifically of Heidegger's treatment of the relation of being and *Dasein*. Now Barth's basic criticism of philosophy has to do with the question of sequence or priority. He holds that philosophy tends consistently to give priority to man, whereas theology must give priority to God. Presumably Barth conceives of Heidegger as giving priority to *Dasein* over being. Yet this "existential misunderstanding" of *Being and Time* does not fit at least the later Heidegger, whose turn consisted in giving being strict priority in his thinking. Thus, in terms of the condition Barth sets up for a positive relation between philosophy and theology, the later Heidegger would seem to provide the kind of philosophy Barth would advocate. Though Barth himself gives no indication of modifying his traditional rejection of Heidegger, one may find here some material justification of Ott's academic position as Barth's successor.

If Ott's dissertation had been in intent a conversation with Bultmann, designed to lead Bultmann toward a revision of his position, one may say that *Denken and Sein* is addressed to Barth or at least to the Barthian position, to lead it, without violating its basic principles, into a confrontation with the later Heidegger. However it should not be overlooked that Ott is also addressing himself to Heidegger, who might be led by Ott's empathetic and noncritical interpretation of his thought to see in its theological development a path for his own reflection. As a matter of fact Heidegger concluded his seminar on "Christian Faith and Thinking" at the conference of Old Marburgers in October, 1959, with the suggestion that although he could not, in view of his repudiation of metaphysics as such, accept a metaphysical concept of God, the door remained open with regard to other possible approaches to theology. And there have been some indications that Heidegger was at least initially more impressed by Ott's theological correlation than were the theologians.

Being and God

Any discussion of God in terms of the philosophy of Heidegger encounters the common association of Heidegger with the atheism of Sartre in distinction to the dimension of transcendence in Jaspers' thought. Ott argues that the association of atheism with Heidegger is part of the basic misunderstanding of Heidegger as if he were an existentialist. This error leads to treating the ontological structures set up as existentials as if they were ontic statements about man's existential dilemma. For example, "being-in-the-world" as a focal existential is at times taken to mean that man's existence is only worldly or immanent, so as to exclude the possibility of contact with a transcendent God.

Heidegger himself had already corrected this misunderstanding as early as 1929.

> The ontological interpretation of *Dasein* as "being-in-the-world" makes neither a positive nor a negative decision about the possibility of being in relation to God. Rather it is only the clarification of transcendence that achieves an *adequate concept of Dasein,* in terms of which being (*Seiendes*) one can now *inquire* as to how the matter stands ontologically with regard to *Dasein's* relation to God.[72]

This is further explained in the "Letter on Humanism."

> In the designation "being-in-the-world," "world" does not at all mean earthly beings in distinction from a heavenly being, nor does it refer to the "worldly" in distinction from the "spiritual." "World" in that designation does not refer to any being or realm of beings, but to openness for being. Man is and is man to the extent that he is ek-sistent.[73]

Not only does Heidegger explicitly reject the attribution to him of atheism;[74] he even goes on to say that his leaving open the question as to God is not a matter of indifference, but is rather intended to point out that a more adequate category than metaphysics is needed for theology.

> Only from the truth of being can the essence of the holy be thought. Only from the essence of the holy is the essence of deity to be thought. Only in the light of the essence of deity can that be thought and said which the word 'God' should name. Do we not have to be able first to understand and hear carefully all these

---

72. Heidegger, *Vom Wesen des Grundes* (4th ed.), 39 n. 1.
73. Heidegger, *Über den Humanismus,* 35.
74. Ibid., 36. Schrey, "Die Bedeutung," 15, speaks in the context of these remarks by Heidegger of an "ironic atheism" that, as a form of negative theology, is "nothing other than an indirect indication of a feeling of the inadequacy of our human conceptions of God."

words, if we as men, i.e., as ek-sistent beings, are to experience a relation of God to man? For how could man in contemporary world history even ask seriously and rigorously whether God is drawing near or withdrawing himself, if man neglects first of all to think his way into the only dimension in which such a question can be asked? But that is the dimension of the holy, which even as a dimension remains closed if the openness of being does not become clear and in its clearing is not near to man. Perhaps the outstanding characteristic of this age consists in the closedness of the dimension of the whole. Perhaps that is the sole bane.[75]

Ott's basic assumption with regard to Heidegger's attitude toward the relation of philosophy to Christian faith is that Heidegger maintains that only a metaphysical philosophy should be regarded by faith as "foolishness,"[76] This would leave open the possibility of a positive relation of Heidegger's own philosophy to faith. Ott builds on such quotations as the following:

Thus the theological character of ontology is not merely due to the fact that Greek metaphysics was later taken up and transformed by the ecclesiastical theology of Christianity. Rather it is due to the manner in which beings as beings have from the very beginning disconcealed themselves. It was this unconcealedness of beings that provided the possibility for Christian theology to take possession of Greek philosophy—whether for better or for worse may be decided by the theologians, on the basis of their experience of what is Christian; only they should keep in mind what is written in the First Epistle of Paul the Apostle to the Corinthians: "Has not God made foolish the wisdom of the world?" (1 Cor. 1:20). The "wisdom of the world," however, is that which, according to 1:22, the "Greeks seek." Aristotle even calls "philosophy proper" "what is sought." Will Christian theology make up its

---

75. Heidegger, *Über den Humanismus*, 36–37. The religious overtones in *heil* ("whole") and *Unheil* ("bane") are more evident in German (cf. *Heilsgeschichte*) than in English.

76. Ott, *Denken und Sein*, 147 and passim. The alternate position, to the effect that Heidegger regards all philosophy, including his own, as "foolishness" for Christian faith, is advocated by Helmut Franz (cf. 58–62 below), who explicitly rejects Ott's position in "Das Denken Heideggers und die Theologie," *ZTKB* 2 (1961) 114. (Cf. Franz, *kerygma und kunst*, 65.) Cf. Ott's reply in "What is Systematic Theology," 106 n. 13.

mind one day to take seriously the word of the apostle, and thus also the conception of philosophy as foolishness?⁷⁷

In Ott's view, this opens the door to a theology that would join Heidegger in his "step backwards" to overcome metaphysics.

Such an understanding of Heidegger's relation to theology becomes clearer in the essay on "The Onto-theo-logical Nature of Metaphysics," where Heidegger says of the uncaused cause or *causa sui*:

> This is the fitting name for the god in philosophy. To this god man can neither pray nor sacrifice. Before the *causa sui* man can neither fall to his knees in awe nor sing and dance. Accordingly, godless thinking that must give up the god of philosophy, god as *causa sui*, is perhaps nearer to the divine God. This means only that such thinking is freer for him than onto-theo-logics would like to admit. This comment may let some small light fall on the path toward which a thinking that carries through the step backwards, back out of metaphysics into the essence of metaphysics, is moving.⁷⁸

As long as this step backwards has not been made, the most appropriate thing to do with regard to God would be to remain silent:

> He whose experience of theology, both that of Christian faith and that of philosophy, is rooted in an unbroken heritage, prefers nowadays to remain silent about God in the realm of thought. For the onto-theo-logical character of metaphysics has become questionable to thought, not on the basis of any atheism, but because of the experience of a thinking that has seen in onto-theo-logics the still unthought unity of the essence of metaphysics.⁷⁹

Yet now that Heidegger has advanced beyond (or stepped behind) metaphysics into more primal thought, Ott sees the possibility of moving beyond a silence with regard to a metaphysical concept of God into explicit nonmetaphysical language about God.

Ott takes his point of departure in the following statement by Heidegger: "Readiness for anxiety is a Yes to the urgent call to fulfill the

---

77. Heidegger, *Was ist Metaphysik?* (8th ed.), 19–20 = *Existentialism from Dostoevsky to Sartre*, 218.

78. Heidegger, *Identität und Differenz*, 35–73, esp. 70 = *Essays in Metaphysics*, 33–67, esp. 65.

79. Ibid., 51 = *Essays in Metaphysics*, 47–48.

highest claim, which only man's nature encounters. Only man of all the beings experiences, when called upon by the voice of being, *the wonder of all wonders: that beings are.*"[80] Heidegger maintains that when man is held out into nothing he becomes aware of the contingency of beings and thus is struck with the fact that they are at all. Their being calls to him. Now Ott infers that if their being is experienced as a wonder, this amounts to experiencing them as God's creation.[81] To be sure such a concept of God the Creator would have to be clearly distinguished from a metaphysical first cause, if such a theology is to correspond to Heidegger's thought. For it was the metaphysical concept of a first cause that provided an answer so fully "settling" the question as to stultify it and even to lead to the question being forgotten. Ott denies that this would be the outcome in terms of the biblical concept of God as Creator. The Bible "answers" the question as to why there are beings by giving the question permanence, in that the awe in the question is carried over in the answer, as awe before the Creator. For God the Creator is not at man's disposal, but in his independence and sovereignty holds the believer in awe. Faith in this Creator is the continuing experience of the strangeness that beings are, it is "the uncompromising persistence of the basic question as to 'why there are beings rather than nothing.'"[82] Thus Ott finds a correspondence between the biblical faith in God the Creator and the philosopher's basic question. He even describes this as the philosopher's encounter with God, the "secularized Christianity" of Heidegger's thought.[83]

The first attempt to work out a correlation between the Christian concept of God and Heidegger's philosophy consisted in a correlation between the believer's numinous awareness of the world as creation and the philosopher's amazement at the being of beings. The being of beings is understood as creation. The theological term "creation" indeed tends to correspond to the philosophical term "being," precisely in the parallel ambiguity of both terms. Being has often been understood metaphysically as the sum total of all beings, thus obscuring the Heideggerian meaning of being, the awareness that the beings are at all. Just so the theological term "creation" is often taken to mean the sum total of all creatures,

---

80. Heidegger, *Was ist Metaphysik?* (8th ed.), 46–47 = *Existence and Being,* 1949, 386; paperback ed., 355.

81. Ott, *Denken und Sein,* 86.

82. Ibid., 88.

83. Ibid., 87.

thus obscuring the more basic meaning of the term, the awareness that all creatures are God's creation. The Christian language corresponding to the being of beings would then be the creation of creatures. Again and again in the Bible the people of God experience their being as the wonder of deliverance, and commemorate this awareness in the language of blessing or thanksgiving. When one recalls that for Heidegger primal thinking is gratitude for the favor of being and thus becomes thanking,[84] one may suspect that the biblical analogy, rather than being a derivative of philosophical thought, is indeed the ultimate origin of Heidegger's insight. For here the thanksgiving emerges as the linguistic formulation of the reverent awareness that one's being is God's creation.[85]

It was in this direction that Ott's thinking was directed in the first, historical part of *Denken und Sein,* consisting of lectures given in the Winter Semester, 1957–58. In the latter, systematic half of *Denken und Sein,* consisting of lectures given in the Summer Semester of 1958, Ott enters into another avenue of correlation.[86] Rather than correlating the doctrine of creation with amazement at the being of beings, Ott now seeks to fit the concept of God into the philosophical position provided by Heidegger. If being is not God—and it is clear that such an identification is contrary to Heidegger's intention, since being is not a being and is not to be hypostasized—then God must be a being. And indeed Heidegger, when emphasizing that man is the only being that "exists," lists other beings that "are" but do not "exist"—and here God is listed alongside a rock, a horse, and an angel as things that are, that is to say, as a being.[87] Ott infers that if one is to talk about God in Heideggerian terms one would speak of God as a being[88]—which immediately confronts Ott with Barth's rejection of the *analogia entis.*

Ott argues that the Heideggerian understanding of being makes it possible to share the two basic objections that led Barth to reject the

---

84. Heidegger, *Was ist Metaphysik?* (8th ed.), 49 = *Existence and Being,* 389; paperback ed., 358–59.

85. This latter point is the thesis of my essay: Robinson, "Heilsgeschichte und Lichtungsgeschichte," 113–41. This essay appeared in English under the title "The Historicality of Biblical Language." Cf. also Fuchs, *Hermeneutik,* 2nd ed., 72.

86. Cf. esp. "The Question as to the Being of God," in *Denken und Sein,* 138–52.

87. Heidegger, *Was ist Metaphysik?*, 8th ed., 15–16.

88. Ott, *Denken und Sein,* 142.

analogia entis and still affirm the being of God.[89] Barth's objection to subsuming God under the highest generalization, being, is that man in his thinking thereby gains control over God; God becomes a concept at man's disposal. Now this objection envisages the subjectivistic approach to thought, in which beings are reduced to objects of the subject's thoughts, against which Heidegger himself is reacting in his rejection of metaphysics. Hence the nonmetaphysical concept of being advocated by Heidegger is a concept intentionally freed of that to which Barth takes exception. Being, for Heidegger, is precisely not a most general concept that thought has at its disposal. Quite the reverse. Being is an occurrence of unveiling, a fate-laden happening upon thought. As thought's fate or lot, being is precisely not at thought's disposal. To speak of God's being and to speak of his freedom in self-revelation are for Ott congruous formulations.

Barth's other objection to the *analogia entis* had to do with the concept of analogy as a static similarity between God and man. Barth rejected the term analogy until he came to conceive of analogy (*analogia fidei* or *relationis* or *operationis*) as a correspondence effected by God in the act of faith. Now Ott holds that this emphasis is more radically carried through by Heidegger, who moves from the concept of analogy to that of correspondence, and affirms that thinking is simply the "response" to the call of being as it unveils itself and gives itself to thought.

Here again one has to do with a Heideggerian play on words. The German word for correspondence is *Entsprechung*, which, like the English "cor-re-spondence," had lost for the average ear its etymological affinity to "re-sponse" (*ent-sprechen*). "Correspondence" had lost the dynamic implications of "an-swering" and had taken on static implications, until heard in its primal etymological meaning by Heidegger. Thus, in the case of "analogy" just as in the case of "being," Ott holds that Heidegger has provided a way for implementing Barth's criticism of the *analogia entis* that is more adequate than Barth's own solution. Ott argues that Barth's valid criticisms of the *analogia entis*, which led him to remove the term "being" while retaining the term "analogy," can be better implemented in terms of Heidegger by removing the term "analogy" (in favor of "response") and retaining the term "being."[90]

---

89. Ibid., 143–46.

90. Jüngel, "Der Schritt zurück, 116–22, argues that the position Ott presents on the basis of Heidegger as a criticism of Barth is in substance Barth's own position.

Having in this way protected his Barthian and Heideggerian flanks, Ott moves constructively toward a clarification of God's being. The Bible says without inhibition[91] that God "is." Yet, as the cryptic name of God in Exod 3:14 "I am who I am" indicates, to say God "is" does not for the Bible imply subsuming God under a higher generalization. Rather this predicate for God brings to expression his absolutely unique self-hood: "God is simply himself: He is he who he is, mysterious, glorious, unapproachable, not part of the world."[92] This is also for Ott the way Heideggerian philosophy would think of God's being:

> *The being of God signifies,* in terms of the way we have understood "being" thus far, *an occurrence of unveiling:* that God unveils himself to thought as he who he is; that he strikes upon thought as a fate and gives himself to thought as the subject matter to be thought, that he encounters thought as a claim upon it and requires of the thinking person a correspondence in freedom.[93]

God's being is not to be compared with that of beings in general, as if God shared in their being as the supreme being or the cause of all other beings. Rather God's being is to be conceived of as the fate-like occurrence that "God is thought about."[94] Thus Ott conceives of God as a being whose being is his revelation of himself, comparable to Heidegger's understanding of being as unveiling.

The two correlations Ott makes between Heidegger's ontology and the doctrine of God stand in some tension to each other. If amazement at the being of beings corresponds to numinous awareness that their being is God's creation, then awareness of God would seem to be latent in awareness of a being's being. When this correlation is applied to God as himself a being, the second correlation Ott proposes, confusion emerges. If awe-inspired awareness of a being's being corresponds to sensing a being as a creature, is then God a creature? If such awe at a being's being is ultimately reverence for a being's Creator, does God, as a being, have a Creator? It seems impossible thus to move from Ott's first correlation

---

91. Franz, "Das Denken Heideggers und die Theologie," 109, brands this an "illusion." "It is precisely the Bible—both Old and New Testament—that speaks of God's being in anything but an uninhibited way."

92. Ott, *Denken und Sein,* 146.

93. Ibid., 148.

94. Ibid., 149.

to his second correlation. Nor is the situation easier when one goes at the matter in the other direction. If God is a being, how then can amazement at the being of beings be correlated to God as their Creator, when Heidegger is fundamentally opposed to the grounding of being in a being? The objection to metaphysics is not just that it stultified the question of being, but that it grounded being in a supreme being. If God is a being, the second correlation Ott proposes, how is Ott to avoid the criticism that his first correlation is by implication metaphysical?

In the light of such problems and the discussion following his presentation at the 1960 meeting of Old Marburgers, Ott has assumed a more cautious position. Whereas his address "What is Systematic Theology?" spoke of his theology "fitting into" Heidegger's philosophy, the printed form of the address only speaks of a "correspondence" with Heidegger's philosophy. Heidegger introduced into the discussion at the 1960 meeting the idea of an *analogia proportionalitatis*: A is to B as C is to D. As philosophical thinking is related to being, when being speaks to thinking, so faith's thinking is related to God, when God is revealed in his word. Ott adopts this formulation, seeing in it primarily an emphasis upon the experiential nature of philosophical and believing thought. Thus theology in its speaking of God is not required to choose whether God is in Heideggerian terms a being, or nothing, or being itself, or that which is implicit in the awesome awareness of the being of beings. God would not "fit into" the Heideggerian system, but the whole of theology, operating within its own language, would have a structural correspondence to philosophy of the Heideggerian kind. It remained to be seen whether Ott could produce a theology under this definition that is still meaningfully related to Heidegger.

Thinking and Theology

For the later Heidegger, thinking is directly related to his understanding of the nature of man. Existence is a term used to define man not because of the traditional distinction between existence as actuality and essence as possibility; rather ek-sistence refers to man as the being who moves out of his subjectivity and stands out where being becomes clear. Man stands ec-statically within the truth of being. Man takes place as man when he is addressed by being. Man is the place where being clears so that one catches sight of it and exclaims "There!" This is the meaning the later Heidegger attributes to his designation of man as "being-there," *Da-sein*. Thus both Heideggerian terms for man, existence and *Dasein*, envisage man as the place where being opens up and reveals itself.

It is the place of man thus defined that is the origin of thinking. Thinking "carries out" man's nature. If man is the being where being itself dawns on the beings, then this basic "clearing" of being, which constitutes man's nature, is synonymous with thinking about being. Thus the act most fundamentally related to man's nature is the act of thinking. Thinking is indeed the form in which the action of being upon man manifests itself.

To be sure, Heidegger does not have in mind any and all thought, but rather thinking in the pregnant sense he sometimes refers to as basic or primal thinking. The objectifying conceptualization carried on by metaphysical philosophy and the mathematical calculation carried on by natural science are in this sense not "thought." Real thinking restricts itself to the unveiling of being. It has no practical goal. It does not, like science, provide information, or, like traditional philosophy, seek to solve the ultimate puzzles of the universe, nor does it produce wisdom for living or guidance for action. Real thinking has "renounced" such pragmatism and persists in understanding itself only as the unveiling of being. Such thought is called forth by being itself, so that thought has a fate-laden character. In distinction from scientific calculation, which derives from the initiative of the scientist, real thinking comes to the thinker from his subject matter. It is this receptive structure of thought, based in man's nature as ek-sistence, that is for Ott the basic insight of relevance for perceiving the nature of theology. "Here lies the key to understanding the whole of Heidegger's work and the key to the whole relevance of this thinker for theology!"[95]

This distinction between the self-appointed calculation of the scientist and the response of primal thinking to the call of being can also be expressed in terms of a path of thought. Thought is not a road upon which one can simply stand and observe its course. Rather it is like a woodland trail that can be seen only as one goes along it, so that the trail seems to open up only in one's movement along it—and yet the course of one's movement is determined by the trail. Thinking consists in following the trail of being by pushing aside the underbrush as one works one's way

---

95. Ibid., 164.

down the path, thereby revealing the clearing that is in fact the path upon which one is led.

In his published works Heidegger has been more involved in relating thinking to poetry than to theology.

> The poet's naming is of a like origin [to the thinker's speaking]. However what is alike is alike only in that it is something different from what it is like. Although composing poetry and thinking are most alike in the care in the use of words, they are at the same time furthest separated in their nature. The thinker speaks being. The poet names the holy. To be sure the question must be left open here as to how, when thought about in terms of the nature of being, composing poetry and thanking and thinking are dependent on each other and at the same time different.[96]

This association of poetry with Rudolf Otto's concept of "the holy," as well as the introduction of the third category of thanking alongside poetic composition and thinking, suggest that we are in close proximity to the thinking involved in theology.

Ott's point of departure for defining theology in correspondence to Heidegger's understanding of thinking and of poetic composition is the conviction that theology of necessity is to be understood as primal thinking, rather than as an instance of the secondary thinking characteristic of metaphysics and science. Otherwise theology would be subordinate to and under the control of another dimension of thought that would be more primal. Theology could hardly accept this subordination in view of its responsibility to devote itself fully and hence freely to the critical explication of Christian faith. Nor does Ott think that one should make a sharp cleavage between preaching and theology, with the one understood as primal thinking, the other as secondary, "scientific" thinking. For this would leave theology in the subject-object dilemma, in the subjectivism that distorts a true understanding of the subject matter.[97]

> What then follows from Heidegger's interpretation of thinking for theology? Theology should not understand itself, its thinking, as freely carried on by a subject who subjectivistically observes

---

96. Heidegger, *Was ist Metaphysik?* (8th ed.), 50–51 = *Existence and Being*, 391–92; paperback ed., 360.

97. Cf. Ott's criticism of Ernst Fuchs in this regard in Ott's book, *Dogmatik und Verkündigung*, 19–20. The alternate position to Ott's is suggested by Ebeling, "Verantworten des Glaubens," 123–24 (cf. pp. 62–63 below).

an object and talks about it. Rather theology should understand itself as an element of encounter, as encounter with what is to be thought, which shows itself, "unveils" itself to thought and thus determines thought. What is to be thought by theology is faith. Faith, however, is not something in itself; instead, it is faith in God. He who does the thinking in theology is himself the believer. Hence theological thinking is the thinking of faith and from faith, a thinking from within the encounter. When theology speaks of God, it does not speak "about" God *outside* the encounter of faith; rather it speaks *out of* the encounter. Its talk about God is the encounter of faith explaining itself. Theology is the movement of faith wishing to clarify itself: *fides quaerens intellectum*. A theology that was something other than thinking out of the encounter, something other than thinking *as encounter*, could from Heidegger's point of view be designated in no other way than as subjectivistic and metaphysical."[98]

The extent to which this Heideggerian approach to theology converges in Ott's mind with reflection from within theology itself becomes clear when one consults Ott's inaugural address as *Privat-Dozent* at the University of Basel, entitled "Theology as Prayer and as Science."[99] Theology is classified among those sciences that are based in experience, in distinction from *a priori* sciences such as logic and mathematics based in reason itself. Now the "experience" that theology explicates is prayer. For in prayer the believer "gives his response to God's word that corresponds to this word.... In human language God's own language makes itself heard."[100] Prayer is the experience in which God can be experienced, not as a psychic phenomenon, but as a response in which God's word comes to expression. It is upon this experience of God that theology is based.

Here the structural parallel to Heidegger's understanding of being pressing itself into thought and hence finding expression in language that "cor-re-sponds" to being can be clearly sensed. And just as Heidegger finds in the language of such poets as Hölderlin the "text" for his thinking, Ott explicates his position in the same essay by means of an interpretation of Anselm of Canterbury's *Proslogion*, which was

98. Ott, *Denken und Sein*, 173-74. Cf. the whole of the section on "The Thinking of the Theologian," 171-75.

99. Ott, "Theologie als Gebet und als Wissenschaft."

100. Ibid., 123.

Anselm's "address" to God in prayer.[101] This treatise, itself composed in the form of prayer, reflects the understanding of theology Ott had in mind. "Teach me to seek thee, and show thyself to me as I seek, for I am not able to seek thee unless thou teachest, nor to find thee unless thou showest thyself" (Chapter 1). Here theology's relation to God corresponds to thinking's relation to being as seen by Heidegger. The fate-laden character of thinking, as response to the unveiling of being that is given to it to think, could hardly be more adequately stated in terms of theological thinking. Thus, as poetry most authentically reflects man's ek-sistence as standing in the clearing of being, so prayer is the mode that best represents the believer's being as response to the word of God.

The relation of theology to prayer need not rob theology of its critical rigor or scholarly character. To be sure the goal of theological scholarship is not a proof convincing to one standing outside of faith. Yet the structure of prayer as response to God's word includes a responsibility before God for one's theological formulations. Just as one can discuss previous decisions and with responsibility reaffirm or revise them, just so theological discussion is possible with those who share the encounter with God and for whom the theologian speaks (church dogmatics!). The rigor of theological responsibility also expresses itself in the rigor of its presentation, the systematic, methodical nature of its utterance. Thus theology is to be defined as a system of analytic statements, explicating the experience of encounter with God that Ott focuses in the term "prayer."

Bultmann has taken exception to this understanding of the relation of theology to Christian experience, by insisting in a letter to Ott on the occasion of the publication of *Denken und Sein* that theology in distinction from faith is an instance of objectifying thought. He illustrates his point by quoting Ott's statement that "theology alone permits the Thou, namely God, to remain a Thou."[102] Here God is not addressed as Thou, but is talked about as a Thou, so that the divine Thou becomes a neuter category rather than a personal address. Bultmann argues that this relative objectification is inevitable. To be sure faith itself implies thought, so that there is a continuity. But the continuity is paradoxical. Theology

---

101. Cf. also Ott's article: "Anselms Versöhnungslehre." Wilhelm Anz, "Verkündigung und theologische Reflexion," 57, in dependence on Ernst Haenchen ("Anselm, Glaube und Vernunft"), argues that Ott's use of Anselm is invalid, since according to Anselm it is temptation that necessitates theology.

102. Ott, "Theologie als Gebet," 124.

is on the one hand the self-explication of faith's encounter. Yet theology has turned from faith's stance of hearkening into the stance of reflective thinking. Lectures and publications are not a witness in which the theologian presents himself as a believer, but are more nearly an "unbelieving" thought-process of an objectifying kind. Bultmann senses some awareness of this on Ott's part when Ott describes theology as moving beyond the horizon of the existence of the individual, and when Ott distinguishes theology's methodological reflections from theology as prayer.[103] Indeed, one may inquire whether Ott conceives of his own publications as theology, and, if so, whether they are not at least as much on the objectifying or methodological side of the dialectic as they are on the encounter or prayer side of the dialectic.

Language and Hermeneutic

Any Heideggerian discussion of being and thinking already involves by implication a discussion of language. For Heidegger, the term language (*Sprache*) does not merely designate audible or verbal articulation. It is more basically related to the conveying of meaning. For example, a thing's identity with itself "speaks" this identity to us, calls upon our thinking to correspond and our speaking to respond to this speech that comes to us from the subject matter.[104] Hence human language that says nothing is not true language. And on the other hand, man may speak without vocal articulation.[105]

Being, as that which calls forth thinking, takes place as authentic language; and thinking, as the "answer to the word of the silent voice of being," "seeks the word" in which being can "become language" and thus be communicated.[106] Language, like thinking, is rooted in *Dasein* as the place where being clears and becomes perceived. Already in *Being and Time* language is understood as having its roots "in the existentialist

---

103. Ibid., 130–31.

104. Heidegger, *Identität und Differenz*, 17ff. = *Essays in Metaphysics*, 16–17.

105. The fact that Heidegger's term "language" does not coincide fully with what the term usually designates can lead to confusion. However, Heidegger tends to some extent to replace "language" with a term designating its essence when he is not referring to man's speaking. Such terms are "calling" (*Ruf*), "tolling" (*Geläut*), "saying" (*Sage*), "showing" (*Zeige*). Man's role in these instances is that of listening.

106. Heidegger, *Was ist Metaphysik?* (8th ed.), 49–50 = *Existence and Being*, 389–91; paperback ed., 358–60.

constitution of *Dasein*'s disclosedness."[107] But for the later Heidegger this means that language does not originate in man as his activity;[108] man's language is his response to being's call upon him.

Heidegger maintains that his approach to language is different from that current in philosophical and theological circles.[109] Language is not to be understood as functioning as a sign, to designate a given content by means of commonly accepted sounds. Nor is language to be understood as functioning to express ineffable inner experience, whereby it would be the speaker himself who comes to expression in his language, and language itself would always be inadequate because of its derivative, objectifying overtone. Such an understanding of language is regarded by Heidegger as secondary, resultant upon the forgetfulness of being characteristic of the West, which has produced a "degeneration of language," e.g., into scientific terminology. Heidegger himself defines language as "the house of being" in which man lives and over which the thinkers and poets stand watch, as their speech carries out the revelation of being.[110] "Language is the clearing-concealing arrival of being itself."[111] For being as it unveils itself calls attention to itself, calls forth thought, calls for a response. When thus identified with the unveiling of being, language rather than man can be said to do the speaking: "Language speaks."[112] Language itself speaking is the condition of the possibility of man having something to say, the condition of the possibility of authentic human language. Just as a human is by one's very nature caught up into the unveiling of being, just so language takes the person up into its occurrence, so that one makes audible through one's own speaking the silent voice of being. Language *needs* the human as its loudspeaker and hence *uses* the human.[113]

Language is conceived of as a movement, a path.[114] This path can be detected when one retraces its steps. A poem "calls up" things in such a way that they are present in their significance, in their little "world."

---

107. Heidegger, *Sein und Zeit*, 160 = *Being and Time*, 203.
108. Heidegger, *Unterwegs zur Sprache*, 249ff., and passim.
109. Heidegger, *Über den Humanismus*, 16; *Unterwegs zur Sprache*, 14ff.
110. Heidegger, *Über den Humanismus*, 5; *Unterwegs zur Sprache*, 267.
111. Heidegger, *Über den Humanismus*, 16.
112. Heidegger, *Unterwegs zur Sprache*, 12, and passim.
113. The German term *brauchen* means both to "need" and to "use." Heidegger seems to intend both meanings. Cf. *Unterwegs zur Sprache*, 30, 256.
114. Heidegger, "Der Weg zur Sprache," in *Unterwegs zur Sprache*, 239–68.

Now this world is not the poet's subjective feeling, but rather the historic significance of beings. The world that the poet calls up is in fact called up to the poet by the things themselves in their being. The poet harkens to the silent tolling in things as their being unveils itself. One's answer only carries into audible language (so that less perceptive persons may hear) what the things themselves have to say as they speak their world. Thus human language is basically "answer," and shares in the fate-laden character of thinking. Primal language is being itself, to which our language corresponds. This path of language from being to human words is the actual dimension in which thinking and being take place.

It is in terms of this particular understanding of language that Heidegger's study of linguistic articulation is to be understood. His fascination with etymology is not primarily directed toward reviving archaic usages, nor is it primarily directed toward a philologically exact statement of the use of terms at a given period, such as the pre-Socratic usage of the term *alētheia*.

> The point is rather, on the basis of the early meaning of a word and its transformation, to catch sight of the material area into which the word speaks, and to reflect upon this area as the area within which the subject matter named by the word moves. Only in this way does the word speak, and this in connection with the meanings with which the subject matter has unfolded itself throughout the history of thinking and poetic composition.[115]

It is in this way that poets serve an inspirative function for Heidegger, in that they lead him into a realm that had been closed off by the metaphysical-scientific tradition, a realm into which he seeks entry. Rather than presenting a historical-critical exegesis of a poem, he enters into dialogue with the poem about the subject matter to which the poem admits him. Thus the poet's word is not an *object* of our study, but is an event calling up to us a subject matter that calls forth a response from us. The crucial issue is not whether the interpreter confines oneself to exegesis to the exclusion of eisegesis, but rather whether one succeeds in entering into the movement of the poet's words, which are derived from the subject matter. The decisive issue is whether one hears the call of being to which

---

115. *Vorträge und Aufsätze*, 48–49. With regard to the philological validity of Heidegger's use of *a-lētheia* see note 60 above.

the poet's words answered—whether one hears that call with sufficient clarity to be oneself called upon to answer. The understanding of a text consists in hearing through the human language what that language has to say, namely, the showing of being that once called forth that language and that still calls upon us in that language.

Heidegger traces the roots of his concern for language to the theological discipline traditionally called "hermeneutic."

> The title "hermeneutic" was familiar to me from my study of theology. At that time I was especially disturbed by the question as to the relation between the word of Holy Scripture and theological speculative thought. It was, if you wish, the same relation, i.e., between language and being, only obscured and inaccessible to me, so that I sought in vain via many detours and false leads for a guiding thread. . . . Without this theological origin I would never have arrived on the path of thought. But origin remains always future.[116]

This is one of the places where the later Heidegger seems to be maintaining a position diverging from *Being and Time,* and yet claiming that this position corresponds to his original intention. In *Being and Time* "hermeneutic" investigates being in terms of an "interpretation of the being of *Dasein*," "an analysis of the existentiality of existence."[117] Now it is part of the turn in Heidegger's thought that hermeneutic in this sense disappears, and Heidegger concedes that the term "hermeneutic" has also disappeared.[118] Yet in precisely this context the term "hermeneutic" is revived in its connection with language.

> The expression 'hermeneutical' is derived from the Greek verb *hermēneuein*. This verb is related to the substantive *hermēneus,* which one can connect with the name of the god Hermes, by a thought-play that is more binding than the rigor of science. Hermes is the messenger of the gods. He brings the message of fate. *Hermēneuein* is the presentation that brings news to the extent that it is itself able to hearken to a message. Such a presentation becomes the exposition of what has already been said by the poets, who, according to the saying of Socrates in Plato's discourse

---

116. Heidegger, *Unterwegs zur Sprache,* 96.
117. Heidegger, *Sein und Zeit,* 37–38 = *Being and Time,* 62.
118. Heidegger, *Unterwegs zur Sprache,* 98.

> *Ion* (534e), are "messengers of the gods." ... From all this it is clear that the hermeneutical does not primarily refer to exposition, but more basically to the bringing of the message and of news.[119]

If hermeneutic both for the early and the later Heidegger has to do with interpreting being, the later Heidegger does this in terms of the path of language rather than in terms of the structures of *Dasein*. The ontological difference between being and beings lays its claim upon man, who corresponds to this claim with the response of his language.

This new correlation of hermeneutic to the later Heidegger's understanding of language provides the potentiality for a new correlation between God's word and man's understanding. If in the first half of this century the Barthians have tended to focus upon the one and Bultmannians upon the other, the possibility of a new theology that would take its point of departure in their unity seems to be possible. It is this possibility that is stated programmatically in Gerhard Ebeling's essay "Word of God and Hermeneutic,"[120] which provides the point of departure for the volume *The New Hermeneutic*.

Although Ott finished *Denken und Sein* before the publication of Heidegger's *Unterwegs zur Sprache*, he had access in unpublished form to some of the essays in that volume on language. And since the appearance of *Denken und Sein* he has himself entered into the new hermeneutical discussion with a then unpublished essay of 1960 on "Language and Understanding as the Basic Problem of Contemporary Theology."[121]

> The hermeneutical problem poses the question: What is understanding and how does a given text become understandable? The language problem poses the question: What is the nature of language and how does a given text speak to us? Yet both problems converge, indeed they are ultimately identical.

From this correlation Ott derives (in a then unpublished essay) the thesis that theology is essentially hermeneutic: "Theology is by its very nature the constant effort to eliminate empty talk from preaching, the incessant attempt to keep open or find ever anew access to the subject matter via authentic understanding. This effort takes place, however, in a twofold

---

119. Ibid., 121–22.
120. Ebeling, "Wort Gottes und Hermeneutik" = "Word of God and Hermeneutic."
121. Ott, "Sprache und Verstehen." Cf. also idem, *Dogmatik und Verkündigung*, 10–11.

direction: toward the understanding of the biblical texts on the one hand and toward the understandability of the gospel in the present on the other."

This leads to the statement that hermeneutic is basically "translation," meaning the trans-portation of the subject matter from then to now, as the event of language in the past speaks in our language today. Here again we have to do with an etymological reflection: The Greek verb *hermēneuein* means to bring to understanding, and from this focal meaning the verb was used in three specific but related senses: to speak, to interpret, and to translate.[122] The first two meanings (to speak and to interpret) suggest the close affinity of the problem of language and the problem of interpretation, since both are "hermeneutic" in the broad sense of bringing something to understanding. In a similar way the affinity of the last two meanings (to interpret and to translate) suggests the interrelatedness of exegesis and translation. At this point, however, a peculiarity of German usage is brought into play. The German word for "translate," *übersetzen,* retains in current usage a meaning that is perhaps rarer in English. To cross from one shore of a river to the other in a ferry is to *übersetzen*—much as in Christian legend a saint could be "translated" into the realm beyond, and his body could be "translated" into an earthly equivalent such as Westminster Abbey. This usage serves in the German discussion to point out that the task of interpretation is to "transport" the meaning of the text into the life of the modern congregation.

Biblical exegesis has not reached its goal in the historical-critical method, but should learn from new hermeneutical reflection to penetrate through to the subject matter, the revelation of God, and, led by the biblical answer to the word of God, to answer to that word with the exegete's own words. Although biblical language is not simply identified with God's revelation, but is rather an answer to God's word, it is the linguistic path to God's word, the linguistic "room" of the revelation, as Ott puts it.[123] Just as one encounters being in this or that historic, fate-laden conceptualization, just so Christian language is not completely irrelevant or optional, but is rather the historic, fate-laden medium in which God's word speaks to us. Similarly our answer to God's word is not abstract, prior to or apart from our words, as if they were some optional

---

122. Cf. Ebeling's article on "Hermeneutik," in *RGG*³, 243.

123. Ott, *Denken und Sein,* 190. Cf. the whole section on "The Word in Theology," 188–92.

or dispensable, secondary or incomplete expression of a response already made. Rather existence is itself essentially linguistic, and faith takes place within our language, which is our answer—not just a secondary *expression* of our answer—to God. The inadequacy of our linguistic response is the inadequacy of our response as a whole, and it would be to ignore our historicness to assume that the "accidents" of linguistic formulation were somewhere transcended in a truer "essential" response. The limits of our language are limits of our historic existence as such—and all the more so when language is understood to mean not just our vocabulary, but the encompassing medium for understanding and conveying meaning in which we exist. Thus language receives a more material relation to the theological enterprise than is often accorded it, by being freed from the stigma of being no more than an inevitably secondary, objectifying expression of a purer inner awareness.

Since it is basically language itself that speaks, Heidegger's study of language has taken the form of seeking to understand such concrete linguistic phenomena as poems. Ott infers that theological reflection upon language should not take place in the abstract, but rather in the concrete effort to understand the linguistic phenomena of theology's subject matter. Hence Ott accompanies his discussions with instances of "practical hermeneutic," the encounter with specific biblical texts, to derive from such experience further clarification of the nature of the language with which theology has to do. Yet if this approach to hermeneutic by listening to biblical language is to be carried out, it must become a task for biblical scholarship as such. It is quite possible that biblical scholarship will react to the new hermeneutic much as it did to Barth's *Romans,* by pointing pedantically to historical-critical inexactitudes, and missing the significance of what is happening. Certainly Heidegger's own interpretations of poetry are open to similar criticism, which has not been slow in emerging.[124] If, however, biblical scholarship will join with philosophical thought in this enterprise, the gulf between the two disciplines may be bridged and a new access to theology achieved.[125]

---

124. Cf. the bibliography given by Löwith, *Heidegger* (2nd ed.), 13 n. 13. Walter Uhsadel's review of *Unterwegs zur Sprache* in *TLZ* (1961) is on this level. Of importance is the "Briefwechsel mit Martin Heidegger," which Emil Staiger published in the latter's *Die Kunst der Interpretation,* 34–49, and Staiger's article "Ein Rückblick."

125. This proposal is made in detail in my essay: Robinson, "Heilsgeschichte und Lichtungsgeschichte" = "The Historicality of Biblical Language."

The World and the Saving Event

One may recall that Ott's point of departure was his criticism of Bultmann's view of history, which in its distinction of *Historie* and *Geschichte* seemed to Ott to end in a dualism of two spheres of reality. Hence *Denken und Sein* defined its approach as follows: "The question that we bring with us is, generally speaking, the question as to the nature of the history in which we in faith know ourselves to be, the history between God and man."[126]

Ott consequently appended to his discussion of being in *Denken und Sein* a section on being as "historic room,"[127] to provide a basis for relating Heidegger's understanding of being to the theological problem of history. Of course the concept of being as historic room does not mean simply a passive space where beings are placed ("in history"), but rather refers to being as providing "room" for beings. Heidegger can speak of being's "roominess," in that being makes it possible for beings to be. To speak of being as the historic room of beings calls attention to the essentially historic nature of beings, their historicness. Since the being of beings occurs as an event, it corresponds to the occurrence of history, and hence being's roominess is "historic room as a whole, the horizon and sum total of all occurrence."[128] If being is the bridge between thinking and beings, in that it is both the condition of the possibility of thinking and the being of beings, then historic room is the center for an all-embracing understanding of reality.

Ott's designation of being as historic room derives from the various historic aspects of being to which Heidegger has drawn attention. For being is not a static concept distinguished and set over against more historic factors such as becoming, appearance, thinking, ethical obligation. Instead, being includes them.[129] Hence Heidegger is concerned to understand as historic various categories previously conceived of in static fashion. *Wesen* is not static *essentia*, but rather a "taking-place"; truth is not a static correlation, but an unveiling; *physis* is not a static nature, but

---

126. Ott, *Denken und Sein*, 27. Cf. also Ott's pamphlet *Die Frage nach dem historischen Jesus*.

127. Ott, *Denken und Sein*, 152–57.

128. Ibid., 153.

129. Heidegger, *Was ist Metaphysik?* (8th ed.), 17 = *Existentialism from Dostoevsky to Sartre*, 215.

the being of beings as it comes forward, shows itself. (The Greek verb *phyein* means to put forth shoots, engender, grow.) Being is itself not a static "is-ness" (*Seiendheit*), but an unveiling. Even the ontological difference between being and the beings is not a fixed separation, but is itself the unveiling of being.

The outcome of this transformation of categories traditionally regarded as static into historic categories designating the event of being is that the word "event" is itself given a deeper significance in terms of Heidegger's philosophy. The German term *Ereignis*, "event," is etymologically related to the term *Auge*, "eye." From the root idea of catching sight of, Heidegger moves to the idea of calling to oneself with a glance, and thus appropriating.[130] "Event" comes to mean "appropriation," and refers basically to being and man appropriating each other. Being is put in the trust of man as the shepherd of being, and man for his fulfillment must be given over to being. The unveiling of being to man's thought, the call of being to man's language, is this mutual appropriation. In this pre-eminent sense the unveiling of being is "event."

If being takes place as thinking and as speaking, a third dimension in which it takes place is called "world." Here "world" is not used in the common meaning of a place (the universe) in which things happen; rather world consists in the event of being, just as this event calls forth thinking and speaking. Nor are the three dimensions, thinking, speaking, and world, different events side by side; rather they are the structures of the one event of being, inseparable in occurrence, though having distinguishable *foci* of discussion.

If being is for Heidegger always the being of beings, world is always the world of things. World is the context of meaning that inheres in things. It is not an interpretation belatedly superimposed on things, but is the very way in which they are. Hence one gains access to Heidegger's understanding of world through his analysis of the essential nature of things.[131]

---

130. Heidegger, *Identität und Differenz*, 28–29 = *Essays in Metaphysics*, 27.

131. Cf. esp. Heidegger, "Das Ding," in *Vorträge und Aufsätze*, 163–85. In *Identität und Differenz*, 9 = *Essays in Metaphysics*, 9, Heidegger says that the essay "Der Satz der Identität," ibid., 11–34 = "The Principle of Identity," in *Essays in Metaphysics*, 11–32, looks forward into the realm discussed in "Das Ding." The essay "Die Sprache," in *Unterwegs zur Sprache*, 9–33, clearly presupposes the analysis in "Das Ding." Cf. also *Die Frage nach dem Ding*.

Heidegger takes his point of departure in the etymology of the word for "thing," *Ding*. The corresponding German verb *dingen* (cf. the Anglo-Saxon verb *thingan*) means to negotiate in court. Hence the noun *Ding* or "thing" means the issue at stake in such an assembly. One may note that other designations of real entities have much the same origin: German *Sache*, Latin *res* and *causa*, and Greek *rhēma* all refer to the issue at stake at a court. Thus a thing is originally a meaning-laden issue at stake, and the common view of a thing as a completely neutral, objective entity is a secondary degeneration of the term.

Heidegger also explicates the primal meaning of "thing" by reference to the original use of the word to refer to the meeting or assembly itself at which an issue is at stake. The Anglo-Saxon name for an assembly, *thing*, is preserved in the Scandinavian designations for a parliament: *Althing* or *Storting*. Heidegger starts from the idea that a thing is a meeting, an assembling. There meet or are assembled in a thing the four sides of a square, which Heidegger characterizes as earth and heaven, the divine and the mortal. It is in this assembling that a thing has its being and its meaningfulness, its world.

A jug, for example, is not to be defined in terms of the technology of producing it, nor in terms of the material composing its bottom and walls, as if this were what it is. Rather a jug is to be understood in terms of its capacity for containing and pouring. This is the actual "essence" of the jug, what makes it a jug. For the scientist to say an empty jug is not actually empty since it is full of air is not to make a more accurate statement about the jug, but rather to lose sight of the jug's reality. A jug full of air is in the most meaningful sense empty, that is to say, it is ready for its contents. A jug is made for wine, not air. In terms of such a jug, Heidegger reflects upon how a thing is a meeting, an assembling. In the wine the strength of the earth and the warmth of the sun meet to quench the thirst of the mortals and to present offerings to the divine. This thing, by assembling the square, constitutes world.

This is further developed in the essay on "Building, Dwelling, Thinking."[132] Here "building" (*bauen*) is traced etymologically to a basic meaning of inhabiting, dwelling. One may compare the English word "neighbor," which means etymologically "nigh-dweller." If building is for the sake of dwelling, then dwelling itself (*wohnen*), as the basic aspect of

---

132. Heidegger, "Bauen Wohnen Denken," in *Vorträge und Aufsätze*, 145–62.

man's existence in the world, is in turn a "husbanding" (*schonen*) of the world, sparing it, letting it be itself; positively, caring or providing for it. This ultimate implication of "building" can be sensed for example in a bridge, which "assembles" the two shores at this point, provides passage for the flood water coming from the storm in the sky, provides the mortals passage on their way, and as it arches them over the stream points them up to the divine. The bridge assembles the square, makes place for it. Such a building is a dwelling since it husbands or provides for the earth.

This can also be described by Heidegger as saving the earth. For the verb for save (*retten*) means basically to "rid" something of what impedes it from being itself, to set it free to be what it is. In distinction from technology, which masters the earth, building saves the earth, lets it be. This relation of building and dwelling to the care of being is rooted in man's nature as ek-sistence, his standing out in or dwelling in the clearing of being, so that man is the "shepherd of being." This nature of man has previously been explicated by Heidegger in terms of thinking as the dimension in which man's nature takes place. Now building and dwelling are put alongside of thinking as basic structures of man.

Walter Schulz[133] locates in the new understanding of a thing the central element in the turn in Heidegger's thought. The Cartesian effort to make man the fixed point upon which all depends can be described as the desire to make man absolute or "unconditioned." The German word for unconditioned (*unbedingt*) contains the word for "thing," and means literally "not dependent on a thing." The later Heidegger, as the completion of his move toward understanding thought as given to man in a fate-laden way, accepts man's existence as conditioned (*bedingt*), dependent upon things to assemble the square that provides man with his world.[134] Thus the subjectivism of the metaphysical tradition is eliminated by renouncing the understanding of man as basically the subject of meaning in the universe. To be sure, this does not reduce man to a mere object upon which such meaning happens, for he is a side of the square that assembles when a thing happens. The thing is no longer a meaningless entity, but is the central meaningful occurrence, in which

---

133. Schulz, "Über den philosophiegeschichtlichen Ort Martin Heideggers," 221–22.

134. Cf. Heidegger, *Vorträge und Aufsätze*, 179: "We are—in the strict sense of the word—conditioned (*die Be-Dingten*). We have left behind us the presumption of all that is unconditioned (*Unbedingten*)."

man as well as nature participates and finds his historicness. Things do not become symbols only when and if they are given meaning by man. Instead, meaning is constituted by things as they happen, and in this meaning man participates.

The Bultmannian use of the concept of the historicness of existence was a first step toward overcoming the subjectivism of the Cartesian epoch, in that it pointed out the basic relatedness of one's self-understanding to one's world. Yet this historicness was largely a matter of man's history in which the world partook, as when the tool or utensil partook in the purposefulness of the person who made it so as to have it at hand. The focus of meaning in *Being and Time* remained man. Ott argues that the later Heidegger's understanding of a thing as an assembling of the square provides a more balanced meaning-structure of the earth and heaven, the divine and mortal, and hence a more fitting correlation for the theologian's understanding of the saving event.[135]

This also implies that what is meaningful for man does not lie outside the world of things or only on the borderline, but rather in the simple everyday things, the jug, the bridge, a peasant's shoes. Thus the Gnostic, a-cosmic overtone often attributed to existentialism would be replaced by a concrete corporeality of historic meaning. Dietrich Bonhoeffer's call for a biblical down-to-earthness rather than a mystic other-worldliness in our doctrine of salvation would seem to find its concrete answer in terms of the later Heidegger. Ott envisages a doctrine of salvation that keeps its feet on the ground, yet, in terms of Heidegger's square, is open to the divine as one dimension of life on earth. With Heidegger's help he proposes to do justice to the eschatological understanding of salvation in the New Testament, which is oriented to the bodily resurrection of Christ and the coming kingdom of God on earth.[136] This corporeality would also have its implications for doctrines of creation, the Lord's Supper, the church, providence, prayer.

To this Bultmann replies that the "corporeality"[137] Heidegger has in mind is not to be understood as physical materiality, but rather as an existential, much as Bultmann presented the Pauline concept of body in his

---

135. Ott, "The World-Dimension of Revelation," in *Denken und Sein*, 222–25.

136. Cf. Ott's booklet, *Eschatologie*.

137. Bultmann distinguishes between two terms for corporeality: *Körperlichkeit*, the physical body, and *Leiblichkeit*, corporeal existence.

Theology of the New Testament.[138] The mere physicality of things is rejected so as to make their corporeality in the true sense intelligible. Bultmann finds himself misunderstood when his position is taken to involve the irrelevance of existence in time and space. Rather he emphasizes that encounters and decisions are not merely between persons, but between persons and fate. Man's history cannot be cut off from what happens in nature. Bultmann fears that Ott's emphasis upon the material corporeality of theology would replace or obscure this existential corporeality.

Rather than the divine side of the square providing a dimension of transcendence, as Ott assumed, Bultmann argues that this is an "immanent transcendence,"[139] and that Ott has misunderstood this and fallen back into a metaphysical understanding of transcendence. The doctrines of creation, providence, and the final consummation do not find in Heidegger's square their structural foundation. Ernst Fuchs senses that Ott's use of the Heideggerian square to argue that man exists in constant confrontation with the divine, or transcendence, or an ultimate limit, is a return to natural theology,[140] in spite of the repeated denials on Ott's part.[141] Helmut Franz argues that Heideggerian thought is incompatible with Ott's interest in bodily resurrection, since for Heidegger corporeal existence is confronted with death, which would hardly be the case with the resurrected body, and for Heidegger a "thing" does not die, so cannot be used as a model for the body, which dies and rises.[142]

It is thus apparent that the relation of the later Heidegger's thought to the structure of theological doctrines is still in need of clarification. If Ott's *Denken und Sein* is only a first word rather than the last word as to the correlation of the later Heidegger and theology, it has nevertheless served the function of precipitating the discussion. It is not surprising that the theological debate about the later Heidegger has become acute only since the appearance of Ott's book, and has to a predominant extent taken the form of a debate with Ott.

138. Bultmann, *Theology of the New Testament*, 1:192–203.

139. In a conversation with R. Scherer, cited by Heinz-Horst Schrey, "Die Bedeutung," 16, Heidegger stated that philosophy cannot speak of God. Rather, what it calls God is a sublimated worldly concept, something immanent, everything else but the Christian concept of God.

140. Fuchs, "Denken und Sein?" 107.

141. Ott, *Denken und Sein*, 15 and passim. With regard to the square, 224.

142. Franz, "Das Denken Heideggers und die Theologie," 84.

THE LATER HEIDEGGER AND BULTMANNIAN THEOLOGY

The initial correlation of *Being and Time* with theology was worked out by Rudolf Bultmann and his pupils. It was to be expected that this school should be the first to take up the discussion of the relevance of the later Heidegger for theology. Not only are they equipped by long familiarity with Heidegger for such a debate; they are also directly challenged by Ott's presentation. Bultmann's own letter of reply to Ott is a defense of the superior theological relevance of the early Heidegger over the later Heidegger. Bultmann's pupils tend to concede that theology must work out a correlation with the later Heidegger, although they disagree basically with the correlation suggested by Ott. An alternative correlation in terms of the tensions between law and gospel began to emerge.

Bultmann begins his reply to Ott by acknowledging the value of *Denken und Sein* as an interpretation of the later Heidegger. Yet he challenges the validity of the relation between philosophy and theology envisaged by Ott. This relation cannot be that of a dialogue, since a dialogue presupposes a common seeking for truth made possible by a common relation to the truth. Yet theology based on faith believes that in distinction from philosophy it knows the truth. Theology does not even share its point of departure with philosophy, for, as Ott himself affirms, theology begins "consciously and strictly in faith in the revelation of God in Christ."[143] Nor can such a conversation be grounded, as Ott assumes,[144] in a common "problem of existence." For theology's problem of existence in distinction from that of philosophy is how man as sinner can exist before God.

The possibility and necessity of a relation of theology to philosophy is, according to Bultmann, rooted in the need to make biblical statements intelligible to humans if they are to appropriate them. They must be intelligible as statements about human existence. Now this necessity for "existentialist interpretation" presupposes the philosopher's clarification of what existence is. When one establishes, for example, that existence is what each person commits himself to, then room is left open for human existence before God—but a "dialogue" with philosophy on this specific existence is not possible. Theology is dependent upon philosophy in that it must use current philosophy's analysis of humanity; it cannot ignore

---

143. Ott, *Denken und Sein*, 13.
144. Ibid., 15.

what the philosophers are saying and simply decide to prefer for example an idealistic or moralistic anthropology. If the theologian wishes to argue this anthropological point, one is functioning not as a theologian but as a philosopher, so that such a discussion would not be a dialogue between theology and philosophy, but a debate within philosophy.

Bultmann agrees that if theology is to remain related to reality, it must be able to give account of itself to philosophy. This relation to philosophy is for Bultmann a dependence upon philosophy, for example upon its analysis of man, rather than a dialogue. Now it is this dependence of theology upon philosophy that Ott, as a Barthian, denies. Yet Bultmann asks how Ott can avoid the inference that Heidegger's philosophy formally determines theology, when theology to be understood must speak in terms of the historicness of existence worked out by Heidegger.[145]

Bultmann denies that philosophy can include the idea of God as Creator and of the world as creature. Philosophy does not go beyond the problem of the eternity or finitude of the world. To be sure, philosophy like science can correct traditional conceptualizations of creation. To this extent theology presupposes philosophy. But Christian theology cannot claim to be philosophy, as Ott assumes, since philosophy cannot recognize a revelation that is both a historical and an eschatological event. It is the relation of philosophy to this event that Ott has not clarified. If philosophical thinking has a history, the history of being, would not theological thinking have its own history, the history of revelation? To be sure philosophy can define what the *term* revelation or the *term* sin means, so that the nonbeliever can know what preaching is driving at. Philosophy can clarify ontologically the existentialist structure relevant to an ontic discussion of revelation or sin. For example, sin is a kind of guilt. Hence when theology expresses itself in the categories of existentialist anthropology, it has a positive relation to philosophy. Yet philosophy is not able to move beyond an ontological discussion about the categories into an ontic discussion about sin or revelation as such. Philosophy is not able to discuss theologically.[146]

---

145. Ibid., 157.

146. Jüngel, "Der Schritt züruck," 122ff, criticizes Ott's interpretation of the relation of philosophy and theology in a way that is in general though not in all details like the criticism of Bultmann. Bultmann's position is like that of Schrey, "Die Bedeutung," 9–21, esp. 14. Schrey states that this position is that of Heidegger himself, presented in an unpublished address of 1927 on "Phenomenology and Theology." It is the position repre-

Bultmann is not only dissatisfied with Ott's general position on the relation of philosophy to theology; he is especially dissatisfied with Ott's position on the relation of the later Heidegger to theology. Bultmann maintains that the theologian should be basically critical of the later Heidegger,[147] and he sketches the direction that such a criticism might take. In substance this sketch serves as a defense of Bultmann's use of the "existentialism" in the early Heidegger.

Bultmann begins by calling attention to the dialectic relation of being and beings: being does not occur apart from beings, and beings do not occur apart from being. Similarly, the relation between "primal" and "secondary" for Heidegger is not a chronological separation, but a material relation of possibilities that are present together. When Heidegger says that language's speaking is the condition of the possibility of human speaking, this does not mean that language speaks before humans can speak. Rather language speaks only in human speaking. Now human words always involve an objectifying element (although this is not necessarily that of scientific conceptualization), and yet human speech is united with the primal language that calls it forth. Both belong together in a dialectic relationship. Similarly, the relation between language speaking and humans expressing their experiences is dialectic rather than antithetic. A poem expresses an experience and as the poem "calls" or "tolls," it makes an impression corresponding to the experience it expresses. If language is the condition of the possibility of human speaking, humanity is the condition under which language becomes verbally articulate. Here one catches sight of Bultmann's reason for emphasizing the dialectic nature of Heidegger's position: He is concerned to emphasize its inescapable relation to humans, which Ott, in his reaction against existentialism, had minimized. Hence Bultmann asks why language addressed from one human to another human, in command or exhortation, is omitted from Ott's discussion of language.

Bultmann presses his point of the focal role of the human by asking whether the historicness that Ott, with Heidegger, roots in things is not in

sented in the unauthorized but widely circulated student's notes of Heidegger's lecture in Marburg of Feb. 14, 1928 on "Theology and Philosophy."

147. Although the Bultmannians have not shared Bultmann's basic reserve with regard to the later Heidegger, Ott has been consistently criticized for his uncritical stance toward Heidegger. Cf. Jüngel, "Der Schritt züruck," 107; Fuchs, "Denken und Sein?" 108; Franz, "Das Denken Heideggers," 89. Ebeling, "Verantworten des Glaubens," 123, rejects a "global appropriation [of Heidegger's thought] and a neglect of critical debate."

fact derived from the human's historicness. The jug, the peasant's shoes, the bridge, speak forth human history and derive from humans their historicness. The world they provide is that of one's own history. When a thing assembles the square and thus speaks, it is not the thing that is historic, but rather the human who stands in the world of things. It is to humans that things speak, and what they say is actually their relation to humanity's fate.

What Bultmann misses in Heidegger's treatment of things is the relation of person to person. Heidegger's analysis of the peasant's shoes neglected to state that they speak of the love with which one works to help another. Similarly with regard to the jug. It often speaks my history, the human relations in which I stand, as would be the case if I inherited it from my father or received it as a gift from a friend. This person-to-person relation characteristic of man is missing from the later Heidegger.[148] Good and evil, duty and responsibility, guilt and forgiveness are not treated. Yet things when they assemble *can* speak of these human relationships, and to this extent Heidegger's philosophy is only a limited analysis of reality.

Bultmann's criticism should not be misunderstood as if he were calling for philosophy to theologize. Rather it is the task of philosophy to provide philosophical analyses that theology presupposes. Guilt and responsibility, for example, are not theological doctrines, but rather dimensions of human existence as such. Theology needs philosophy to provide clarity with regard to just such dimensions. For example, theology is concerned with a human as a person, and hence needs clarity as to what being a person means. If *Being and Time* understood historicness as that of each particular person, it thereby provided an understanding of humans as persons. When now historicness is instead located in reality as such, the question of the nature of the human as a person is left dangling. What is selfhood for the person who is at the disposal of the fate-laden occurrence of being? Where is the human as responsible to God? To the extent that the later Heidegger does not provide structures for such theological concerns, his philosophy is of limited relevance to theology.

Ott's book was not only a critique of Bultmann's use of the early Heidegger, but also a debate with Ernst Fuchs over the use to be made of the later Heidegger. Hence it is not surprising that the debate with Ott has been carried on primarily by Fuchs and his pupils. Eberhard Jüngel was an

---

148. Ebeling, "Verantworten des Glaubens," 124, points out that the concrete place where language occurs, person-to-person relations, remains in need of clarification.

assistant in the New Testament department of the *Kirchliche Hochschule* of Berlin when Fuchs was Professor there, and it is he who has published an article with the subtitle "A Debate with Heinrich Ott's Interpretation of Heidegger."[149] The essay is entitled "The Step Backwards," which is of course a play on Heidegger's term referring to the step back out of metaphysics into the ground of metaphysics. Jüngel means it as a criticism of Ott for falling back into metaphysics.[150]

Jüngel's charge that Ott has returned to metaphysics is based on Ott's use of traditional terminology whose roots are ultimately to be found in the subjectivism of the metaphysical tradition. Ott can speak of a "project of thought," whereas thought is not "projected" from the subject, but comes to him from the subject matter. Ott distinguishes between a formal and a material relation of philosophy to theology, whereas such Aristotelian categories as form and matter are to be replaced. Ott describes Heidegger's thought as "static" prior to the shift, "dynamic" after the shift, and draws diagrams of it, whereas Heidegger regards thought as historic, as event. Jüngel most of all takes exception to Ott's defining Heidegger's approach as transcendental.[151] This suggests that the movement of thought comes from the thinker, as he moves step by step into the presup-*posit*ions of thought. But thinking is for Heidegger no longer what the thinker "posits" but that which comes to the thinker from being. Hence Heidegger should not be described as inquiring as to presuppositions of thought. Instead, he hearkens to what being bids him; his thinking corresponds to being. Thus Ott, in describing being as the presupposition of thought, is using a vocabulary that has not yet been brought into conformity to the subject matter of Heidegger's thought—an inconsistency frequently and perhaps unavoidably encountered in these initial stages of the discussion of the later Heidegger's thought.[152]

149. Jüngel, "Der Schritt züruck," 104–22.

150. Ibid., 110.

151. Ibid., 105ff. Similarly Fuchs, "Denken und Sein?" 108. Franz, "Das Denken Heideggers," 85, criticizes Ott for trying to "reproduce Heidegger's thought in the language of German idealism."

152. Jüngel ("Der Schritt züruck," 104–5) appeals to Franz's book, *kerygma und kunst*, as the proper use of the later Heidegger in relation to theology, by way of contrast to Ott's *Denken und Sein*. Yet Franz, "Das Denken Heideggers," 86, 100, uses the term "dynamic" as equivalent to "historic," and makes use (ibid., 100) of diagrams like those of Ott. Cf. Heidegger's comment: "It belongs to the nature of such transitions that they to a certain extent must still speak the language of what they are helping to overcome." *Was ist*

Ernst Fuchs' own review of Ott's book, although sharing quite decidedly in the general Bultmannian criticism of Ott, is primarily of relevance in that it sketches some of the outlines of his own position. Fuchs meets Ott's criticism of him for not following Heidegger's path of thought[153] with the reply that he never intended to do so, since "faith is no path of thought." Fuchs understands Ott's talk of Heidegger's "path of thought" in the same way Jüngel understands Ott's description of Heidegger's method as transcendental: a "path of thought" suggests Cartesian subjectivism. Hence Fuchs sets up the antithesis: "If the 'path of thought' leads into the square, the *path of language* will lead again—to us." Human efforts at thought are one's works righteousness; thought is equivalent to law,[154] while language is equivalent to gospel. Being has its place not in thought but in language, for the hearing of the voice of being calls forth speech. Fuchs poses the "decisive" question to Heidegger: "When will the thinker finally give up thinking about being? If he has experienced that being speaks, then he will understand why I pose my question this way. The theologian, and Barth specifically, knows of being as 'being for . . .'"[155] Here Fuchs seems to identify being and God, an identification not made by Heidegger himself.

Another of Fuchs' former pupils, Helmut Franz, has moved via a critique of both Ott[156] and Fuchs[157] in their use of Heidegger to an independent position. Fuchs' rejection of Heideggerian thinking is for Franz a misunderstanding of what thinking means for Heidegger. Thinking is for Heidegger responding to being, and hence does not derive from human

---

Metaphysik? (8th ed.), 43 = *Existence and Being,* 380–81; paperback ed., 350.

153. Ott, *Denken und Sein,* 186. Actually, Ott is here criticizing Fuchs for not following Heidegger's understanding of language.

154. Ebeling, "Verantworten des Glaubens," 122, questions "whether faith in the sense of primal Christian living tolerates theology at all, that is to say, whether faith can be 'thought.'" He raises the question as "whether theology is not essentially bound to metaphysical thinking." Yet on 123 he describes theology since Luther as involved in the effort to overcome metaphysics. On 124 he wonders "whether the segregation of thinking from believing and the expectation that God could be promised to thought, together with the talk of the 'square,' may not be clinging to metaphysics."

155. All quotations of Fuchs are from 108 of his review of Ott's book. This review is significantly entitled "Thinking and Being?" ("Denken und Sein?"), which is both a play on the title of Ott's book and a suggestion of Fuchs's criticism.

156. Franz, "Das Denken Heideggers," 83–85 and passim. He characterizes Ott's method as eclecticism.

157. Ibid., 89–90. Cf. also *kerygma und kunst,* 57.

initiative. Hence thinking is in this regard no more a works righteousness than is language. Nor is being understood as "being for . . ." only by the theologian. Heidegger himself understands being as "being for" beings, and so speaks of the favor of being.

Franz also presents a critique of Fuchs' earlier use of Heidegger in his *Hermeneutik*.[158] Here Fuchs had already interpreted Heidegger in terms of the latter's understanding of language almost a decade before the appearance of *Unterwegs zur Sprache*. He understands Heidegger to be presenting a complaint about the breakdown of language. Since for Fuchs authentic language is the word of God, he interprets Heidegger's complaint about the breakdown of language as posing the question of God. The question about God is then answered when Jesus' call of love responds as authentic language to the complaint and turns it into thanksgiving. Thus the unveiling of being as authentic language and the appearance of Jesus with his word tend to coincide. Franz suspects that theology here emerges simply as a dialectic transformation of complaint into its opposite. But most of all Franz expresses doubt that Heidegger can be correctly understood as the philosopher of man's collapse and complaint. That is to say, Franz sees in Fuchs' use of Heidegger the "existential misunderstanding" of Heidegger against which Ott argues.[159] Indeed, Ott's criticism of Fuchs' use of Heidegger consisted in asserting that Fuchs understood Heidegger to be interested in language in terms of its role in achieving authentic existence, rather than being interested in language "as language," as the voice of being.[160]

Franz himself advocates a clearer distinction between Heidegger's thought and Christian faith than was characteristic of the original positions of Fuchs and Ott. Indeed he interprets Heidegger as himself calling for a clear distinction not only between metaphysics and faith, but also between his own philosophy and faith.[161] Alongside remarks distinguish-

---

158. Fuchs, *Hermeneutik*. Cf. chapter 5: "The Question about God (M. Heidegger)," 62–72. In his review of Ott, Fuchs states that this chapter was written in 1950. Franz's discussion of Fuchs's *Hermeneutik* is scattered through *kerygma und kunst* and is summarized in "Das Denken Heideggers," 86–88.

159. Franz, "Das Denken Heideggers," 82–83, makes the same criticism of Bultmann's use of Heidegger as he did of Fuchs. Heidegger's analysis of *Dasein* does not portray man's collapse as a pre-understanding for the gospel.

160. Ott, *Denken und Sein*, 185–86.

161. Franz, *kerygma und kunst*, 62ff.; "Das Denken Heideggers," 92, 113–14, passim.

ing *Being and Time* from existentialism occur remarks distancing it from theology, and specifically from dialectic theology.[162] Heidegger holds that his basic question as to why there are beings at all rather than nothing is stultified by faith, with its glib answer that God created them.[163] Actually, Heidegger argues, faith should regard his basic question as "foolishness," since it has no relation to faith's own concerns.[164] According to Heidegger, "the unconditionedness of faith and the questionableness of thinking are two different spheres separated by a chasm."[165] "Faith has no place in thinking."[166] Although in both these contexts "faith" refers to the authoritarianism and absolutism traditionally associated with religion, rather than to faith as the specific Christian self-understanding, Franz uses these quotations as support for his position that Christian faith in Heidegger's view requires a clear distinction from his philosophical thought.

When Franz comes to discuss the passages where Heidegger takes a more positive stance toward Christian faith, he defines such statements as only "on the fringe of his thought." He distinguishes Heidegger's experience in thinking from Heidegger's experience of Christianity and locates within the latter the statements that Ott uses to relate Heidegger's thinking to Christianity.[167] Thus Franz in his own way carries through a distinction—even within Heidegger—between thinking and believing, although not the same distinction Fuchs made,[168] and, like Fuchs, brings

---

162. Heidegger, *Vom Wesen des Grundes* (4th ed.), 42 n. 59.

163. Heidegger, *Einführung in die Metaphysik* (2nd ed.) 5 = *An Introduction to Metaphysics*, 6–7.

164. Heidegger, *Einführung in die Metaphysik* (2nd ed.) 6; *An Introduction to Metaphysics*, 7. Franz, *Kerygma und Kunst*, 64, draws attention to the diverging assumption of Bultmann, when in *Das Evangelium des Johannes*, 18, Bultmann says: "The philosopher's question 'Why is there not nothing?' would also be answered by this sentence: 'In the beginning was the word.'" One may also cite Carl Michalson, *The Hinge of History*, 126, where Heidegger is treated as an existentialist and his basic question translated "why am I something and not nothing?" Compare Heidegger, ibid., 3 [ibid., 4]: "If our question 'Why are there beings rather than nothing?' is taken in its fullest sense, we must avoid singling out any special, particular being, including man."

165. Heidegger, *Was heisst Denken?*, 110.

166. Heidegger, *Holzwege* (3rd ed.), 343.

167. Cf. Franz, "Das Denken Heideggers," 112ff.

168. In *kerygma und kunst*, 97, Franz explicitly rejects Fuchs's association of Jesus' word with Heidegger's language theory (Fuchs, *Hermeneutik*, 72), and associates the latter with the rest of Heidegger's philosophy as the world out of which Jesus calls us.

this distinction into correlation with the theological distinction between law and gospel.[169]

Franz explains the place of God in Heidegger's thought by clarifying Heidegger's answer to the question of how God entered metaphysics. The realm of being that calls forth thinking and language is the divine realm. In its own unveiling and calling, being does not present itself as God, for being is not a being. When, however, thinking ascends through logical processes toward that divine realm, it takes being for a supreme being, God. Now since this logical ascent of thought is a fate-laden occurrence of being (even though being veils itself thereby), the concept of God is just as inevitable as is metaphysics. Yet Heidegger's overcoming of metaphysics would involve a replacement of God with the divine realm, just as being as a supreme or universal being is replaced by being in its distinction from beings.

This analysis could suggest as one alternative the position taken by Walter Schulz in his address of 1956 on "The 'God of the Philosophers' in Modern Metaphysics."[170] Schulz argues that Heidegger has in his understanding of being achieved a kind of transcendence without God, and in the turn in his thought has gone through the equivalent of conversion. But rather than this suggesting that Heidegger has "found God," this suggests that a modern person can get along even in one's religious life without God or Christianity. This is the outcome that was feared by various theologians when *Being and Time* appeared.[171] Whether today Dietrich Bonhoeffer's program of a "nonreligious interpretation of Biblical categories" suited to a "world come of age"[172] opens an avenue to a positive reception of this alternative by theologians remains to be seen. There are some indications that point in this direction.[173]

---

169. Franz identifies thinking with the law and with works righteousness in "Das Denken Heideggers," 110.

170. Schulz, "Der 'Gott der Philosophen' in der neuzeitlichen Metaphysik," in *Der Gott der neuzeitlichen Metaphysik* 33–58.

171. Cf. Schrey, "Die Bedeutung," 10, quoted in my review of Ogden's *Christ without Myth*, 440.

172. Bonhoeffer, *Prisoner for God*.

173. Ebeling, "Elementare Besinnung auf verantwortliches Reden von Gott," in *Wort und Glaube*, 359: "A doctrine of God is today abstract speculation if the phenomenon of modern atheism is not present in it from the very beginning." With regard to Heidegger's thought, Ebeling ("Verantworten des Glaubens," 124) says theology must speak of God nonmetaphysically, "and this means, according to the dominant theological tradition,

Franz himself follows a different alternative.¹⁷⁴ When Heidegger on occasion speaks of the "divine God" in distinction from the metaphysical God,¹⁷⁵ Franz does not, like Ott, assume that this may be leading in the direction of the Christian God.¹⁷⁶ Instead, he identifies the realm of being as the "god-world," and the god emerging from it the "world-god." He points out that Heidegger derives his concept of the world from the New Testament, arguing that primitive Christianity, precisely in being called out of the world, first clearly caught sight of "world."¹⁷⁷ Then he quotes Heidegger with regard to the New Testament: "A world separates all this from Heraclitus."¹⁷⁸ Hence we should follow Heidegger's advice to take seriously the Christian subject matter and regard philosophy as foolishness.¹⁷⁹ This Christian subject matter is once defined by Heidegger as "the Christian life that existed for a brief time before the writing of the gospels and before the missionary propaganda of Paul."¹⁸⁰ From this Franz argues that we should obey Jesus' call for repentance, his call out of the world.¹⁸¹ Such faith is freedom from the world as law.

Although Fuchs, Jüngel, and Franz have not agreed in all respects, there does emerge from their presentations of the relation of theology to the later Heidegger a general direction, which has been brought into fo-

---

godlessly." Herbert Braun's address at the meeting of the Old Marburgers in 1960, intended to present the exegetical aspect of the relation of Heidegger to theology as Ott's address presented the systematic aspect, presupposes a basic difference between New Testament times and our times in that God's existence can no longer be assumed. Hence his normative reinterpretation of God is an instance of such a "godless," that is to say, nonmetaphysical understanding: God is the dialectic of "you may" and "you ought" in interpersonal relations. Cf. "Die Problematik," 3–18, esp. 3.

174. Franz, *kerygma und kunst*, 83, identifies Schulz's position as "an amazing misunderstanding." This would be true if Schulz really identifies being and God, as Diem assumes in his reply, *Gott und die Metaphysik*.

175. Heidegger, *Identität und Differenz*, 71 = *Essays in Metaphysik*, 65.

176. Ebeling, "Verantworten des Glaubens," 124, identifies the "divine God" with the Christian God.

177. Franz, *kerygma und kunst*, 89ff.

178. Heidegger, *Einführung in die Metaphysik*, 103 = *An Introduction to Metaphysics*, 135. Franz, *kerygma und kunst*, 80, 88, and passim; idem, "Das Denken Heideggers," 111.

179. Heidegger, *Was ist Metaphysik?* (8th ed.), 20 = *Existentialism from Dostoevsky to Sartre*, 218.

180. Heidegger, *Holzwege*, 202.

181. Franz, *kerygma und kunst*, 88, 95ff.; idem, "Das Denken Heideggers," 119–24.

cus by Gerhard Ebeling in the theses with which he concludes the Beiheft of the *Zeitschrift für Theologie und Kirche* devoted to this debate.[182] While conceding that the emergence of a philosophy that overcomes metaphysics and that is consequently distinct from traditional Western philosophy presents a "completely new situation" for the discussion between philosophy and theology,[183] he argues that the distinction between philosophy and theology remains clear. Since Protestant theology is oriented to the distinction of law and gospel,[184] this pattern is proposed for the definition of the distinction between the later Heidegger and theology. Heidegger's thinking is an interpretation of the law, which corresponds to theology in that theology too interprets the law, but is in tension with theology in that Heidegger's thought does not understand itself as law. Since Heidegger, just as the law to a considerable extent, speaks what the times call for, faith is responsible to listen, since it is responsible for our times as they are. Yet it would be regression into metaphysical thinking to theologize about Heidegger's ontological difference between being and the beings. Instead, one could speak of a theological difference of God and creature. Yet, lest this be confused with a metaphysical difference between two worlds, such a theological distinction should be understood concretely. It is the difference between man the sinner and the God who justifies, a distinction that happens in the preaching of the word.

---

182. Ebeling, "Verantworten des Glaubens," 119–24

183. Ibid., 121.

184. Cf. Ebeling's programmatic essay, "Die Notwendigkeit der Lehre von den zwei Reichen" = "The Necessity of the Doctrine of the Two Kingdoms."

Bibliography 1

Anz, Wilhelm. "Verkündigung und theologische Reflexion." *ZTKB* 2 (1961) 47–80.
Barth, Karl. "Philosophie und Theologie." In *Philosophie und christliche Existenz: Festschrift für Heinrich Barth zum 70. Geburtstag am 3. Februar 1960*, edited by Gerhard Huber, 93–106. Basel: Hebling und Lichtenhan, 1960.
Bonhoeffer, Dietrich. *Prisoner for God: Letters and Papers from Prison*. Translated by Reginald H. Fuller. New York: Macmillan, 1954.
Braun, Herbert. "Die Problematik einer Theologie des Neuen Testaments." *ZTKB* 2 (1961) 3–18.
Bultmann, Rudolf. *Das Evangelium des Johannes*. 1941. 16th ed. Göttingen: Vandenhoeck & Ruprecht, 1959.
———. *The Gospel of John*. Translated by G. R. Beasley-Murray et al. Philadelphia: Westminster, 1971.
———. *Theology of the New Testament*. 2 vols. Translated by Kendrick Grobel. New York: Scribner, 1951. Reprinted, Waco, TX: Baylor University Press, 2007.
———. "Untersuchungen zum Johannesevangelium." *ZNW* 27 (1928) 113–63.
Diem, Hermann. *Gott und die Metaphysik*. ThSt 47. Zurich: EVZ, 1956.
Ebeling, Gerhard. "Hermeneutik." In *RGG³* (1959) 3:243–58.
———. "The Necessity of the Doctrine of the Two Kingdoms." In *Word and Faith*, 386–406.
———. "Die Notwendigkeit der Lehre von den zwei Reichen." In *Wort und Glaube*, 407–28.
———. "Verantworten des Glaubens in Begegnung mit dem Denken M. Heideggers." *ZTKB* 2 (1961) 119–24.
———. *Word and Faith*. Translated by James W. Leitch. Philadelphia: Fortress, 1963.
———. "The Word of God and Hermeneutic." In *Word and Faith*, 305–32. Reprinted in *The New Hermeneutic*, edited by James M. Robinson and John B. Cobb Jr., 78–110. New Frontiers in Theology 2. New York: Harper & Row, 1964.
———. "Wort Gottes und Hermeneutik." *ZTK* 56 (1959) 224–51. Reprinted in *Wort und Glaube*, 319–48.

———. *Wort und Glaube*. Tübingen: Mohr/Siebeck, 1960.
Franz, Helmut. "Das Denken Heideggers und die Theologie." *ZTKB* 2 (1961) 81–118.
———. *kerygma und kunst*. Saarbrücken: Minerva, 1959.
Friedländer, Paul. *Plato*. 3 vols. Translated by Hans Meyerhoff. Bollingen Series 59. New York: Pantheon, 1958–69.
———. *Platon*. 3 vols. 2nd ed. Berlin: de Gruyter, 1953–60.
Fuchs, Ernst. *Hermeneutik*. Bad Cannstatt: Müllerschön, 1954. 2nd ed., 1958.
———. "Denken und Sein?" *PhR* 8 (January, 1961) 106–8.
Gogarten, Friedrich. *Demythologizing and History*. Translated by Neville Horton Smith. London: SCM, 1955.
———. *Entmythologisierung und Kirche*. Stuttgart: Vorwerk, 1953.
———. *The Reality of Faith: The Problem of Subjectivism in Theology*. Translated by Carl Michalson. Philadelphia: Westminster, 1959.
———. *Wirklichkeit des Glaubens: Zum Problem des Subjektivismus in der Theologie*. Stuttgart: Vorwerk, 1957.
Haenchen, Ernst. "Anselm, Glaube und Vernunft." *ZTK* 48 (1951) 312–42.
Heidegger, Martin. "Aufzeichnungen aus der Werkstatt." *NZZ* 5.2898 (69) (Sept. 27, 1959).
———. *Aus der Erfahrung des Denkens*. Pfullingen: Neske, 1954.
———. "Aus einer Erörterung der Wahrheitsfrage." In *Zehn Jahre Neske Verlag*, 19–23. Pfullingen: Neske, 1962.
———. "Bauen Wohnen Denken." In *Vorträge und Aufsätze*, 145–62.
———. *Being and Time*. Translated by John Macquarrie and Edward Robinson. New York: Harper & Row, 1962.
———. "Brief über den Humanismus." In *Platons Lehre von der Wahrheit*, 53–119. Bern: Franke, 1947. Republished separately as *Über den Humanismus*. Frankfurt: Klostermann, 1949.
———. "Ein Briefwechsel mit Martin Heidegger." In Emil Staiger, *Die Kunst der Interpretation: Studien zur deutschen Literaturgeschichte*, 34–49. Zurich: Atlantis, 1955. 2nd ed., 1957.
———. "Das Ding." In *Vorträge und Aufsätze*, 163–85.
———. *Einführung in die Metaphysik*. 1957. 2nd ed. Tübingen: Niemeyer, 1958.
———. *Erläuterungen zu Hölderlins Dichtung*. 2nd ed. Pfullingen: Neske, 1951.
———. *Essays in Metaphysics: Identity and Difference*. Translated by Kurt F. Leidecker. New York: Philosophical Library, 1960.
———. *Existence and Being*. Translated by R. F. C. Hull and Alan Crick. London: Vision, 1949. Gateway Paperback ed. Chicago: Regnery, 1960.
———. *Existentialism from Dostoevsky to Sartre*. Translated by Walter Kaufman. New York: Meridian, 1956.
———. *Der Feldweg*. Frankfurt: Klostermann, 1949. 2nd ed., 1956.
———. *Die Frage nach dem Ding*. Tübingen: Niemeyer, 1962.
———. *Die Frage nach der Technik*. Opuscula: Aus Wissenschaft und Dichtung. Pfullingen: Neske, 1962.
———. "Die Frage nach der Technik." In *Vorträge und Aufsätze*, 13–44.
———. *Gelassenheit*. Pfullingen: Neske, 1959. 2nd ed., 1960.

———. *Gespräch mit Hebel.* Schriftenreihe des Hebelbundes Sitz Lörrach 4. 1956. Reprinted in *Hebeldank,* edited by Hanns Uhl. Freiburg: Rombach, 1960.

———. *Hebel—Der Hausfreund.* Pfullingen: Neske, 1957.

———. *Hölderlin und das Wesen der Dichtung.* Munich: Langen und Müller, 1937. Reprinted in *Erläuterungen zu Hölderlins Dichtung,* 1951, 31–43. English translation by Douglas Scott in *Existence and Being,* 291–315; paperback ed., 270–91.

———. *Holzwege.* Frankfurt: Klostermann, 1950. 3rd ed., 1957.

———. *Identität und Differenz.* Pfullingen: Neske, 1957.

———. *An Introduction to Metaphysics.* Translated by Ralph Manheim. New Haven: Yale University Press, 1959.

———. *Kant und das Problem der Metaphysik.* Frankfurt: Klostermann, 1929. 2nd ed., 1951.

———. *Die Kategorien- und Bedeutungslehre des Duns Scotus.* Tübingen: Mohr/Siebeck, 1916.

———. *Nietzsche.* 2 vols. Pfullingen: Neske, 1961.

———. "Die onto-theo-logische Verfassung der Metaphysik." In *Identität und Differenz,* 35–73. Pfullingen: Neske, 1957.

———. *Platons Lehre von der Wahrheit: Mit einem Brief über den "Humanismus."* Sammlung Überlieferung und Auftrag: Reihe Probleme und Hinweise 55. Bern: Francke, 1947. 2nd ed. 1954. 4th ed., 1967.

———. "The Principle of Identity." In *Essays in Metaphysics,* 11–32.

———. *The Question of Being.* Translated by William Kluback and Jean T. Wilde. New York: Twayne, 1958.

———. "Der Satz der Identität." In *Identität und Differenz,* 11–34.

———. *Der Satz vom Grund.* Pfullingen: Neske, 1957. 2nd ed., 1958.

———. *Sein und Zeit.* 8th ed. Tübingen: Niemeyer, 1957.

———. *Die Selbstbehauptung der deutschen Universität.* Breslau: Korn, 1933.

———. *Über den Humanismus.* Frankfurt: Klostermann, 1949.

———. "Überwindung der Metaphysik." In *Vorträge und Aufsätze,* 71–99.

———. *Unterwegs zur Sprache.* Pfullingen: Neske, 1959. 2nd ed., 1960.

———. "Der Ursprung des Kunstwerkes." In *Holzweg,* 7–68. 3rd ed. Frankfurt: Klostermann, 1957.

———. "Der Weg zur Sprache." In *Die Sprache,* 93–114. Darmstadt: Wissenschaftliche Buchgesellschaft, 1959. Reprinted in *Unterwegs zur Sprache,* 239–68.

———. *Vom Wesen der Wahrheit.* Frankfurt: Klostermann, 1949. 3rd ed. 1954. 8th ed., 1997.

———. *Vom Wesen des Grundes.* Halle: Niemeyer, 1929. 2nd ed. 1931. 4th ed. Frankfurt: Klostermann, 1955.

———. *Vorträge und Aufsätze.* Frankfurt: Klostermann, 1954. 2nd ed. Pfullingen: Neske, 1959.

———. *Was heisst Denken?* Tübingen: Niemeyer, 1954.

———. *Was ist das—die Philosophie?* Pfullingen: Neske, 1956.

———. *Was ist Metaphysik?* Frankfurt: Klostermann, 1929. 8th ed., 1960.

———. "The Way Back into the Ground of Metaphysics." In *Existentialism from Dostoevsky to Sartre,* 206–21. Translated by Walter Kaufmann. New York: Meridian, 1956.

———. "Der Weg zur Sprache." In *Die Sprache*, 93–114. Darmstadt: Wissenschaftliche Buchgesellschaft, 1959. Reprinted in *Unterwegs zur Sprache*, 239–68.
———. *What Is Philosophy?* Translated by William Kluback and Jean T. Wilde. New York: Twayne, 1958.
———. *Zur Seinsfrage*. 1956. 2nd ed. Frankfurt: Klostermann, 1959.
Heitsch, Ernst. "Die nicht-philosophische Alētheia." *Hermes* 90 (1962) 24–33.
Jüngel, Eberhard. "Der Schritt zurück: Eine Auseinandersetung mit der Heidegger-Deutung Heinrich Otts." *ZTK* 58 (1961) 104–22.
Löwith, Karl. *Heidegger: Denker in dürftiger Zeit*. Göttingen: Vandenhoeck & Ruprecht, 1953. 2nd ed., 1960.
———. *Meaning in History: The Theological Implications of the Philosophy of History*. Chicago: University of Chicago Press, 1949.
Michalson, Carl. *The Hinge of History*. New York: Scribner, 1959.
Noller, Gerhard. *Sein und Existenz: Die Überwindung des Subjekt-Objektschemas in der Philosophie Heideggers und in der Theologie der Entmythologisierung*. Munich: Kaiser, 1962.
Ott, Heinrich. "Anselms Versöhnungslehre." *TZ* 13 (1957) 183–99.
———. *Denken und Sein: Der Weg Martin Heideggers und der Weg der Theologie*. Zurich: EVZ, 1959.
———. *Dogmatik und Verkündigung*. Zurich: EVZ, 1961.
———. *Eschatologie: Versuch eines dogmatischen Grundrisses*. ThSt 53. Zurich: EVZ, 1958.
———. *Die Frage nach dem historischen Jesus und die Ontologie der Geschichte*. ThSt 62. Zurich: EVZ, 1960.
———. *Geschichte und Heilsgeschichte in der Theologie Rudolf Bultmanns*. BHTh 19. Tübingen: Mohr/Siebeck, 1955.
———. "Sprache und Verstehen als Grundproblem gegenwärtiger Theologie." Unpublished essay.
———. "Theologie als Gebet und als Wissenschaft." *TZ* 14 (1958) 120–32.
———. "Was ist systematische Theologie?" *ZTKB* 2 (1961) 19–46.
———. "What is Systematic Theology?" In *The Later Heidegger and Theology*, edited by James M. Robinson and John B. Cobb Jr., 77–111. New Frontiers in Theology 1. New York: Harper & Row, 1963.
Robinson, James M. "Basic Shifts in German Theology." *Int* 16 (1962) 76–97.
———. "Heilsgeschichte und Lichtungsgeschichte." *EvTh* 22 (1962) 113–41.
———. "The Historicality of Biblical Language." In *The Old Testament and Christian Faith: A Theological Discussion*, edited by Bernhard W. Anderson, 124–58. New York: Harper & Row, 1963.
———. Review of Schubert M. Ogden, *Christ without Myth*, in *TTo* 19 (1962) 439–44.
Sartre, Jean-Paul. *Existentialism*. Translated by Bernard Frechtman. New York: Philosophical Library, 1947.
———. *L'Existentialisme est un Humanisme*. Paris: Nagel, 1946.
Schrey, Heinz-Horst. "Die Bedeutung der Philosophie Martin Heideggers für die Theologie." In *Martin Heideggers Einfluss auf die Wissenschaften aus Anlass seines sechzigsten Geburtstag*, edited by Carlos Astrada, 9–21. Bern: Francke, 1949.

Schulz, Walter. *Der Gott der neuzeitlicher Metaphysik*. Pfullingen: Neske, 1957; 2nd ed., 1959.

———. "Über den philosophiegeschichtlichen Ort Martin Heideggers." *PhR* 1 (1953-54) 65–93, 211–32.

Staiger, Emil. *Die Kunst der Interpretation: Studien zur deutschen Literaturegeschichte*. Zurich: Atlantis, 1955; 2nd ed., 1957.

———. "Ein Rückblick." *NZZ* 5.2868 (Sept. 27, 1959) 69.

Steiger, Lothar. *Die Hermeneutik als dogmatisches Problem: Eine Auseinandersetzung mit dem transzendentalen Ansatz des theologischen Verstehens*. Gütersloh: Gütersloher Verlag Mohn, 1961.

Thurneysen, Eduard. "Warum nicht Gollwitzer? Ein Wort zum Kampf um die Nachfolge Karl Barths in Basel." *KRS* 118–119 (1962). Reprinted in *EvTh* 22 (1962) 271–77.

Uhsadel, Walter. Review of Martin Heidegger, *Unterwegs zur Sprache* in *TLZ* 86 (1961) 217–21.

CHAPTER 2 | *Hermeneutic Since Barth*

HERMENEIA

THE ENGLISH TERM HERMENEUTIC ONLY PARTIALLY CORRESPONDS TO the "equivalent" Greek noun *hermēneia*. The meaning of the Greek term was determined by the Greek verb *hermēneuein*, corresponding to the Latin verb *interpretari*, to "interpret."

Hermēneia meant "interpretation" so broadly that it could be applied to whatever activity was involved in bringing the unclear to clarity. Indeed it is this broad scope of clarification, rather than any one specific kind of clarification, that seems to be basic to *hermēneia*. It is in this way that one is to understand the constant application of *hermēneia* to the messages of the gods, in that they are by their very nature mysterious, obscure, and in need of clarification. The *hermēneia* of the will of the gods doubtless shared in this broad, numinous sensitivity even when the *hermēneia* in question has become specific and concrete.

An instance of this general sensitivity to the numinous quality of theological *hermēneia* is the spiritual gift "*hermēneia* of tongues." This gift, listed in 1 Cor 12:10 alongside of speaking in tongues, is not simply to be identified with the capacity for rational translation. For the speaking in tongues did not (pace Luke) involve foreign languages, but rather ecstatic, divine ("angelic" 1 Cor 13:1) utterance, calling for interpretation, such as is required for various kinds of obscure divine communication. The interpretation itself has revelatory character, and consequently ranks as itself a charismatic gift. Thus, in 1 Cor 14:26, although *hermēneia* is again paired with speaking in a tongue, one could perhaps best translate it "illumination," rather than simply "translation." For the gift has some independent significance in communicating divine will, which makes it suited to stand in this verse alongside of "psalm," "teaching," and "revelation," as well as alongside of "tongue" as its translation.[1]

Hermēneia is already involved in the activity of a herald or spokesperson for the gods, whose function it is to proclaim clearly the will of the gods. This meaning of *hermēneia* as proclamation is implicit in the name of the divine herald Hermes, who invented language as a medium of interpretation. The people of Lystra call Barnabas, Zeus, but Paul, Hermes, "because he was the chief speaker" (Acts 14:12). Since Moses is told that Aaron "shall speak for you" (Exod 4:16), Philo can refer to Aaron as Moses' "spokesperson" (*hermēneus*).[2] But the inspired prophet himself is designated with the same term, as God's "spokesperson."[3] Similarly Plato refers to the poets as "nothing but spokespersons (*hermēnēs*) of the gods," and to rhapsodists, whose function it was to recite Homeric poems, as "spokesmen for spokesmen" (*hermēneōn hermēnēs*).[4] In this case interpretation takes the form of a continuing recurrence of language, from the poet's utterance to the rhapsodist's recital. Here language is itself interpretation,[5] not just the object of interpretation. Hence *hermēneia* can mean "linguistic formulation" or "expression," and it can be used to designate a work on logical formulation or artistic elocution,[6] the discipline we today call "speech."

If this understanding of language as itself interpretation has been hardly sensed in traditional hermeneutics, it has become central in the new hermeneutic, and is indeed one of its distinguishing characteristics. Gerhard Ebeling begins his encyclopedia article on hermeneutic with the

---

1. In Sir 47:17 countries are amazed at Solomon "for songs and proverbs and parables and for illuminations (*hermēneiai*)." Cf. further 1 Cor 12:30; 14:5, 13, 27, 28.

2. Philo, *That the Worse Attacks the Better* 39.

3. Cf. the passages from Philo collected by Johannes Behm, "ἑρμηνεύω κτλ.," in *TWNT* 2:661 = *TDNT* 2:664-65.

4. Plato, *Ion*, 534E, 535A.

5. The term interpretation retains a somewhat analogous significance in the arts, where a musician or actor's "interpretation" refers to his rendition or performance of the work of art, rather than to a commentary on the work of art.

6. Georg Heinrici, "Hermeneutik," 719, and Gerhard Ebeling in "Hermeneutik," 243 cite for the former Aristotle's *Peri hermēneia* and for the latter (Pseudo-) Demetrius of Phaleron's use of the same title.

statement: "The etymological origin of *hermēneuein* and its derivatives is contested, but it points in the direction of roots with the meaning 'speak,' 'say' (connected with the Latin *verbum* or *sermo*)."[7] If this etymology is admittedly uncertain, and yet serves to open the presentation, it is because it symbolizes the scope of the new hermeneutic. This embraces the whole theological enterprise as a movement of language, from the word of God attested in Scripture to the preached sermon in which God speaks anew, and is not confined to a subdivision within Biblical studies treating of the theory of exegesis.

The "interpretation" involved in *hermēneia* could also take the specific form of "translation" out of a foreign tongue.[8] This meaning of *hermēneia* was not carried over into traditional hermeneutics. But it is distinctive of the new hermeneutic that it does understand its task as translating meaning from one culture to the other, from one situation to the other. The deeper implication involved in translating from one language to another, namely, the constitutive role attributed to man's historicness in appraising the hermeneutical task, is a significant aspect of the contemporary renewal of the hermeneutical question.

This deeper implication involved in translation can be brought to attention within English usage by recalling a meaning of the term "trans-

---

7. Ebeling, "Hermeneutik," 243. Indeed the Latin *verbum* is derived from the root *wer* or *wre* meaning to "say." This has as its Greek cognate a form originally using a Greek letter *digamma* subsequently dropped from the Greek alphabet and replaced by the rough breathing transliterated in English with "h." Consequently, the Latin stem *verb-* and the Greek stem *herm-* could be cognates of each other and of the German *Wort* and English "word." One Greek term for "word," *rhēma*, is also involved in this group of cognates. The Latin *sermo* may be related to the verb *sero*, meaning to arrange in a row, or thread, whose Greek cognate form was originally *serjo*. Since such an initial *s* tended to be replaced by the rough breathing (transliterated in English with "h"), this Greek root survived as *her-* (e.g., *herma*, which means "earring"). Thus the Latin stem *serm-* could also be related to the Greek stem *herm-* involved in *hermēneuein*. But *hermēneuein* can hardly be derived from the root beginning with *digamma* meaning "to say" and from the root beginning with *sigma* meaning "to arrange in a row," in spite of the fact that both roots came to be written with the rough breathing and thus to converge with each other and with the Greek stem of *hermēneuein* (and perhaps each to produce a distinct verb of identical spelling, *eirein*). Furthermore, *sermo* is more probably derived from a root *swer* meaning to speak and cognate to the German *schwören*, English "swear." Cf. Menge and Güthling, *Enzyklopädisches Wörterbuch der lateinischen und deutschen Sprache*, 792, s.v. *verbum*, and 692, s.v. *sermo*; Boisacq, *Dictionnaire étymologique de la langue grecque*, 282–83, s.v. *hermēneus*, etc., and 229–30, s.v. *eiro*.

8. John 9:7: "Siloam, which is translated (*hermēneuetai*) 'Sent.'" Cf. similarly Matt 1:23; Mark 5:41; 15:22, 34; John 1:38, 41, 42; Acts 4:36; 9:36; 13:8; Heb 7:2.

lation" that has passed out of common usage and is largely confined to ecclesiastical concepts derived from the past. One can speak of "translating" a bishop from one see to another, just as one used to speak of a saint's "translation" to heaven. This usage of the term "translate" to refer to a movement from one place to the other has largely been replaced by other terms, such as the term "transfer," derived from the same Latin verb. In German one can still speak of "trans-lating" a person or thing across a river in a ferry, whether or not the river be Jordan. And the Greek verb *hermēneuein* betrays much the same sensitivity in its proclivity for the use of the prefixes *dia-* and *meta-*, equivalent to the Latin prefix *trans-*, when meaning "to translate." Indeed Plato made the same analogy without benefit of the play on words, when he referred to "translating and ferrying (*hermēneuon kai diaporthmeuon*) to gods what comes from men and to men what comes from gods."[9] The new hermeneutic has to do with this slippery business of "translating" meaning.

Another specific form of *hermēneia* was that of a commentary, where no foreign language was involved but where the obscurity of an utterance or text called for some clarification. In Luke 24:27 the resurrected Lord "interpreted (*diermēneusen*) to them in all the Scriptures the things concerning himself."[10] Thus in Greek usage one meaning of *hermēneia* is synonymous with *exēgēsis*, a synonymity carried over into their Latin translations, *interpretatio* and *expositio* respectively,[11] and thus into the English synonyms interpretation and exposition. Hence our modern distinction between hermeneutics as the theory and exegesis as the practice of the art of interpretation cannot be attributed to antiquity. In the introduction to his "*Exēgēsis* of the Lord's Sayings," Papias speaks of what is to follow as "interpretations" (*hermēneiai*).[12] Hence *hermēneia*

---

9. *Symposium* 202 E. Miskotte, *Zur biblischen Hermeneutik*, 4, arrives at a similar understanding of hermeneutic as translation without recourse to the play on words.

10. The numinous nature of such revelatory interpretation is reflected in the parallel statements "he opened to us the Scriptures" (v. 32) and "he opened their minds to understand the Scriptures" (v. 45); the role of such interpretation as itself proclamation is reflected in the parallel statement "beginning with this Scripture he told him the good news of Jesus" (Acts 8:35).

11. E.g., the Latin translation of Photius' *Bibliotheca* by Andreas Schott, SJ of 1605 (printed 1653) follows consistently this translational policy for the instances of *hermēneia* listed in n. 13 below, with the exception of the anonymous *Hermēneia* on the Octateuch, where *hermēneia* is translated *expositio*. Cf. PG 103 (1900).

12. Cited by Eusebius, *Ecclesiastical History* 3.39.3. *The Gospel according to Thomas*,

became a patristic name for "commentary," in which meaning it is only now being revived.¹³ One significant aspect of the new hermeneutic is its return to this close association of hermeneutic with the *practice* of the art of interpretation, so that "hermeneutic" can become coterminous with Christian theology as the statement of the meaning of Scripture for our day.

The Greek noun *hermēneia* thus embraced the whole broad scope of "interpretation," from "speech" that brings the obscure into the clarity of linguistic expression, to "translation" from an obscure, foreign language into the clarity of one's own language, and to "commentary" that explicates the meaning of obscure language by means of clearer language. The profound implication that these three functions belong together as interrelated aspects of a single hermeneutic was lost in traditional hermeneutics, which was the theory of but one aspect of *hermēneia*, exegesis. This narrowing of the concept may suggest that some of the dimensions of the hermeneutical task had been lost from sight. Thus the rather explicit return to the breadth of *hermēneia* on the part of the new hermeneutic is to be seen not as etymological pedantry, but rather as a new grasp of the proportions and nature of the hermeneutical task.¹⁴

It is an initial indication of the approach of the new hermeneutic that its understanding of the hermeneutical task has been here worked out in seeking to translate the meaning of the term *hermēneia* into our language. Involved has been the assumption characteristic of the new hermeneutic that the language pointing to the subject matter is not simply in need of interpretation, but is already itself an initial interpretation of that subject matter. This is not meant as an invitation to seek that subject matter in

---

edited by A. Guillaumont et al., has as its first introductory saying "Whoever finds the *hermēneia* of these words will not taste death" (3). Thus *hermēneia* seems early to have been the standard term for an interpretation of the sayings of Jesus.

13. A ninth-century library catalogued by Photius, Patriarch of Constantinople, listed a *Hermēneia* on Daniel by Hippolytus of Rome (who also wrote a *Hermēneia* on Ruth), one on Genesis by Theodore of Mopsuestia, head of the Antiochene school of exegesis, another on Daniel by the Antiochene Theodoret of Cyrrus, and an anonymous *Hermēneia* on the Octateuch (as well as Theodoret's *Exēgēsis* on the Octateuch). Cf. *PG* 103 (1900), Codices 202, 38, 203, 36, 204. An international critical commentary series initiated with the focus on the interacting meanings of the Greek term has been entitled *Hermeneia: A Critical and Historical Commentary on the Bible*.

14. Ebeling, "Hermeneutik," 243: "Therein emerges the complexity of the hermeneutical problem, to which not merely one of these meanings, but rather their structural relatedness, points."

intuitive immediacy apart from the language interpreting it. Quite to the contrary, it is intended to indicate the positive and indispensable role of language in understanding. Rather than the language being a secondary, distorting objectification of meaning that must be removed to free the meaning behind the language, the language of the text is regarded positively as an interpretative proclamation of that meaning and hence as our indispensable access to it. Similarly the understanding of this meaning is not held in speechless profundity, but rather within our language. For only when the subject matter has been translated into our language, in spite of the historicness and finiteness of that language, has it been interpreted into our historic and finite world of understanding and hence been really understood. The insistence upon the unbroken linguisticality of understanding is an insistence upon the thoroughgoing historicness of the process of understanding. Thus one may say that the new hermeneutic, guided by the basic recognition of the historicness of man and of his understanding, has elevated language and translation, the more historic dimensions of interpretation, into positions of principle significance in the understanding of hermeneutic.

To listen to the Greek term *hermēneia* as an interpretation of the subject matter of hermeneutic—and to listen to it means to translate it into our language as "interpretation" in the three senses of "speech," "translation," and "commentary"—is not to stay on the outside of hermeneutical reflection, merely within linguistic objectifications behind which some neglected realm of immediacy is assumed to lie. Rather it is to understand hermeneutic as best man in his historic finiteness can understand, i.e., within the hermeneutical structures of his own existence, of which his linguisticality is primary.

HERMENEUTICS

Hermēneia, interpretation, is constantly being carried on without calling attention to itself, as people seek to understand one another and make themselves understood. Only when such normal communication breaks down due to some serious impediment to understanding (such as a foreign language) is attention drawn to the understanding process itself in such a way as to call forth reflection upon the *theory* of interpretation.

The factors that have usually combined to produce the main efforts at theorizing about interpretation in Western civilization have been two.

First, theorizing has emerged in the process of interpreting bodies of literature whose authority is in one way or the other binding and whose meaning is therefore crucial. Second, theorizing has been especially required when these classical or canonical literatures are to assert their authority in a situation to which they no longer directly speak, and into which their meaning must be translated if they are to be heard at all. This necessity for translating authoritative literature has been the *agens* in the history of hermeneutical theory.

In antiquity it was, on the one hand, classical Greek literature, binding aesthetically, morally, and religiously, whose authority was put in question by enlightenment and was vindicated, e.g., in the allegorical method of the Stoics. On the other hand, it was the Old Testament whose canonical authority for Jew and Christian was to be vindicated—in spite of the replacement of theocracy and temple by synagogue and church— by its translation into Rabbinic casuistry, Qumranian and primitive Christian eschatological exegesis, and Philo and Origen's allegory. When the Renaissance and the Reformation coupled a revival of the authority of the classics and the Bible with a sense of the newness of the times, the hermeneutical question again became a focus of attention. The necessity to interpret the *corpus juris* so as to reach a legal decision in cases to which that body of law does not directly speak has, alongside Homer and the Bible, provided the third main subject matter for hermeneutical reflection over the years. Thus the history of hermeneutical theory[15] has in each case been determined by a very practical dimension, the necessity of man to act in the present, and yet to act correctly in terms of traditional norms. For hermeneutic itself is rooted in man's historicness, namely, the call placed upon him to encounter the history of the past in such a way as not to deny his own existential future and present responsibility.

The Greek term *hermēneia* had long since disappeared from the Latinized vocabulary of scholarship when the theory of interpretation emerged as a science as a result of the Renaissance and Reformation.[16]

---

15. The detailed history is presented in most standard treatments. Cf., e.g., Blackman, *Biblical Interpretation*; Wood, *Interpretation of the Bible*; Ebeling, "Hermeneutik," 245–58; Grobel, "Interpretation." Cf. further Smalley, *Study of the Bible in the Middle Ages*; Grant, *Bible in the Church*; Grant, Terrien, and McNeill, "History of the Interpretation of the Bible."

16. Cf. Dilthey, "Die Entstehung der Hermeneutik," 323ff. Classical philology developed rules known as *ars critica*, "but the final constituting of hermeneutic is to be attributed to Biblical interpretation" (324). "The definitive founding of a scholarly her-

The vogue to return to the original Greek during the pseudo-classicism of the seventeenth century is responsible for coining—alongside the already existing Latin expression *ars interpretandi*—the Greek-sounding term *hermeneutica*,[17] from which the English term "hermeneutics" is derived.[18]

The precedent for the neologism (but not its plural form) is provided by Plato's allusion to (*hē*) *hermēneutikē* (*technē*), "(the) hermeneutical (art)," which, in distinction from the critical arts that judge between true and false, belongs to those arts that merely give commands, and this not in one's own name, but, like the prophet and the herald, under another's authority. It is one of the arts that do not impart wisdom since they "only know what is said, but have not learned whether it is true."[19]

An analogy to this distinction is to be found in more recent times in that between hermeneutics and criticism, a distinction quite characteristic in the period of traditional hermeneutics,[20] but, significantly enough,

---

meneutic" is attributed first to Schleiermacher (327).

17. Von Dobschütz, *Vom Auslegen des Neuen Testaments*, 5 n. 2. The first work to use this in a title was J. C. Dannhauer, *Hermeneutica Sacra* (1654).

18. *The Oxford English Dictionary*, 5:243, lists as the first instance of the term the following formulation from the 2nd ed. of Daniel Waterland's *Eucharist* of 1737: "Taking such liberties with sacred Writ, as are by no means allowable upon any known rules of just and sober hermeneuticks." Although *hermeneutica* was construed as feminine singular, the frequency of neuter plural names for sciences with the same ending *-ica* made it almost inevitable that the plural form "hermeneutics" would prevail in English. Up until the present (when the singular form is gaining ground) the plural form has been so prevalent that it can function in the present essay to designate the discipline as it was understood up until the emergence of the new hermeneutic.

19. *The Statesman* 260D; the Pseudo-Platonic *Epinomis* 975C.

20. E.g., Ernesti distinguishes the "hermeneutical" from the "critical" use of biblical allusions in the church fathers, "one pertaining to understanding, the other to judging as to the integrity of the words." *Institutio interpretis Novi Testamenti* (cited from 4th ed., 1776), 130. Schleiermacher taught in sequence hermeneutics and criticism, so that the two were published posthumously in one volume by Friedrick Lücke under the title *Hermeneutik und Kritik mit besonderer Beziehung auf das Neue Testament*, in the *Sämmtliche Werke*, 1:7. The "General Introduction" began as follows: "Hermeneutics and criticism, both philological disciplines, both arts, belong together, since the execution of each presupposes the other. The former is in general the art of understanding correctly the speech of another, especially when it is written down. The latter is the art of judging correctly the authenticity of the writings and passages, and of establishing on the basis of adequate attestation and data." This passage is cited by Martin Heidegger, *Unterwegs zur Sprache*, 97. Heinz Kimmerle omits the material on criticism from his edition, "for the development of Schleiermacher's thoughts on hermeneutics shows that hermeneutics

put in question by the new hermeneutic.[21] Conversely, hermeneutics did not build upon *hermēneia* in its rich suggestiveness of the interpretive interrelatedness of language, translation, and exegesis, but rather limited itself to but one dimension of interpretation, exegesis. Even here the original synonymity of *hermēneia* with exegesis was replaced by a distinction, in terms of theory and practice, into hermeneutics and exegesis.[22] It is this narrowing inherent in the term hermeneutics, set off on the one side from criticism and on the other from exegesis, that gave the discipline in recent times a specialized, technical connotation partly responsible for its neglect in theological education. Even Schleiermacher, who first posed the broad hermeneutical problem as to how understanding takes place at all, separated hermeneutics proper from linguistic and historical study of the text on the one hand and from the modern formulation and application of the text's meaning on the other.[23] With the increasing complexity of theological scholarship, hermeneutics became such a narrow

---

is an independent theme in the context of his thought." Schleiermacher, *Hermeneutik,* newly edited from the manuscripts and introduced by Heinz Kimmerle, 13. For the association of hermeneutics and criticism Schleiermacher is dependent upon Friedrich Ast, *Grundlinien der Grammatik, Hermeneutik und Kritik.*

21. Ebeling, "Hermeneutik," 243. Cf. also the criticism of Emilio Betti's distinction between cognitive, normative, and reproductive functions of interpretation in Gadamer, *Wahrheit und Methode,* 293–94 = *Truth and Method,* 309–10.

22. "Exegetical theology or *exēgesis* and the verb *exēgeisthai* can be regarded as synonymous with *hermēneuein* and *hermēneutica* and are indeed used in such a significance, so that *theologica hermeneutica* and *exegetica* are one and the same. More fittingly, however, these two expressions are distinguished from each other, so that a new subdivision into *exegetica theoretica* and *practica* can be avoided. Thus hermeneutics actually embraces the theory of the rules of the interpretation of Holy Scripture, while *exēgēsis* or exegetical theology refers to the real execution or application of these rules in individual cases on real passages and books of Holy Scripture." D. Siegmund Jacob Baumgartens *ausführlicher Vortrag der Biblischen Hermeneutic* (sic!), 5–6.

23. Cf. Kimmerle, "Hermeneutische Theorie," 115 = "Hermeneutical Theory," 108.

subdivision within a subdivision[24] as to be often omitted as a discipline altogether.[25]

Yet when one considers what was normally treated in the discipline called hermeneutics, one immediately observes that it is not these contents themselves that have ceased to be the subject of scholarly discussion. For example, hermeneutics normally began with a discussion of

24. Cf., e.g., Georg Heinrici's designation of the place of hermeneutics in theological scholarship: "It is not directed to the history of Israel and primitive Christianity in general, but rather to the specific products of the religious spirit that are united into a canon of Old and New Testament, i.e., to the sources and documents collected in the Bible. In that it teaches one to establish and apply the principles and methods for their fitting interpretation, it presupposes all the information that the research disciplines of Biblical scholarship provide, as this information is collected in Biblical linguistics, introduction, archaeology, and the history of Biblical times. Similarly it requires prior work in criticism with regard to the transmission of the text of its materials. Their hermeneutical treatment can lead to reliable results only if the question as to the reliability or the corruption of the text is set clear and, to the extent the sources permit, rectified. On the other hand, hermeneutics must have done its work and have presented its results in the exposition of Scripture if the descriptive disciplines of Biblical scholarship, the history of Israel and of the gospel, the history of apostolic times and especially of Biblical theology, are not to become a playground for the dilettante with his curious and arbitrary hypotheses or with his dogmatic prejudice," "Hermeneutik," 723.

25. One may compare with Heinrici's classification of the subdivisions of New Testament scholarship that presented a generation later by A. Meyer, "Bibelwissenschaft," in RGG^2 (1927) 1:1085:
   I. Research into the *language*, Koine Greek . . .
   II. The establishment of the *text* and its history
   III. The history of the New Testament *canon*
   IV. The history of New Testament *times*
   V. *Interpretation* of New Testament writings
   VI. *Introduction* to the New Testament. . . . The objective is a *history of primitive Christian literature* . . .
   VII. *Historical* presentation
      a) *'Life of Jesus'* . . .
      b) *Paul*
      c) *the apostolic period* . . .
      d) *the sub-apostolic period* . . .
      e) *the history of primitive Christianity as a whole*
   VIII. *Biblical theology* . . . The objective is a *history of the religion of primitive Christianity*. . . ."

Here hermeneutics has ceased to be a subdivision within the discipline of New Testament scholarship. Perhaps the fact that the term interpretation tends to embrace both hermeneutics and exegesis is partly responsible for its greater popularity in recent times, as this instance would tend to indicate.

the language of the text.²⁶ In the case of the New Testament this had to do with the problem that the vocabulary and grammar are not those of classical Greek, but rather those of Hellenistic Greek with more or less Semitic influence. He who has familiarized himself with "Bauer-Arndt-Gingrich"²⁷ and "Blass-Debrunner-Funk,"²⁸ with some awareness of what is involved, such as is provided by Walter Bauer's "Introduction to the Lexicon of the Greek New Testament"²⁹ and E. C. Colwell's article on "The Greek Language,"³⁰ has as accurate a knowledge of this division of hermeneutics as was provided for an earlier day by the textbooks on hermeneutics. Hermeneutics as a discipline became irrelevant in spite of the continuing relevance of such philological lore. For it failed to go beyond what such specialized philological resources can be expected to provide and investigate the relation of language itself to the process of interpretation.

A second major segment of hermeneutics had to do with the historical setting of the Biblical literature, in terms of which its original meaning is to be understood.³¹ Its advice ranged from the necessity of such historical analogy if one is to avoid modernizing, to the danger of drawing parallels where the similarity is very superficial. Here too the debate and refinement of method has continued without benefit of the discipline of hermeneutics. One need merely consider the immense literature about Gnosticism in its relation to primitive Christianity, or that concerning Qumran and the New Testament, from Hermann Gunkel's prediction of the discovery of such a sect, made while emphasizing the hermeneutical relevance of such comparative religious parallels,³² to Samuel Sandmel's

---

26. Cf., e.g., Heinrici, "Hermeneutik," 724–25, Part 2a, "Linguistic Explanation"; Torm, *Hermeneutik des Neuen Testaments*, chap. 2: "New Testament Greek," 39–96.

27. Bauer, *A Greek-English Lexicon*. This has now been revised and edited by Frederick W. Danker in a 3rd edition (2000).

28. Blass and Debrunner, *A Greek Grammar of the New Testament and Other Early Christian Literature*.

29. Bauer, *Greek-English Lexicon*, ix–xxv.

30. Colwell, "The Greek Language."

31. Cf., e.g., Heinrici, "Hermeneutik," 726–27, Part 2b, "Historical Explanation"; Torm, *Hermeneutik des Neuen Testaments*, chap. 6: "Special Problems of Understanding (The Relations of the Text to Its Contemporary Background)," 170–207.

32. Gunkel, *Zum religionsgeschichtlichen Verständnis* = "Religio-historical Interpretation."

more recent warning against "parallelomania."³³ Yet such research has often worked in terms of a rather superficial grasp of the hermeneutical task, as when "understanding" is taken to mean simply explaining where ideas or influences come from, rather than penetrating into the meaning of the text. The unique position held by Hans Jonas' work within the study of Gnosticism³⁴ stands hermeneutically in judgment upon such research that, though philologically more exacting, never moved beyond explaining, i.e., never really entered in upon the task of understanding the deeper meaning of the text.

Krister Stendahl has pointed out that the purely descriptive approach of the *religionsgeschichtliche Schule* "does not necessarily imply the disintegration of the Biblical material into unrelated bits of antiquated information." Indeed "the result of descriptive Biblical theology has raised the hermeneutical problem in a somewhat new form," in that it forces upon us the recognition of systematic theology's task to translate the Biblical message into modern categories.³⁵ Yet it is this profound hermeneutical significance of the purely descriptive achievement of the *religionsgeschichtliche Schule* that was first recognized as such by the new hermeneutic.

Another major subdivision within hermeneutics has been variously characterized as "psychological" or "technical" (terms used by Schleiermacher), or "generic" (Boeckh), or "stylistic" (Heinrici). Here the text is to be classified in terms of the rhetorical or other stylistic figures it employs and the literary category to which it belongs. The significance of the individual text, i.e., what the author was at, can be sensed from the style he is using. Here is where the deeper task of interpretation emerges within traditional hermeneutics.³⁶ And yet this relation of form to meaning came into its own after traditional hermeneutics had faded away, when form criticism emerged in all its theological relevance for what the text is trying to say.³⁷ Traditional hermeneutics had tended to

---

33. Sandmel, "Parallelomania."

34. Jonas, *Gnosis und spätantiker Geist*; idem, *The Gnostic Religion*.

35. Cf. Stendahl, "Contemporary Biblical Theology," esp. 425 and 427.

36. Heinrici, "Hermeneutik," 728, cites Luther's focus upon the *scopus* of the text, and declares (729): "Here the hermeneut has reached his goal."

37. Apart from Old Testament *Gattungsgeschichte*—whose classic instances are Hermann Gunkel, *Die Sagen der Genesis* = *The Legends of Genesis*; and idem, *Die Einleitung in die Psalmen* = *Introduction to the Psalms*—one should cite as classic primarily Martin

use the literary categories as a foil for determining the originality, individuality, and thus personality of the author, his personal "style."[38] The scope as a whole that is to be brought into a fruitful interaction (a hermeneutical circle) with the specific text was the "author's personality."[39] Schleiermacher's term "psychological" did indeed characterize the net outcome.[40] Consequently, the subject matter of the text itself tended to be lost from view as the goal of interpretation. It is here that Barth's criticism found its point of departure.

It was often in connection with the special rhetorical figures and literary forms of Biblical literature that one came to treat the problems of allegory, typology, prophecy, and, in general, the Christian interpretation of the Old Testament. This part of hermeneutics had in a sense been replaced by the debate about the critical historical method, so that the decline of hermeneutics was in this regard in direct proportion to the rise of critical scholarship. Liberalism and conservatism tended to divide criticism and hermeneutics between them. This may in part explain the fact that hermeneutics as a discipline has survived in conservative circles even down to the present.[41] And yet the creative work on the problem of

---

Dibelius, *From Tradition to Gospel*; Bultmann, *History of the Synoptic Tradition*; and Schmidt, "Die Stellung der Evangelien in der allgemeinen Literaturgeschichte," where the theological issue is posed with an acuteness unequaled since the outsider Franz Overbeck published "Über die Anfänge der patristischen Literatur" forty years earlier.

38. Heinrici, "Hermeneutik," 724.

39. This is the concept dominating Torm's *Hermeneutik des Neuen Testaments*.

40. It may be indicative that Heinrici's criticism of this term was that it was too broad, in that "historical explanation" also provides a psychological interpretation ("Hermeneutik," 724). Lütgert, "Bibelerklärung des NT," 1016, also associates "psychological explanation" with "historical" explanation. This broadening of the "psychological" is partly a missing of the deeper point and justification for the designation of formal analysis as "psychological." Whereas traditional rhetoric has regarded composition as a mechanical applying of rules adorned with literary figures, Schleiermacher traced literary form back to the author's individuality, his form or "style," so that the literary form reflects the author's personal scope. This could lead to psychologizing, but it could also lead to Heidegger's hearing of "world" in language, and to the Heideggerian literary criticism of Emil Staiger, *Die Zeit als Einbildungskraft des Dichters*.

41. Without a doubt Milton S. Terry's *Biblical Hermeneutics: A Treatise on the Interpretation of the Old and New Testaments* has been *the* American textbook in the field. First published in the Library of Biblical and Theological Literature, edited by George R. Crooks and John F. Hurst (1883), it was republished in a revised edition in 1890 and in a further revision in 1911, only to be reprinted (1952) for use as a textbook today. Indicative of the persistence of hermeneutics in conservative circles are the fol-

the Christian interpretation of the Old Testament has gone on quite apart from the conservative discipline of hermeneutics.[42]

Of particular interest is the apologetic role that the study of the "forms or kinds of speech" and "literary modes" used in the Bible play in Roman Catholic hermeneutics. "By this knowledge and exact appreciation of the modes of speaking and writing in use among the ancients can be solved many difficulties, which are raised against the veracity and historical value of the Divine Scriptures, and no less efficaciously does this study contribute to a fuller and more luminous understanding of the mind of the Sacred Writer."[43] Thus form criticism has provided a her-

---

lowing: Dungan, *Hermeneutics: A Textbook* (1888); Burnham, *The Elements of Biblical Hermeneutics* (1916); Schodde, *Outlines of Biblical Hermeneutics: A Handbook for Students of the Word* (1917); Hartill, *Biblical Hermeneutics* (1947); Chafer, *The Science of Biblical Hermeneutics: An Outline Study of Its Laws* (1939). More recently the term hermeneutics has been relegated to the subtitle, in favor of the more popular term interpretation: Berkhof, *Principles of Biblical Interpretation (Sacred Hermeneutics)* (1950; 2nd ed., 1952); Ramm, *Protestant Biblical Interpretation: A Textbook of Hermeneutics for Conservative Protestants* (1950; rev. ed., 1956).

42. For the period since World War II cf. the programmatic double issue of *Evangelische Theologie* 12.1-2 (1952), leading to the Biblischer Kommentar: Altes Testament, edited by Martin Noth (Neukirchen-Vluyn: Neukirchener, 1955-). Most of these essays have appeared in English in *Interpretation* 16 (1961): Martin Noth, "The 'Re-presentation of the Old Testament in Proclamation," 50-60; Gerhard von Rad, "Typological Interpretation of the Old Testament," 174-92; Walther Zimmerli, "Promise and Fulfillment," 310-38; Hans Walter Wolff, "The Hermeneutics of the Old Testament," 439-72. Cf. also *Vergegenwärtigung: Aufsätze zur Auslegung des Alten Testaments* (Berlin: Evangelische Verlagsanstalt, 1955); and the discussion following upon the programmatic essay by Wolfhart Pannenberg, "Heilsgeschehen und Geschichte," 218-37, 259-88, English translation of the Old Testament part in Westermann and Mays, eds., *Essays on Old Testament Hermeneutics* (1964). The symposium edited by Pannenberg, including contributions by him, Rolf Rendtorff, Ulrich Wilckens, and Trutz Rendtorff, *Offenbarung als Geschichte*, Beiheft 1 of *KuD* (1961; 2nd ed., 1963) = *Revelation as History*, led to a discussion in a double issue of *EvTh* 22.1-2 (1962). Volume 3 of New Frontiers in Theology, entitled *Theology as History*, is devoted to a discussion of this position. Most of these and other essays from the decade 1950-1960 are included in the volume edited by Westermann, *Probleme alttestamentlicher Hermeneutik* (1960) = *Old Testament Hermeneutics* (1963).

43. The Papal encyclical *Divino Afflante Spiritu* (Sept. 30, 1943) §39. Published in pamphlet form by the National Catholic Welfare Conference, Washington, DC. English translation provided by the Vatican. Cf. also the section *De generibus litterariis in S. Scriptura* in the encyclical of Oct. 20, 1943, *De Sacrorum Bibliorum studiis*, quoted in Denzinger and Umberg, editors, *Enchiridion symbolorum definitionum et declarationum de rebus fidei et morum*, 26th ed. (1947), §2294. An instance of the application of this hermeneutical principle is provided, e.g., by Bourke, "The Literary Genus of Matthew

meneutical principle for the acceptance of critical positions that would otherwise have been dogmatically inadmissible.

If one can then hardly say that the subject matter traditionally handled in hermeneutics had dropped out of scholarly discussion with the disappearance of the discipline, one *can* say that the disappearance of hermeneutics is in any case indicative of a disintegration of the principle discussion of the hermeneutical problem within critical scholarship at the opening of the century. Part of the shock caused by Barth's *Romans* is due to this vacuum into which it exploded.

Symptomatic of this situation is the following remark made at about that time: "In the period from 1720–1820 almost every year a hermeneutics appeared; now, since J. Chr. K. von Hofmann's *Biblische Hermeneutik*, which appeared posthumously in 1880, nothing worth mentioning has appeared."[44] Georg Heinrici had written the article on "Biblical hermeneutics" called for by an encyclopedia in 1899,[45] but in a supplementary volume in 1913 he could only comment on this topic:

> The scholarship of the present collects and catalogues facts with especial interest; it rejoices in statistical investigations and concerns itself with making use of insights of natural science even for one's world view. The drive toward a fundamental grounding of the problems, the interest in philosophical speculation, in methodological investigations, has been repressed. The basic tone determining wide circles of scholars is provided by the empiricists of England and America.[46]

1–2." This article, while distancing itself at the beginning from Renan's argument that, being a haggadic commentary, Matthew 1–2 does not have "the slightest historical basis," concludes with a position whose most striking difference from Renan consists in that such a position has become ecclesiastically acceptable: "Admittedly, the gospel presents Jesus' ministry, death and resurrection as events which really happened. But that the author of such a work might have introduced it by a midrash of deep theological insight, in which Jesus appears as the true Israel and the new Moses (thus containing the theme of the entire gospel), and in which the historical element is very slight, seems to be a thoroughly probable hypothesis."

44. Von Dobschütz, *Auslegen des Neuen Testament*, 6 n.2. He concedes that there has been some activity on the part of Roman Catholic scholarship, and mentions Eduard König's *Hermeneutik des Alten Testaments* (1916), which however treats only the Old Testament. It is indicative of the waning of the term "hermeneutics" that von Hofmann's work has been published in English under the title *Interpreting the Bible* (1959).

45. Heinrici, "Hermeneutik," 718–50.

46. Heinrici, *PRE* 23:643.

It is perhaps not surprising that the next treatment of hermeneutics also derives from the exigencies of an encyclopedia. Ernst von Dobschütz supplied the article on "Interpretation" in Hasting's *Encyclopaedia of Religion and Ethics*[47] and used the fruits of his research for his rectoral address at Halle in 1922,[48] which began as follows:

> The interpretation of the New Testament has made astounding achievements precisely in the last decades. It is all the more striking how little time it has found for reflection as to its nature, goals and paths. Yet without this the best practice threatens to sink back to a technician's skill, and dilettantism and lust for originality crop up on all sides. What one calls hermeneutics, once the discipline carried on most actively, then criminally neglected for two generations, must be awakened to new life.[49]

Since the theological faculty of the University of Copenhagen in the 1920s still required New Testament hermeneutics in the curriculum and on comprehensive examinations, their Professor of New Testament, Frederik Torm, published in Danish in 1928 a textbook on hermeneutics,[50] without pretense of doing more than temporarily filling a practical pedagogical need. But its usefulness in view of the vacuum to which von Dobschütz had called attention was recognized,[51] and a German translation appeared in 1930.[52] Yet this work does not alter the situation, but rather documents the hermeneutical sterility of the traditional approach. It marks the end of an epoch, rather than a new beginning. One must

---

47. Von Dobschütz, "Interpretation," 390–95. Von Dobschütz, *Auslegen des Neuen Testaments*, 6 n.2, dates the encyclopedia article in 1914.

48. Von Dobschütz, *Vom Auslegen insonderheit des Neuen Testaments* (1922). Von Dobschütz's *Auslegen* of 1927 includes the rectoral address and two others of 1926, one entitled "Ein neuer Weg zum Verständnis des Neuen Testaments, die formgeschichtliche Methode"; the other, "Die Pneumatische Exegese, Wissenschaft und Praxis."

49. Von Dobschütz, *Auslegen des Neuen Testaments*, 5. Cf. his statement in "Interpretation," 7:392: Exegetical theology has "striven to the utmost to gain a grammatical and historical comprehension of Scripture. Nevertheless, it has failed to provide its ever-expanding industry with a proper rationale in a theoretic discussion of the hermeneutical problem. This failure is now beginning to bring its retribution, inasmuch as an art that does not reflect upon its own essential function readily degenerates into a mechanical routine."

50. Torm, *Nytestamentlig Hermeneutik*.

51. Cf. the review by Erling Eidem in *TLZ*.

52. *Hermeneutik des Neuen Testaments* (1930).

close the chapter on hermeneutics with a comment by Schleiermacher: "As long as hermeneutics is still treated as an aggregate of individual observations of a general and special nature, no matter how fine and commendable they may be, it does not yet deserve the name of an art."[53]

UNDERSTANDING

At the turn of the century a distinction was emerging in philosophical discussion of the Dilthey type between "explaining" (*Erklärung*) and "understanding" (*Verstehen*). "Over against the explaining of occurrences of nature there emerged, as a fundamentally different way of human knowing, historic 'understanding.'"[54] "We explain nature, we understand the life of the soul."[55]

One may trace in the opening third of the century the gradual shift in hermeneutical discussion from the one to the other term. Heinrici's presentation of 1899 uses the rubrics: A. Linguistic Explanation; B. Historical Explanation; C. Stylistic Explanation.[56]

Hermann Gunkel does not seem to sense any distinctive implication in his title "On the Religio-historical Understanding of the New Testament" (1903), but rather speaks of the *religionsgeschichtliche Schule* "with broad vision bringing Western and Eastern material together into an explanation," and thus "explaining not a little in the New Testament."[57] Indeed he identifies the two terms when he opposes those who prefer merely "exact reproduction" to those who seek "explanation," i.e., "historical classification," which then is called "genuinely living, historical understanding."[58] A generation later in 1927 the second edition of the standard German encyclopedia *Die Religion in Geschichte und Gegenwart*[59] still

---

53. Schleiermacher, *Kurze Darstellung*, 59–60 (¶133).

54. Windelband and Heimsoeth, *Lehrbuch der Geschichte der Philosophie*, 589.

55. Cf. Dilthey, *Gesammelte Schriften*, 5:144. Max Weber's uncompleted work, posthumously published under the title *Wirtschaft und Gesellschaft*, was intended by Weber to be an "outline of understanding-psychology." "Max Weber calls this sociology 'understanding,' since its object is the intended meaning of social activity." Gadamer, "Hermeneutik und Historismus," 245.

56. Heinrici, "Hermeneutik," 724–29.

57. Gunkel, *Zum religionsgeschichtlichen Verständnis des Neuen Testaments*, 4–5 = "Religio-historical Interpretation of the New Testament."

58. Ibid., 6.

59. *RGG*² 1:1011–18, by Baumgärtel (OT) and Lütgert (NT).

treated hermeneutics under the title "Explanation of the Bible." Yet by the time the last volume appeared in 1931 an article on "understanding" by Joachim Wach was included.[60] Indeed it was Wach's three-volume work on "Understanding"[61] that marked the clear shift to the preference for "understanding."[62] Thus the term understanding in its distinction from "explanation" characterized the first move toward the new hermeneutic.

It was Wilhelm Dilthey who relativized traditional hermeneutics in terms of the deeper role of understanding. He had detected in the history of hermeneutics an inner logic, in that thought had penetrated deeper and deeper into the problem until it had finally arrived at "the analysis of understanding" as "the sure point of departure for working out the [hermeneutical] rules."[63] If the sum of such rules is hermeneutics, then the analysis of understanding is a discipline prior to, more fundamental than, hermeneutics. It is in this sense that Erich Fascher defined his treatise "On Understanding the New Testament" as "a contribution to laying the foundation for a modern hermeneutic."

> We do not wish to do what is done in textbooks on hermeneutics, simply to develop the skills of interpreting on the basis of exegetical practice. Nor do we wish to do what happens in the discussion today, namely describe the qualities the exegete must have. Rather we turn to the question prior to all hermeneutics and exegesis: How then is understanding possible, what means are there for understanding? This is not the same as hermeneutics. Rather its parts are here put in an epistemological light.[64]

Thus one can say that the new hermeneutic began to emerge in a recognition of the superficiality of hermeneutics, and hence in an intentional distinction of its deeper concern for understanding from that of hermeneutics. It is not surprising that the dominant term in the first movement toward the new hermeneutic has been "understanding."

60. Wach, "Verstehung."

61. Wach, *Das Verstehen* (1926, 1929, 1933).

62. Cf., e.g., Erich Fascher's title *Vom Verstehen des Neuen Testaments: Ein Beitrag zur Grunlegung einer zeitgemässen Hermeneutik,* esp. 100ff., where the distinction is derived primarily from Gomperz, *Über Sinn und Sinngebilde, Verstehen und Erklären,* and Bultmann's collected essays entitled *Glauben und Verstehen* (1929, 1952, 1960).

63. Dilthey, "Die Entstehung der Hermeneutik," 320. He attributes this decisive step to Schleiermacher, 327ff.

64. Fascher, *Vom Verstehen,* 12.

When Dilthey focused the hermeneutical task upon literature, he did so with the justification "that in language alone does what is inside man find its complete, exhaustive and objectively intelligible expression. Hence the art of understanding has its center in the interpretation of the remains of human existence contained in writing."[65] Here language is evaluated only as the objectification through which one must penetrate to the understanding of the existence expressing itself in the text. In somewhat the same way Heidegger in his analysis of understanding regarded understanding as a basic existential whose articulation in interpretation may (but does not necessarily) lead to "expression" as but a "derivative mode."[66] It is this secondary role of linguistic "expression" in the Heidegger of *Being and Time* that provided the context for relating language to understanding in the Bultmannian school in the postwar generation.

Into the void left by the collapse of hermeneutics exploded Karl Barth's *Romans*.[67] This book is not hermeneutics, a theory about interpretation, but rather *hermēneia:* a commentary, in which the subject matter of Paul's language is radically translated and proclaimed anew in the language of our day. It is this *fait accompli* that has called forth the hermeneutical reflection of our times.

Only the beginnings of this reflection were provided by Barth himself. With a few swift strokes of the brush he sketched its direction in the Preface to the first edition of *Romans*, written in 1918:

> The critical historical method of Biblical research has its validity. It points to the preparation for understanding that is never superfluous. But if I had to choose between it and the old doctrine

---

65. Dilthey, "Die Entstehung der Hermeneutik," 319. The word translated "existence" is *Dasein,* which was later to become the technical term in Heidegger used in Bultmannian hermeneutic.

66. Heidegger, *Sein und Zeit,* 9th ed. (1960), 153ff. ET = *Being and Time,* 195ff. The published translation of *Aussage* as "assertion" has been here replaced by "expression," so as to retain the implication heard in the German word that something inward is being "spoken out." The following section on discourse and language (203ff.) defines discourse as being as basic an existential as is understanding, and thus points toward the post-Bultmannian development.

67. Barth, *Der Römerbrief* (1919; reprinted, 1963); the 2nd ed. of 1922 was thoroughly rewritten and has been reprinted substantially unaltered. Citation is from the German original, the 8th printing of the 2nd ed. (1947). There is also an English translation by Edwyn C. Hoskyns (1933). Gadamer, "Hermeneutik und Historismus," 246, declares Barth's *Romans* to have been a "hermeneutical manifesto."

of inspiration, I would decidedly lay hold of the latter. It has the greater, deeper, more important validity, for it points to the actual work of understanding, without which all preparation is useless. I am happy not to have to choose between the two. But my whole attention was directed to looking through the historical to the spirit of the Bible, which is the eternal Spirit. What once was serious is still serious today, and what today is serious, and not just accidental and peripheral, stands in direct relation to what was once serious. Our questions, if we understand ourselves aright, are the questions of Paul, and Paul's answers, if their light illumines us, must be our answers.... The understanding of history is a continuous, increasingly open and urgent discussion between the wisdom of yesterday and the wisdom of tomorrow, which are one and the same.[68]

Here the view of the relation of subject to object basic to the critical historical method, to the effect that the subjective element is to be eliminated so as to attain the highest possible objectivity, has been relativized by the basic recognition of the hermeneutical relevance of the subject. This basic insight is what Hans Jonas has called the "metaphysical *a priori*" of the history of ideas.[69]

The question with regard to the subject is not simply whether he can eliminate his subjectivity as a source of prejudice, but whether he "understands himself aright," i.e., whether he is grappling with what is "serious," or, as we might say today, whether he is asking the right questions, whether his concern is with the ultimate. If that be the case, his subjectivity provides an access to the subject matter of the text that is indispensable as a heuristic medium of interpretation, if it is really that subject matter, serious both then and now, that he is seeking to understand. One's subjectivity does not simply introduce distortions; it insures that the phenomena with which the text was grappling—if it is a serious text—are not overlooked or distorted into curiosities. It is this relevance of "Bultmannian" hermeneutic for the understanding of the past in its own right (in distinction from any modern appropriation of the message of the past) that is often overlooked.[70] Hans Jonas' *Gnosis und spätantiker*

---

68. Barth, *Römerbrief*, v of the 1st ed. and of the 8th printing of the 2nd ed.

69. Jonas, *Augustin*, 6.

70. This is the case with Stendahl's penetrating discussion of "Contemporary Biblical Theology."

Geist (and its more popular English form *The Gnostic Religion*), more unambiguous even than Barth's *Romans*, demonstrated this *ad oculos*.

Thus the flow of the traditional relation between subject and object, in which the subject interrogates the object, and, if one masters it, obtains from it one's answer, has been significantly reversed. For it is now the object—which should henceforth be called the subject matter—that puts the subject in question. This is true not simply at the formal level, in inquiring as to whether one understands oneself aright, i.e., is serious, but also at the material level, in inquiring as to whether the text's answers illumine the person.

The first at the formal level is a more ontological, philosophical query, as to whether one is asking the right questions, irrespective of the way one is answering them. Bultmann's recourse to Heidegger's existentialist analysis was an attempt to meet this question. For Bultmann's objective was to penetrate beneath a superficial theology of moralism to one that came to grips with the problem of humanity's very being.

> "God's will is the requirement of the good." . . . This is not a genuinely religious concept of God, but rather, as is always characteristic of naive thinking, the binding power of the good appears under the mythical conception of a God who demands and punishes, pardons and rewards. This faith does not become religion simply in that special psychic conditions—being shaken up or inspired—accompany it, but only when it gains a new content. That is to say, when the person who bows to the requirement of the good experiences thereby an inner history in which one lays hold of a reality that is not that of the ethical ideal, but rather a reality of life from which one feels oneself growing, to which one feels oneself quite subjected, and by which one feels oneself carried; when the person who stands in obedience to the good feels that one thereby experiences a fate through which one is transformed; when experiences that lead through depths and heights, experiences that in religious language are called sin and grace, lead one—not to fulfilling the ethical requirements, but rather to fulfilling one's being. In religion it is not a matter of doing, but rather of being, not of the intention directed to the goal of the good but rather of the experience of passing away in the presence of God's reality and of being endowed by divine grace, of transfor-

mation, new creation to a being whose deed is not the fulfillment of a requirement but rather the portrayal of one's being.[71]

It was Heidegger who provided Bultmann with structures ("existentials") for talking more adequately about humanity's being, one's "existence." With this aid it would become possible to determine whether a "mythical conception" contains "religion" or not.

The second query at the material level is more ontic, theological, as to whether the interpreter decides to understand one's being the way the text understands existence. This question as to how humanity understands one's being, one's very existence, is the "existential" question that theology helps preaching to pose.

Something of what is involved hermeneutically begins to emerge in Barth's debate with Adolf von Harnack in 1923.[72] To Harnack it is obvious that theology's task is to "establish the content of the gospel," i.e., "to get intellectual control of the object."[73] Barth replies that "the 'scholarliness' of theology consists in being bound to the recollection that its object was *first subject* and must again and again become subject.[74] What is emerging here is the recognition that God is not a phenomenon at the disposal of scientific investigation as are phenomena of the world. Barth hurls the category of revelation into opposition to that of scholarship as known in that day. All this seemed to Harnack no better than a pious platitude, to which he could only reply that scholarship's sole task is "the pure knowledge of its object."[75]

Yet it is precisely here that Barth was in fact moving decisively beyond Harnack, even though it would take a generation for his advance to be recognized fully and elevated to a new understanding of hermeneutic. For Barth first sensed the odd incongruity between the results of the rigid application of "method" in contemporary scholarship and the dimension of truth in which we actually live—an incongruity that has been raised to

---

71. Bultmann, "Ethische und mystische Religion im Urchristentum," 741. This quotation reveals clearly the positive influence of Wilhelm Herrmann in Bultmann's rejection of "religious moralism" in favor of "ethical religion." Cf. the summary of Herrmann's position in this regard in my "For Theology and the Church."

72. "Ein Briefwechsel mit Adolf von Harnack."

73. Ibid., 8, 14

74. Ibid., 10

75. Ibid., 31

a basic issue of philosophical hermeneutic only within the last few years. Barth states the issue as follows:

> I think I am acquainted with 'thinking persons' in earlier and later centuries who as theologians went in ways completely different from those considered normal since the eighteenth century, and whose 'scholarliness' cannot be denied (if 'scholarship' means 'doing justice to the subject matter'!). When one appeals to the theology of Paul or Luther, you seem to be able to explain it only as a proud attempt at imitation. On my side of the "chasm" separating us the situation looks this way: The material superiority of these and other earlier theologians, no matter how poorly they fit today's club standards, forces itself upon us so irresistibly that . . . we cannot regard ourselves as relieved of the duty to take their basic approach more seriously into consideration in terms of its possible validity than has been the case of late, in spite of all Pauline research and enthusiasm for Luther. This has nothing to do with repristination. Of course it is my private opinion that practicing the repristination of a classic theological train of thought regarded as "theology" in the medieval period or during Protestant scholasticism would probably be more instructive than the chaotic business of our faculties today, for whom the concept of an authoritative *object* has become foreign and uncomfortable over against the pervasive normativeness of *method*. But I think I also know that the *same thing* cannot and should not return, and that we have to think *in* our time *for* our time. And my objective is not to remove from theological research the critical historical method of studying the Bible and history that has developed in the last centuries. Rather my objective is to identify the relevant place for it and the sharpening of the issue for theological research that it has effected.[76]

This is precisely the point of departure for the philosopher Hans-Georg Gadamer's magnum opus on *Truth and Method*, whose critical analysis of wide segments of contemporary interpretation is represented by the following quotation: "What gives dignity to scholarly opinion is giving proofs, methodical verification (and not doing justice to the subject matter in and of itself). In the eyes of the Enlightenment lack of proofs does not leave room for other kinds of certainty, but rather implies that

---

76. Ibid., 19–20.

the opinion has no basis in the subject matter itself, i.e., is 'unfounded.'"[77] It is the task of the present introductory essay to trace this development from Barth's intuitive insights to the explicitly hermeneutical formulations of Gadamer.

At the time Barth wrote his *Romans*, the incomprehension expressed in Harnack's response was all that could be expected. For here not only two generations, but two worlds, meet—or, more precisely, fail to meet, but rather bypass each other. Perhaps Barth senses this when he refuses to be determined by "the protest of the spirit of modern times (which must perhaps first learn to understand itself!)."[78]

In retrospect we can to some extent understand what Harnack did not, since the spirit of modern times is gradually becoming audible for what it really is. Perhaps Martin Heidegger has analyzed it in the way most relevant to the point at issue in his book *Der Satz vom Grund*.[79] Here he draws attention to the fact that the principle of sufficient cause, namely, that nothing is without a cause, was first clearly formulated in the Cartesian period and, consequently, was immediately identified with the idea that everything must give account of itself, state its cause, to the investigating subject to which it is answerable. Thus nature ceases to be for itself, but *is* only as that which gives account of itself to us, that which we put before us for our investigation, that which we objectify. The objective world, since it is defined by a science that understands reality as answerable to the inquiring subject, is a world seen from this viewpoint of the investigating subject, and hence is actually subjective, the subject's world view. This Cartesian subjectivism of the objectified world is responsible for the subject-object schema that gained ascendancy in the natural sciences and was then carried over to the humanities. This objectifying approach is all Harnack could conceive of science as being, so that theology as a science necessarily consisted in gaining intellectual mastery over its object of inquiry.

Only if we can relativize and to this extent transcend this Cartesian mentality can we even conceive of a scholarly relation to reality that would not consist in our pinning objects down, but that would instead consist in beings calling up their being to us, so that the scholar's role would be to

---

77. Gadamer, *Wahrheit und Methode*, 255 = *Truth and Method*, 271.
78. Barth, *Theologische Fragen und Antworten*, 19
79. Heidegger, *Der Satz vom Grund*.

answer responsibly with one's own words this tolling of the being of beings as it comes to oneself. Yet this emerging insight into the nature of the Cartesian epoch, which is itself potentially the transcending of that epoch, is of more recent date, at least in the form here under consideration, so that we must return to what was the immediate outcome of Barth's *Romans*. It suffices at this stage to call attention to the clearly audible way in which the supposed objectivity of Harnack's critical historical method reveals what Heidegger was subsequently to identify as the subjectivism of the Cartesian epoch, whereas Barth was gropingly speaking in terms of a post-Cartesian world.

It is not surprising that the New Testament scholars of Harnack's generation did not understand what had happened in Barth's *Romans*. Their reviews associated Barth's failures in mastering critical historical detail with his achievement in letting the subject matter of the text put us in question, to conclude that his commentary is merely practical and edifying, i.e., of no further interest to scholarship.[80] The failure of such reviews to see what was going on was the direct result of the hermeneutical vacuum at that time, as was further documented by the dismal debate about "pneumatic exegesis" in the mid-twenties. Although set in motion by Karl Girgensohn's *Die Inspiration der heiligen Schrift*,[81] it took on proportions explainable only in terms of the hermeneutical embarrassment scholarly circles sensed in trying to cope with Barth's *Romans*.[82] It is significant that it was Rudolf Bultmann who called pneumatic exegesis terminologically "repulsive" and materially "senseless," and said the sooner

---

80. Cf. the reviews by such leading New Testament scholars as Adolf Jülicher, "Ein moderner Paulus-Ausleger"; idem, Review of *Der Römerbrief* by Karl Barth; and Hans Windisch, Review of *Der Römerbrief* by Karl Barth. Jülicher's first review was answered by Friedrich Gogarten, "Vom heiligen Egoismus der Christen," who introduces Kierkegaard's "subjectivity" into the debate.

81. Girgensohn, *Die Inspiration der heiligen Schrift*.

82. E.g., Bachmann, "Der Römerbrief verdeutscht und vergegenwärtigt," 518, referred to Barth's "pneumatic-prophetic exegesis." For the debate on pneumatic exegesis, cf. Procksch, "Über pneumatische Exegese," in Girgensohn's periodical *Christentum und Wissenschaft*; Behm, *Pneumatische Exegese?*; the lectures of 1926 by Heinrich Frick, *Wissenschaftliches und pneumatisches Verständnis der Bibel*, and by Ernst von Dobschütz, "Die Pneumatische Exegese: Wissenschaft und Praxis"; R. Seeberg, "Zur Frage nach dem Sinn und Recht einer pneumatischen Schriftauslegung"; E. Seeberg, "Zum Problem der pneumatischen Exegese"; Macholz, "Pneumatische Exegese," 705–24; Friedrich Traub, "Wort Gottes und pneumatische Schriftauslegung"; Torm, *Hermeneutik*, 17ff.; Fascher, *Vom Verstehen*, 25–30.

the discussion was terminated the better[83]—for it was Bultmann who had something better to say. He had recognized the theological validity of Barth's *fait accompli*—at least in its second edition—and thereupon devoted himself to working out a hermeneutic in terms of which such an outcome could be defended by purifying and clarifying the method and thus making it available to scholarship as a whole.

Bultmann identified the basic weakness of the first edition as residing in the incompleteness of Barth's translation of the subject matter of Pauline theology into our modern world, in that Barth retained myth and dogma.

> The artificiality of a Catholicizing repristination of the ancient cult, as well as the orthodox transfiguration of Pauline myth and ecclesiastical dogma, are condemned from the outset. This applies also to the fanatical renewal of the Pauline myth in Barthian polish. As much as I welcome the religious criticism of culture in Barth's *Romans,* I cannot see, in what he presents positively, anything other than an arbitrary adaptation of the Pauline myth of Christ. The judgment that Barth passes upon 'liberal theology' strikes Barth himself to the same extent.[84]

The second edition seemed to Bultmann to have overcome this major limitation to an extent that made it possible to systematize its position in terms of a philosophy of religion, or what Barth would call a normative statement of the nature of faith.

> Although in the original form of a commentary, it falls in line with works such as Schleiermacher's *Speeches on Religion* and Otto's *Idea of the Holy,* with modern attempts to work out a religious *a priori,* and finally with Romans itself, whose radical antithesis between works and faith is really attempting to do the same thing. No matter how different these may be in details, all of them are attempts to express in language the awareness of the distinctiveness and absoluteness of religion.[85]

---

83. Bultmann, *Glauben und Verstehen,* 1:127–28.

84. Bultmann, "Ethische und mystische Religion," 740.

85. Bultmann, "Karl Barths 'Römerbrief' in zweiter Auflage," esp. 320. It is because of this that Jülicher opened his negative review of the 2nd ed. with a slap at an unnamed "well-wishing review," his junior colleague at Marburg, Rudolf Bultmann; idem, Review of *Der Römerbrief* by Karl Barth, 538.

Hermeneutic Since Barth 95

Yet even here Bultmann criticized Barth's unwillingness to concede that Paul himself at times gave inadequate expression to this normative subject matter.

> The "measuring by the subject matter" of "all words and groups of words" contained in the source to be explained, rightly insisted upon by Barth in the Preface, cannot take place without criticism, if it is meant seriously. . . . It is the consistent implementation of the principle, recognized as correct, that the text is to be understood from the subject matter. In terms of the subject matter one must then in fact measure to what extent in all words and statements of the text the subject matter has really achieved adequate expression. For what else could "measuring" mean? . . . The subject matter is greater than the interpreting word. . . . When in exegeting Romans I identify tensions and contradictions, heights and depths, when I exert myself to show where Paul is dependent upon Jewish theology or upon common Christianity, Hellenistic enlightenment, or Hellenistic sacramentalism, I am not merely carrying on historical philological criticism (at least if I do not conceive mechanically my task as exegete). Rather I do it to show where and how the subject matter comes to expression, in order that I may lay hold of the subject matter itself, which is greater even than Paul. And I am of the opinion that such criticism can only aid the clarity of the subject matter. For the more strongly I sense that with this subject matter it is a question of uttering the unutterable (and Barth knows this quite well), the more clearly I also sense and as exegete point out the relativity of the word. And it is a matter not only of the relativity of the word, but also of the fact that no one—not even Paul—can always speak only from the subject matter. Other spirits also come to expression through him than the Spirit of Christ. Hence criticism can never be radical enough.[86]

Here Bultmann is calling for what became known as *Sachkritik*, criticism in terms of the subject matter, "content-criticism."

Barth's reply to this criticism actually bypasses the point, for he treats it only as a recognition of the inadequacy of language, which he is willing enough to concede.[87] What he was not willing to face squarely

---

86. Bultmann, "Karl Barths 'Römerbrief' in zweiter Auflage," 372–73. Cf. already Jülicher, review of *Der Römerbrief* by Karl Barth, 466, 468, and the arguments of Traub, "Wort Gottes," 88ff., and Fascher, *Vom Verstehen*, 36–40.

87. "What is expressed in words in Romans are simply the 'others,' the Jewish, com-

is the question as to whether in given places the point Paul makes—not just the language he uses—is inadequate to the subject matter basic to Paul himself. Hence Bultmann presses the issue again in his discussion of Barth's commentary on 1 Corinthians.[88] Yet here again *Sachkritik* is at times formulated by Bultmann as a criticism of the language employed, just as his original criticism of the first edition of the *Romans* commentary was directed at the use of myth and dogma, as if these were by their very nature a language unsuited to faith. And indeed the problems of inadequately making the point and of inadequate language are interrelated, in that objectifying language inappropriate to the subject matter can lead away from that subject matter by focusing attention on the inconsistent element in the language as if it were precisely that foreign ingredient that is intended. Thus the concern for language emerges in the hermeneutical discussion primarily in the context of *Sachkritik*, where language is envisaged as an objectification inappropriate to the subject matter, a source of distortion rather than an aid in understanding.[89]

This defective aspect of language is most prominent in the case of mythological language. For here the objectification can easily be meant literally, so that the language itself speaks and drowns out the understanding of existence coming to expression in it.

> It seems to me just as certain that in 1 Cor. 15 Paul is talking of such history of final things (*Schlussgeschichte*) as that in truth he cannot and does not wish to speak of such a history. That is to say, one cannot get by in 1 Cor. 15 without thoroughgo-

---

mon Christian, Hellenistic, and other 'spirits' he [sc. Bultmann] cites. Or on what place can one lay one's finger with the claim that precisely *there* the *pneuma Christou* comes to expression in words? Or, put the other way around: Is the Spirit of Christ, e.g., a spirit that can be conceived of as competing *along side of other* spirits? . . . Everything is *litera*, voice of the 'other' spirits. Whether and to what extent everything can also be understood in connection with the 'subject matter,' as voice of the *spiritus (Christi)*, that is the question with which the *litera* must be studied." Preface to the 3rd ed., xix of the 8th printing of the 2nd ed.

88. Barth, *Die Auferstehung der Toten* = *The Resurrection of the Dead*. Cf. Bultmann's review article, *Glauben und Verstehen*, 1:38–64.

89. "God remains always subject in the relationship that is created by this witness. He does not transform himself into the object, man's possession, man's being in the right, man's having the last word' (*Die Auferstehung der Toten*, 4)—correct! But in our talking, to the extent we must undertake it (e.g., in affirming the 'from God' of 1 Cor.), God is object." *Glauben und Verstehen*, 1:41. Cf. also the allusions to "uttering the unutterable" and "the relativity of the word" ("Karl Barths 'Römerbrief' in zweiter Auflage," 373).

ing *Sachkritik* (not only occasionally, as Barth does in verse 29 in spite of himself). For however little Paul proclaims such a thing as a "Weltanschauung," there still is for him, as for any one else, the necessity to say what he says in the terminology of his *Weltanschauung*. And it is not permissible simply to regard the ideological (in this case mythological) elements as "parable" or to eliminate them by twisting their meaning. What Barth concedes for later Christian eschatologists that they construct of the Biblical material a history of final things (*Schlussgeschichte*) that is in truth not at all historic in an ultimate sense (*endgeschichtlich*)—is true for Paul too, who derives his material from Jewish or Jewish-gnostic apocalypticism.[90]

Thus the language comes to say nothing about the subject matter, human existence, and ceases to be relevant, "serious." "In that the myth is narrated, nothing is said about my existence, about the reality in which alone I could hear God. For how should I know about all the things the myth is talking about (archons, the camouflage of the divine being, the deception of the demons, etc.)?"[91]

Thus one can detect two kinds of *Sachkritik* intertwined in Bultmann's position, one in which the subject matter coming to expression in the language is criticized as inconsistent with the subject matter dominant in the text, and the other in which the use of mythological language as such is criticized as an objectification, in which worldly categories are simply elongated to express what actually is wholly unworldly. Such objectified language is even prone to have its own say at the objectified level and thus to spin itself out without any existential meaning behind it.

It is interesting that even after the emergence of the program of demythologizing the inadequacy of mythological language can continue to be treated in the context of *Sachkritik*.

> But from the fact that theological statements are by nature the explication of believing comprehension it also follows that *these statements may be only relatively appropriate, some more so, others less so*. The possibility exists that in some of them the believing comprehension may not be clearly developed, that it may be hindered— bound perhaps by a pre-faith understanding of God, the world, and man and by a corresponding terminology—and consequently may speak of God's dealing and of the relation between God and man

---

90. Bultmann, *Glauben und Verstehen*, 1:52.
91. Ibid., 1:43.

in juristic terms, for instance. Or it may speak of God's relation to the world in mythological or cosmological terms which are inappropriate to faith's understanding of God's transcendence. Or the consequence may be that it expresses God's transcendence in the terminology of mysticism or of idealistic thinking. From this possibility arises the task—even in the case of the New Testament writings of *content-criticism* (*Sachkritik*) such as Luther, for example, exercised toward the Epistle of James and the Revelation of John.[92]

Here the basic inadequacy of objectifying mythological language to its own nonobjective subject matter is cited in the midst of a list of situations calling for *Sachkritik*.

It is this second ingredient originally included within *Sachkritik*, the criticism of the dangerous inadequacy of mythological and dogmatic language, that has now been largely lifted out of the broader context of *Sachkritik* and developed into the hermeneutic distinctive of Bultmannianism: demythologization, or, put positively, existentialist interpretation. The obscuring of the interrelation between *Sachkritik* and demythologizing is doubtless due in part to the apologetic necessity to distinguish liberalism's "elimination" of the incredible from demythologizing as a "decoding" of the myth's meaning. Yet demythologizing does "eliminate" the inadequate mythical conceptualization for the sake of stating more adequately the myth's meaning, and, if the objectifying conceptualization has been spun out into speculative *theologoumena* without existential meaning, such meaningless arabesques are to be "eliminated."

It is the contribution of Hans Jonas, the student of Heidegger and Bultmann, to have opened the way to this development. Bultmann wrote a revealing Preface to Volume I of *Gnosis und spätantiker Geist*, which is omitted from the published bibliographies of Bultmann's works and hence is easily bypassed, in which the indebtedness to Jonas is explicit.

> I would like to say that I, who for years have devoted a large part of my work to the study of gnosticism, have learned from none of the previous studies in this area—and one knows that there are very excellent ones—so much toward a real grasp of gnosticism as a phenomenon in the history of ideas as from this work. Indeed it was here that the significance of this phenomenon was first made clear to me in its full dimension. . . . The method of the author, of laying hold of the real meaning of a historical phenomenon by means of the principle of the analysis of existence, seems to me to

---

92. Bultmann, *Theology*, 2:238.

have proven brilliantly its fruitfulness. I am certain that this work will fructify research in the history of ideas in many regards, and not least also the interpretation of the New Testament.[93]

Jonas' analysis of the dogmatic controversy between Augustine and Pelagius was directed to

> analyzing which things this struggle is basically concerned with, and how these basic phenomena get along in this struggle, in the grip of the concepts and formulae needed in argument; what becomes of the phenomena in the expressedness of a given rational structure; what of their own subject matter was misunderstood and covered over by the debaters themselves and missed in the 'logical' exposition; finally, how the truth does not reside in a position, but rather is to be reconstructed out of it in a distinctive hermeneutical correction.[94]

Thus Jonas brought to focus a recognition that had been emerging already among historians of the *religionsgeschichtliche Schule,* to the effect that myths bear meaning that lies behind the uncongenial language, from which that meaning must be freed by a procedure of reconstruction. In the same year in which Bultmann was publishing this work of his pupil Jonas in a monograph series of which he was editor, he republished in the same series an older work by Hermann Gunkel in which that insight is clearly enunciated:

> It will frequently be shown in what follows that New Testament material is reminiscent of *myths* and the *mythical.* But a word of warning is in place lest without further ado one connect with these words the negative connotation of the pagan, the wildly fantastic, the confused. The mythical emerges everywhere that a naive spirit regards the divine in a living way and paints it to himself in his fantasy. Hence in itself the mythical is in no sense a perversion, but rather a necessary phase of religious thought. Even the *most*

---

93. Jonas, *Gnosis und spätantiker Geist,* 1:vii. In his original essay on demythologizing, "Neues Testament und Mythologie," Bultmann refers (25) the reader seeking to understand "the critical interpretation of myth" to "the important explanations about the hermeneutical structure of dogma in Hans Jonas, *Augustin und das paulinische Freiheitsproblem,* pp. 66–76"; and, as a model of demythologizing, he refers (28) to Jonas' *Gnosis und spätantiker Geist,* vol. 1. Here as elsewhere, the English translation by Reginald H. Fuller (edited by Bartsch), *Kerygma and Myth* 12, 16, has been so free as to omit completely part of the text.

94. Jonas, *Augustin,* 6.

precious treasures of religion can conceal themselves in mythical form. Hence we should guard against throwing away the mythical unexamined, before we have carefully released its precious kernel from the foreign husk.[95]

For Jonas it is not simply the problem of myth, but rather the problem of language as such, or, more precisely, a problem inherent in the human spirit, whose nature it is to symbolize meaning in objective formulae that lead away from the very meaning they intend to convey.[96] And it is precisely in this context, in describing the turn away from the language back to that meaning, that the term demythologizing is first attested, in describing the consciousness that seeks the path back from the symbolic language to the existential meaning it was intended to convey.

> All this derives from an unavoidable fundamental structure of the spirit as such. That it interprets itself in objective formulae and symbols, that it is "symbolistic," is the innermost nature of the spirit—and at the same time most dangerous! In order to come to itself, it necessarily takes this detour via the symbol, in whose enticing jungle of problems it tends to lose itself, far from the origin preserved symbolically in it, taking the substitute as ultimate. Only in a long procedure of working back, after an exhausting completion of that detour, is a demythologized (*entmythologisiert*) consciousness able terminologically to approach directly the original phenomena hidden in this camouflage (cf. the long path of the dogma of original sin up to Kierkegaard!).[97]

---

95. Gunkel, *Zum religionsgeschichtlichen Verständnis*, 14–15. When the 3rd ed. appeared, Bultmann was editor of the series, and its republication coincided with the publication the same year of Jonas' work, *Augustin und das paulinische Freiheitsproblem*, as vol. 44 of the same series.

96. The understanding of language is in the context of Ernst Cassirer's *Philosophie der symbolischen Formen* = *The Philosophy of Symbolic Forms*.

97. Jonas, *Augustin*, 67. The history of the term demythologizing may be traced further in Jonas' *Gnosis und spätantiker Geist*, 2:1, which, though published only in 1954, had already been printed in 1934 in its relevant parts and hence was known to Bultmann, editor of the series, if not to the public at large. Here Jonas says (3–4): "In the metaphysical emanation and deprivation schema we find gnostic myth in depersonalized (*entpersonalisiert*), logicized form, i.e., in a sense indeed demythed (*entmythisiert*), and yet, because of its nature as hypostasized, still mythical. We will run across these mythological, philosophical mediating forms in the *metaphysics* of Origen and Plotinus. But we first turn to an anthropological, ethical sphere of concepts, in which we would not in principle expect such mythographic analogies, and in which we too are primarily concerned with something else: to show how the assumed existential basic principle,

Thus Bultmann's program of demythologizing is embedded in a specific view of language as the objectification of understanding, an objectification that is itself contrary to the understanding seeking expression in it:

> The real intention of myth is not to provide an objective world view. Rather in it is expressed the way man understands himself in his world. Myth is not intended to be interpreted cosmologically, but rather anthropologically, or, better still, existentialistically. Myth speaks of the power or powers that man thinks he experiences as ground and limit of his world, of his own action, and of what happens to him. To be sure it speaks of these powers in such a way that it incorporates them conceptually into the sphere of the known world, of its things and forces, and into the sphere of human life, of its emotions, motives, and possibilities. For example, it speaks of a world egg or world tree, to provide a picture of the basis and origin of the world. Or it speaks of battles of the gods, from which the conditions and principles of the known world emerged. It speaks of the unworldly in a worldly way, of the gods in a human way.
>
> In myth there is expressed the faith that the known and controllable world in which man lives does not have its ground and goal in itself. Rather its ground and its limit lie outside the known and controllable. This known and controllable sphere is constantly interpenetrated and threatened by the weird powers that are its ground and limit. And, along with this, myth expresses the knowledge that man is not master of himself, that he is not only dependent within the known world, but that before all he is dependent on the powers ruling beyond the known, and that in this dependency he can become free from just these very known powers.

---

the 'gnostic' principle, if it really is capable of separation from the mythological world of symbol and of treatment as a more general *arche*, is here in a quite distinctive way drawn back out of the outward mythical objectification and transposed into inner concepts of *Dasein* and into ethical practice, i.e., it appears as it were 'resubjectivized'—just as on the other hand also in this sphere the mythical element is not really overcome. Rather even in 'immanence' (i.e., even without mythological transcendence) the concepts of *Dasein*, with regard to their ontological structure, remain in a very broad sense 'mythical'—because of their pervasive origin in a basic *objectification*." One may see here a groping toward the concept and term *Entmythologisierung*, especially in the aspect of the steps toward demythologizing taken within the sources themselves, to which Bultmann calls attention in *Kerygma und Mythos*, 1:24, 31ff. = *Kerygma and Myth*, 12, 20ff.

Hence in the myth itself there is contained the motive for criticizing itself, i.e., for criticizing its objectifying conceptualizations, to the extent that its own intention of speaking of a power beyond to which the world and man are subjected is restricted and obscured by the objectifying nature of its statements.[98]

The characteristic flow of Bultmannian hermeneutic is thus away from language—of which mythological language serves as model—back to the understanding prior to, and more authentic than, the language. It is at this point that Ebeling seeks to supplement Bultmann's hermeneutic with a more positive correlation of language and hermeneutic.[99]

The emergence of the term understanding was not—any more than that of *hermēneia* and *hermeneutics* before it—an irrelevant terminological fluctuation. Rather, like them, it stated the particular hearing of the subject matter characteristic of its day. Its implication of getting behind the words to the existence objectifying itself in them calls to attention both the depth and the limitation characteristic of this first step toward a new hermeneutic.[100] The reintroduction of the term *Hermeneutik* in our day presumably calls up a different scope, which, while not "hermeneutics," is not simply "understanding" either;[101] it is this scope that the following pages seek to make audible in the term hermeneutic.

---

98. Cf. Bultmann, *Kerygma und Mythos*, 1:23 = *Kerygma and Myth*, 10–11. Translation is from the German original. A complete survey of the demythologizing debate has been provided by Günther Bornkamm, "Die Theologie Rudolf Bultmanns in der neueren Diskussion: Zum Problem der Entmythologisierung und Hermeneutik," (the full bibliography on 33–46 is by Egon Brandenburger). The omission here of such an analysis should not imply that the demythologizing issue is past (which would in fact suggest it might well be bypassed), but rather that it was the vanguard of a movement that has emerged in the new hermeneutic. "In fact in Rudolf Bultmann's own view the issue and concept of demythologizing is relatively speaking confined to the surface of the matter. It is not new, and calling attention to it is really a *testimonium paupertatis*. For it has necessarily been always taking place in various ways, although usually without adequate hermeneutical reflection. According to Rudolf Bultmann it has its real theological meaning only within the context of comprehensive hermeneutical reflection" (125).

99. Cf. Fuchs, "The New Testament and the Hermeneutical Problem," 84.

100. Gadamer, "Verstehen," 1.381–82, distinguishes between understanding the subject matter coming to expression in language and understanding the psychic, inner element in an expression. When he then refers the reader for the former to the article on "Hermeneutik" and treats only the latter in his article on "Understanding," he has by implication carried through a systematic distinction confirming the historical distinction made in the present paper.

101. Indicative of the fact that "understanding" has not continued to be a reliable

HERMENEUTIC

It is a central recognition of the new hermeneutic that language itself says what is invisibly taking place in the life of a culture. An instance of this would be the sudden re-emergence of the term *Hermeneutik* within post-Bultmannian German theology. If the last textbook in hermeneutics, the German translation of Torm's *Nytestamentlig Hermeneutik*, had appeared in 1930, it was indicative of something when in 1954 another New Testament scholar, Ernst Fuchs, published a volume entitled *Hermeneutik*.[102] Then in 1959 the term suddenly appeared on all sides. The third edition of the standard German theological encyclopedia, *Die Religion in Geschichte und Gegenwart*, published an article on "Hermeneutik" by Gerhard Ebeling,[103] an entry missing from the first two editions. In the same year Ernst Fuchs published a volume of collected essays under the title *Zum hermeneutischen Problem in der Theologie: Die existentiale Interpretation*.[104] In 1962 the University of Zürich created an Institut für Hermeneutik under the directorship of Gerhard Ebeling, and in 1963 a similar institute was founded at the University of Marburg directed by Ernst Fuchs. Together with their close friend Manfred Mezger, Professor of Homiletics at Mainz, they also founded a monograph series entitled *Hermeneutische Untersuchungen zur Theologie*.[105]

These developments were counterbalanced by a new prominence of the term from the other side of Continental theology. The Dutch theologian Kornelis Heiko Miskotte published in 1959, in the series *Theologische Studien* edited by Karl Barth, four radio speeches on *Biblische Hermeneutik*.[106] Then a pupil of Hermann Diem in Tübingen, Lothar Steiger, wrote in 1960 a dissertation *Die Hermeneutik als dogmatisches Problem*.[107] This was followed in 1961 by a volume from the

---

hallmark of the *avant garde* discussion is Magnusson, *Der Begriff "Verstehen."*

102. Fuchs, *Hermeneutik* (1954; 2nd ed., 1958 with *Ergänzungsheft*).

103. Ebeling, "Hermeneutik," 242–62.

104. Fuchs, *Zum hermeneutischen Problem in der Theologie* (1959).

105. Volume 1 is Gerhard Ebeling's essays entitled *Theologie und Verkündigung: Ein Gespräch mit Rudolf Bultmann* (1962); vol. 2 is Eberhard Jüngel's dissertation, *Paulus und Jesus: Eine Untersuchung zur Präzisierung der Frage nach dem Ursprung der Christologie* (1962).

106. Miskotte, *Zur biblischen Hermeneutik* (1959). The radio speeches were given in 1957.

107. Steiger, *Die Hermeneutik als dogmatisches Problem* (1961).

Professor of Practical Theology at the University of Erlangen, Kurt Frör, entitled *Biblische Hermeneutik*.[108] Yet in spite of such works retaining more continuity with traditional hermeneutics, the term *Hermeneutik* has clearly received a new overtone oriented to the position of Fuchs and Ebeling. As such it has come to serve as a label for their position, and has been countered by a call to return to the more customary practice of the historian's trade. Thus Oscar Cullmann calls for objectivity in the sense of an exegesis without presuppositions:

> I myself am a theologian. But I present my lectures in Paris at the Ecole des Hautes-Etudes and at the Sorbonne—where I hold a strictly neutral "comparative religions" chair for the New Testament branch of science under the secular designation "Histoire des origines du Christianisme"—no differently than in Basel, where I belong to the Theological Faculty. This is possible for me since I regard the non-violation of the limits imposed on the New Testament scholar in studying New Testament texts as precisely a *theological* duty applicable to all, not only to the scholars: first, before all evaluation, all judging, perhaps even prior to all "being addressed" in my "understanding of existence," prior to all believing, simply to be obedient to what the men of the new covenant want to communicate to me as revelation, even if it is quite foreign to me. I am aware that I thereby stand in contradiction to a "hermeneutical" trend widely prevalent today. Whether listening with understanding is possible at all without faith and whether it cannot precisely in this way lead to faith, is to be worked out in my next book frequently anticipated here.[109]

108. Frör, *Biblische Hermeneutik* (1961). Cf. Eduard Schweizer's review in *NZZ*.

109. "Retrospect upon the Effect of the Book in Post-War Theology," written in the summer of 1962 in the place of a new Preface to the 3rd ed. of *Christus und die Zeit*, 25–26. One may compare the argument of Gilmour, in his article "Jesus Christ," 494, that "a careful distinction must be drawn between the functions of 'historical' and of 'theological' exegesis." The former involves "the rigid exclusion of the interpreter's personal, apologetic, or polemical interests," whereas the latter runs the danger that "occasionally the theologian reinterprets and recasts his source material so as to force it into the service of the theological or philosophical position he represents." The assumption that the historian can hold off his historicness until he is ready to shift consciously into the category of theologian is naïve, and avoids rather than meeting the thrust of Bultmann's question, "Is Exegesis without Presuppositions Possible?" The discussion of hermeneutic has come to the center of the Bultmannian movement precisely because these scholars know they must face this issue squarely. Cf. my review article of Gilmour's essay in *ANQ*. Cf. also Krister Stendahl's comment in his essay on "Contemporary Biblical Theology," 421: "It is not quite clear how Cullmann understands the relation between such a de-

The extent to which such a statement does not meet the Bultmannian position can be seen by comparing it with the following methodological statement by Bultmann himself.

> The theological investigator obviously cannot presuppose his own faith as an epistemological instrument and make use of it as a presupposition for methodical work. What he can and should do is keep himself ready, open, free. Or, better, keep himself questioning—or knowing the questionability of—all human self-understanding, in the knowledge that existential understanding of one's self (in distinction from existentialist interpretation of man's being) is real only in the act of existing and not in the isolated reflection of thought.[110]

Somewhat sharper is the reservation about the new hermeneutic expressed by Ernst Käsemann from within the Bultmannian school itself (if that term had not already become an anachronism).

> Not everyone can do everything, and in the present high tide of "interpretation" some must devote themselves to administering the estate left by the historians, if for no other reason than to disturb the interpreters.... This state of affairs awakens the suspicion that *sub rosa* historiography and interpretation are exchanging the roles appropriate to them, in that interpretation no longer serves historiography in need of clarification, but rather turns it into a quarry for its buildings arbitrarily erected for contemporaries in need of a roof. Ultimate hermeneutical problems emerge here, as already the discussion between Ebeling, Fuchs, and myself proves. It seems to be, e.g., a quite inappropriate category taken over invalidly from traditional natural science into the realm of history, when one speaks of the occurrences of the past as objectively at hand and under our control. That can be asserted just as well and just as poorly about things in the present. The mistakes of historians and interpreters and the misunderstanding of the neighbor belong very much together, are not in the least merely the result

---

scriptive Biblical theology in its first- and second-century terms and its translation into our present age; his hermeneutical discussions have nothing of the radical penetration of Bultmann's.... Cullmann (and Stauffer) have not clarified their answer to why or how they consider the NT as meaningful for the present age. Because of this lack of clarification, their works are read by many—perhaps most—readers as being on the same level of present meaning as Bultmann's or Barth's highly 'translated' interpretations; and there are indications that they do not mind such a use of their works."

110. Bultmann, *Theology*, 2:241.

of stupidity, and indeed prove that one is victim of a short circuit when one makes what is foreign in a contemporary or past history into something objective in the sense of being subject to our control. I regard the confusion of understanding and decision as no less dangerous. The assumed compulsion of having always to take a stand, rather than first hearing for once and waiting for what is given or taken by that which is foreign, is usually the death of understanding, the strangling of the real question, the missing of the chance to grow by learning. How many of our students still perceive that understanding is always a process of one's own growth, and hence requires time and leisure even to the extent of self-forgetfulness; that only unripe fruit is shaken from the tree of knowledge by him who does not himself ripen in the handwork of the historian's trade? The cardinal virtue of the historian and the beginning of all meaningful hermeneutic is for me the practice of hearing, which begins simply by letting what is historically foreign maintain its validity and does not regard rape as the basic form of *engagement*.[111]

Thus the German theological debate of the sixties has become to a large extent a debate about *Hermeneutik*.[112]

The fate of the term *Hermeneutik* in our century—where "fate" means *fatum*, "what is spoken"—can be illustrated by the case of Martin Heidegger. He was first introduced to hermeneutics as a student at the Roman Catholic Theological Faculty of the University of Freiburg im Breisgau.[113] He took the term hermeneutics up into his own philosophical vocabulary when he began to write *Being and Time* in 1923, in seeking

---

111. Käsemann, "Zum Thema der urchristlichen Apokalyptik," 258–59 [it appeared February 1963] = "On the Subject of Primitive Christian Apocalyptic," 109–10.

112. One may contrast with the admissions of hermeneutical lethargy from the turn of the century the recent comment by a nontheologian: "The contemporary discussion of the hermeneutical problem is certainly nowhere so vigorous as in the area of Protestant theology." Gadamer, "Hermeneutik und Historismus," 256.

113. "The title 'hermeneutics' was familiar to me from my study of theology. At that time I was especially tormented by the question as to the relation between the word of Holy Scripture and theological speculative thought. It was, if you will, the same relation, namely that between language and being, only concealed and unavailable to me, so that I sought in vain on many detours and blind alleys for a guiding thread.... Later I found this title *Hermeneutik* again in Wilhelm Dilthey in his theory of those humane sciences which are historiological in character. Dilthey was familiar with hermeneutics from the *same* source, his study of theology, especially his study of Schleiermacher." Heidegger, *Unterwegs zur Sprache*, 96.

to distinguish his phenomenology from that of Husserl.[114] For Heidegger, hermeneutic was the analysis of the existentiality of existence, i.e., of the "existentials" in terms of which existence is to be understood. By deriving ontologically the historicness of *Dasein,* his hermeneutic provided a foundation for Dilthey's methodology of the humanities. For if Dilthey had sought to establish a distinctively historic method for the humane sciences that was not borrowed from that of the natural sciences, such a "critique of historic reason" logically presupposed some such analysis of man's historic being as that provided by Heidegger. Thus, just as Dilthey's concern for understanding had superseded hermeneutics, in that the problem of understanding is prior to the rules of interpretation, Heidegger's hermeneutic opened up a possibility for superseding Dilthey.[115]

Yet in the actual analysis of the existentials that followed, Heidegger came to see that "interpretation," which he correctly recognized as the translation of *hermēneia* and thus presumably would equate with hermeneutic,[116] was itself grounded in "understanding," which was the "fundamental existential."[117] Thus his "existentialist interpretation" itself led back from the term hermeneutic to the term understanding. The task

---

114. Ibid., 95. ". . . Hermeneutical phenomenology . . . the name was intended to designate a new direction for phenomenology."

115. "Our investigation itself will show that the meaning of phenomenological description as a method lies in *interpretation.* The *logos* of the phenomenology of *Dasein* has the character of a *hermēneuein,* through which the authentic meaning of being, and also those basic structures of being which *Dasein* itself possesses, are *made known* to *Dasein's* understanding of being. The phenomenology of *Dasein* is a *hermeneutic* in the primordial signification of this word, where it designates this business of interpreting. But to the extent that by uncovering the meaning of being and the basic structures of *Dasein* in general we may exhibit the horizon for any further ontological study of those entities which do not have the character of *Dasein,* this hermeneutic also becomes a 'hermeneutic' in the sense of working out the conditions on which the possibility of any ontological investigation depends. And finally, to the extent that *Dasein,* as an entity with the possibility of existence, has ontological priority over every other being, hermeneutic, as an interpretation of *Dasein's* being, has the third and specific sense of an analytic of the existentiality of existence; and this is the sense which is philosophically *primary.* Then so far as this hermeneutic works out *Dasein's* historicality ontologically as the ontical condition for the possibility of historiology, it contains the roots of what can be called 'hermeneutic' only in a derivative sense: the methodology of those humane sciences which are historiological in character." Heidegger, *Being and Time,* 61–62.

116. Ibid., 201.

117. Ibid., 182

logically prior to Dilthey was redefined as that of getting to the basis of "understanding,"[118] and the term hermeneutic faded out of Heidegger's vocabulary.[119]

In the later Heidegger's writing the term hermeneutic reemerges just long enough to indicate the sense in which it is now heard. Negatively, it does not mean a theory of interpretation, but rather the process of interpretation itself.[120] And it is decisive that interpretation has its focus not in terms of understanding existence, but rather in terms of language. Indeed the term hermeneutic is heard primarily in terms of the meaning of *hermēneia* as "speech."

> The term "hermeneutical" is derived from the Greek verb *hermēneuein*. This refers to the noun *hermēneus*, which can be associated with the name of the God *Hermes* in a game of thought that is more binding than the rigor of science. Hermes is the messenger of the gods. He brings the news of fate. *Hermēneuein* is that exposition that brings news, to the extent that the exposition is itself able to hear the message. Such exposition becomes interpretation of what has already been said by the poets, who themselves, according to the saying of Socrates in Plato's discourse Ion (534 E), "are messengers (*hermēnēs*) of the gods." . . . Socrates carries the connection even further in thinking of the rhapsodists as those who bring news of the word of the poets. . . . From all this it becomes clear that the hermeneutical does not mean only the interpretation, but prior to that already the bringing of the message and the news."[121]

Here hermeneutic is primarily the speaking of meaning, and it is a subordinate remark that of course it is a speaking that has itself understood what it has to say. This priority of proclamation is the reason the herme-

---

118. Ibid. "'Understanding' in the sense of *one* possible kind of cognizing among others (as distinguished, for instance, from 'explaining') must, like explaining, be interpreted as an existentialist derivative of that primary understanding which is one of the constituents of being and of the 'there' in general."

119. Heidegger, *Unterwegs zur Sprache*, 98.

120. Ibid., 120. This passage is in the context both of interpreting *Being and Time* and of defining the subsequent "turn" in Heidegger's thought. On the complex problem of the extent to which such subsequent interpretations of *Being and Time* are themselves representative of the position of the later Heidegger, see above in chapter 1: "The German Discussion of the Later Heidegger," esp. 40–46.

121. Heidegger, *Unterwegs zur Sprache*, 121–22.

neutic of the later Heidegger is worked out less under the topic "hermeneutic" than under the topic "language."[122]

Language in the new hermeneutic is not viewed as an objectification behind which one must move in establishing the understanding of existence objectifying itself therein. It is indeed not man at all who is ex-pressing himself in language. Rather it is language itself that speaks.[123] It is in this sense that Helmut Franz warns against the subjectivism involved in letting "not the exegete as subject, but rather the author as subject dominate. This subject stands somewhere in isolation and composes texts with contents, truths, intentions. But such a subject is not seen as moving and being moved in history."[124] He describes the hermeneutical orientation that avoids this unsuspected form of subjectivism as follows:

> The basic thing about a text is not what the author intended to express in words by following up a given point of view. Rather, basic is what wills fundamentally to show itself and have its say prior to or apart from any subjective intent. The question to the text would then not be the question as to the [author's] perspective, but rather: "What shines forth in this text? What shows itself in this text?"[125]

Such phraseology is not intended to eliminate man from the language process,[126] but merely to emphasize that the subject matter "addresses itself" to man's thought,[127] to which man answers with his words. "Primal thinking is the echo of being's favor, in which what is unique clears and lets it happen that beings are. This echo is the human answer to the word of the silent voice of being. Thought's answer is the origin of the

---

122. The new hermeneutic of Heidegger is most explicit in the volume entitled *Unterwegs zur Sprache* (On the Way to Language). The titles of the lectures and essays brought together into this volume are also indicative of the prominence of the term "language" in designating the new hermeneutic: "Language"; "Language in the Poem"; "From a Discussion of Language"; "The Essence of Language"; "Word"; "The Path to Language."

123. Ibid., 20 and throughout.

124. Franz, "Das Wesen des Textes," 190.

125. Ibid., 204.

126. Cf. the play on words with the German verb *brauchen*, which means both to use and to need. Language, the silent tolling of reality, uses man and indeed needs man's voice as its spokesperson. Ibid., 20, 256, and throughout. This play on words recurs in Fuchs, *Zur Frage nach dem historischen Jesus*, 427.

127. Heidegger, *Identität und Differenz*, 13

human word, which word first lets language emerge as the enunciation of the word into words."[128]

The subject matter of which language speaks is primarily being. It is man's very nature to hearken to the call of being. "Man is actually this relation of cor-'respond'-ence, and only this."[129] In this way language is located at the center of man's nature, rather than being regarded primarily as an objectification of an otherwise authentic self-understanding. For man's nature is defined as linguistic, in that his role is to re-speak, to respond, to answer, the call of being.

> Since flora and fauna are yoked to their respective surroundings, but never set free into the clearing of being—and only this clearing is 'world'—for that reason they lack language. Yet in this term 'surroundings' the whole puzzle of living creatures is compressed. Language in its essence is not the objectification of an organism, nor is it the expression of a living creature. Hence it can never be thought in a way that does justice to its nature by being thought of as a sign or even as a signification. Language is the arrival of being itself, both clearing and concealing.[130]

Heidegger's new understanding of language is thus derived from an understanding of humanity that is not oriented to existentialism but rather to "ontology,"[131] if this term is valid for the distinctively

---

128. Heidegger, *Was ist Metaphysik?*, 49. Translation is from the original rather than being derived from the thoroughly confused English translation by R. F. C. Hull and Alan Crick in *Existence and Being*, 358.

129. Heidegger, *Identität und Differenz*, 22. Translation is from the German original rather than being derived from the English translation, *Essays in Metaphysics: Identity and Difference*, 21.

130. Heidegger, *Über den Humanismus*, 16.

131. It should be noted that Heidegger regards "ontology" as referring metaphysically to the science of being, which obscures the question as to being and is hence to be repudiated. Cf. *Was is Metaphysik?*, 19 = *Existentialism from Dostoevsky to Sartre*, 217; and the essay "Die onto-theo-logische Verfassung der Metaphysik," in *Identität und Differenz*, 33–73 = *Essays in Metaphysics*, 33–67. Hence it is ironic to see him criticized as an ontologist by those who learned from him to transcend traditional ontology. Cf. Carl Michaelson's contrast between "Theology as Ontology and as History," and Emil Staiger's criticism: "But it must be immediately added that Martin Heidegger does not himself interpret in this way [sc. *Being and Time*]. He is not concerned to acknowledge that which is unique in a historical figure as unique, although he likes to make use of the ambiguous expression 'let be' for designating the correct encounter of *Dasein* with beings. Rather than ordering the wealth of purely grasped historic life with the aid of his temporal concepts [Staiger's method], he sees in every text—and this is something

Heideggerian sense of the basic question as to why there are beings at all and not simply nothing—the question as to being. Humanity is where being's voice is heard and given room. Humanity is the loud-speaker for the silent tolling of being. When one fulfills this role, one is truly human. It is for this reason that Heidegger regards the poet as humanity's true priest. It is the human who names the gods, who speaks forth the world of meaning that being addresses to humanity; it is the human who calls humanity out of the forgetfulness of being into one's true role as shepherd of being. It is because of this new understanding of humanity as being's spokesperson that Heidegger's hermeneutic has moved from an interpretation of *Dasein* to an interpretation of poets such as Hölderlin. Indeed Heidegger has become fascinated with such pre-Hellenic heroes as Tantalus, Prometheus, and Sisyphus, who occur in Hellenic mythology as personages to be punished, "tantalized," for having revealed the secrets of the gods—figures whom Heidegger restores to their original position of honor as hermeneuts of the gods. Thus the primary orientation of *hermēneia* to the numinous messages of the gods emerges in the later Heidegger's hermeneutic, and the role of the new hermeneutic as a new orientation for theology is prefigured by his work.

It was Ernst Fuchs who first translated the hermeneutical discussion from the categories of inauthentic and authentic existence derived from *Being and Time* into the later Heidegger's analogous distinction between the everyday language of the subject-object dilemma and the uncorrupted language of being. From Heidegger Fuchs has learned that humanity's location in a given historical tradition means that the human hears reality in terms of a certain "world," a context of meaning, that a person simply takes over from one's culture in its language. If "world" is thus experienced in language, and if the term existence suggests that "out there, as world, is to be decided what is to be worked out inside, in the human, as *Dasein*,"[132] then the decision with regard to one's self-understanding takes place as a decision with regard to language. Thus language becomes constitutive of self-understanding, rather than merely its secondary objectification.

---

quite different—only a contribution to his problem of ontology." "Ein Rückblick." In actuality Heidegger's concern with being is an effort to understand reality as historic and linguistic.

132. Fuchs, *Hermeneutik*, 67.

Helmut Franz clarifies this primacy of language in a commentary on Calvin's phrase *subest locutioni relatio*, "relation is subordinate to language":

> What precedes every relation and makes such a thing as relation first possible is *"locutio."* It is not true that the relation, our being involved, is fulfilled and manifested in our being addressed. Rather the opening of an area of "mutual understanding" as a language area is the primary thing that penults involvement and relations to occur.[133]

Although Fuchs has learned this inherent relation of language to existence in Heidegger primarily with regard to inauthentic existence, he also sees in it a potentiality for a positive theology. For he hears Heidegger's lament about inauthentic language as an indirect witness to true language, somewhat as the law is related to the gospel.[134]

> For the lament as *language* no longer belongs to lostness, but rather supplies a person with the plus that as the *essence* of language reminds a person that one belongs to a communication, a ... *nearness* to the power at work in language prior to all human participation. For it is not true that a person has given birth to language. Rather a person is born out of language. That a person then has made language a means of usurped existence merely proves that a person is accustomed to exist in daily life having missed the mark.[135]

The drag of the past upon humanity takes place primarily as the language one inherited predisposing a person to inauthenticity, so that a person is constantly walking in the rut it provides and thus falling into its trap. But this recognition that language is where the past becomes our future can also be stated positively. Indeed such inauthentic language is only the perversion of authentic language, and if authentic language is also part of our past, it can meet us as our future that holds open to us the dimension of our own authenticity into which we can enter. Fuchs finds authentic language in Jesus' language of love, and thus moves from

---

133. Franz, "Das Wesen des Textes," 198.

134. Cf. the definition of the relation of Heidegger to theology in terms of law and gospel that increasingly emerged in the school of Fuchs and Ebeling, summarized above in "The German Discussion of the Later Heidegger," 53–63.

135. Fuchs, *Hermeneutik*, 63.

Heidegger into a "christological understanding of language."¹³⁶ This is a somewhat different understanding of language from that of Heidegger himself, as detailed study of Heidegger would subsequently indicate,¹³⁷ and it is a different grasp of the nature of the new quest of the historical Jesus from that intended by its main proponent at that time, Ernst Käsemann.¹³⁸ Yet such observations should not distract attention from the point of major significance in the present context: Fuchs's own combination of these various ingredients emerged as a basically new step in the development of hermeneutic, of which his *Hermeneutik* of 1954 is the first landmark.

When one opens Ernst Fuchs's *Hermeneutik*, aware that it is the first New Testament hermeneutic since Torm's *Hermeneutik des Neuen Testaments* a quarter of a century before, the contrast between the two works is so overpowering that one is inclined to conclude that they belong to completely different fields and only by mistake came to share the name *Hermeneutik*. Hence it is necessary to point out that there is some continuity between the two volumes, which at least makes it possible to recognize that Fuchs's intention is to move out from the literary genre known as a textbook on hermeneutics. Indeed his point of departure for arriving at his particular understanding of the title *Hermeneutik* is the traditional definition of hermeneutics as the theory of exegesis.

> But to the extent that exegetical theology's way of operating in specific cases calls for an accounting as to its presuppositions, there is a need for explicit reflection upon the presuppositions of exegesis. Exegesis too must discuss the communicability of the revelation, but [it must do this] in view of the historical and indeed on the basis of its experiences with the historical. So there is a need for a systematic introduction to the exegesis of the New Testament, in distinction from an introduction in terms of the history of literature. This is the task that we wish to follow up in this *Hermeneutik* with regard to the New Testament. We could equally well have

---

136. Ibid., 78. Cf. the criticism of Franz, "Das Denken Heideggers und die Theologie," 89: "But it is not Fuchs in danger, with this 'solution' of the problem, of dissolving also the inner tension that *maintains* itself in Jesus' language, and indeed that first becomes acute in the very fact that Jesus 'speaks.'"

137. Cf. chapter 1 above, 59

138. Cf. my essay: Robinson, "The Recent Debate on the 'New Quest,'" 201. Käsemann has published a critical analysis of the turn the new quest has taken: "Blind Alleys in the 'Jesus of History' Controversy."

spoken of a "theological introduction" to the New Testament, but we have not done so since we must go beyond the area of theology in various directions.[139]

Fuchs's *Hermeneutik* is also divided rather traditionally into general and applied (i.e., special)[140] hermeneutic, the latter devoted rather traditionally to a treatment—but what a treatment!—of the various literary and oral forms. Thus Fuchs clearly proposes to be doing what hermeneutics should have been doing, and when one, after reading Fuchs, recalls in Torm the long sections on the language and time of the New Testament, one can only be amazed that none of the depth dimension that Fuchs at least exposed to view had even been dimly sensed by Torm.[141] Hermeneutic is clearly a challenge to hermeneutics that cannot be simply brushed aside by Biblical scholarship as the responsibility of some other discipline.

Of course the material position of Fuchs's New Testament hermeneutic can best be approached from its point of departure in Bultmannian hermeneutic, rather than from that of Torm. It is perhaps relevant in this regard to observe that Fuchs accentuates the critical side of demythologizing that it shares with *Sachkritik*. "But since this text [sc. John], in spite of its demythologizing intention, still uses mythological terms, its own intention demands its critical analysis, since of course one cannot presuppose *a priori* that the evangelist was also able to carry through his intention completely."[142]

It is this critical function in demythologizing that is the connecting link with the step Fuchs takes beyond Bultmann. If for Bultmann the interpreter's own self-understanding is involved in the hermeneutical process as a pre-understanding, this self-involvement is for Bultmann still subordinated to the purpose of interpreting the text, which thus remains the ultimate objective of interpretation. For Fuchs, however, there is a decisive development in the scope of hermeneutic, in that the text in

---

139. Fuchs, *Hermeneutik*, 100–101.

140. Cf. ibid., 101.

141. Schleiermacher had already related the forms of literary expression with the transcendental forms in which man perceives, among which forms time is primary since Kant, so that the hermeneutical recognition of language and time as structures of man's existence was long overdue. Cf. Dilthey, "Die Entstehung der Hermeneutik," 327–28.

142. Fuchs, "Schluss der Vorlesung über das Johannesevangelium, Berlin S.S. 1958 (24.7.1958)," in *Ergänzungsheft* to the *Hermeneutik*, 9.

turn interprets us, and the involvement of our pre-understanding carries beyond its heuristic function in interpreting the text into a criticism of our own self-understanding in terms of the self-understanding the text addresses to us.[143]

> Who is now the object of demythologizing? Neither God, nor Jesus, nor the world, nor even language oriented toward walking,[144] but rather humanity caught in a distorted relation to itself, at a standstill, indeed in collapse, who thinks either too highly or too lowly of oneself, indeed who does not even know that one lives from a movement that is terribly obscured by one's common understanding of space as stationary and of time as only seeming to move. It is not valid to subject the revelation to a stationary space and to a time that only seems to move. Rather one must let oneself be drawn by the gospel back to where space and time make sense in terms of a movement, in terms of a path and walking, as space for others and time for us. For this reason I have in this course replaced Bultmann's program and method of demythologizing with what seems to me a more radical existentialist interpretation, so as to bring the text anew on the road and put it in motion. What resulted was at least an analysis of Jesus' love. It should confirm itself as a movement of our own existence. What in all of this is theory should be brought to an end for now, in order that love itself can begin to speak. What does love say? "Arise, let us leave theory!"[145]

Such hermeneutic, intended to interpret our existence, flows as directly over into preaching as do passages in Barth's *Romans*.

Since for Fuchs the interpreter's self-understanding is not merely the *pre*-understanding in the hermeneutical process, but is also the *goal* of that process itself, it is not surprising that the concept of a pre-understanding has to some extent been replaced by another concept, that of

---

143. It is indicative of the bond of continuity with Bultmann that Fuchs works toward his position as an interpretation of Bultmann. "Bultmann's attempt at demythologizing also takes place as a question, as a critical interpretation of the pre-understanding of being that determines each existence (since it is traced out on each existence), i.e., as existentialist interpretation of being." Ibid., 12.

144. "Such an analysis of love [sc. as in John] is however no mythology, since it does not enter in upon concepts *about* love, but rather is intent only upon pointing the way, i.e., is intent on love itself." Ibid., 12.

145. Ibid., 13.

the "hermeneutical principle."[146] A hermeneutical principle is that with which the text is confronted to call forth from it what it has to say. Put otherwise, a hermeneutical principle is the "place" where the text is to be put if it is to begin to speak. Put a cat before a mouse and the cat gets into action and shows what a cat is.[147]

With regard to the hermeneutical principle for theological exegesis, Fuchs observes that it is the confrontation with our need that reveals what we mean by the term God.[148] Hence, the hermeneutical principle, the "indication of the place for the truth of the gospel," is the unremitting plaint of Rom 7:24 as to who will deliver us from this existence of death.[149] Put otherwise, history, existence in the flesh, is the place of the encounter with God,[150] and so the hermeneutical principle must be of the nature of history.[151] The hermeneutical principle is the presupposition that man has a relation to himself, or, more exactly, the question as to ourselves.[152] It is ourselves that we place before the text. The text unfolds itself, speaks up, in what it says about us. Here one can see interpretation taking place less as "understanding" than as "language," in that the text interprets itself by what it has to say about us.

Under "language" Fuchs does not mean simply the act of oral speaking.[153]

---

146. Fuchs, *Hermeneutik*, 103–18.

147. Ibid., 109. Cf. the definition on 111: "'Hermeneutical principle' designates what bestows on understanding the power and truth of an *occurrence*. It is the *power* of understanding in the birth of *the language naming the truth*. The hermeneutical principle points out the 'place' of truth." Cf. also the illustration in Fuchs, "The New Testament and the Hermeneutical Problem," 138, of putting a football in front of a person to see whether he is a person interested in football.

148. Fuchs, *Hermeneutik*, 110.

149. Ibid., 111.

150. Ibid., 114.

151. Ibid., 116.

152. Ibid., 116–17.

153. "Bultmann reproaches me for confusing language (*Sprache*) and speaking (*Sprechen*), since I talk of a language event (*Sprachereignis*) rather than being satisfied with the expression 'event of speaking' (*Sprechereignis*), which in his view would be more suitable for what I mean. I am amazed." Fuchs, *Zur Frage nach dem historischen Jesus*, 424. It is to avoid this misunderstanding that I have translated *Sprachereignis* as "language event" rather than as "speech event."

> Language is not even necessarily talk. Language is rather primarily a *showing* or *letting* be seen, an indication in the active sense: I intimate to you or instruct you what you yourself should "perceive" (take notice of or watch out for).... That can take place through a simple movement, even by turning away from another.[154]

It is such "language" that in Fuchs's hermeneutic receives the primary role, which is another point at which he conceives of himself as going beyond Bultmann.

> Of course language is directed to man and being is related to existence. Here I do agree with Bultmann. But, on the other hand, both being and man are directed to language. And to this extent we are related to God.... The responsibility for speaking resides already in language, not outside it. That is my *thesis*. He who notices recognizes that language "grants." Language is not the abbreviation of thinking, but thinking is an abbreviation of language. Language is gift.... Like Bultmann, I deny that a person has faith "at his disposal." But the reason does not reside in the actuality of sin, but prior to that in the dependence of faith on word, God's word... Hence I took the further step of exhibiting the historicness of existence as the linguisticality of existence.[155]

It is at this point that the term hermeneutic attains the specific profile characteristic of the new hermeneutic, as "faith's doctrine of language."[156]

> Being emerges from language, when language directs us into the dimension of our existence determinative for our life. Is that the "meaning" of the word of God? Then hermeneutic in theology would indeed be nothing else than the "doctrine of the word of God" (Ebeling), faith's doctrine of language. The reverse also is true: The theological doctrine of the word of God would be the question as to being in the horizon of Biblical language. The content of human historicness would then not be named questionability but rather linguisticality.[157]

154. Fuchs, *Hermeneutik*, 131.
155. Fuchs, *Zur Frage nach dem historischen Jesus*, 427–29.
156. Fuchs, *Hermeneutik*, III, 101–2; idem, "Response," 241.
157. Fuchs, *Zum hermeneutischen Problem in der Theologie*, 115. Cf. the definition of reality in terms of language, Fuchs, *Hermeneutik*, 130: "Reality is hence not at all simply what is, as we said to begin with in adopting the current view. Rather the real is only that which can become present as language (even though this be in recollection!). What

In this way the problem of understanding aright biblical history becomes the problem of right language. Bultmann had originally made use of the term *Heilsgeschichte,* "salvation history." Yet he came to reject this term,[158] and Fuchs traces the inadequacy of the *Heilsgeschichte* approach to the inauthentic, objectifying understanding of language it presupposes:

> Faith and faith's *expression* (*Aussage*) are not the same, even though admittedly they condition each other. For faith must always have already been transposed in a quite specific manner into language if it wishes to understand itself as confession, i.e., is to be faith in (Jesus Christ). This structure of intentionality[159] (faith *in*) is for us inherent only at the level of language. It does not derive from faith itself, which is originally obedient answer, as we saw.[160] But our language usually has the structure of *logos tinos,*[161] although this structure is not the only one, just as a word can be equally well word from something as word to someone. But faith's *expression* shares in the intentional structure of language and is today characterized by this structure. For example, only in this structure can it be meaningful to insist on the confession to "objective saving facts," in which context it is quite irrelevant whether or not the theology that insists on the confession to "objective saving facts" is aware of the structural dependency, i.e., the *logical* presuppositions, of its expression. Of course as "theology" it should recognize *which* logic its confessional formulation aids to ascendancy, i.e., to which logic it is submitting itself. Friedrich Gogarten has rightly named this logic the "subject-object schema."[162] But the

---

is now unutterable seems on the contrary to be unreal, which does not mean it is or was impossible. Thus reality has not yet been fully defined when we locate it only in the context of beings, but rather as a 'category' it is even more basically built into the nature of another realm, that of *language.*" Ebeling shares the concern for language without departing from an emphasis upon "the all-embracing questionability of the whole." "Die Evidenz des Ethischen und die Theologie," 350.

158. This is most explicit in Bultmann's review of Cullmann's *Christ and Time,* entitled "History of Salvation and History," in *Existence and Faith,* 226–40; German ed. in *TLZ* 73 (1948) 659–66.

159. It should be pointed out that Fuchs uses the term "intentionality" here to refer to objectification, a usage quite the reverse of that of Dillenberger, "On Broadening the New Hermeneutic," 154.

160. Fuchs, *Hermeneutik,* 84.

161. "Word of or about something." Cf. *Being and Time,* 201.

162. Fuchs, *Hermeneutik,* 79.

subject-object schema is only *one* of its possible forms. Its basis is intentionality, i.e., its worldliness. "Objective saving facts" are hence only the reverse of "objective worldly facts," i.e., merely an apologetic antithesis, as if God were simply the opposite of the world.[163]

Bultmann himself had met this problem by replacing the term *Heilsgeschichte* with the term *Heilsgeschehen* (or *Heilsereignis*), "saving event." But now that authentic language has come to have such a close association with God's word admitting man to authentic existence, the refinement of terminology can be carried a step further, when Fuchs designates the saving event as "language event" (*Sprachereignis*) and Ebeling as "word event" (*Wortgeschehen*). This terminological development is obvious in such a statement as the following:

> All this may be called "*Heilsgeschehen.*" Paul even gives the impression that we had to do with a *Heilsgeschichte*. But one could call the *Heilsgeschehen* a "*Heilsgeschichte*" only as a *Heilsgeschichte* of love. I cannot discuss this further here, for I would have to show Paul's interpretation of Jesus' person to be a genuine interpretation of the historical Jesus, a task that would take us too far afield. It suffices that we retain the *Heilsgeschehen* as a *Wortgeschehen* that happens in the Spirit for faith.[164]

Fuchs's use here of the term characteristic of Ebeling rather than of himself indicates that *Sprachereignis* and *Wortgeschehen* are synonyms and that the choice depends upon which Bultmannian term serves as the point of departure, *Heilsereignis* or *Heilsgeschehen*.

Fuchs can illustrate what is meant by a language event by pointing out that one does not name a person brother simply because of a biological fact, i.e., it is not that one is first a brother and then automatically calls the other brother; rather the other becomes brother by my naming him brother. It is the meaningful relationship of brotherhood that is primary, without which the biological tie would be a mockery of the name of brother.[165] The calling of the other "brother" affirms that relationship, lets

---

163. Ibid., 93–94.

164. Fuchs, "Die Spannung im neutestamentlichen Christusglauben," 41. Cf. also his essay "Proclamation and Speech-Event."

165. Fuchs, *Zur Frage nach dem historischen Jesus*, 426. Fuchs once made this point in terms of the local color of his Württemberg background by calling attention to the fact that when at the birth of a calf the cow licks down the newborn calf, this is the cow's

it be what it is, "justifies" it.[166] Language thus "lets being 'become' temporally, makes it an event."[167] Language can also be termed "admission," in that it admits something into its real being.[168] The language event can also be described as carrying out the assembling function of being to which Heidegger had called attention.[169] Theologically speaking, proclamation is such a language event in which the body of Christ is constituted, assembled. The church as assembly takes place in the language event of proclamation.[170] Here the distinctively Protestant definition of the church in terms of the preaching of the word has been restated in terms of the new hermeneutic's understanding of language.

Fuchs seems to have been the first to introduce the play upon the term trans-lation, as the language of the text conveys its meaning into the language of today. "Truth is always immediate. Hence translating succeeds only by trans-lating (*Über-setzen*) truth to us."[171] Hence Fuchs's close friend in the homiletical field, Manfred Mezger, can begin his "guidance for preaching" with a section on "the problem of trans-lation: the text and its freedom," in which the concrete experience of translating the text of the sermon is recognized in its basic hermeneutical relevance for the whole procedure of preaching the text's meaning in the language of today.[172]

---

acknowledgment of the calf as its own, and hence is a "language event."

166. Ibid., 425. Fuchs can refer to his saying "I love you" to his wife as "justifying" her existence.

167. Ibid. Here the term translated "become" is *anwesen*, a term for "being" revived by Heidegger to accentuate the event character of being. Cf. *The Later Heidegger and Theology*, 22, and cf. the Greek term *parousia*, meaning presence in the sense of arrival.

168. The German term is *Einlass*, referring to the granting of entry. Fuchs provides as illustration: "If I . . . say the sheep there are beautiful, I of course refer to the beautiful sheep there. But prior to that I have with this statement also already admitted the beauty of the sheep as that which is and prevails between them and us, in that I entered in upon this occurrence of being." *Zur Frage nach dem historischen Jesus*, 425.

169. "Language picks up the essential trait of being, that it assembles. And the assembling of being *needs* language, *in order to be*. Only in language is being necessarily event." Ibid. Cf. *The Later Heidegger and Theology*, 59.

170. Fuchs, *Zur Frage nach dem historischen Jesus*, 426.

171. Fuchs, *Hermeneutik*, 109. Cf. also Heinrich Ott's use of the idiom in volume 1 of this series, *The Later Heidegger and Theology*, 80, and my discussion of it in the section of the introduction to that volume on "Language and Hermeneutic," reprinted above, 40–46, esp. 45. Cf. also my essay: Robinson, "Theology as Translation."

172. Mezger, "Anleitung zur Predigt," esp. 381–87. Cf. Fuchs's response, "Übersetzung

> Translation does not simply mean finding a word for each word, but rather seeking and finding as well the new place where this text, without detriment to its historical individuality, strikes home to us. The short cut of putting myself in the skin of Moses or Paul is popular but no good, for my name is neither Moses nor Paul.[173]

Thus hermeneutic as translation stands in contrast to the Schleiermacher-Dilthey hermeneutic of becoming "contemporary" with the author—reliving the author's experience.[174]

> [Guidance for preaching] includes and tests the whole path of translation over the cleft of the historical distance into our life. Since it sees to it that what was once said is not simply repeated but is to be said anew, it must show what understanding means and make clear how what is understood comes to expression, i.e., becomes sayable, for people listening today.[175]

Confronted with such a text as John 20:6–7, the burial clothes neatly placed in the empty tomb, one can neither ignore them as irrelevant to us, nor treat them as symbol or allegory. Rather

> the statement of the text is translatable today only in radically contrary formulation to that of the text. . . . Guidance for preaching does not consist in sparing the student the trials provided by the text or teaching the student some kind of tricks for avoiding the questions traditionally left open or deferred to some vague future for treatment. Rather one must give the student courage and charge the student to trust the text so unconditionally that the text retains its intention to say something right through the whole procedure of genuinely attempting to translate, especially where—for the sake of the witness intended to create faith—the statement of the text must be repeated *in completely different language, i.e.,* in some circumstances *contra versionem explicatam*.[176]

Fuchs's understanding of language is well summarized in a passage whose own form illustrates the central role of language in hermeneutic.

---

und Verkündigung."

173. Mezger, "Anleitung zur Predigt," 384.

174. This particular point is that of Gadamer, *Wahrheit und Methode,* 361ff. = *Truth and Method,* 383ff.

175. Mezger "Anleitung zur Predigt," 378.

176. Ibid., 387.

For this summary occurs in an interpretation of the prologue of John, which interpretation takes the form of a discussion of the way to translate it. That is to say, understanding it means naming the words that speak its meaning. Fuchs begins with the famous translation by Faust, "in the beginning was the deed." This is then corrected, on the basis of John 13:34 (the "new commandment" to love), to the translation "in the beginning was love...." Then, in view of 1 John 4:16 ("God is love"), "love" becomes the translation for *theos* rather than for *logos*. "In the beginning was the word, and the word was with love, and the word was love." Then, since this instance of hermeneutic has to do with what hermeneutic itself is, Fuchs continues with a classical formulation of his understanding of language:

> Yet what then does "word" mean? For we wish to achieve with the term word the expression that is able to grasp Christ once for all. In the supplement to my *Hermeneutik*[177] I made the attempt to understand word as that Yes that forestalls and precedes every No, as the Yes ultimately constitutive of every language event. For word is, after all, language; it speaks, as its very nature. In genuine language do we not, even before any affirmation, say simply this Yes, when we speak? And even more: With our language do we not correspond from the very first to a Yes that grants us entry, entry into that being in which we are with ourselves and yet precisely not left alone? Even though language usually alienates itself from the word, its ground, and builds all sorts of words that are only signs, does it not still in its own-most ground live from that Yes that is the word of all words? To be sure language would then be originally the language of God, and its basic trait would then rightly be named love.[178]

Perhaps nowhere more clearly than here does one hear the sense in which the "saving event" is a "language event," since language, when it is true language, is God's saving word. And perhaps nowhere more clearly than here does one hear the central role of language in a new theology that

---

177. Since in the *Ergänzungsheft* discussion of "word" was in an appendix reproducing the conclusion of a course on John, Fuchs's allusion in the present quotation back to the *Ergänzungsheft* does not involve a contradiction but rather a confirmation of the point made above that this understanding of "word" was worked out in the context of interpreting the Johannine prologue. The same is true of the parallel discussions of "word" in the article "Logos," in *RGG*³, esp. 439–40.

178. Fuchs, "Das Christusverständnis."

has its two foci in the historic Jesus and hermeneutic. For the "historic Jesus" is heard not as "objective factuality," but as "word of address"; and "hermeneutic" is heard not as "understanding in speechless profundity," but as "translation into language that speaks today." Thus hermeneutic is the method suited to the historic Jesus, and the historic Jesus is the material point of departure for a recovery of valid hermeneutic.

The nub of Bultmann's opposition to the new quest of the historical Jesus is formulated in his two rhetorical questions: "Does Jesus' eschatological consciousness mediate an eschatological self-understanding to him who perceives it as a historical phenomenon? . . . Does Jesus' claim of authority, perceived as a historical phenomenon, reach beyond the time of his earthly activity?"[179] These rhetorical questions anticipating a negative answer are posed in terms of the method of the original quest, so that the historical Jesus and the proclaimed kerygma are incommensurable. Bultmann even regards his own *Jesus and the Word*[180] as historiography and therefore not as kerygma.[181] But when his questions are heard in terms of the language event of the new hermeneutic, they are subject to a positive answer.[182] Fuchs and Ebeling would argue that Jesus' word—not just the Easter kerygma—happens as recurring word today and thus mediates an eschatological self-understanding to him who hears it; that Jesus' claim of authority, heard as the word of love, reaches beyond the time of his earthly activity to speak to us today. If Bultmann can say that Jesus rose into the kerygma,[183] Fuchs and Ebeling would say that the word event inaugurated by Jesus' word happens today in the church's proclamation. Thus the term "kerygma"—which has functioned to separate the church's proclamation from the historical Jesus—tends to pass out of the vocabulary of the new hermeneutic,[184] and to be explained and replaced by the term language event or word event, in which Jesus' and

---

179. Bultmann, *Das Verhältnis*, 17.

180. Bultmann, *Jesus and the Word*, 1934; 2nd ed., 1958. German ed., *Jesus*, 1926.

181. *Kerygma und Mythos*, 1:148 = *Kerygma and Myth*, Torchbook ed., 117.

182. It is thus in terms of hermeneutic that the question of Van A. Harvey and Schubert M. Ogden, "Wie neu ist die 'Neue Frage nach dem historischen Jesus'?" is to be answered.

183. Bultmann, *Das Verhältnis*, 27.

184. The turning point in this development is marked by Ebeling's volume *Theologie und Verkündigung*.

the church's proclamation belong together.[185] That this can be asserted not simply as an uncritical harmonization but as a scholarly viewpoint is due to the fact that theological scholarship has attained a new methodology, a new hermeneutic, which traces the translation of meaning in the recurring event of language.

Hans-Georg Gadamer, Bultmann's leading pupil within the field of philosophy and Germany's leading authority on hermeneutic from the philosophical point of view, has described this hermeneutical development in the Bultmannian school as follows:

> In [Fuchs's] essay on "Translation and Preaching" it becomes clearer to what extent this hermeneutical doctrine seeks to transcend what Bultmann meant by existentialist interpretation. It is the hermeneutical principle of translation that points the direction. It is incontestable that "the translation should create the same room that the text sought to create as the Spirit spoke in it." But the bold and yet inescapable consequence is that the word has primacy over the text, for the word is language event. This is obviously meant as the assertion that the relation between word and thought is not that of belatedly catching up with the thought by means of the word expressing it. Rather the word is like a flash of lightning that strikes.[186]

If the new hermeneutic thus proposes to bridge the gulf between historical and systematic theology in terms of a recurrent event of language that moves from Jesus' word to that of the preacher, then the new hermeneutic has become in fact a new understanding of theological scholarship as a whole. It is this overarching implication moving far beyond hermeneutic's point of departure as a subdivision within Biblical scholarship that becomes most apparent in the work of Gerhard Ebeling. He, like Ernst Fuchs, had studied under Rudolf Bultmann.[187] Yet he began

---

185. Most of Fuchs's contributions to the topic are in the second volume of his collected essays, *Zur Frage nach dem historischen Jesus,* and in subsequent issues of *ZTK.* For Ebeling's contributions, cf. esp. "Jesus and Faith." Cf. also his *Das Wesen des christlichen Glaubens* = *The Nature of Faith*: chap. 4: "The Witness of Faith"; chap. 5: "The Basis of Faith," esp. 70–71. See also his essay "The Question of the Historical Jesus and the Problem of Christology."

186. Gadamer, "Hermeneutik und Historismus," 263. The reference in the quotation is to Fuchs's essay "Übersetzung und Verkündigung," 409.

187. Ebeling studied in Marburg from the Summer Semester of 1930 through the Winter Semester of 1931–32. Then he studied in Berlin, which was his home, and in

his academic career in the history of doctrine, and moved from there into systematic theology. His dissertation was an investigation of Luther's hermeneutic, and it was thus with the hermeneutical question that he began. And it was indeed from Luther[188] rather than from Bultmann or Heidegger that he received most directly the correlation between word and faith that has become the focus of his theology. Already in his dissertation he had stated:

> The relation between faith and word in the process of understanding and interpretation is not a relation that moves from the subject to the word, but rather from the word to the understanding subject. Faith adds nothing new to the word, but is the becoming effective of the word as that which it claims to be—as God's word. If faith does not correspond to the word, it is not only not believed but also not understood. For it is not in the least grasped in its real nature and significance. This correlation between word and faith belongs to the word not on the basis of its general structure as word, but rather as witness to the incarnation of the Son of God, in which it is this incarnate One who is encountered in the present. In all words of Scripture we have to do with nothing other than the incarnate Son of God, Jesus Christ. The effect of this is that not a single word of Scripture is understood if it is not grasped in its correlation to faith. God's word comes into view as God's word in no other relation at all than that of faith. Hence the relation between word and faith is unique, unrepeatable and indivisible. The relation between word and faith is the only contact between God and existence. The understanding of the word in faith is thus nothing other than the christological interpretation of Scripture. To the inseparable togetherness of the two natures in

---

Zürich, where he completed his doctorate under Fritz Blanke in 1938.

188. In his programmatic essay on "The Significance of the Critical Historical Method for Church and Theology in Protestantism" of 1950 (*Word and Faith*, 23), Ebeling lists among the works appearing just after World War I responsible for the theological shift at that time "Karl Holl with his collection of Luther essays." Among these was one on "Luther's Significance for the Advance of the Art of Interpretation," written in 1920, which Ebeling considers as sharing in the reawakening of interest in the hermeneutical problem. Cf. Karl Holl, *Gesammelte Aufsätze zur Kirchengeschichte*, Vol. 1: *Luther*, 544-82. Ebeling's own dissertation, *Evangelische Evangelienauslegung*, reflects his point of departure in Luther's hermeneutic. Cf. also Ebeling's articles "Die Anfänge von Luthers Hermeneutik"; "Luthers Psalterdruck vom Jahre 1513"; "Luthers Auslegung des 14. (15.) Psalms in der ersten Psalmenvorlesung im Vergleich mit der exegetischen Tradition."

Christ there corresponds the never-ending togetherness of word and faith.[189]

When Fuchs (born in 1903) and Ebeling (born in 1912) were together at the University of Tübingen just after World War II, there grew up not only a unique personal friendship but also a material unity of position that has made of the new hermeneutic a single school of thought with a shared leadership. Ebeling began as did Fuchs with the subject matter of his own field, which in his case was church history. He entered the postwar discussion with a programmatic document proposing a basically new understanding of church history as "the history of the interpretation of Holy Scripture."[190] This hermeneutical understanding of church history gives this discipline a more direct relation to the theological enterprise as a whole than it had had, for example, in the Barthian system.[191]

When in 1950 the leading German theological periodical, the *Zeitschrift für Theologie und Kirche,* was reopened with Ebeling as its editor, he began with a programmatic essay that recast the whole of theology in terms of hermeneutic.

> The question of hermeneutic forms the focal point of the theological problems of today. A brief glance at the individual theological disciplines can elucidate this assertion. That Old Testament and New Testament scholars come up against the problem of hermeneutic in a special way is obvious at once. But the same is true also of the discipline of church history—here, indeed, in two respects: first in so far as it is likewise continually concerned with the interpretation of sources, but then also and above all because of course the process of exposition of Scripture that goes on in the history of the church presents the hermeneutical problem in its full compass, and thus the question of the theological grasp of the nature of church history opens straight into the basic problem of hermeneutic. The difficult problem of theology's systematic

---

189. *Evangelische Evangelienauslegung,* 1st ed., 382–83.

190. Ebeling, *Kirchengeschichte als Geschichte der Auslegung der Heiligen Schrift.*

191. Cf. Barth, *Church Dogmatics* I/1, 3: "Thus as *Biblical* theology, theology is the question as to the *foundation,* as *practical* theology it is the question as to the *aim,* as *dogmatic* theology it is the question as to the *content,* of the language peculiar to the Church." Then in fine print: "Church history so-called answers, from the point of view of Christian language about God, to no question that need be put independently, and is therefore not to be regarded as an independent theological discipline. It is the indispensable *auxiliary science* to exegetical, dogmatic, and practical theology."

method can be properly solved only when it is likewise set in the light of the question of hermeneutic. For resting on the exposition of Scripture and the history of theology, dogmatics has the task of bringing the church's teaching into contact and discussion with contemporary principles of thought, there to submit it to critical sifting and present it in its full inner coherence. Thus here the struggle for the momentarily required translation of the kerygma is brought to its issue in the most comprehensive way—whereby, however, the hermeneutical question in its basic methodological significance is also momentarily brought to a decision. And it is likewise plain that for so-called practical theology, above all in its teaching on sermon, instruction, and pastoral care, the hermeneutical question presents the one central problem underlying all questions of detail, in so far as the *applicatio* must not stand unrelated and all on its own alongside the *explicatio*. More particularly also in the study of missions, with its difficult questions (so highly instructive for theological work as a whole) of translating the Biblical message into the languages of totally different civilizations, the hermeneutical problem proves to be of fundamental significance.[192]

This lead essay on "The Significance of the Critical Historical Method for Church and Theology in Protestantism" also faced squarely the issue of the positive significance of critical scholarship for the church. This too Ebeling worked out in terms of hermeneutic, as the freeing of the word event from impediments. He has summarized his thesis as follows:

> Criticism is an element of integration in the effort to understand the text. For the sake of what the Biblical text seeks to bring to understanding, criticism is directed against everything that obstructs this hermeneutical function of the text. It is levelled in principle against distortion of the text—whether distortions in the form of the text resulting from the process of transmission, or distortions in the understanding of the text resulting from traditional prejudices, inappropriate systems of interpretation and unsuitable approaches to the problem, or distortions of the matter itself with which the text as a Biblical text has to do, resulting from confusion in the linguistic medium of the text. The purpose of the critical historical method therefore lies ultimately in the

---

192. "Die Bedeutung," 11–12, reprinted in *Wort und Glaube*, 12–13 = *Word and Faith*, 27.

interpreter's self-criticism in view of all the conceivable possibilities of deceiving himself as to the aim of the Biblical text.[193]

If the basic hermeneutical task of translating meaning from one culture to another had been laid hold of by Bultmann primarily in terms of the shift from a mythopoetic culture through enlightenment into a post-mythical world, Ebeling opens this translational task of hermeneutic out into the total theological enterprise. Here he revives Dietrich Bonhoeffer's call for a "nonreligious interpretation of Biblical concepts" suitable for a "world come of age."[194] Thus in Germany Ebeling has become, like R. Gregor Smith in Scotland, John A. T. Robinson in England, and William Hamilton in the United States, the theologian who has carried out the legacy of Bonhoeffer.

In this way Ebeling has achieved a hermeneutic that has embraced the doctrine of the word of God and become the focus to a total theological position. The new hermeneutic is a new theology, just as were dialectic theology and Ritschlianism before it. Indeed it is Ebeling's conviction that theology itself is hermeneutic, for it consists in translating what the Bible has to say into the word for today.

Perhaps the maturest statement of the material theological position of the new hermeneutic is the following attempt by Ebeling to summarize his position in a way that clarifies misunderstandings that had arisen:

> The criticism to make against a theology that has become traditionalistic and positivistic is not that it abides by the given, the tradition. Quite the contrary. It is precisely under the appearance of especially loyal allegiance to the tradition that *de facto* it is given up. For it is "presented" as *traditum* and thus as *praeteritum*, rather than by responding responsibly in pointing into the future with a word happening today, so that what is transmitted, the *traditum*, can take place as *traditio*, the act of transmitting. The *traditum* becomes what it is transmitted for only when it enters in upon the act of transmission, i.e., when the text fixed in letters becomes the spiritual occurrence of the oral word. The thesis that the object of dogmatic theology is not to be defined as a textual object is not intended to make the text irrelevant, but rather to be

---

193. Ebeling, *Wort und Glaube*, 451 = *Word and Faith*, 428.

194. Ebeling, "The 'Non-religious Interpretation of Biblical Concepts'"; cf. also the brief essay entitled simply "Dietrich Bonhoeffer," in *Wort und Glaube*, 294-99 = *Word and Faith*, 282-87.

what really lets it count. Dogmatic theology completes the task of interpretation not in the sense of a method competing with historical exegesis, but rather in the sense of a turn, called for by the subject matter itself, from the historical to the dogmatic way of understanding.[195] In dealings with the text its being interpreted by us turns into *our* being interpreted by the text. The interpretation of the text in the sense of an objective genitive becomes an interpretation of the text in the sense of a subjective genitive. Instead of the text being that which is to be interpreted and is in need of interpretation, what the text is there for emerges as that which is to be interpreted, clarified and delivered. For the text is not there for its own sake, but rather for the sake of the word event that is the origin and hence also the future of the text. Word event is the event of interpretation taking place through the word. Hence the text is there for the sake of the event of interpretation, which is the text's origin and future. For the word that once happened and in happening became the text must again become word with the help of the text and thus happen as interpreting word. What happens in the word event can thus be called interpretation, since it is the essence of word to clarify what is obscure, to bring light into darkness, and thus, if it is the word that concerns every man absolutely, to name the reality of man's being as what it truly is. The depth of such event of interpretation is of course only grasped when it is recognized that this bringing into truth is at the same time the exposure and the alteration of reality. Thus the object of dogmatic theology is the word event itself, in which the reality of man comes true.[196]

One of the most significant aspects of this new theology is that it stands within the context of a new assessment of the nature of the liberal arts in general. It was Dilthey's recognition of hermeneutics as the methodology of the humanities, deepened by Heidegger, that gave to the hermeneutic of Bultmann critical rapport with the cultural life of our times. For Bultmann was doing in terms of Biblical interpretation what, e.g., the Heideggerian philosopher Hans Jonas was doing in terms of Gnosticism and Emil Staiger in terms of German literature.[197] But in

195. Cf. Ebeling, "Word of God and Hermeneutic," 93ff.
196. Ebeling, *Theologie und Verkündigung*, 14–15.
197. *Die Zeit als Einbildungskraft des Dichters*. It is significant that Staiger, whose indebtedness to the early Heidegger is quite explicit (cf. "Ein Rückblick") came increasingly into an antithetic relationship to the later Heidegger. Cf. "Ein Briefwechsel

the present situation Dilthey and increasingly Heidegger have been superseded by the Heidelberg philosopher Hans-Georg Gadamer, a former pupil of Heidegger and Bultmann, whose *magnum opus* grounds the humanities in a hermeneutic oriented not to psychologism or existentialism, but rather to language and its subject matter.[198]

Gadamer criticizes Dilthey to the effect that his orientation to the individual's psychic structures as the context for interpreting the text produces a hermeneutic not fully commensurate to historic reality.

> The basis upon which [Dilthey] sought to erect a construction of the historic world in the humanities is the recognition that experiences are characterized by inwardness, so that here there is no problem of knowing the other, of knowing what is not myself, such as was at the basis of the Kantian approach. Yet the historic world is no experiential relation such as is history, e.g., in autobiography, where it portrays itself in the inwardness of subjectivity. Historic relation must ultimately be understood as a relation of meaning that basically transcends the experiential horizon of the individual.[199]

Gadamer's own positive alternative begins to emerge in the following critical appraisal of Dilthey:

> His point of departure, the taking of "experiences" into oneself, could not build the bridge to historic realities, for the great historic realities society and the state—are actually already determinative prior to every "experience." Self-reflection and autobiography—Dilthey's point of departure—are not primary and do not suffice as a basis for the hermeneutical problem, since they re-private-ize history. In reality history does not belong to us but we to it. Long before we understand ourselves in retrospection we understand

---

mit Martin Heidegger." To a considerable extent this is the antithesis of the professional literary critic to the philosopher's interpretations of literature sometimes lacking in professional exactitude; but it is also to some extent the tension between an interpretation in terms of the existence whose temporality comes to expression in literature and an interpretation in terms of language in which being speaks. The presence of Professor Staiger at the University of Zürich immediately gives to Ebeling's hermeneutic a universe of discourse shared with the humanities. The practical relevance of this rapport is enhanced when one recalls that many theological students, planning to teach in the public schools, divide their studies between theology and literature.

198. Gadamer, *Wahrheit und Methode* = *Truth and Method*. Cf. also his essay "Vom Zirkel des Verstehens" = "On the Circle of Understanding."

199. Gadamer, "Hermeneutik und Historismus," 243.

> ourselves as a matter of course in the family, society, and state in which we live. The focus in terms of subjectivity is a distortion. The individual's self-reflection is only a flash within the unbroken flow of historic life. Hence the individual's prejudgments, much more than his judgments, are the reality of his being.[200]

This historic "prejudice" with which our experience is loaded is primarily our language.

Gadamer's pupil Heinz Kimmerle[201] has traced this deficiency in Dilthey, upon whom the modern development of hermeneutic had been built, back to Schleiermacher, from whom Dilthey derived his hermeneutic. Dilthey's inadequacy with regard to the "historic world" is due to Schleiermacher's inadequacy with regard to "language"—as indeed the new focus on language in hermeneutic is an effort to do justice to the historic aspects of hermeneutic. Dilthey's Schleiermacher was, however, not the whole Schleiermacher, for Friedrich Lücke's edition of Schleiermacher's hermeneutics omitted the early manuscripts as too fragmentary for publication, whereas Kimmerle maintains that Schleiermacher increasingly departed from an earlier, hitherto unknown, hermeneutical position, and progressively fell into the defect Gadamer detects in Dilthey.

> The late Schleiermacher tends (from 1819 on) more and more toward a different, a psychological, understanding of individuality. The specific linguistic expression is no longer related to language as the general dimension, but rather to the totality of the individual life that produced it. He is primarily concerned to explain (reproduce) how an individual speech or act is an element of the whole life (by means of what he called psychological interpretation). The individual's life experience becomes the hermeneutical principle that guides the effort at understanding.[202]

Kimmerle has published a new edition of Schleiermacher's hermeneutical writings in which for the first time the early fragments are made available to the public. It is Kimmerle's thesis that they show Schleiermacher to have oriented the hermeneutical task originally to language, and thus to be materially a precursor of the new hermeneutic.

---

200. *Wahrheit und Methode*, 261 = *Truth and Method*, 276–77.

201. Kimmerle's unpublished dissertation of 1957 was on "The Hermeneutic of Schleiermacher in the Context of His Speculative Thought."

202. Kimmerle, "Hermeneutische Theorie," 116.

> The decisive productive thought of Schleiermacher's hermeneutic, as it comes to expression primarily in the early sketches, resides, however, in its strict and conscious orientation to the concrete procedure of living speaking. In Manuscript I there is the statement: "All that is to be presupposed in hermeneutics as well as all that is to be found is language alone. Where the other objective and subjective presuppositions belong must be found from the language" (p. 8); and in Manuscript II much the same is said and actually in a more explicit way: "Everything that (can) be the task of hermeneutics is part of a sentence" (p. 11).[203]

Gadamer's own point of departure is the recognition that much of truth has not come to us by means of scholarly method and yet commands our acknowledgment as true. His approach is

> to seek, wherever it is to be found, the experience of truth that transcends the area under the control of scholarly methodology and to investigate the legitimation peculiar to it. Thus the humanities unite with kinds of experience that lie outside science: the experience of philosophy, of art, and of history itself. All these are kinds of experience in which truth that cannot be verified with the methodical means of science makes its presence known.[204]

It is his interest in the philosophical legitimation of such ways of knowing that lie outside science that leads Gadamer to hermeneutic. "In my opinion the contemporary relevance of the hermeneutical phenomenon resides in the fact that only by penetrating into the phenomenon of understanding can such a legitimation be provided."[205] The result is a new approach to understanding. "Understanding is itself not to be thought of so much as an action of one's subjectivity, but rather as entering into an occurrence of transmission in which past and present are constantly be-

---

203. Schleiermacher, *Hermeneutik,* 17 in Kimmerle's Introduction. Gadamer uses the first of these previously unknown statements by Schleiermacher as the motto at the head of Part III of *Wahrheit und Methode,* 361 = *Truth and Method,* 381. Christoph Senft, in reviewing Kimmerle's edition of Schleiermacher's *Hermeneutik* (*PhR* 10 [1962] 288-90), suggests that the hermeneutic of the younger Schleiermacher, which Kimmerle identified, may have been consistently retained by Schleiermacher in later years, contrary to Kimmerle's own assumption. Yet one should be cautious in rewriting history to make it conform to the current view.

204. Gadamer, *Wahrheit und Methode,* xiii-xiv = *Truth and Method,* xxii.

205. Ibid., xiv.

ing mediated. That is what must gain acceptance in hermeneutical theory, which is much too dominated by the idea of procedure, method."[206]

Gadamer does not simply set up a theory about understanding, but rather investigates the conditions under which understanding does in fact take place. Thus, aspects of hermeneutic that may not otherwise have been regarded as of principal significance for scientific interpretation emerge, in view of their constant presence in the interpretation that really takes place, as basic ingredients that must be recognized as such. One of these neglected aspects is the temporal gulf between text and interpreter. One reason it had not been given constitutive importance in previous hermeneutic is that it had been usually bridged in terms of some unhistoric element common to both the past and the present. Dilthey described this as follows:

> The possibility of universally valid interpretation can be derived from the nature of understanding. Here the individuality of the interpreter and that of his author do not stand over against each other as two incommensurable facts. Both have been formed on the basis of universal human nature, and therein is made possible man's capacity for community in speech and understanding.[207]

Heidegger's existentials seemed to make such common ground available even on the assumption of the historicness of existence, so that his pupil Hans Jonas could boldly refer to this common ground of existentials as the "metaphysical *a priori*" of the history of ideas. "The phenomena in question . . . , to the extent authentic fundamental existentialist phenomena are involved, are also still available to us in such a way as to permit us to measure what was said then by the phenomena themselves."[208] And yet in retrospect Jonas has recognized that the Heideggerian existentials were not themselves beyond the historic flux, but were indeed historically conditioned and not universally valid.

> When, many years ago, I turned to the study of gnosticism, I found that the viewpoints, the optics as it were, which I had acquired in the school of Heidegger, enabled me to see aspects of

---

206. Ibid., 275. The term "occurrence of transmission" (*Überlieferungsgeschehen*) is analogous to Ebeling's term "language event" (*Wortgeschehen*). Both involve a continuing occurrence rather than a single event.

207. Dilthey, "Die Entstehung der Hermeneutik," 329.

208. Jonas, *Augustin*, 6.

gnostic thought that had been missed before. And I was increasingly struck by the familiarity of the seemingly utterly strange. ... The fitness of its categories to the particular matter was something to ponder about. They fitted as if made to measure: *were* they, perhaps, made to measure? At the outset, I had taken that fitness as simply a case of their presumed general validity, which would assure their utility for the interpretation of any human 'existence' whatever. ... Thus the meeting of the two, started as the meeting of a method with a matter, ended with bringing home to me that existentialism, which claims to be the explication of the fundamentals of human existence as such, is the philosophy of a particular, historically fated situation of human existence; and an analogous (though in other respects very different) situation had given rise to an analogous response in the past.[209]

In a somewhat similar way Kimmerle criticizes the use of the existentialist analysis of *Dasein* to bridge the historical distance between text and interpreter:

Has here historical relativity been thought through in a sufficiently radical fashion? Is it not possible that a *metaphysical* entity has been introduced here as a hermeneutical principle, an entity that does not stand up to a Kantian-type epistemological critique applied to history? Dilthey himself wished to put alongside the Kantian "critique of pure reason" a "critique of historical reason." Would not such a critique have to insist radically that every period can really only be understood in its own terms, from its own center, without reference to any trans-temporal instance? The idea of individual life, no matter what general formulation is given it, cannot provide the principle for understanding each particular phenomenon in all periods of time, nor even for the historical context in general in which we ourselves stand. The analysis of *Dasein* as being in the world is metaphysicized, contrary to its own self-understanding, when it is expected to provide the schema of categories for every scholarly effort at understanding.[210]

Gadamer sees as of fundamental hermeneutical significance the fact that the interpretation of documents of the past involves a separation in time that no assumed "contemporaneity" can really overcome, and hence that the interpretation is always a translation from one situation to an-

---

209. Jonas, "Epilogue," esp. 320–21.
210. Kimmerle, "Hermeneutische Theorie," 120.

other. One always understands the text, if not better, at least differently than does the author himself.

> Every historian and philologian must reckon with the fundamental openendedness of the horizon of meaning in which he moves as he understands. Historic tradition can only be understood by recalling the basic continuing concretizing taking place in the continuation of things. Similarly the philologian who has to do with poetic or philosophic texts knows about their inexhaustibleness. In both cases it is the continuation of the occurrence that brings what is transmitted into new aspects of meaning. New actualization in the process of understanding involves the texts just as much in an authentic occurrence as is the case with events when they are involved in occurrence by their own continuation. That is what we designated the "effective history" aspect within hermeneutical experience. Every actualization in the process of understanding can be aware of itself as a historic possibility of what is understood.[211]

The fact that the interpreter has an interest in his subject matter that no assumed "objectivity" of method has ever fully succeeded in eliminating points to another often neglected but nonetheless basic hermeneutical insight: The subject matter of hermeneutic is the *relation* between the interpreter and the text he is studying, the "interest," the material issue involved. The objective of understanding is material agreement. "Understanding is always the process of welding [the interpreter's and the text's] horizons that only seem to exist independently."[212] The interpreter assumes the text is answering some question, and attributes to the text adequacy to reveal that question. Thus the interpreter enters into the text's dimension of meaning and seeks to make sense of what it says. Hence Gadamer speaks of an "anticipation of perfection" as an aspect of the hermeneutical circle. One anticipates not only that there is a consistent view in the text, but also that it is true to the subject matter, until the text itself no longer permits such an assumption. At that point critical operations must begin because the text is no longer "intelligible." "Understanding means primarily to understand each other on the subject matter, and only secondarily to clarify and understand the view of the

---

211. Gadamer, *Wahrheit und Methode*, 355 = *Truth and Method*, 373.
212. Ibid., 289 = *Truth and Method*, 306.

other person as such."²¹³ It is significant that Gadamer places as a motto at the head of this section of his book the following quotation from Luther: "*Qui non intelligit res, non potest ex verbis sensum elicere*"—a person who does not understand the subject matter under discussion cannot elicit the meaning of the words.²¹⁴

Gadamer's position has been questioned as to the scholarliness of interpretation of this kind by the leading contemporary exponent of the Dilthey tradition, the Italian historian of law Emilio Betti. To him Gadamer replies in a letter, later cited and expanded in an essay, as follows:

> Basically I do not propose *a method,* I only describe *what is.* I do not think one can seriously contest that the situation is as I describe it. . . . E.g., you too, when you read a classic study by Mommsen, immediately detect in what period all that could have been written. Even a master of historical method is not able to remain completely free from the prejudices of his time, his social environment, his national position, etc. Is that to be taken for a deficiency? And even if it were, I regard it as a philosophical task to reflect as to why this deficiency is never absent wherever something is done. In other words, I regard *acknowledging what is* as the only scholarly way, rather than taking one's point of departure in what should or might be. In this sense I try to think beyond modern science's concept of method (which retains its limited validity), and to think, in explicit universality, what *always* happens.
>
> But what does Betti say to that? That I reduce the hermeneutical problem to the *quaestio facti* ("phenomenologically," "descriptively"), and do not pose the *quaestio juris* at all. As if Kant's posing of the *quaestio juris* to pure natural science had been intended to prescribe how it should really be, rather than attempting to justify the transcendental possibility of natural science as it was. In the sense of this Kantian distinction, thinking beyond the humanities' concept of method, which my book attempts, poses the question as to the "possibility" of the humanities (which certainly does not mean what they really ought to be!).²¹⁵

---

213. Ibid., 277–78.
214. Ibid., 162.
215. Gadamer, "Hermeneutik und Historismus," 249.

This emphasis upon analyzing the possibility of interpretation as it in fact takes place, and thus upon the analysis of what is, is designated by Gadamer as an "ontological turn in hermeneutic."[216] "This *ontological* turn in hermeneutic signifies its elimination as a doctrine of a special art or method. It makes the theory of understanding into a central philosophical problematic."[217] This new turn in German hermeneutic was introduced into the theological discussion at the meeting of Old Marburgers in October, 1962, which was devoted to hermeneutic. Gadamer insisted that it is not a self-understanding that comes to expression in language. Word is "selfless," and what the Biblical author is talking about transcends his self-understanding. What language has to say must be sought in terms of its subject matter, so that the word "disappears" into what it has to say. To be sure, what the word has to say does not lie outside language as understood by the new hermeneutic—a point made by Heidegger and conceded by Gadamer. Yet it is this dialectic between language and its subject matter (*Sprache* and *Sache*) rather than that between mythological language and the existential self-understanding it objectifies, which designates the point at which the hermeneutical discussion in Germany had arrived.

The involvement of Heidegger and Gadamer in the new hermeneutic points to the fact that this hermeneutic provides the prospect not only of a new grasp of the nature of the theological task, but also of the place of theology in the university. It is the purpose of the present essay to investigate the extent to which this new hermeneutic provides as well an adequate point of focus for theology in the context of higher education in America.

---

216. Part III of *Warheit und Methode* is entitled "The Ontological Turn in Hermeneutic [worked out] in Terms of Language," 361–465.

217. Kimmerle, "Hermeneutische Theorie," 121. The title of Kimmerle's essay expresses the same alternative.

Bibliography 2

Ast, Friedrich. *Grundlinien der Grammatik, Hermeneutik und Kritik.* Landshut, 1808.
Bachmann, Ph. "Der Römerbrief verdeutscht und vergegenwärtigt." *NKZ* 32 (1921) 518.
Barth, Karl. *Die Auferstehung der Toten: Eine akademische Vorlesung über 1. Kor. 15.* Munich: Kaiser, 1924.
―――. "Ein Briefwechsel mit Adolf von Harnack." In idem, *Theologische Fragen und Antworten: Gesammelte Vorträge,* 3:7–31. Zollikon: Evangelischer Verlag, 1957.
―――. *Church Dogmatics* I/1: *The Doctrine of the Word of God.* Translated by G. T. Thomson. New York: Scribners, 1936.
―――. *The Epistle to the Romans.* Translated by Edwyn C. Hoskyns. London: Oxford University Press, 1933.
―――. *The Resurrection of the Dead.* Translated by H. J. Stenning. 1933. Reprinted, Eugene, OR: Wipf & Stock, 2003.
―――. *Der Römerbrief.* Bern: Bäschlin, 1919.
―――. *Der Römerbrief.* 2nd ed. Zurich: Evangelischer Verlag, 1947.
Bartsch, Hans Werner, editor. *Kerygma and Myth: A Theological Debate.* London: SPCK, 1953. New York: Harper & Row, 1961.
Bauer, Walter. *A Greek-English Lexicon of the New Testament and Other Early Christian Literature.* Translated and adapted by William F. Arndt and W. Wilbur Gingrich. Chicago: University of Chicago Press, 1957.
―――. *A Greek-English Lexicon of the New Testament and Other Early Christian Literature.* Revised and edited by Frederick William Danker. Chicago: University of Chicago Press, 2000.
Baumgärtel, Friedrich. "Bibelerklärung des AT." In *RGG*² 1 (1927) 1011–15.
Behm, Johannes. "ἑρμηνεύω κτλ." In *TWNT* 2 (1935) 659–62 = *TDNT* 2 (1964) 661–66.
―――. *Pneumatische Exegese?* Schwerin: Bahn, 1926.
Berkhof, Louis. *Principles of Biblical Interpretation (Sacred Hermeneutics).* Grand Rapids: Baker, 1950. 2nd ed., 1952.

Bertram, M. Joachim Christoph, editor. *D. Siegmund Jacob Baumgartens ausführlicher Vortrag der Biblischen Hermeneutic.* Halle: Gebauer, 1769.

Blackman, E. C. *Biblical Interpretation.* Philadelphia: Westminster, 1957.

Blass, Friedrich, and Albert Debrunner. *A Greek Grammar of the New Testament and Other Early Christian Literature.* Translated and revised from the 9th-10th German edition by Robert W. Funk. Chicago: University of Chicago Press, 1961.

Boisacq, Emile. *Dictionnaire étymologique de la langue grecque étudiée dans ses rapports avec les autres langues indo-européennes.* 4th ed. Heidelberg: Winter, 1950.

Bornkamm, Günther. "Die Theologie Rudolf Bultmanns in der neueren Diskussion: Zum Problem der Entmythologisierung und Hermeneutik." *ThR* 29 (1963) 33-141.

Bourke, Myles M. "The Literary Genus of Matthew 1-2." *CBQ* 22 (1960) 160-75.

Bultmann, Rudolf. *Essays, Philosophical and Theological.* Library of Philosophy and Theology. London: SCM, 1955.

———. "Ethische und mystische Religion im Urchristentum." *ChrW* 34 (1920) 725-31; 738-43; 750-53.

———. *Existence and Faith: Shorter Writings of Rudolf Bultmann.* Selected, translated, and introduced by Schubert M. Ogden. New York: Meridian, 1960.

———. *Faith and Understanding.* Translated by Louise Pettibone Smith. Fortress Texts in Modern Theology. Philadelphia: Fortress, 1987.

———. *Glauben und Verstehen.* Vol. 1. Tübingen: Mohr/Siebeck, 1933.

———. *Glauben und Verstehen.* Vol. 2. Tübingen: Mohr/Siebeck, 1952.

———. *Glauben und Verstehen.* Vol. 3. Tübingen: Mohr/Siebeck, 1960.

———. "Heilsgeschichte und Geschichte: Zu Oscar Cullmann, *Christus und die Zeit.*" *TLZ* 73 (1948) 659-66.

———. "History of Salvation and History." In *Existence and Faith,* 226-40.

———. *History of the Synoptic Tradition.* Translated by John Marsh. New York: Harper & Row, 1963; 2nd ed., 1968. German 1st ed., 1921. German 2nd ed., 1931.

———. "Is Exegesis without Presuppositions Possible?" In *Existence and Faith: Shorter Writings of Rudolf Bultmann,* 289-96. Translated by Schubert M. Ogden. New York: Meridian, 1960.

———. *Jesus.* Berlin: Deutsche Bibliothek, 1926.

———. *Jesus and the Word.* Translated by Louise Pettibone Smith and Erminie Huntress Lantero. New York: Scribners, 1934.

———. "Karl Barths 'Römerbrief' in zweiter Auflage." *ChrW* 36 (1922) 320-23; 330-34; 358-61; 369-73.

———. "Neues Testament und Mythologie." In *Kerygma und Mythos: Ein theologisches Gespräch.* TF 1. Hamburg: Reich und Heidrich, 1948.

———. *Theology of the New Testament.* 2 vols. Translated by Kendrick Grobel. New York: Scribner, 1951-55.

———. *Das Verhältnis der urchristlichen Christusbotschaft zum historischen Jesus.* SHAW 1960, 3. Heidelberg: Winter, 1960.

Burnham, Sylvester. *The Elements of Biblical Hermeneutics.* Hamilton, NY: Republic, 1916.

Cassirer, Ernst. *Philosophie der symbolischen Formen.* 2nd ed. Oxford: Bruno Cassirer, 1923. Reprinted, Darmstadt: Wissenschaftliche Buchgesellschaft, 1956.

---. *The Philosophy of Symbolic Forms*. 4 vols. Translated by Ralph Manheim and John Michael Krois. New Haven: Yale University Press, 1953-96.
Chafer, Rollin Thomas. *The Science of Biblical Hermeneutics: An Outline Study of Its Laws*. Dallas: Bibliotheca Sacra, 1939.
Cobb, John B. Jr. "Faith and Culture."In *The New Hermeneutic*, edited by James M. Robinson and John B. Cobb Jr., 219-31. New Frontiers in Theology 2. New York: Harper & Row, 1964.
Colwell, Ernest Cadman. "The Greek Language." In *IDB* 2:479-87.
Cross, Frank Moore, and Helmut Koester, editors. *Hermeneia: A Critical and Historical Commentary on the Bible*. Philadelphia and Minneapolis: Fortress, 1974-.
Cullmann, Oscar. *Christus und die Zeit*. 3rd ed. Zurich: EVZ, 1962.
---. "Retrospect upon the Effect of the Book in Post-War Theology." *Christus und die Zeit*. 3rd ed. Zurich: EVZ, 1962.
Dannhauer, J. C. *Hermeneutica Sacra: sive methodus exponendarum Sacrarum Literarum*. Strasbourg, 1654.
Denzinger, Heinrich, and Johann Baptist Umberg, editors. *Enchiridion symbolorum definitionum et declarationum de rebus fidei et morum*. 26th ed. Freiburg: Herder, 1947.
Dibelius, Martin. *From Tradition to Gospel*. Translated by Bertram Lee Woolf. New York: Scribners, 1933. German ed. 1919.
Dillenberger, John. "On Broadening the New Hermeneutic." In *The New Hermeneutic*, edited by James M. Robinson and John B. Cobb Jr., 147-63. New Frontiers in Theology 2. New York: Harper & Row, 1964.
Dilthey, Wilhelm. "Die Entstehung der Hermeneutik." In *Gesammelte Schriften*, 5:317-38. Berlin: Teubner, 1924.
Dobschütz, Ernst von. *Vom Auslegen insonderheit des Neuen Testaments*. Hallesche Universitätsreden 18. Halle: Niemeyer, 1922.
---. "Interpretation." In *Encyclopaedia of Religion and Ethics*, edited by James Hastings, 7:390-95. New York: Scribner, 1920.
---. "Ein neuer Weg zum Verständnis des Neuen Testaments, die formgeschichtliche Methode." In *Vom Auslegen des Neuen Testaments*. Göttingen: Vandenhoeck & Ruprecht, 1927.
---. "Die Pneumatische Exegese: Wissenschaft und Praxis." In *Vom Auslegen des Neuen Testaments*, 49-64. Göttingen: Vandenhoeck & Ruprecht, 1927.
---. *Vom Auslegen des Neuen Testaments*. Göttingen: Vandenhoeck & Ruprecht, 1927.
Dungan, D. R. *Hermeneutics: A Textbook*. Cincinnati: Standard, 1888.
Ebeling, Gerhard. "Die Anfänge von Luthers Hermeneutik." *ZTK* 48 (1951) 172-230.
---. "Die Bedeutung der historisch-kritischen Methode für Kirche und Theologie in Protestantismus." *ZTK* 47 (1950) 1-46.
---. "Dietrich Bonhoeffer." In idem, *Wort und Glaube*, 294-99.
---. "Dietrich Bonhoeffer." In idem, *Word and Faith*, 282-87.
---. *Evangelische Evangelienauslegung: Eine Untersuchung zu Luthers Hermeneutik*. Forschungen zur Geschichte und Literatur des Protestantismus 10/1. Munich: Lempp, 1942; 2nd ed., Darmstadt: Wissenschaftliche Buchgesellschaft, 1963. 3rd ed. Tübingen: Mohr/Siebeck, 1991.
---. "Die Evidenz des Ethischen und die Theologie." *ZTK* 57 (1960) 318-56.

———. "Die Frage nach dem historischen Jesus und das Problem der Christologie." *ZTK* 56 (1959) 14–30. Reprinted in *Wort und Glaube*, 300–318.
———. "Hermeneutik." In *RGG*³ 3 (1959) 243–58.
———. "Jesus and Faith." In idem, *Word and Faith*, 201–46.
———. "Jesus und Glaube." *ZTK* 55 (1958) 64–110. Reprinted in idem, *Wort und Glaube*, 203–54.
———. *Kirchengeschichte als Geschichte der Auslegung der Heiligen Schrift*. Sammlung gemeinverständlicher Vorträge und Schriften aus dem Gebiet der Theologie und Religionsgeschichte 189. Tübingen: Mohr/Siebeck, 1947.
———. "Luthers Auslegung des 14. (15.) Psalms in der ersten Psalmenvorlesung im Vergleich mit der exegetischen Tradition." *ZTK* 50 (1953) 280–339.
———. "Luthers Psalterdruck vom Jahre 1513." *ZTK* 50 (1953) 43–99.
———. *The Nature of Faith*. Translated by R. Gregor Smith. Philadelphia: Muhlenberg, 1961.
———. "The 'Non-religious Interpretation of Biblical Concepts.'" *ZTK* 52 (1955) 296–360. Reprinted in *Wort und Glaube*, 90–160 = *Word and Faith*, 98–161.
———. "The Question of the Historical Jesus and the Problem of Christology." In idem, *Word and Faith*, 288–304.
———. "The Significance of the Critical Historical Method for Church and Theology in Protestantism." In *Word and Faith*, 17–61.
———. "Die Bedeutung der historisch-kritischen Methode für die protestantische Theologie und Kirche." *ZTK* 47 (1950) 1–46. Reprinted in *Wort und Glaube*, 1–49.
———. *Theologie und Verkündigung: Ein Gespräch mit Rudolf Bultmann*. Hermeneutische Untersuchungen zur Theologie 1. Tübingen: Mohr/Siebeck, 1962.
———. *Das Wesen des christlichen Glaubens*. Tübingen: Mohr/Siebeck, 1959.
———. *Word and Faith*. Translated by James W. Leitch. Philadelphia: Fortress, 1963.
———. "Word of God and Hermeneutic." In *The New Hermeneutic*, edited by James M. Robinson and John B. Cobb Jr., 78–110. New Frontiers in Theology 2. New York: Harper & Row, 1964.
———. *Wort und Glaube*. Tübingen: Mohr/Siebeck, 1960.
Eidem, Erling. Review of *Nytestamentlig Hermeneutik* by Frederik Torm in *TLZ* 54 (1929) 104–5.
Ernesti, J. A. *Institutio interpretis Novi Testamenti*. Havniae: Ex Officina Hallageriana, 1761; 4th ed., 1776.
Fascher, Erich. *Vom Verstehen des Neuen Testaments: Ein Beitrag zur Grundlegung einer zeitgemässen Hermeneutik*. Giessen: Töpelmann, 1930.
Franz, Helmut. "Das Denken Heideggers und die Theologie." *ZTKB* 2 (1961) 81–118.
———. "Das Wesen des Textes." *ZTK* 59 (1962) 182–225.
Frick, Heinrich. *Wissenschaftliches und pneumatisches Verständnis der Bibel*. Sammlung gemeinverständlicher Vorträge und Schriften aus dem Gebiet der Theologie und Religionsgeschichte 124. Tübingen: Mohr/Siebeck, 1927.
Frör, Kurt. *Biblische Hermeneutik: Zur Schriftauslegung in Predigt und Unterricht*. Munich: Kaiser, 1961.
Fuchs, Ernst. "Das Christusverständnis bei Paulus und im Johannesevangelium." In *Jesus Christus: Das Christusverständnis im Wandel der Zeiten: Eine Ringvorlesung der Theologischen Fakultät der Universität Marburg*, edited by Hans Grass and

Werner Georg Kümmel, 11–20. Marburger Theologischen Studien 1. Marburg: Elwert, 1963.

———. *Zur Frage nach dem historischen Jesus*. Gesammelte Aufsätze 2. Tübingen: Mohr/Siebeck, 1960.

———. *Hermeneutik*. Bad Cannstatt: Müllerschön, 1954. 2nd ed. with *Ergänzungsheft*, 1958.

———. *Zum hermeneutischen Problem in der Theologie: Die existentiale Interpretation*. Gesammelte Aufsätze 1. Tübingen: Mohr/Siebeck, 1959.

———. "Logos." In *RGG*³ 4 (1960) 434–40.

———. "The New Testament and the Hermeneutical Problem." In *The New Hermeneutic*, edited by James M. Robinson and John B. Cobb Jr., 111–45. New Frontiers in Theology 2. New York: Harper & Row, 1964.

———. "Proclamation and Speech-Event." *TTo* 19 (1962) 341–54.

———. "Response to the American Discussion." In *The New Hermeneutic*, edited by James M. Robinson and John B. Cobb Jr., 232–43. New Frontiers in Theology 2. New York: Harper & Row, 1964.

———. "Die Spannung im neutestamentlichen Christusglauben." *ZTK* 59 (1962) 32–45.

———. "Übersetzung und Verkündigung: Hermeneutisches Korreferat." In *Zur Frage nach der historischen Jesus*, 405–23.

Funk, Robert W. "The Hermeneutical Problem and Historical Criticism." In *The New Hermeneutic*, edited by James M. Robinson and John B. Cobb Jr., 164–97. New Frontiers in Theology 2. New York: Harper & Row, 1964.

Gadamer, Hans-Georg. "Hermeneutik und Historismus." *PhR* 9 (1962) 241–76.

———. "On the Circle of Understanding." http://faculty.washington.edu/ewebb/R528/Gadamer.pdf.

———. *Truth and Method*. Translation revised by Joel Weinsheimer and Donald G. Marshall. London: Continuum, 2004.

———. "Verstehen." In *RGG*³ 6 (1962) 1381–83.

———. *Wahrheit und Methode: Grundzüge einer philosophischen Hermeneutik*. Tübingen: Mohr/Siebeck, 1960.

———. "Vom Zirkel des Verstehens." In *Festschrift Martin Heidegger zum siebzigsten Geburtstag*, edited by Günther Neske, 24–34. Pfullingen: Neske, 1959.

Gilmour, S. Maclean. "Jesus Christ." In *Dictionary of the Bible*, edited by F. C. Grant and H. H. Rowley, 494. Rev. ed. New York: Scribners, 1963.

Girgensohn, Karl. *Die Inspiration der heiligen Schrift*. Dresden: Ungelenk, 1925. 2nd ed., 1926.

Gogarten, Friedrich. "Vom heiligen Egoismus der Christen." *ChrW* 34 (1920) 546–50.

Gomperz, Heinrich. *Über Sinn und Sinngebilde, Verstehen und Erklären*. Tübingen: Mohr/Siebeck, 1929.

Grant, Robert M. *The Bible in the Church*. New York: Macmillan, 1948.

———, Samuel Terrien, and John T. McNeill. "History of the Interpretation of the Bible." In *IB* 1:106–41.

Grobel, Kendrick. "Interpretation." In *IDB* 2:719–23.

Guillaumont, A., H.-Ch. Puech, G. Quispel, W. Till, and Yassah 'Abd al Masīḥ, editors. *The Gospel according to Thomas*. New York: Harper & Row, 1959.

Gunkel, Hermann. *Die Einleitung in die Psalmen.* Edited by Joachim Begrich. Handkommentar zum Alten Testament. Göttingen: Vandenhoeck & Ruprecht, 1933.

———. *Introduction to the Psalms: The Genres of the Religious Lyric of Israel.* Translated by James D. Nogalski. Mercer Library of Biblical Studies. Macon, GA: Mercer University Press, 1998.

———. *The Legends of Genesis: The Biblical Saga and History.* Translated by W. H. Carruth. 1901. Reprinted, Eugene, OR: Wipf & Stock, 2003.

———. *Zum religionsgeschichtlichen Verständnis des Neuen Testaments.* FRLANT 1. Göttingen: Vandenhoeck & Ruprecht, 1903.

———. "The Religio-historical Interpretation of the New Testament." *The Monist* 3 (1902) 398–455.

———. *Die Sagen der Genesis.* Göttingen: Vandenhoeck & Ruprecht, 1901.

Hartill, J. Edwin. *Biblical Hermeneutics.* Grand Rapids: Zondervan, 1947. Reprinted, 1960.

Harvey, Van A., and Schubert M. Ogden. "Wie neu ist die 'Neue Frage nach dem historischen Jesus'?" *ZTK* 59 (1962) 46–87.

Heidegger, Martin. *Being and Time.* Translated by John Macquarrie and Edward Robinson. New York: Harper & Row, 1962.

———. *Essays in Metaphysics: Identity and Difference.* Translated by Kurt F. Leidecker. New York: Philosophical Library, 1960.

———. *Existence and Being.* Translated by R. F. C. Hull and Alan Crick. 1949. Gateway Paperback Edition. Chicago: Regnery, 1960.

———. *Existentialism from Dostoevsky to Sartre.* Translated by Walter Kaufmann. New York: Meridian, 1956.

———. *Identität und Differenz.* Pfullingen: Neske, 1957.

———. *Der Satz vom Grund.* Pfullingen: Neske, 1957. 2nd ed., 1958.

———. *Sein und Zeit,* 9th ed. Tübingen: Niemeyer, 1960.

———. *Über den Humanismus.* Frankfurt: Klostermann, 1949.

———. *Unterwegs zur Sprache.* Pfullingen: Neske, 1959.

———. *Was ist Metaphysik?* 8th ed. Frankfurt: Klostermann, 1960.

Heinrici, Georg. "Hermeneutik." In *PRE* 7 (1899) 718–50.

Hofmann, J. Chr. K. von. *Interpreting the Bible.* Translated by Christian Preus. Minneapolis: Augsburg, 1959.

Holl, Karl. *Gesammelte Aufsätze zur Kirchengeschichte.* Vol. 1: *Luther.* Tübingen: Mohr/Siebeck, 1921. 7th ed., 1948.

Jonas, Hans. *Augustin und das paulinische Freiheitsproblem: Ein philosophischer Beitrag zur Genesis der christlich-abendländischen Freiheitsidee.* FRLANT 44. Göttingen: Vandenhoeck & Ruprecht, 1930.

———. "Epilogue: Gnosticism, Existentialism, and Nihilism." In idem, *The Gnostic Religion,* 320–40. 2nd rev. ed. Boston: Beacon, 1963.

———. *Gnosis und spätantiker Geist.* 2 vols. Göttingen: Vandenhoeck & Ruprecht, 1934, 1954.

———. *The Gnostic Religion.* Boston: Beacon, 1958. 2nd ed., 1963.

Jülicher, Adolf. "Ein moderner Paulus-Ausleger." *ChrW* 34 (1920) 453–57; 466–69.

———. Review of *Der Römerbrief* by Karl Barth. *TLZ* 47 (1922) 537–42.

Jüngel, Eberhard. *Paulus und Jesus: Eine Untersuchung zur Präzisierung der Frage nach dem Ursprung der Christologie*. Hermeneutische Untersuchungen zur Theologie 2. Tübingen: Mohr/Siebeck, 1962.

Käsemann, Ernst. "Blind Alleys in the 'Jesus of History' Controversy." In idem, *New Testament Questions of Today*, 23-65.

———. *Essays on New Testament Themes*. Translated by W. J. Montague. SBT 1/41. London: SCM, 1964.

———. *New Testament Questions of Today*. Translated by W. J. Montague. Philadelphia: Fortress, 1969.

———. "On the Subject of Primitive Christian Apocalyptic." In idem, *New Testament Questions of Today*, 108-37.

———. "The Problem of the Historical Jesus." In idem, *Essays on New Testament Themes*, 15-47.

———. "Zum Thema der urchristlichen Apokalyptik." *ZTK* 59 (1962) 257-84.

Kimmerle, Heinz. "Hermeneutical Theory or Ontological Hermeneutics." *JTC* 4 (1967) 107-21.

———. "Hermeneutische Theorie oder ontologische Hermeneutik." *ZTK* 59 (1962) 114-30.

König, Eduard. *Hermeneutik des Alten Testaments: Mit spezieller Berücksichtigung der modernen Probleme*. Bonn: Marcus & Webers, 1916.

Lütgert, Willi. "Bibelerklärung des NT." In *RGG*² 1 (1927) 1016-18.

Macholz, W. "Pneumatische Exegese." *Pastoralblätter* 70 (1927) 705-24.

Magnusson, Martin. *Der Begriff "Verstehen" in exegetischem Zusammenhang unter besonderer Berücksichtigung der paulinischen Schriften. I. Allgemeine Probleme des exegetischen Verständnisses*. Studia theologica lundensia 8. Lund: Gleerup, 1954.

Menge, Hermann, and Otto Güthling. *Enzyklopädisches Wörterbuch der lateinischen und deutschen Sprache*. 8th ed. Berlin: Langenscheidt, 1954.

Meyer, A. "Bibelwissenschaft." In *RGG*² 1 (1927) 1085.

Mezger, Manfred. "Anleitung zur Predigt." *ZTK* 56 (1959) 377-97.

Michaelson, Carl. "Theology as Ontology and as History." In *The Later Heidegger and Theology*, edited by James M. Robinson and John B. Cobb Jr., 136-56. New Frontiers in Theology 1. New York: Harper & Row, 1963.

Miskotte, Kornelis Heiko. *Zur biblischen Hermeneutik*. ThSt 55. Zollikon: Evangelischer Verlag, 1959.

Noth, Martin, editor. *Biblischer Kommentar: Altes Testament*. Neukirchen-Vluyn: Neukirchener, 1955-.

———. "The 'Re-presentation' of the Old Testament in Proclamation." Translated by James Luther Mays. *Int* 16 (1961) 50-60. Reprinted in *Essays in Old Testament Hermeneutics*, edited by Claus Westermann and James Luther Mays, 76-88. Atlanta: John Knox, 1963.

Overbeck, Franz. "Über die Anfänge der patristischen Literatur." *Historische Zeitschrift* 48 (1882) 417-72.

The Oxford English Dictionary (A New English Dictionary on Historical Principles). Oxford: Clarendon, 1901.

Pannenberg, Wolfhart. "Heilsgeschehen und Geschichte." *KD* 5 (1959) 218-37; 259-88.

―――, editor. *Offenbarung als Geschichte*. Beihefte zur KD 1. Göttingen: Vandenhoeck & Ruprecht, 1961. 2nd ed., 1963.

Procksch, Otto. "Über pneumatische Exegese." *Christentum und Wissenschaft* 1 (1925) 145–58.

Rad, Gerhard von. "Typological Interpretation of the Old Testament." Translated by John Bright. *Int* 16 (1961) 174–92. Reprinted in *Essays in Old Testament Hermeneutics*, edited by Claus Westermann and James Luther Mays, 17–39. Atlanta: John Knox, 1963.

Ramm, Bernard L. *Protestant Biblical Interpretation: A Textbook of Hermeneutics for Conservative Protestants*. Boston: Wilde, 1950. Rev. ed., 1956. 3rd ed. Grand Rapids: Baker, 1970.

Robinson, James M. "For Theology and the Church." *JTC* 1 (1965) 1–19.

―――. "The Recent Debate on the 'New Quest.'" *JBR* 30 (1962) 198–208.

―――. Review of "Jesus Christ" by S. Maclean Gilmour. *ANQ* 3 (1963) 37–39.

―――. "Theology as Translation." *TTo* 20 (1964) 518–27.

Robinson, James M., and John B. Cobb Jr., editors. *The Later Heidegger and Theology*. New Frontiers in Theology 1. New York: Harper & Row, 1963.

―――, editors. *The New Hermeneutic*. New Frontiers in Theology 2. New York: Harper & Row, 1964.

―――, editors. *Theology as History*. New Frontiers in Theology 3. New York: Harper & Row, 1967.

Sandmel, Samuel. "Parallelomania." *JBL* 81 (1962) 1–13.

Schleiermacher, Friedrich D. E. *Hermeneutik*. Newly edited and introduced by Heinz Kimmerle. Abhandlungen der Heidelberger Akademie der Wissenschaften, Philosophisch-historisch Klasse, Jg. 1959, 2. Abh. Heidelberg: Winter, 1959.

―――. *Hermeneutik und Kritik mit besonderer Beziehung auf das Neue Testament*. Sämmtliche Werke 1. Edited by Friedrick Lücke. Berlin: Reimer, 1838.

―――. *Kurze Darstellung des theologischen Studiums zum Behuf einleitender Vorlesungen*. Berlin: Reimer, 1830.

Schmidt, Karl Ludwig. "Die Stellung der Evangelien in der allgemeinen Literaturgeschichte." In *Eucharistērion: Festschrift für Hermann Gunkel*, edited by Hans Schmidt, 2:50–134. FRLANT 36. Göttingen: Vandenhoeck & Ruprecht, 1923.

Schodde, George H. *Outlines of Biblical Hermeneutics: A Handbook for Students of the Word*. Columbus: Lutheran Book Concern, 1917.

Schott, Andreas, SJ., translator. *Bibliotheca* by Photius. Rothomagi: Sumpt, I. & D. Berthelin, 1653.

Schweizer, Eduard. Review of *Biblische Hermeneutik* by Kurt Frör. *NZZ* 2810 (July 17, 1963) Abendsausgabe, 1–2.

Seeberg, E. "Zum Problem der pneumatischen Exegese." In *Beiträge zur Religionsgeschichte und Archäologie Palästinas: Ernst Sellin zum 60. Geburtstag*, edited by W. F. Albright et al., 127–37. Leipzig: Deichert, 1927.

Seeberg, R. "Zur Frage nach dem Sinn und Recht einer pneumatischen Schriftauslegung." *ZST* 3 (1926) 3–59.

Senft, Christoph. Review of Kimmerle's edition of Schleiermacher's *Hermeneutik*. *PhR* 10 (1962) 288–90.

Smalley, Beryl. *The Study of the Bible in the Middle Ages*. Oxford: Blackwell, 1941. 2nd ed., 1952.

Staiger, Emil. "Ein Briefwechsel mit Martin Heidegger." In idem, *Die Kunst der Interpretation: Studien zur deutschen Literaturgeschichte*, 34-49. Zürich: Atlantis, 1955. 2nd ed., 1957.

———. "Ein Rückblick." *NNZ* (Sept. 27, 1959) Blatt 5, Nr. 2898 (69).

———. *Die Zeit als Einbildungskraft des Dichters*. Zurich: Atlantis, 1939. 2nd ed., 1953.

Steiger, Lothar. *Die Hermeneutik als dogmatisches Problem: Eine Auseinandersetzung mit dem tranzendentalen Ansatz des theologischen Verstehens*. Gütersloh: Gütersloher/Gerd Mohn, 1961.

Stendahl, Krister. "Biblical Theology, Contemporary." In *IDB* 1:418-32.

Terry, Milton S. *Biblical Hermeneutics: A Treatise on the Interpretation of the Old and New Testaments*. New York: Eaton & Mains, 1883. Rev. ed. 1890. 3rd ed. 1911. Reprinted, Grand Rapids: Zondervan, 1952.

Torm, Frederik Emanuel. *Hermeneutik des Neuen Testaments*. Göttingen: Vandenhoeck & Ruprecht, 1930.

———. *Nytestamentlig Hermeneutik*. Copenhagen: Gads, 1928.

Traub, Friedrich. "Wort Gottes und pneumatische Schriftauslegung." *ZTK* 8 (1927) 83-111.

Vergegenwärtigung: Aufsätze zur Auslegung des Alten Testaments. Forward by Hans Urner. Kirche in dieser Zeit 14. Berlin: Evangelische Verlagsanstalt, 1955.

Wach, Joachim. "Verstehung." In *RGG*² 5 (1931) 1570-73.

———. *Das Verstehen: Grundzüge einer Geschichte der hermeneutischen Theorie im 19. Jahrhundert*. 3 vols. Tübingen: Mohr/Siebeck, 1926, 1929, 1933.

Waterland, Daniel. *A Review of the Doctrine of the Eucharist, as Laid Down in Scripture and Antiquity*. Cambridge: Crownfield, 1737.

Weber, Max. *Wirtschaft und Gesellschaft*. Tübingen: Mohr/Siebeck, 1956.

Westermann, Claus, editor. *Probleme alttestamentlicher Hermeneutik*. ThBü 11. Munich: Kaiser, 1960.

———, and James Luther Mays, editors. *Essays in Old Testament Hermeneutics*. Atlanta: John Knox, 1963.

Wilder, Amos N. "The Word as Address and the Word as Meaning." In *The New Hermeneutic*, edited by James M. Robinson and John B. Cobb Jr., 198-218. New Frontiers in Theology 2. New York: Harper & Row, 1964.

Windelband, Wilhelm, and Heinz Heimsoeth. *Lehrbuch der Geschichte der Philosphie*. 14th ed. Tübingen: Mohr/Siebeck, 1950.

Wolff, Hans Walter. "The Hermeneutics of the Old Testament." Translated by Keith Crim. *Int* 16 (1961) 439-72. Reprinted in *Essays in Old Testament Hermeneutics*, edited by Claus Westermann and James Luther Mays, 160-99. Atlanta: John Knox, 1963.

Windisch, Hans. Review of *Der Römerbrief* by Karl Barth. *TLZ* 45 (1920) 200-201.

Wood, James D. *The Interpretation of the Bible: A Historical Introduction*. London: Duckworth, 1958.

CHAPTER 3 | *Revelation as Word and as History*

GERMAN THEOLOGY BETWEEN THE TWO WORLD WARS WAS DOMINATED by what was initially a united movement called "dialectic theology," but which polarized into a Barthian position, usually called the "theology of the word," and a Bultmannian position, often referred to as "kerygmatic theology"—terminologies that suggest the common orientation to the concept of the word of God. That brilliant theological epoch has now drawn to an end, and new theologies are beginning to emerge. One alternative is to pick up dialectic theology's focus upon the word of God as a point of departure, and to bring it into coordination with newly emerging understandings of language, such as the understanding of language as event, as performatory language. The result is the new hermeneutic analyzed in Chapter 2 above. Another alternative is to "forsake" "the context of the 'theology of the word' that has determined theological thinking in one form or another for more than a generation,"[1] and to find instead a focal orientation in an understanding of history. It is this alternative that is to be analyzed in the present essay.[2]

It is not surprising that titles in the literature related to this development have reflected from time to time such a juxtaposition of word and

---

1. Pannenberg, "Postscript," in *Offenbarung als Geschichte*, 2nd ed., 132.
2. The attentive reader will note that this essay has been written by one more oriented to the first alternative. Yet an effort has been made, without losing a participant's sensitivity for what the issues are and where the problems lie, to reduce so far as possible elements that would hinder the reader's open access to the new and creative theological position this essay seeks to introduce as one of the living options in theology today.

history. An advocate of the new position has defended it in an article entitled "History and Word in the Old Testament,"[3] and a critic has entitled his treatment, *Theology of the Word of God and the Hypothesis of Universal History.*[4] Similarly the leader of the new movement has presented a comparison of the two positions in an essay entitled "Hermeneutic and Universal History."[5] The title of the present essay is intended to reflect this usage present in the discussion itself.

Such terminologies are not intended to suggest an either/or relationship between language and history. Rather the discussion has to do with the question: Which provides the more adequate overarching category for bringing to expression their correct relationship? "Hermeneutic," by interpreting language as *event* that recurs in the ongoing translation of meaning, provides an approach to a theological understanding of history. And "universal history," by interpreting events in the context of the history of the transmission of *traditions,* provides an approach to a theological understanding of language. Yet by the nature of the case each would tend to be more adequate in bringing to expression that pole which it has used as the model for the overarching category. Hence the debate between the two positions has often followed the pattern of criticizing the other side of the discussion for its inadequate treatment of the pole that is one's own point of departure, and of claiming to do more justice to total reality by using that pole as a model: the linguisticality of all reality, or all reality as history.

THE THEOLOGICAL EXPERIENCE OF CONTEMPORARY HISTORY

If it is true that reflection upon history emerges in the wake of great historic events, then, conversely, the ways in which such events are themselves experienced should foreshadow the understanding of history operative in the historical study that follows. The contours of Wolfhart Pannenberg's distinctive position in the Christian understanding of history can thus be anticipated by contrasting the divergent ways in which leading German theologians experienced the two World Wars.

In 1920 *Die Christliche Welt,* the leading religious weekly of German Christendom, comparable to *The Christian Century* in America, carried

3. R. Rendtorff, "Geschichte und Wort."
4. Klein, *Theologie des Wortes Gottes.*
5. Pannenberg, "Hermeneutik und Universalgeschichte."

a shocking article that repudiated all that the journal stood for, especially the program of *Kulturprotestantismus* its title expressed. This article by a village pastor, Friedrich Gogarten, was significantly entitled "Between the Times." It began: "It is the destiny of our generation to stand between the times. We never belonged to the period presently coming to an end; it is doubtful whether we shall ever belong to the period which is to come, and, if through our own efforts we could be part of the future, whether it would come so soon. So we stand in the middle—in an empty space."[6] The defeat and dethroning of the Kaiser, and now the ruinous inflation, brought to an end a culture that had proudly inscribed its self-understanding on the buttons of its soldiers, "Gott mit uns" ("God with us"). This grinding halt is seen by Gogarten as a welcomed liberation from an empty theology that had only provided a false security. The final external collapse was all that was to be expected in view of the inner hollowness. Albert Schweitzer's dramatic discovery of primitive Christian apocalyptic eschatology, which prior to World War I had been shocking only in demonstrating how irrelevant Jesus' position was to modern theology, was now followed by a second shock wave: this eschatology, rather than modern liberal theology,[7] seemed to fit the contemporary situation, seen now as the "interim" following upon the collapse of the "present evil aeon." Gogarten argued that it was not yet the time to set up new programs for the future to fill in the void (where Communism and then Nazism would be the live options), but rather the time finally to pause, unburdened by the vested interest of a culture comprised of man's achievements, and for once to listen to what God has to say.

Now, it is significant to Gogarten that the inner hollowness had become visible prior to the external collapse. His generation had caught sight of it by means of critical historical method, in terms of which the great historians of the day had taught the theological student to understand Biblical and church history just as other history is to be understood,

---

6. Gogarten, "Between the Times," 277.

7. For example, the leading theological journal of liberalism prior to World War I, the *Zeitschrift für Theologie und Kirche*, in spite of its programmatic intention to carry on theology as a constant hermeneutical translation of the point of the gospel into the contemporary situation, failed to do precisely that between the two World Wars. Compare the survey of the history of that journal in my essay, "For Theology and the Church," esp. 16. Compare also Schempp, "Randglossen zum Barthianismus," 305 = "Marginal Glosses to Barthianism," 193: "Barth has a following because his theology corresponds better to the present intellectual climate than do other theologies."

i.e., as man's doing. *Heilsgeschichte* had been unmasked as simply a part of the long story of human self-assertion.

> All these things have long since disintegrated. They have long since been explained in terms of historical development, long since been placed in the stream of general history. That happened the moment you handled them scientifically. You could not have done it a moment sooner. Science (should I say "our" science?) directs its attention toward and can comprehend those things which are dead. And what is left of this period that has not been worked over scientifically and that science does not understand? . . . In all the world we see no form of life which is not being dissolved. Did you not teach us to see the work of man in each and every thing? Was it not you who sharpened our sight for the human element by subjecting everything to history and development? We are grateful that you did. You created the tools for us; now let us use them. Now we draw the conclusion: Everything that is somehow a human work not only has a beginning, but passes away again. And it passes away when the human work overruns everything else. I have said already that it happens when science grasps it. It can do just that in the moment that man has won out. Now is the hour of decline. . . . That means we are acutely sensitive to the human element. . . . And we raise the question, in all seriousness, whether today there are any persons who can really conceive of God.[8]

Here the theology that we know today in terms of the "post-Christian era," in which "God is dead," and theology accordingly must be "honest to God," was launched at the moment when the secular approach to history implicit in critical historical method was finding its dramatic vindication in current events: The Christian service of the Kaiser in building God's kingdom on earth was unmasked as just a typical instance of the nationalism, militarism, and colonialism of the twentieth century.[9] It is not surprising that this theology interpreted Franz Overbeck's classification of primitive Christianity as "pre-historic" with regard to the history of Hellenistic literature and culture as a normative statement of what Christianity should be,[10] made a "system" of Kierkegaard's "infinite qualitative difference" between time and eternity,[11] and elevated the name

---

8. Gogarten, "Zwischen den Zeiten," 97–98.

9. For an analysis of the "unmasking" function of critical historical method, cf. Funk, "The Hermeneutical Problem and Historical Criticism," esp. 185–86.

10. Barth, "Unerledigte Anfragen."

11. Barth, *Der Römerbrief,* xiii; = *Epistle to the Romans,* 11. The quotation is from the

of Gogarten's article to the name of its journal, *Zwischen den Zeiten*.¹² And it is not surprising that when the Barthian wing of dialectic theology gradually moved toward *Heilsgeschichte*, it was challenged from within the dialectic theology context itself in the aftermath of World War II by the translation of Paul's phrase in Rom 10:4, "Christ the end of the law," as "Christ the end of history."¹³ Yet, in the decisive first years after World War II, with Bonhoeffer silenced,¹⁴ postwar theology hardly begun,¹⁵ and the occasional attempts to speak to the situation often more well-meant than fully adequate,¹⁶ many were ready for someone to provide a new orientation.

When the University of Heidelberg opened after the war, the first Rector to be elected from the Theological Faculty presented in his Rectoral Address an attempt to provide a theological reinterpretation of the history that was taking place. Hans von Campenhausen spoke on "Augustine and the Fall of Rome."¹⁷ His description of the end of the first Roman Empire, from the raping and looting of the eternal city that left it in ashes (like most German cities in 1945), to the stream of pitiful refugees in regions (like Heidelberg) that had not themselves been devastated by the war, certainly drew into sharp focus the parallel to the fall of the Third Reich.

Foreword to the 2nd edition, written in September 1921.

12. Karl Barth, Friedrich Gogarten, and Eduard Thurneysen were in charge of this publication of their school from 1922–1933. It was edited by Georg Merz.

13. Bultmann, *Das Urchristentum*, 209 = *Primitive Christianity*, 187–88. Similarly, Bultmann in "History and Eschatology," 13, reprinted in *Glauben und Verstehen*, 3:103. Also Fuchs, "Christus das Ende der Geschichte."

14. Executed in April, 1945, Bonhoeffer began his new posthumous influence on theology only with the publication of *Widerstand und Ergebung* (1951) = *Prisoner for God* (1953).

15. The currency reform of 1948 marked more than did 1945 the beginning of postwar German activity. Only then can one note real signs of new theological vigor, such as the publication in 1948 of the first fascicle (vol. 1 of the English edition) of Rudolf Bultmann's *Theologie des Neuen Testaments* and the resumption in 1950 of the publication of the *Zeitschrift für Theologie und Kirche*.

16. Günther Bornkamm's pamphlet of 1946 quoting Jean Paul's "Speech of the Dead Christ from the Firmament that there is no God" succeeded in bringing to expression what many Germans felt at that time. His own "Postscript" may have sounded like the same language of Zion one heard the last time one went to church. Reprinted in *Studien zu Antike und Urchristentum*, 245–52.

17. Von Campenhausen, "Augustin und der Fall von Rom," 253–71 = "Augustine and the Fall of Rome."

Then von Campenhausen outlined in impressive terms the way in which Augustine, in the face of the catastrophe that seemed to deny *ad oculos* any meaning to history and any value to Christianity, had presented in *De civitate dei* the "last, greatest apology of Christian antiquity,"[18] "a refounding of Christian faith itself by developing a concrete theodicy that speaks to the concerns and needs of the day."[19] This apology is not really an attempt to prove Christianity; it is rather an appeal to believe that, in spite of the apparent arbitrariness and hence meaninglessness of what happens, there will be on the last day, before God's judgment throne, a solving of the puzzle, a vindication of God's justice and of Christian faith.[20]

Von Campenhausen's concern is to correct a "pietistic and individualistic"[21] understanding of Augustine, in terms of which his response "could be understood as a wholly resigned retreat from the world of reality and its political decisions, as the final founding of a purely individualistic, ascetic stance toward life, which gives up forming world history at large and turns it over without a struggle to the purely earthly demonic forces."[22] Rather Augustine confronts the *civitas terrena* with the *civitas dei*, with "reality and real community."[23]

> Augustine feels that the pagan appeal to the nation's greatness and to its past has brought into play a moral power and a passion that the church cannot bypass and simply turn over to its pagan opponents, having condemned them without examination. One must speak to the issue, and the religious apology thus becomes a critical revision of the dominant historic consciousness, a struggle for the proper possession of one's own past and of political history as a whole.[24]

Augustine opposes "the dominant national ideology of pagan historians and philosophers" and recognizes in the pride that separates the

18. Ibid., 256.
19. Ibid., 259.
20. Ibid., 261.
21. These are also the terms with which von Campenhausen had described a position falsely identified as Christian "since Augustine," in his address at the University of Heidelberg on the four hundredth anniversary of the death of Martin Luther (Feb. 18, 1946), "Gottesgericht und Menschengerechtigkeit in der Geschichte," esp. 65. The position of Luther presented in this address is similar to the position of Augustin as presented in the Rectoral Address.
22. Von Campenhausen, "Augustin und der Fall von Rom," 262 = "Augustine and the Fall of Rome."
23. Ibid.
24. Ibid., 263.

individual from God the driving power behind the Roman state, which led to its fall.²⁵ In this way Augustine achieves a Christian understanding of the history of Rome from Romulus' murder of his brother down to the degeneracy of Augustine's own time. And to this view of past history there corresponds a new Christian society of the future in which "political virtues emerge again in a new spirit."²⁶ Thus Augustine rose to the occasion created by the fall of Rome, presented the gospel in terms of the situation he confronted, and thereby became "the first universal historian and theologian of history in Western civilization."²⁷

Von Campenhausen concluded his address with a program for orienting contemporary theology to Augustine's Christian philosophy of history.

> At least the *church* historian has no reason to give up today the task Augustine posed. He has only to take it up again with new means. Of course, it is a long road before we shall possess a total history of the church that meets the requirements of modern research in church history and history of religions and that nonetheless relates each epoch directly to Christ and measures it by Jesus' original proclamation, as is called for by what 'church' means. Furthermore it would be necessary, in order to have a real whole, to achieve a corresponding theological grasp of Israelite and Near Eastern history as a movement toward Christ, at whose center would of course be the presentation of primitive Christianity and of Jesus, a presentation that points both backward and forward. Only so would the disciplines of historical theology be able to perform theologically in their unity and totality that which the single individual Augustine once called for and accomplished.²⁸

At the time this program would seem to have had its implementation in such a work as Oscar Cullmann's *Christ and Time*.²⁹ Von Campenhausen had spoken of *Heilsgeschichte,* and, though his teachers had been Bultmann and Hans von Soden, he could present his under-

---

25. Ibid., 263–64.
26. Ibid., 266.
27. Ibid., 270.
28. Ibid., 271.

29. *Christus und Zeit* (1946) = *Christ and Time* (1950). The objective validity of this work in its historical aspects seemed in a way verified by the use made of it, though with a different ideological orientation, by Karl Löwith, *Meaning in History* (1949); German ed. *Weltgeschichte und Heilsgeschehen* (1953).

standing in language reminiscent of Cullmann. "All the lines of history from the beginning on converge toward a point in time and meet at Jesus Christ, in whom the meaning and goal of the whole movement are mysteriously unveiled. Here begins the history of our present, which flows irresistibly toward the same Christ, i.e., his return at the end of time for the consummation and the judgment."[30] Yet this *Heilsgeschichte* was soon replaced by Rudolf Bultmann's concept of the "saving event," and the nascent philosophy of history gave way to existentialism's historicness of existence as the current partner to theology.

Meanwhile the impact of von Campenhausen's Rectoral Address continued to work among the theological students, who crowded into Heidelberg until there was standing room only in the reading rooms of the University Library and Theological Seminar. The systematic theologians Peter Brunner and Edmund Schlink, with their strict Lutheran dogmatics, seemed at the time to present a bold Christianity that did not seek to curry favor with the cultural fads and the modern mind but was content to give an unambiguous witness. And the Old Testament theology of Gerhard von Rad began working out on a grand scale the basic Old Testament segment of the thesis that theology is ultimately an interpretation of history.

A group of young graduate students, drawn together by such influences, crystallized into a small but lasting discussion group that gradually became visible as dissertations and *Habilitationsschriften* (second dissertations prerequisite in Germany to entering the academic career) began to appear in print. Wolfhart Pannenberg,[31] then Professor of Systematic Theology at the University of Mainz, published his *Doctrine of Predestination*

---

30. Von Campenhausen, "Augustin und der Fall von Rom," 271 = "Augustine and the Fall of Rome."

31. Pannenberg (born 1928) came to Heidelberg as a student in 1951 after a year in Basel, where he had received strong influences from Barth but had reacted against Barth at two points: He recognized, in a constitutive way Barth did not, the need for critical historical study of the Bible (with a modified methodology) and was thus directed to the historical disciplines in Heidelberg; and he recognized, in distinction from Barth, the need to involve oneself more seriously in general, nontheological thought. He had studied philosophy under Nicholai Hartmann in Göttingen in 1948-49 and under Karl Jaspers while in Basel in 1950-51, and he continued these studies under Karl Löwith in Heidelberg from 1951 to 1953. Indeed Pannenberg's own road to Christianity had been more one of rational reflection than of Christian nurture or a conversion experience.

in Duns Scotus in 1954,³² the same year in which Rolf Rendtorff, then Professor of Old Testament at the University of Heidelberg, published his *Laws in the Priestly Document: A Study in the History of Gattungen*.³³ The latter's brother, Trutz, then *Dozent* of Systematic Theology at the University of Münster, published in 1958 *The Social Structure of the Congregation: The Ecclesiastical Forms of Life in the Social Change of the Present*.³⁴ In 1959 Klaus Koch, then Professor of Old Testament at the University of Hamburg, followed up Rolf Rendtorff's work on the Priestly Document with his own work, *The Priestly Document from Exodus 25 to Leviticus 16*.³⁵ Ulrich Wilckens, then Professor of New Testament at the Kirchliche Hochschule in Berlin, published the same year his dissertation, *Wisdom and Foolishness: An Exegetical and Comparative Religious Investigation of 1 Cor. 1 and 2*,³⁶ and two years later his *Habilitationsschrift*, entitled *The Missionary Speeches in Acts: Investigations in Form Criticism and the History of Traditions*.³⁷ Meanwhile Dietrich Rössler published in 1960 his dissertation in the department of New Testament at Heidelberg, entitled *Law and History: Investigations in the Theology of Jewish Apocalypticism and Pharisaic Orthodoxy*;³⁸ and in the same year Martin Elze, then *Dozent* in Church History at the University of Tübingen, published his dissertation, *Tatian and His Theology*.³⁹ Rössler then shifted into Practical Theology with a small volume entitled *The "Whole" Man: The Concept of Man in More Recent Pastoral Counseling and Modern Medicine in Relation to Anthropology in General*,⁴⁰ and became Professor of Practical Theology at the University of Tübingen.

Lest one overlook the inner unity in this series of scattered monographs reaching from the Old Testament to the social structure of the church and to psychiatry in the present, a programmatic essay by

---

32. Pannenberg, *Die Prädestinationslehre des Duns Skotus*.
33. R. Rendtorff, *Die Gesetze in der Priesterschrift*.
34. T. Rendtorff, *Die soziale Struktur der Gemeinde*.
35. Koch, *Die Priesterschrift*.
36. Wilckens, *Weisheit und Torheit*.
37. Wilckens, *Die Missionsrede der Apostelgeschichte*.
38. Rössler, *Gesetz und Geschichte*.
39. Elze, *Tatian und seine Theologie*.
40. Rössler, *Der "ganze" Mensch*.

Pannenberg on "Redemptive Event and History"[41] appeared on the crest of this wave of monographs in 1959, with a footnote to the title:

> The following discussion is a slightly revised lecture given in Wuppertal on January 5, 1959, at a meeting of teachers from the theological schools of Bethel and Wuppertal. Especially in the first part, it deals with a theme on which a theological circle originally from Heidelberg has worked regularly for seven years. Although I am responsible for the following considerations, many of them could not be expressed as they are without my continuing conversations with M. Elze, K. Koch, R. Rendtorff, D. Rössler, and U. Wilckens.[42]

A new school had been launched. This new movement, usually referred to as the "Pannenberg circle,"[43] is the first to emerge from the German generation that was born well after World War I had passed, was raised in the throes of the Third *Reich,* World War II, and the collapse of 1945, and has reached maturity in the *Bundesrepublik.* It is also the first theological school to emerge in Germany within recent years that is not in one form or the other a development of the dialectic theology of the twenties.

---

41. Cf. below, note 44.

42. "Heilsgeschehen und Geschichte," 218 = "Redemptive Event and History," 314. Compare the opening footnote of Ulrich Wilckens's essay "Die Bekehrung des Paulus als religionsgeschichtliches Problem," 273: "Inaugural address presented on December 10, 1958, in Heidelberg and on December 12, 1958, in Marburg. The thesis which is intentionally only sketched here originated in connection with theological work shared over a period of years with Martin Elze, Klaus Koch, Wolfhart Pannenberg, Rolf Rendtorff, and Dietrich Rössler." Robert L. Wilken, "Who is Wolfhart Pannenberg?" 140, says the group consisted initially of only Wilckens, Rössler, Koch, and Rendtorff. Lothar Steiger, "Offenbarungsgeschichte und theologische Vernunft," 89, comments: "The Old Testament scholar Klaus Koch, and in the area of Church History, Martin Elze, give less clear indication of belonging to this group." However, Koch's essays, "Spätisraelitisches Geschichtsdenken" and "Der Tod des Religionsstifters," and Elze's essay, "Der Begriff des Dogmas in der Alten Kirche," are oriented to Pannenberg's position. The brother of Rolf Rendtorff, Trutz Rendtorff, identified himself with the group in the symposium, *Offenbarung als Geschichte* (*Revelation as History*) with his essay "Das Offenbarungsproblem in Kirchenbegriff" = "The Problem of Revelation in the Concept of the Church." August Strobel's book, *Die apokalyptische Sendung Jesu,* indicates that he has adopted the new position with the uncritical zeal characteristic of the convert, as Ulrich Wilckens's somewhat cool review indicates (in *TLZ,* 1964).

43. Pannenberg refers to the movement as a "working circle" and their position as a "theological conception of history" (*Grundzüge der Christologie,* 9 = *Jesus—God and Man,* 12).

THE LOCATION OF THE NEW POSITION WITHIN THE THEOLOGICAL SPECTRUM

The position emerging from this movement was first presented as such in the programmatic essay by Pannenberg entitled "Redemptive Event and History."[44] That essay includes both a critical assessment of the then current theological options in Germany and the main lines of an alternative to them. And indeed one can best begin an evaluation of the importance of this new movement and of the role it has played in German theological discussion by clarifying where its first thrust lies in relation to these alternate positions. The discussion was initially hampered by overhasty assumptions on both sides in this regard. For the older positions have available certain rejected categories in terms of which it is all too convenient to classify any and all divergent opinions. And the younger movement, not having experienced the older views in their original vigor and excitement of discovery, but as "safe doctrine," handed down and watered down, may not do full justice to the theologies it is opposing. Hence it is the purpose of this section to work through such initial assessments to a more accurate identification of the points of divergence.

The programmatic essay began by setting out its location within the spectrum as follows:

> History is the most comprehensive horizon of Christian theology. All theological questions and answers are meaningful only within the framework of the history that God has with humanity and through humanity with his whole creation—the history moving toward a future still hidden from the world but already revealed in Jesus Christ. This presupposition of Christian theology must be defended today within theology itself on two sides: on the one side, against Bultmann and Gogarten's existential theology that dissolves history into the historicness of existence; on the other side, against the thesis, developed by Martin Kähler in the tradition of redemptive history, that the real content of faith is suprahistorical. This assumption of a suprahistorical kernel of history, which was in substance present already in von Hofmann's delimi-

---

44. Pannenberg, "Heilsgeschehen und Geschichte." The first part was reprinted in slightly shortened form in *Probleme alttestamentlicher Hermeneutik* (1960) = *Essays on Old Testament Hermeneutics* (1963). (It is odd that 233–35 of the original essay, in which Pannenberg expresses most agreement with the other side, in this instance Kierkegaard and Gogarten, are omitted from the reprint, which resumes where the criticism, in this instance of Bultmann and Fuchs, resumes.)

tation of a theology of redemptive history (*Heilsgeschichte*) over against ordinary history (*Historie*), and which is still alive today especially in the form of Barth's interpretation of the incarnation as "prehistory" (*Urgeschichte*), necessarily depreciates real history, just as does the reduction of history to historicness. Both theological positions, that of pure historicness and that of the suprahistoric ground of faith, have a common extratheological motive. Their common starting point is to be seen in the fact that critical historical research as the scientific establishment of events did not seem to leave any room for redemptive events. Therefore the theology of redemptive history fled into a harbor supposedly safe from the critical historical flood tide, the harbor of suprahistory, or, with Barth, of prehistory. For the same reason the theology of existence withdrew from the meaningless and godless "objective" course of history to the experience of the significance of history in the "historicness" of the individual. The historical character of the redemptive event must therefore be asserted today in debate, with the theology of existence, with the theology of redemptive history, and with the methodological principles of critical historical research.[45]

This position would seem to oppose equally the Barthian and Bultmannian alternatives. However, the concept of *Urgeschichte*, "prehistory," was limited to the early Barth, so that the quotation is not as direct a criticism of the Barthians as it might seem. To be sure there does seem to remain in the later Barth a vestige of a supernatural precinct.[46] Yet the emphasis in the Barthian movement has moved in the direction of a view of revelatory history nearer to that out of which the Pannenberg movement arose. Thus Barth could express his approval of such Old Testament views with regard to "faith and history"[47] as that of von Rad, from which

---

45. "Heilsgeschehen und Geschichte," 218 = "Redemptive Event and History," 314.

46. Cf. Bornkamm, "Die Theologie Rudolf Bultmanns," 88–89: "In Barth on the other hand it seems as if the revelation not only calls upon us for faith but also for the concession of another advantage, namely the separating out in advance of an area of mysterious things that, as was customary in the orthodox tradition, I exclude in advance with the help of a formal concept of scripture and canon and that I may no longer make the object of critical inquiry." In note 1 on 89 he comments that he had already registered this criticism in 1951, and that in the interim his hopes of having misunderstood Barth have "become fainter." Pannenberg senses in Barth's neglect of critical historical method a continuation of his "prehistory" position.

47. Cf. Barth, "How My Mind Has Changed," 75: "To me it is significant that present-day Old Testament scholars, especially in regard to the old yet always new theme of

Pannenberg's view of history emerged, and that of Walter Zimmerli, who provided a basic ingredient for the theology of the Pannenberg group and found it difficult to distinguish his position from theirs, as the next section of this introduction will indicate. Hence, when the Barthian journal, *Evangelische Theologie*, called a meeting of its editorial board in September, 1961, to carry through a reorganization along more scholarly lines and to appraise critically "a theology of history emerging again in somewhat different form,"[48] the series of papers presented for discussion more nearly revealed the extent to which the two movements were converging.[49] The main theological paper was presented by Jürgen Moltmann, known as the editor of the collection of important articles from the twenties reprinted as the *Beginnings of Dialectic Theology*,[50] as well as for his own *Theology of Hope*.[51] His presentation parallels very closely the thought of Pannenberg, and only in a somewhat peripheral way echoes the "theology of the word of God."[52] And Bohren's applica-

---

'faith and history,' are on the whole on much better ground than the authoritative New Testament men."

48. Cf. *EvTh* 21 (1961) 529-30. The editor, Ernst Wolf, expressed the personal dissatisfaction of the Barthians with this new movement by thus suggesting a parallel to the theology of history presented by the notorious "German Christians," an innuendo subsequently retracted, *EvTh* 22 (1962) 223-24.

49. The reorganized journal opened with a double issue for January–February, 1962, which included the papers discussed at the meeting: Günther Bornkamm, "Geschichte und Glauben im Neuen Testament," which did not address itself directly to the position of Pannenberg; Walter Zimmerli, "'Offenbarung' im Alten Testament," which will be discussed in the next section; Jürgen Moltmann, "Exegese und Eschatologie der Geschichte"; Rudolf Bohren, "Die Krise der Predigt als Frage an die Exegese." It was only a supplementary article by another participant at the meeting, Hans-Georg Geyer, that brought out any extensive divergence from Pannenberg: "Geschichte als theologisches Problem." In his "Postscript" to *Offenbarung als Geschichte*, (2nd ed., 147 n. 35), Pannenberg relativizes the difference between their positions.

50. Moltmann, *Anfänge der dialektischen Theologie*; see also Robinson, ed., *The Beginnings of Dialectical Theology*.

51. Moltmann, *Theologie der Hoffnung* = *Theology of Hope*.

52. In his preface to *Anfänge der dialektischen Theologie*, 1:XII, Moltmann argues that "theology of the word" is the only "appropriate" designation for dialectic theology. In "Exegese und Eschatologie der Geschichte," 58, one finds a passing echo of that theology: "The revelation of the special history that grounds faith in Christ takes place in the word that effects history.... Thus history does not become revelation, but it does become the sphere of revelation." But this is then led in a direction nearer to Pannenberg on 59: "The eschatological proclamation effects and provokes the experience of reality as history, ... makes the reality in which men live together a historical process." In Moltmann's *Theologie*

tion of Moltmann's paper to the homiletical problem, while sensing in Pannenberg's emphasis that facts speak for themselves "a complete defeat for preaching,"[53] goes on to affirm that over against the other alternatives this emphasis is "simply liberating,"[54] and then to sketch a concept of preaching oriented to remembering and narrating history that could well be a homiletical implementation of Pannenberg's theology.

Dialectic theology had originally waged its polemic against an objectivizing idealistic interpretation of history in favor of an encounter with history in which history is not ultimately under man's control but rather opens up access to that which is not at his disposal, and for that reason encounters him as a real, irreplaceable, and authoritative event.[55] It was that new understanding of history that came to expression more adequately in terms of a historic concept of word, to which it was then coordinated.[56] Now this coordination seems to be fading among the

der Hoffnung, 49 = *Theology of Hope*, 56–57, he defends Barth against Pannenberg's association of Barth's understanding of the word of God with Gnosticism and personalism.

53. Bohren, "Die Krise der Predigt," 78.

54. Ibid., 82–83.

55. Cf., e.g., Bultmann's criticism of his predecessors, "Das Problem einer theologischen Exegese des Neuen Testaments," reprinted in *Anfänge der dialektischen Theologie*, 2:51 = "The Problem of a Theological Exegesis of the New Testament," 239: "That means that the connection of the existing [*existentiell*] subject with history does not take place at all—or only if the existence of man does not lie in the sphere of the universal or rational, but in the individual, in the concrete moment of the here and how. For the Idealist, there is nothing in history which places demands on the individual in the sense that something new is said which is not already potentially one's own, which is not at one's disposal by virtue of one's participation in universal reason. One finds nothing which encounters oneself as authoritative; one finds only oneself in history; this one does by reducing the content of history to the movement of the ideas impressed on one's reason. One thus controls all possible historical occurrences from the outset."

56. Ibid., 53 = ibid., 240–42: "In each of these cases the word of the text is unable to speak in any real sense to the interpreter, since the interpreter is a priori thoroughly in control of all the possibilities which may be expressed, by means of the principles of his approach. However, the original and genuine meaning of the word 'word' is that it intends to refer to something outside the speaker, to disclose this to the hearer, and by so doing to become an event for him. The potential objection raised by Idealist exegesis, which insists that it does not exclude such a definition, rests on the fact that it does not conceive the speaking individual as a psychically or historically determined subject and can therefore interpret his statements as references to transsubjective matters. But such matters are not intended here, since they cannot become events for the hearer. Rather, since their content is the system of reason, the essence of the spirit of rationalism, such matters include only that which the interpreter as a rational subject controls a priori. Objective exegesis seeks to deal responsibly with the original and genuine meaning of

Barthians, with the result that the concept of the word tends to merge with that of the interpretation given in the tradition—which Pannenberg includes within his concept of history. Thus the Barthian tends not to realize how much his own position has become like that of Pannenberg, with the result that he is able to mark the difference only by presenting Pannenberg's view as nearer to that of positivism than in reality it is. For example, Eduard Schweizer summarizes critically:

> With [the Pannenberg circle] the revelation of God is to be found exclusively in history. It is not the interpreting word of the prophet or of the witness in [the] early church; it is the course of history itself which reveals God to anyone who is not blind.... We cannot deal extensively with this [position]. It may suffice to say that according to the Old and New Testament God's acts [in] history are not at all visible to everybody. It is the word of the prophet; it is the preaching of the Apostles; it is the special instruction of Jesus granted to the disciples, which solves the riddles; and it is, above all, always the miracle of God's Spirit, which opens hardened hearts. With Pannenberg, the fundamental difference between scientific perception and faith as a gift of God becomes blurred... Stressing with Pannenberg exclusively the mere facts leads us astray. The mere fact is a birth, and nobody could see its relevance, its real meaning, without the interpretation of faith.[57]

Yet in actuality the Pannenberg group does not maintain a revelation in historical fact apart from the context of traditions and interpretations in which it took place.[58] Their divergence from dialectic theology is in the

---

'word' by understanding it as a reference to the subject matter."

57. Schweizer, "Some Trends," 5, 7. For the extent to which Schweizer's position is actually like that of Rendtorff, cf. below, note 186. For the extent to which the Barthians have in general been moving away from the original understanding of the word characteristic of dialectic theology, one may compare an exchange between Heinrich Ott and Bultmann. In his pamphlet *Die Frage nach dem historischen Jesus und die Ontologie der Geschichte*, 40, Ott appeals, in his opposition to brute-fact positivistic historiography, to Martin Buber for the fact that "saga," the meaning of events, goes back to the inspiration with which the events themselves were experienced. To this Bultmann replied in a letter: "Your quotations from Buber show how much he is still stuck in historicism. For the inspiration whose function he perceives in the historical tradition is after all a phenomenon thoroughly visible to the positivistic historian. The kind of encounter which is the presupposition of genuine understanding of historical reality is surely my own encounter as I question history, expose myself to it; but it is not the encounter of various reporters."

58. Apart from an occasional remark, later by implication withdrawn; cf. below, notes

area of history as present address, and when on this topic the Barthian, much like the traditional Lutheran Althaus,[59] speaks simply of "the miracle of God's Spirit," Pannenberg can with some justification feel such a view is in need of demythologization. That is to say he is at least in part to be understood as reacting in his way, i.e., in terms of a theology of history, against the same symptoms of decline within the "theology of the word" as is Ebeling in his, i.e., in terms of a hermeneutical understanding of language.

There is, on the other hand, some degree of justification for Oscar Cullmann to sense a convergence between his and Pannenberg's views of history. For although Cullmann is hardly a dialectic theologian, his position is in fact that toward which the Barthian school has been moving. In the "Retrospect on the Effect of the Book in Theology since the War" that Cullmann uses in the place of a preface to the third German edition of *Christ and Time* (1962), he finds himself in the propitious moment "where the theological situation seems to be developing such that in the future one can perhaps expect even in Germany more understanding for what I was at, than was the case in the period now coming to an end, characterized by the inroads of existentialism into New Testament exegesis." This hope is documented in a footnote with the remark: "I have in mind, e.g., the circle around W. Pannenberg (without yet assuming a position with regard to it)."[60] Even this reservation is removed in Cullmann's newer book, whose title, *Salvation as History*,[61] stands in striking parallel to that of the symposium of the Pannenberg group, *Revelation as History*,[62] of which Cullmann says: "To be sure [it] does not play up the term '*Heilsgeschichte*,' but in spite of all deviation in detail its position comes near to that advocated by myself in *Christ and Time*."[63]

157, 158, 185.

59. Cf. below, 200-203.

60. Cullmann, *Christus und die Zeit*, 3rd ed., 9-10.

61. Cullmann, *Heil als Geschichte* = *Salvation in History*.

62. *Offenbarung als Geschichte*, 1961; 2nd ed., 1963 = *Revelation as History*, 1968. Since this is the first *Beiheft* to *Kerygma und Dogma*, there is prefaced to it a brief note by the "editors" of the journal, of whom Cullmann is one, to the effect that the value of the essays in the volume led them to introduce the series format for this symposium and similar materials.

63. Cullmann, *Heil als Geschichte*, 39 = *Salvation in History*, 57. Cullmann recognizes here that his soteriological focus is a "quite different perspective" from the focus of the Pannenberg group on revelation, a distinction that becomes quite explicit in Pannenberg's *Grundzüge der Christologie*, esp. chap. 2 on "Christology and Soteriology,"

If however there is hardly a sharp line of demarcation between the Pannenberg group and the place at which the Barthian movement has in fact by and large arrived, so that the Pannenberg group may in retrospect seem more its heir than its opponent, a clearer alternative would seem to exist with regard to the Bultmannian position; for this position has retained more of the original correlation of history and word by means of which dialectic theology had distinguished itself from the antecedent idealistic view of history. Unfortunately the version of this position prevalent at Heidelberg,[64] and apparently sanctioned by the fact that it had been propagated by the Bultmannian on the faculty,[65] was in fact misleading. Yet Pannenberg appeals to Bornkamm's criticism of Bultmann[66] as "showing convincingly that Paul is not concerned with a new self-understanding, but with a 'new history and existence,' in which I am taken up into Christ's history."[67]

Johannes Körner had already challenged the validity of the interpretation of Bultmann implicit in this either/or formulation. For if it does not advocate a dualistic view of history, which Bornkamm hardly intended, it presupposes a misunderstanding of Bultmann.[68] However,

---

32-44 = *Jesus—God and Man*, 38-51. The Cullmannian concept of the Christ event as "the center of *Heilsgeschichte*" emerges in the Pannenberg group, e.g., Dietrich Rössler, *Göttinger Predigtmeditationen* 16 (1962) 159, although Pannenberg subordinates it to the futurity of eschatology (*Grundzüge der Christologie*, 405-6= *Jesus—God and Man*, 389-90), and prefers to speak of Jesus as the "proleptic end" of history, "Heilsgeschehen und Geschichte," 224 = "Redemptive Event and History," 322. The focus of Ernst Fuchs's review of *Offenbarung als Geschichte*, entitled "Theologie oder Ideologie? Bemerkungen zu einem heilsgeschichtlichen Programm," is to draw the parallel between the Pannenberg circle and Cullmann.

64. On the general breakdown of real communication between the leading positions in Germany, the rigidifying of fronts, the misrepresentation, and hence the general degeneration of the relevance of the discussion between groups (in contrast to the more accurate and profound interpretation and discussion especially of Bultmann coming from Roman Catholic and English language theology), cf. Günther Bornkamm's survey, "Die Theologie Rudolf Bultmanns in der neueren Diskussion."

65. Bornkamm, "Mythus und Evangelium."

66. Ibid., 25.

67. Pannenberg, "Heilsgeschehen und Geschichte," 222 = "Redemptive Event and History," 322.

68. Körner, *Eschatologie und Geschichte*, 124. "But what is meant by this new history of Christ? That is the problem. Does this call for a historic dualism to the effect that there is an old history, world history, and alongside of it a new history of Christ different in content? Does that mean that first two kinds of history are shown objectively to

Pannenberg maintains that Körner's interpretation is "automatically refuted"⁶⁹ by Bultmann's own presentation in *The Presence of Eternity*, where Bultmann says: "But although the history of the nation and the world has lost interest for Paul, he brings to light another phenomenon, the historicity of man, the true historical life of the human being."⁷⁰ Körner argues

---

exist, of which one is mine, the other Christ's, histories that I can observe even before being taken up into them? That would correspond, e.g., to the dualism of Manicheeism or Marcionitism, or Flacius' doctrine of justification, and would necessarily contradict every scholarly view of history, which can only be monistic. Or does it merely mean that, in believing, reality all at once appears to me as completely new, that [in this sense] Christ takes me into his history and hence prior history is now indeed 'no longer mine'? But Bultmann himself means the same thing—and Bornkamm himself [ibid., 27] concedes that Paul speaks of the new history 'to be sure not in a descriptive way, but only indirectly, through a renewed exposition of what now comprises man's being in faith.'" In a blurb attached to Körner's book, Bultmann is quoted as regarding it as "one of the most important recent publications in the field of theology," which "will advance the theological discussion fruitfully." Bultmann wrote me: "my view [on the relation of the ontological to the ontic] is accurately presented in the excellent book of Johannes Körner." Bornkamm ("Die Theologie Rudolf Bultmanns," 69 n. 1) has expressed reservations concerning his previous formulation of Bultmann's position in this regard, and (orally) specifically of the use Pannenberg made of it. Cf. Bultmann's "Answer to Ernst Käsemann": Käsemann may criticize the fact that this constant (sc. between Jesus and the kerygma) is seen in the self-understanding. But he does so obviously because he conceives of the self-understanding as an anthropological phenomenon visible to a distancing, objectifying view. The self-understanding in Braun and Robinson's sense includes in any case a self-understanding of man in his relation to a transcendent reality confronting him." *Glauben und Verstehen* 4:195.

69. "Heilsgeschehen und Geschichte," 225 n. 13 = "Redemptive Event and History," 322 n. 13.

70. Bultmann, *The Presence of Eternity*, 41ff. The quotation is on 43 and is quoted by Pannenberg in "Heilsgeschehen und Geschichte," 224 = "Redemptive Event and History," 322. The quotation from Bultmann continues: ". . . the history which every one experiences for himself and by which he gains his real essence." Thus Bultmann's talk of man's historicness would not seem to replace or "dissolve" history. In such statements Bultmann is contrasting a relation of salvation to the history of a whole nation or people, Israel, with the Christian understanding of salvation for which "there is neither Jew nor Greek." Cf. Bultmann, "History and Eschatology in the New Testament," esp. 13, reprinted in *Glauben und Verstehen*, 3:91–106, esp. 112; idem, *The Presence of Eternity*, 31. Thus Bultmann's point in the quotation under discussion is that salvation is independent of the course of international political history. Of course, this is not meant in the sense of the common distinction between "particularism" and "universalism," where preferring the latter to the former would move in the direction of Pannenberg's own position. Rather Bultmann is here distinguishing the Christian understanding of history not only from an understanding oriented to the national history of Israel, but also to an understanding in terms of world history. This latter distinction is to be understood in

that Bultmann does occasionally speak of a "new history," a "God-led history," and is indeed not replacing history with anthropology. Rather Bultmann's reserve in referring to eschatological existence as history and his preference for referring to it as a possibility of man's existence is to prevent much the kind of thing Pannenberg seeks,[71] namely the understanding of that history in its revelatory nature as demonstrable to the historian apart from (even though presumably leading to)[72] faith as one's own commitment.[73]

Bultmann himself expresses his view as follows:

Gogarten's sense: "A person will have one relation to history when he regards the whole span of its development as the proper revelation of God, and he will have another when he sees the proper revelation in God's original action which does not enter into its own effects and consequences and is not modified by and recognizable in them, but which must be grasped ever and again in its pure original nature beyond its historical effects and forms, however important these may be." "Vom heilen Egoismus des Christen," 548; reprinted in *Anfänge der dialektischen Theologie*, 1:101 = "The Holy Egoism," 84.

71. In connection with a (valid) use made by Pannenberg of an exegetical insight from Bultmann's *Theology*, Georg Muschalek, SJ, comments: "Bultmann's real concern in Section 37, which Pannenberg quotes in support of his thesis, is a diametrical contradiction of Pannenberg's thesis to the effect that 'the truth (of revelation) lies so patently before everyone's eyes that the natural and only possible result, in terms of the matter itself, is that it would have to be perceived." Cf. Georg Muschalek, SJ and Arnold Gamper, SJ, "Offenbarung in Geschichte; Parts 1 and 3 are by Muschalek, and Part 2 by Gamper. The quotation is from 192.

72. Pannenberg, "Postscript," 147; idem, "Einsicht und Glaube," 86, 90-91; and below, 219-21; and Pannenberg's lead essay, "Focal Essay," 129-31.

73. Körner, *Eschatologie und Geschichte*, 123: "But since this 'history' is exclusively a fact to faith, a fact that in principle can never be demonstrated as a factual event, which is what historiography has as its objective—since otherwise it would become rigidified into an empirical condition and then would no longer have anything to do with eschatological occurrence—hence Bultmann usually avoids the term history. This history is to be made intelligible only ontologically as a possibility. Hence it is more fitting to speak of it as 'authentic historic being' or as 'eschatological existence.' By means of this circumlocution the indirectness of the revelation is brought to expression . . . , i.e., the fact that man as a being in history has no unmediated relation to God in which he could have definitive hold of his authenticity. The ontological formulation is more suited as a scholarly means to this purpose than is history, because the intention of the ontological talk is to give up any pictorial description of a so-called Christian history and to point only to the possibilities of Christian existence in terms of man's being. . . . It is possible . . . to speak this way . . . because Bultmann roots history ontologically in historicness, i.e., every human actualization of being always must in some way be 'history' and the 'new history' is basically history in general, under the promise of faith."

> Faith also speaks of God acting in his control of nature and history, as Creator and Ruler. Indeed faith must so speak. For if man in his existence knows himself both called into life and sustained by God's omnipotence, then he knows also that the nature and history within which his life takes place are permeated by God's action. But this knowledge can be expressed only as confession and never as a general truth such as a theory of natural science or a philosophy of history. Otherwise God's action would be objectified to a worldly transaction. The statement of God's creatorship and dominion has its legitimate ground only in man's existential self-understanding.[74]

In reply to a critic advocating an interpretation of him analogous to that of Pannenberg, Bultmann has said:

> He overlooks the fact that existential understanding is not subjectivity, and that the nature of revelation as encounter is not denied in that it is designated as inaccessible for objectifying historical research. He fails to see that revelation is not thereby separated from history because he does not see the paradox that dominates the whole presentation of the Gospel of John, namely that the historical activity of Jesus is at the same time eschatological occurrence.[75]

Bultmann has addressed himself explicitly to the question of his own view of history as distinguished from that of von Campenhausen, which lies in the background of that of the Pannenberg group. For a Czechoslovakian pastor, J. A. Dvoracek, had been corresponding with

---

74. Bultmann, "Zum Problem der Entmythologisierung," 26. Cf. similarly *Glauben und Verstehen*, 2:101–4 = *Essays Philosophical and Theological*, 115–18.

75. Bultmann, "Zur Interpretation des Johannesevangelium," 8. Bultmann is here reviewing Holwerda's dissertation at the Free University at Amsterdam, *The Holy Spirit and Eschatology in the Gospel of John*. He answers the analogous criticism of Käsemann similarly: "Can one then deny that the consciousness of belonging to the people, to the new eschatological covenant, determines the self-understanding of each individual?" Bultmann, "Ist die Apokalyptik die Mutter der christlichen Theologie?," 65. In a further "Answer to Ernst Käsemann" Bultmann says: "To this (criticism) is to be said first of all that I do indeed distinguish existentialistic interpretation from objectifying (interpretation), but that I do not separate the one from the other. I would have thought I had emphasized often enough, over against the misunderstanding of existentialistic interpretation as subjectivistic, that existentialistic interpretation cannot be separated from the objectifying view of the historical phenomena." *Glauben und Verstehen*, 4:192. Pannenberg's position would be to the effect that contrary to his intention Bultmann's position involves subjectivism.

von Campenhausen on this point, and sent their correspondence to Bultmann, who replied in a letter of October 6, 1961:

> You understand correctly that it is my opinion that historical research can only produce data that can be objectively established, and this only with relative certainty. Demonstrating the origins of the Christian message by means of historical research would only establish this message as an historical phenomenon, and would not, however, establish it as the authentic, faith-producing "message," as the word of God addressing me. Further, you understand very correctly that I do not wish to free the message from history (and not from the church, either). Rather the relationship between history (as world history) and the event of revelation is a dialectical one, that is to say, the Christian faith asserts the paradox that a purely historical event is, at one and the same time, an eschatological event. With this assertion we include the statement that the event of revelation must at the same time be proclaimed as an historical event. Otherwise we could surrender the paradox. The Christ event must, therefore, to use your words, be proclaimed as a "hidden mystery" that happens in this empirical-historical world and its history. It is just this dialectic or paradox that Professor von Campenhausen does not appear to have fully grasped. Otherwise he could not characterize the resurrection of Jesus as an event that breaks through the created order and causality of the world right in the middle of its historical continuity, as an event 'in which the old world with its laws really comes to an end'—in other words, as a miracle. The end of the old world through the eschatological event, as that which continually comes to pass through proclamation and in faith, is open only to faith, and is for every other view (therefore, also for historical science) hidden. In the place of this dialectic, von Campenhausen puts the miraculous rupturing of the reality of this world.[76]

Thus the situation in which Pannenberg's theology emerges is not simply that of history having been eliminated in favor of existentialism by Bultmann, but rather that of different versions of the Christian under-

---

76. Quoted by Bowen, "Toward Understanding Bultmann," 34–35. Cf. also Bultmann's "Answer to Ernst Käsemann": "Do I advocate a dualism when I distinguish between the church as institution and as eschatological event . . . ? No! For it is of course clear to me that there is no such thing as an eschatological event in history without corporeality. But in this case it is I who speak of dialectic. The relation between the church as institution and as eschatological event is a dialectic (relation)." *Glauben und Verstehen*, 4:198.

standing of history and hence different implications for the structuring of theology. Pannenberg does not regard man's historicness as a universal ontological reality, but rather as an acquired trait of Western man, the effect on him of Biblical history.[77] Hence it cannot function for him as an all-embracing category as it does for Bultmann. Instead Pannenberg speaks directly of "history" as "reality in its totality."[78] What Pannenberg is seeking to do is to carry through in a way somewhat analogous to Whitehead the replacement of static ontological categories by those for which history provides the model. "The historic process as such has become the bearer of meaning."[79] It is not, however, his purpose to produce a Christian narration of history, what he calls a "total conception of history," i.e., "a conception of the whole course of history in terms of revelational history,"[80] which would indeed, as Kierkegaard argued, limit both the freedom of God and man and the contingency of history;[81] rather he wishes to achieve a "total view of reality as history directed by promises toward fulfillment."[82]

Pannenberg traces the development of this understanding of reality as history from ancient Israel to the present. In the course of Israelite history the fulfillment is progressively extended out into the future toward the end of history, so that the whole historical process takes on the directional character inherent in the prophetic vision and finds therein its unity. The completion of this development is found in Jewish apocalypticism, which is in turn the context in terms of which primitive Christianity

77. "Heilsgeschehen und Geschichte," 232 = "Redemptive Event and History," 332–33.

78. Ibid., 222 = ET 319.

79. Ibid., 219 = ET 315–16.

80. Ibid., 235 = ET omits at 333.

81. Ibid., 234–35 = ET omits at 333.

82. Ibid., 237 = ET 335. Although such formulations indicate the direction, they are an exploratory effort to break new ground and hence at times fall short of the intention and are subject to immanent criticism in terms of intention. The defining of history as coterminous with reality leaves unclarified what reality is to be attributed to the end of history when God is fully revealed, and suggests a dualism inherent in the timeless reality after history's end, if that is more than a limiting concept for Pannenberg. The reality of such a position as is able to look back upon ended history is emphasized subsequently by such statements as the following: "The revelation grounded by the course of history can be an event only at its end, i.e., after the totality of occurrences run their course, which in turn receive their ultimate light only from the end." So in the "Postscript," in *Offenbarung als Geschichte*, 2nd ed., 142 n. 25.

is to be understood.[83] Hence Christianity is seen carrying on the Biblical understanding of reality as history through the development of Western civilization, until, with the Enlightenment, man replaced God as the agent held to be at work in history. This elimination of God from historiography has as its outcome theology's failure to maintain the historical basis of its faith. Pannenberg's objective, in the light of this analysis, is to create a situation in which faith can rest on historically proven fact. This is not simply a matter of proving objective facts, to which the Christian attributes a significance not shared by the historian as such. "If the really decisive thing, the revelatory and saving significance of what happened to Jesus of Nazareth, can be seen only by faith and is on principle inacces-

---

83. In apocalypticism, "end-of-history eschatology has merely replaced the prophets' within-history eschatology," "Heilsgeschehen und Geschichte," 223 = "Redemptive Event and History," 321. This is the reverse interpretation of apocalypticism from that, e.g., of Gerhard von Rad, *Theologie des Alten Testament*, 2:314-21 = *Theology of the Old Testament*, 2:301-8, which is largely followed by Jürgen Moltmann, *Theologie der Hoffnung*, 120-24 = *Theology of Hope*, 133-38, and would imply that apocalyptic thinking is "history-less" (121 = 134). "This contradictory impression is due to the fact that in prophetic eschatology the horizon of promise both in its breadth and in its depth reaches the limits of what we can designate cosmic finitude. But when the historic horizon of the historic hopes has in its development reached these *eschata*, then one is confronted with the possibility of forsaking the historic location of one's perspective and of reading the historic course of the world backwards from the end one envisions, as if universal history is a *universum*, a predetermined historic cosmos. Ancient cosmological speculations about numbers are introduced in order to establish the order o the periods of world history in a way that corresponds to the order of space. The world kingdoms are fixed. The *eschaton* becomes fate. Then, in the place of election that directs one to hope and obey, there emerges—providence, which determines events. In the place of promise, in which one hopes in spite of what appears as the only hope, there emerges—the end drama. In the place of the eschaton that God calls forth in his freedom, there emerges—the finale of history that comes to be by the passage of time. In the place of God's faithfulness in which one trusts for the fulfillment of the promised future in God's freedom, there emerges—the plan of God that is fixed from the beginning of time and is unveiled successively by history. A historic theology becomes a theology of history and a historic eschatology becomes an eschatological view of history. Just as in the *Heilsgeschichte* theology of the eighteenth century, there lurks in apocalypticism a noticeable deism of the distant God. On the other side one should not overlook the fact that there is always an element of exhortation in the speculative apocalypses. It is the exhortation to persevere in the faith of the just. He who holds out to the end will be blessed. But faith and unbelief, good and evil, election and reprobation, the righteous and the unrighteous, are fixed, and one remains what one is. This in turn corresponds completely to the setting of apocalypticism in the life of the withdrawn conventicle" (ibid., 121-22 = 135). Cf. similarly Gerhard Sauter, *Zukunft und Hoffnung*, especially the section on "Revelation and History," 239-51 of the chapter on "Apocalypticism and Eschatology."

sible to rational research into what happened, then it is impossible to see how the historicity of pure facts is to protect faith against the suspicion of resting on illusion and arbitrariness."[84] Luther's insistence upon the clarity of the word of Scripture is applied to the clarity of history as bearing within itself its nature as revelation.[85]

The meaning of historical occurrence can ultimately be grasped only in terms of the total sweep of history, just as individual units of research are carried on in terms of a working hypothesis concerning their relation to an overarching concept. This universal scope may not however be permitted to weaken the recognition of the contingency of history. Hence the universality may not be conceived in terms of an evolutionary or morphological pattern to which history conforms. The tension one senses in retaining both values can be overcome by identifying a common base for universality and contingency. This cannot be the human, "since [the human's] spirit always exists only as an individual and for the individual."[86] Hence a transcendent ground in God is to be inferred by rational argumentation,[87] as an *a posteriori* confirmation of the Old Testament understanding of history. His freedom is the source of contingency, his faithfulness the source of continuity; the latter is visible to man only in retrospect, not in terms of a plan for the future. Hence only at the end of history will the total wholeness of contingent history be apparent. This position is identified with the Israelite-Christian view of God and history, which is thus the condition of the possibility of comprehending the unity and contingency of history.[88]

84. Pannenberg, "Heilsgeschehen und Geschichte," 275.

85. Ibid., 275–76. In criticism of this interpretation of Luther's emphasis on the clarity of Scripture, cf. Steiger, "Offenbarungsgeschichte und theologische Vernunft," 113.

86. Ibid., 284.

87. Geyer, "Geschichte als theologisches Problem," esp. 96–97 criticizes Pannenberg here to the effect that his position is "a postulate of historical reason," a "transcendental deduction of the concept of history." Pannenberg replies in his "Postscript" to the second edition of *Offenbarung als Geschichte*, 138 n. 15, that Geyer "fails to note that it is not only a matter of rational construction, but also of the presuppositions, in terms of the history of the transmission of traditions, for modern thought about history." Moltmann (*Theologie der Hoffnung*, 68 n. 98 = *Theology of Hope*, 77–78 n. 7) questions whether Pannenberg's procedure of inferring a doctrine of God from history, which Moltmann sees as parallel to the Greek procedure of inferring a first principle from the cosmos, is appropriate to the biblical understanding of history.

88. Pannenberg, "Postscript," 287. Cf. Geyer, "Geschichte als theologisches Problem," 98: "For the logical construction of that mode [sc. of retrospectively connecting events

Revelation as Word and as History   171

The historiographical execution of this program must take account of the fact that the meaning of universal history cannot be derived from a small segment of history, but only from the total sweep of history visible only at the end of history. Yet the role of Jesus' resurrection as the proleptic anticipation of that end of history to some extent removes it from the category of just a particular and makes of it the key for attaining a universal grasp of history before the end comes. Thus the historical proof of the resurrection can serve as a materially decisive model for Pannenberg's procedure, as an alternative to Bultmann's access to the resurrection in the existential encounter with the historic witness of the church.

Pannenberg takes his point of departure in a critical scrutiny of a basic principle of historical method, the use of analogy: comparison with what is already known provides a touchstone for evaluating the probability that a reported thing actually occurred and for establishing its specific contours. Pannenberg argues that at times an ideological element intervenes, in that we assume an overarching similarity of all phenomena, which in effect limits the freedom of history. Troeltsch had argued for the "principle similarity of all historical occurrence, which to be sure is not identity, but rather leaves all necessary room for differences, but for the rest presupposes in each case a kernel of common similarity, on the basis of which the differences are to be understood and tested."[89]

For Pannenberg, comparison is for the sake of establishing that which is individual and distinctive about the phenomenon under consideration. Hence such comparison may not be used to obscure that which is distinctive, by classifying it as just another instance of a given category. The result of this corrective is that the lack of historical analogy loses any decisive role in determining the historicity of an event.

> If analogies that have been found are used in this way in awareness of the limit of their validity, they hardly can serve in Troeltsch's way as the criterion for the reality of an event affirmed by the tradition. The fact that a reported event breaks the analogy of what

---

into a broader context], the claim of a transcendent ground is a superfluous axiom, to the extent that the categories of the unity of history and the individuality of the historical suffice as presuppositions."

89. Troeltsch, *Gesammelte Schriften*, 2:732, cited by Pannenberg, "Heilsgeschehen und Geschichte," 264.

is otherwise customary or frequently attested is not in itself sufficient grounds to contest its factuality.⁹⁰

Thus Pannenberg thinks he could overcome "the main argument against the historicity of the resurrection of Jesus."⁹¹ The common denial that the resurrection is *historisch* "rests on remarkably weak grounds."⁹² The argument from analogy can be used to indicate nonhistoricity only indirectly, in terms of finding formal analogies, i.e., "if in historical sources positive analogies to unreal forms of transmission (such as myths, but also legends) or [to unreal] phenomena of consciousness (such as visions) can be identified."⁹³ By arguing there are not such formal analogies for Jesus' resurrection, Pannenberg proposes to make room for it as an "event without analogy," as von Campenhausen argues,⁹⁴ without making it necessary to affirm it to be a miracle, as Bultmann found to be the case with von Campenhausen's position.⁹⁵

We can to some extent trace the way this proof of the resurrection has been subsequently carried out. In a public debate with Herbert Braun on February 19, 1965, Pannenberg presented a series of theses about Jesus'

---

90. Pannenberg, "Heilsgeschehen und Geschichte," 266.

91. Ibid., 266 n. 22.

92. Ibid.

93. Ibid., 267–68. For Pannenberg's subsequent adjustment of his position with regard to the appearances as visions, cf. *Grundzüge der Christologie*, 88–93 = *Jesus—God and Man*, 93–94, and below, 177–78.

94. Bowen, "Toward Understanding Bultmann," 34.

95. Pannenberg for his part rejects the concept of miracle as being in tension with the concept of creation. "If God were not the creator, then his will could be carried through in the world only through naked miracles, by eliminating all other forces affecting history. But his will is not done in this way at the expense of human activity, but is actualized precisely through the experiences, planning and action of men, in spite of and within their sinful distortion. Theological historiography, by laying hold of God's activity in such directness, i.e., by searching for relationships among occurrences, in concrete immanent circumstances (to be sure without interpreting away what is novel and more or less without analogy in events), witnesses to God as creator of the world," *KuD* 5 (1959) 288. In Pannenberg's opinion it would in any case be difficult to argue that an occurrence is to be regarded as miraculous in the common connotation of the term as referring to a breaking of the laws of nature. For with appeal to modern physics he argues: we do not know all the laws of nature; natural law controls only an aspect of events; the validity of natural law is itself contingent. Since the natural scientist can make no definitive judgment, the decision as to whether an unusual event occurred is left to the historian. *Grundzüge der Christologie*, 95–96 *Jesus—God and Man*, 97–99. Thus the miraculous as a functional category is eliminated from consideration.

resurrection that point the direction of a "theological historiography" that would provide the basis for a historical argument for the resurrection. He again identified as the major hindrance the ideological element in historiography that uses analogy to argue that the dead do not rise: "The contesting of the historicity of Jesus' resurrection is based *primarily* on general ideological considerations. In generalizing the experience that, as far as we can see, the dead remain dead, the possibility of a dead person becoming alive again, however it may take place, is precluded *a priori.*"[96] (Thesis 8.) Then the conditions that would have to be met to be able legitimately to classify the resurrection as an instance of a non-historical narrative or experience are so sharply defined as not only to place the burden of proof upon those who would deny its historicity but also to suggest that such a proof is not likely to succeed. Thesis 9 reads: "The traditions of Jesus' resurrection would be subject to evaluation as unhistorical if:

"a) the Easter traditions were demonstrable as *literarily secondary constructions* in analogy to common comparative religious models not only in details, but also in their kernel,

"b) the *Easter appearances* were to correspond *completely* to the model of self-produced *hallucinations* (owing to organic peculiarities or medicines),

---

96. The average reader probably takes this to be what is involved in Bultmann's position, since his emphasis has in fact been directed toward rejecting any historical description or proof of the resurrection and toward presenting instead its kerygmatic meaning as providing the Christian interpretation of the cross. Hence his talk of the Lord Jesus being encountered in the kerygma has perhaps been taken as more figurative than he really intends. Cf. the following statement in the discussion with von Campenhausen by Bowen, "Toward Understanding Bultmann," 37: "You are correct that 'the all-embracing effectiveness of the preaching of Christ is brought into question in so far as it does not give as its basis the real Christ event and as its goal the living fellowship with Christ.' We agree also 'that eternal life through the presence and future of Christ has a concrete eschatological dimension even beyond death.' And I agree when you characterize the hope as a real hope for a final victory over death and the fulfillment of the gift of fellowship and the new existence out of grace alone. This is no mythological speculation. I would only characterize a hope in this way that pictures objectively the new existence 'out of grace alone,' and that would be the case if one understood the new existence in eternal life as a once-for-all possession. But can it ever be anything other than a gift that continually retains its character as a gift? . . . In the new existence there is no more opposition [of "the old 'I,'" as "in earthly life, life in time"] (continual temptation). The distinctions end in the new existence, in eternity. Is that mythological speculation? I think not, even as surely as we must refuse every visualization."

"c) the tradition of the empty tomb of Jesus were to be evaluated as a late (Hellenistic) legend."

It is not an evaluation of the synoptic tradition that provides the basis of Pannenberg's argument for the empty tomb. His argument on this point is the historical rather than literary consideration that the church in Jerusalem would have had to reach clarity about the grave very early and hence can be safely assumed to have assured itself of its emptiness. "Even if the report we have of the finding of Jesus' grave should turn out to be a late legend conceived first in the Hellenistic church, the weight of the arguments presented [for this historical consideration] would remain intact."[97] Thus the proof of c) would not in fact disprove the empty tomb, which in any case is not a primary factor for Pannenberg in the argument for the resurrection.

With regard to condition a), which has in its background the question whether the appearances can be classified as instances of "unreal forms of transmission," such as myth or legend, Pannenberg points out the "penetrating material difference" between eschatological resurrection and revival of persons who return to normal earthly life and presumably will die again.[98] Some have affirmed on the basis of this distinction that only the latter of these conceptions was characteristic of apocalypticism and that Paul's concept of resurrection as transformation was his distinctive departure from apocalypticism. Pannenberg rejects this view, affirming that "Paul did not arrive at his view of the resurrection as transformation first under the impression of his encounter with the resurrected Jesus. The view of the differentness of the resurrection life as imperishableness, in distinction to the present perishable body, has Jewish parallels."[99] Thus, he is concerned to identify in a more than external way the Easter expectation with forms of expectation provided by Jewish apocalypticism.[100] "The fact that the completely other reality that was experienced in these appearances could be understood as the encounter with one risen from the dead can only be explained on the presupposition of a particular form of apocalyptic expectation of the

---

97. *Grundzüge der Christologie*, 99 = *Jesus—God and Man*, 101.

98. Ibid., 73 = 77.

99. Ibid., 77 = 81.

100. Pannenberg follows Gerhard Kittel in affirming there is "hardly the slightest trace" of the cults of dying and rising gods in first-century Palestine; ibid., 88 = 91.

resurrection of the dead."[101] This might seem to suggest that the reality experienced at Easter was not in itself a resurrection, but that "resurrection" was simply one of the languages in which it was interpreted.[102] And indeed Pannenberg can speak of "resurrection" or "rising" from the dead as a metaphor built upon the concept of rising from sleep. "Resurrection" can hence be called a "picture," a "parable," of the reality intended. "The intended reality and the way it is spoken about are essentially different.... Rather there is involved a parabolic way of speaking of an event that is still hidden from us in its true essence."[103]

At this point a person who, in distinction from Pannenberg, regards resurrection language as mythological, could think of demythologizing as a way of expressing this essence more comprehensibly than is possible in the language of apocalypticism. Or one might take the language in which the essence comes to expression somewhat more seriously than does Bultmann by regarding the whole as a language event in which the language is involved in the event, but can in turn give way to other language, as the point scored in the original language event is translated into new situations and thought forms. This would move in the direction of the hermeneutical theology of Gerhard Ebeling, who says on this point: "Both Jesus' assurance, becoming audible after his death, and faith's con-

---

101. Ibid., 89–90.

102. Willi Marxsen, *Die Auferstehung Jesu*, follows through this alternative in discussion with Ulrich Wilckens. Rather than describing the original experiences of the disciples as "appearances of the Resurrected" (cf. Pannenberg, ibid., 87), Marxsen thinks it is more accurate to describe them as experiences of recognizing Jesus, and hence as "appearances of the Crucified" (16). He points out that Paul, in describing his Damascus road experience, does not speak of an appearance of the Resurrected, but rather of "Jesus our Lord" (1 Cor 9:1), "God's Son" (Gal 1:15). It was then an inference, an interpretation, a way of bringing to expression the encounter with Jesus alive, when reflection as to how it was that he was encountered as alive led to the use of the apocalyptic language of resurrection. And Marxsen argues it was not the only such language. When appearances are interpreted as the commissioning of the disciples, resurrection language is lacking in early traditions, not only in Paul, but Matt 28:16–20 and John 20:19–23, although the merging of the two interpretations and their language does take place (Acts 10:40–42). From this role of resurrection language as only one of alternate interpretations of the appearances Marxsen concludes that "in the case of the resurrection one cannot in a real sense speak of a datum," but rather of an interpretation of the datum that the event of God that was taking place in the public ministry of Jesus, "which was really over with his death, began anew with the experience of seeing him" (33). To refer to resurrection as itself the event is a "forbidden historicizing of an interpretation" (34).

103. Ibid., 70.

currence that enters in upon that assurance, came to expression as Jesus' resurrection, since it is Jesus' life becoming revealed—to be sure by borrowing apocalyptic conceptualizations, and yet as the arrival of the eschaton already, which breaks down the essence of apocalypticism."[104] Yet Pannenberg maintains that this statement regards apocalypticism as "just any means of expression among others," and rejects it with the assertion "that this significance of the event, even if it 'breaks down' the apocalyptic expectation, could be expressed only in the language of the apocalyptic tradition and hence remains related to the apocalyptic horizon of expectations precisely in its uniqueness."[105] Apparently Pannenberg means by this that Easter remains related to apocalypticism in a sense that goes beyond the truism that a historical occurrence cannot escape from its original context; rather the implication is that the Easter event may not be translated completely out of apocalyptic categories by theology today. "Though apocalyptic portrayals of the end of the world may be false in many details, yet their main lines, the expectation of a resurrection of the dead in connection with the end of the world and the final judgment, remain true also for us."[106]

Pannenberg holds that resurrection is an "absolute metaphor." "It is metaphorical, and indeed in the sense of the 'absolute metaphor' that is not more or less interchangeable with other pictures and cannot be reduced to a rational kernel different from it, but is itself the only appropriate expression for a certain situation."[107] To some extent this is meant in the sense that metaphorical language is as near to reality as we can get, so that the metaphor is not to be transcended by rational conceptualization. In part the inescapability of metaphorical language seems to imply a literal reality that is not usually implied in the concept of metaphorical

---

104. Ebeling, *Theologie und Verkündigung*, 91, cited by Pannenberg, *Grundzüge der Christologie*, 93–94 = *Jesus—God and Man*, 95–96. Willi Marxsen, *Die Auferstehung Jesu*, 25–26, develops Ebeling's position by referring to the Easter message as "the carrying on of Jesus' subject matter," "set in motion by the experience of seeing him," for which the source Q is an instance. Incidentally, Q, like the *Gospel of Thomas*, lacks resurrection language (except in an Old Testament quotation, Luke 7:22). He presents this as an alternative to Wilckens' view, *Offenbarung als Geschichte*, 58–63, to the effect that Jesus' ministry was in need of God's ratification by the resurrection, which for Marxsen would make of the earthly Jesus "only a prelude," "the precursor of the Resurrected" (31–32).

105. *Grundzüge der Christologie*, 93–94 n. 94 = *Jesus—God and Man*, 96 n. 96.

106. Ibid., 78–79 = 82–83.

107. Ibid., 189 = 187.

language. Anthropological considerations of man's need to hope in an afterlife, which can today be conceived only in psychosomatic terms of the union of body and soul,[108] provide the argument for this literal apocalyptic ingredient in resurrection faith, which Pannenberg hence refers to as "an anthropologically interpreted apocalyptic expectation."[109] Thus the recognition that the Easter event conforms in its essence or kernel to a comparative religious model, the Jewish apocalyptic view, rather than implying nonhistoricity at the literal level, becomes part of an argument for retaining the main lines of the apocalyptic picture.[110]

With regard to the form of experience that would suggest nonhistoricity, Pannenberg speaks in Thesis 9 b) of hallucinations rather than visions, since subsequent to his negative evaluation of visions in "Redemptive Event and History" Hans Grass had convinced him the resurrection appearances were, in form, visions.[111] Hence the term "vision" is now taken to say "something about the subjective way of experiencing, but not something about the reality of the occurrence experienced in this

---

108. Ibid., 79ff. To this Johannes Wirsching, "Ein neues theologisches System?," 607, poses critically the rhetorical question: "The resurrection reasonable because it fits men's longing?"

109. Pannenberg, *Grundzüge der Christologie*, 104 = *Jesus—God and Man*, 107

110. An alternate position to that of the Pannenberg circle has been presented by Willi Marxsen, who argues that since "resurrection" is an interpretation derived from reflection on the fact of Jesus' appearances, we should work back through this interpretive process to come to grips with what was being interpreted and then seek to say in our language what that which was being interpreted means in our language today: "Since God resurrected Jesus, and since Jesus consequently is the Resurrected, then he did not remain in death. So he is the Living One. Hence his 'subject matter' is not ended with his death. Therefore what he brought is not simply past and lost to the past, but is also valid today still. Hence when I say Jesus has been raised, then this conviction those people gained by means of reflection is quite literally uninteresting so long as I do not say at the same time: He is the Resurrected because he, identical with the Earthly One, also still comes today with the same (old) claim. But if I say that, then I must clearly realize that I do not absolutely need to appropriate the concept 'the Resurrected,' but that I must indeed of necessity speak of 'the Living One.' And that is actually more, for to refer to him as 'the Resurrected' only gives him a designation, in a conceptualization provided by the history of religion, and this by moving onesidedly from the return of the Crucified to life to just this conceptualization given in the historical context." Marxsen, *Die Auferstehung Jesu*, 27. Thus Marxsen would understand the Easter kerygma to the effect that the "event of God" in the public ministry of Jesus has begun to happen again in the living Christ.

111. Pannenberg, *Grundzüge der Christologie*, 90 = *Jesus—God and Man*, 93, citing Hans Grass, *Ostergeschehen und Osterberichte*, 229.

form."[112] Visions lacking "extra-subjective" reality are hence designated "hallucinations"; but such nonobjective phenomena "only rarely" occur.[113] "Especially in the area of the history of religions, where it is always exceptional occurrences that are recounted, the psychiatric concept of vision [i.e., hallucination] cannot at all be postulated in cases where there are no more exact indications for that fact in the tradition."[114] Thus the possibility of proving the resurrection appearances to be hallucinations becomes very remote, and their conformity to the form of visions no longer weighs against their historicity.

---

112. Pannenberg, *Grundzüge der Christologie*, 91–92 = *Jesus—God and Man*, 94–95. In effect the indirect historical argument about an alleged incident's historicity, in terms of formal analogy to kinds of narration or experience, seems to be evolving into a more direct argument in terms of positive historical analogy. In a letter Pannenberg clarifies his position as follows: "Does not the formation of our concepts of myth, legend, and vision [sc. insofar as they imply nonhistoricity] rest precisely on positive analogies, in that we experience in the present that in the creation of legends today things are claimed that never happened (whereas instead something else happened). Hence where we find positive analogies in old traditions, we regard them likewise as legendary and are skeptical of their claims with regard to their having happened." Thus the argument against historicity would seem to rest less in the classification of a reported incident within certain narrational or psychological categories than upon the close similarities of the reported incident to a modern incident known to be nonhistorical. When such is lacking, as would often be the case, no argument from analogy would function.

113. Pannenberg, *Grundzüge der Christologie*, 91–92 = *Jesus—God and Man*, 94–95. Contrast the rejection of such considerations by Karl Barth, *Die Auferstehung der Toten*, 78 = *Resurrection of the Dead*, 137–38. "May it not be described as simple tactlessness, to make of 'He appeared,' or what takes its place in the Gospels (appearances of angels and subsequently personal meetings with Jesus), with the liberals, so-called visions (with the extraordinarily profound distinction between 'objective' and 'subjective' visions), or, with the 'positives,' equally banal 'historical facts,' respecting which one can refer to the 'sources' for support, as in the case of all other facts, with only the distinction that what happens here is marvellous beyond comparison and that one is constantly exposed to the danger of running into the arms either of the Scylla of a gross mythology or the Charybdis of a coarse or refined spiritualism—quite apart from the bad historical conscience which we would develop, and which might suddenly drive us once more to the liberal friends of visions! As if this 'positive' manner of asserting the resurrection of Jesus were not in fact the secret denial of the very thing we would fain assert, the resurrection as the deed of God, which no eye has seen nor ear heard, which has entered no human heart, neither outwardly nor inwardly, neither subjectively nor objectively, neither mystically nor spiritualistically nor flatly historically, but as a historic divine fact, which as such is only to be grasped in the category of revelation and in none other."

114. Pannenberg, *Grundzüge der Christologie*, 93 = *Jesus—God and Man*, 96.

The outcome of this remarkable tour de force is the claim of a proof of the historicity of the resurrection, which Pannenberg carefully formulates as follows:

> In this sense then the resurrection of Jesus is to be designated as a historical event: If the origin of primitive Christianity that, quite apart from other traditions, is traced back also by Paul to appearances of the resurrected Jesus, is, in spite of all critical testing of the tradition, intelligible only if one regards it in the light of the eschatological hope of a resurrection from the dead, then that which is so designated is a historical event, even though we do not know anything more specific about it. Hence an event is to be maintained to have happened historically that can only be expressed in the language of the eschatological expectation.[115]

This materially decisive instance of the relation of historiography to theology is the model for the general approach to the perennial problem of "faith and history." On this issue the alternative Bultmannian position is shared not only by Barthians, but also by such conservative Lutherans as Paul Althaus and Walter Künneth, namely that the resurrection is not historically demonstrable.[116] Bultmann comes to this position from the following considerations: For modern historiography, as for modern science in general, the "God hypothesis" is not necessary (Laplace).[117] Bultmann has no theological reason to contest this situation of modern science, since for him God, understood in terms of the theology of the cross, is known only paradoxically or dialectically. The meaning of history is furthermore not scientifically ascertainable, but is experienced by the person open to history in one's confrontation with it in current events, as a possibility for one's own living."[118] Thus Bultmann's position

---

115. Ibid., 95 = *Jesus—God and Man*, 98.

116. Cf., e.g., the reservation in the otherwise favorable reception of Pannenberg's programmatic essay by Ulrich Kühn, "Das Problem," 16, with regard to "a few daring formulations about the verifiableness of the historic saving action of God."

117. *Kerygma und Mythos*, VI, 1, 20; *ZThK* 60 (1963) 337 = *JThC* 2 (1965) 85.

118. Cf. *Kerygma und Mythos*, VI, 1, 22: "*Being future* is the reality in which man stands. This becomes clear in the history of mankind in that the historic meaning of an event always becomes intelligible only in terms of its future. The future belongs essentially to the event. Only from the end of history is consequently the meaning of historic occurrence finally intelligible. But since such a view from the end is impossible for human eyes, a philosophy that seeks to understand the meaning of history is not possible. One can speak of the meaning of history only as the meaning of the moment that has

involves a dialectic relation between the objective establishment of facts and of their traditional interpretation, on the one hand, and the existential encounter with current events or with the present witness to past events, on the other.

Pannenberg concedes there is "something correct" about the view behind the denial of the historical verifiability of Easter, to the effect that "the reality of the new aeon of course could not be perceived with the eyes of the old aeon; the historian has to judge in terms of the rules of the old aeon and hence can say nothing of the resurrection of the dead."[119] Yet to this view Pannenberg adds: "Since the life of the Resurrected has to do with the reality of a new creation, the Resurrected is indeed not perceptible as an object among others in this world. For that reason he could be experienced only by means of the exceptional kind of experience, the vision, and could be designated only in a symbolic language. But in this way he nonetheless made himself known in our reality, at a quite definite time, in a limited number of events, to certain specific persons. Hence these events are also to be affirmed or contested as historical events, as occurrences that actually took place at a quite fixed time in the past. If we were to give up the concept of a historical event, then it would no longer be possible to maintain that the resurrection of Jesus or the appearances of the resurrected Jesus really took place in our world at a given time. There is no valid ground to claim the resurrection of Jesus as an event that really took place if it is not as such to be maintained to be historical."[120]

From these historically verifiable facts man can gain knowledge of God, if such facts are not seen in isolation but in a context of traditions that speak of God in an "understandable way."

> *Then* it is true that in an event—not equally in every event!—God is *recognized again,* to be sure in a new way, in modified form; and only in this context and in this sense would one "infer" God from an event—to the extent that all recognition implies the logical structure of an inference.[121]

---

meaning as the moment of decision."

119. Pannenberg, *Grundzüge der Christologie,* 96 = *Jesus—God and Man,* 99.
120. Ibid.
121. Quotation is from a letter of clarification from Pannenberg. He apparently does not accept the distinction made, e.g., by Marxsen, ibid., 12: "The fact that in encountering Jesus during his lifetime one encountered God remains hidden to historical knowledge.

It is in this sense that revelation can be seen as history, once criticism of the presuppositions of historical method has produced a theological historiography, that is to say, a historiography maintained by theologians to be valid for all history. Systematic theology would provide a Christian view of history as a model or working hypothesis in terms of which the Christian historian would do his detailed research, with its conclusions in turn filling in and modifying that picture. Lest this remain a ghetto separating off the Christian historian from his secular colleague, Pannenberg would argue that the Christian working hypothesis is more adequate than that implicit in secular historiography. Thus the dualism of a sacred and a profane historiography would be overcome in theory by denying the validity of secular historiography at those points where the two diverge.

THE DEBATE IN OLD TESTAMENT SCHOLARSHIP

If a constitutive ingredient of the position here under discussion is the theological role it attributes to historical research, then one would expect that the issues can be presented in historical terms. This is especially true in the case of Old Testament research, where the school found its initial point of departure. One may compare the way in which Bultmannian theology can be debated in terms of New Testament research as well as in terms of contemporary theology. Indeed when Pannenberg was described[122] as having a "system" for which his colleagues in the historical disciplines only provided "preliminary studies," he clearly rejected such an "honor." "Rather the first impulse came from Rolf Rendtorff, who brought the problem of revelation into relation with Zimmerli's studies on the 'word about [God] demonstrating [himself]' (*Erweiswort*) and characterized this 'word of demonstration' as the most important contribution of the Old Testament to this question."[123] For Pannenberg's

---

Historical knowledge (i.e., historical exegesis) can always take note only of the claim of the witness to have encountered God in Jesus." Pannenberg has not yet made fully clear the step from the historical observation that an event occurred in a context in which people believed in God and his action to the theological knowledge by the historian that their belief is true, and the differentiation of such knowledge brought by the historian to the specific occurrence from the view, rejected by Pannenberg, that a theological understanding of the event is limited to the believer.

122. Lothar Steiger, "Offenbarungsgeschichte," 90-91.
123. "Postscript" to *Offenbarung als Geschichte*, 2nd ed., 132.

insight to the effect that contemporary theology means by revelation primarily the revealing of God himself[124] would seem to put in question not only a theology anthropologically oriented, but also one oriented to an understanding of history. It was Zimmerli's research on the "word of demonstration" that made it possible to interpret Old Testament history as a revelation about God himself.

Zimmerli's basic discovery came within the context of preliminary studies for a commentary on, of all things, Ezekiel, which he himself approached in Barthian terms of a theology of the word of God. His inaugural address as a Professor in Göttingen in 1951 had been on "The Word of God in the Book of Ezekiel,"[125] where Ezekiel's "call to genuine decision in the here and now" is God's word of promise answering man's word of despair or is a reactualizing of God's word given by an earlier prophet in terms of the new situation of the exile.[126] And the first major breakthrough in Zimmerli's form critical study of Ezekiel[127] seemed to point in the same direction: He discovered a "self-presentation formula," in which the deity introduces himself: "I am Yahweh." Although this formula was subsequently expanded with predications about Yahweh (". . . thy God," ". . . who brought thee out of the land of Egypt," etc.), the form critical analysis suggested to him that the brief form is prior, in that the formula is not intended to make predications about the god, but rather to present him.[128] We have to do with "the full, personal presentness of Yahweh in his word."[129] The very fact that Yahweh is described as raising his hand, i.e., taking an oath, as he gives his name, indicates that he is giving his

---

124. Pannenberg, ibid., laid before his group this factor in contemporary theology as still in need of adequate "grounding." Cf. his "Introduction" to *Offenbarung als Geschichte*, 7–20.

125. Cf. "Das Gotteswort des Ezechiel" = "The Word of God in the Book of Ezekiel." The title of Zimmerli's collected essays, *Gottes Offenbarung* ("God's Revelation"), is due to the inclusion of the same essays Rendtorff builds upon, which according to Zimmerli "inquire how God, according to the Old Testament witness, steps forward from his mystery and how human knowing is able to encounter him as he steps forward" ("Preface," 8). Thus the volume is intended to present thematically his alternative to Rendtorff, which his article "'Offenbarung' im Alten Testament," presents more in a form conditioned by the debate. For this reason (according to the Preface) the latter essay is omitted from the collected essays.

126. *Gottes Offenbarung*, 143ff.

127. "Ich bin Jahwe" = "I am Yahweh."

128. *Gottes Offenbarung*, 14.

129. Ibid., 17.

word. "This revelation of Yahweh's name is a revealing of God that happens to certain men, binds him to them, [so that he] remains true to them for the sake of his oath."[130]

Thus far Zimmerli's research could well have led him, e.g., in the direction of Ebeling's "word event," a term that in fact occurs in Zimmerli's writing.[131] Yet growing reserve about the Bultmannian alternative[132] and further research on Ezekiel led gradually into a somewhat different emphasis: God is faithful to his word by carrying out what he promises in history. Thus the history that God brings forth is the carrying out of the revelation of God's person that took place in revealing his name. History is seen not as an end in itself, leading to an "understanding of history," but rather as revealing God, and the focus of this revelation tends to shift from God giving his word to the history vindicating that word. "Yahweh's history with Israel is the place where the truth of his revelatory word is knowable in that it is carried out."[133]

Zimmerli works out this position in analyzing a larger formula in which the "self-presentation formula" is quoted: ". . . and they are to know that 'I am Yahweh.'"[134] This larger formula he calls the "cognition formula." It stands normally at the end of a prediction about God's action in history, through which the self-revelation in his name is vindicated. The addition of the "cognition formula" to the prophet's prediction turns the prediction about history into a "pointer to Yahweh's historic self-demonstration in his action, to be known by man."[135] This whole "prophetic word

---

130. Ibid., 21.

131. Ibid., 110. Cf. also, 86: "Old Testament faith is of the opinion that in such a report of Yahweh's deed a full re-actualization happens, in which complete, not just secondary, knowledge can be attained."

132. Zimmerli on occasion presents his position in rejection of terms that, though vague and anonymous, do point to Bultmann, or, more precisely, to the prevalent misunderstanding of his position. Ibid., 80: knowledge of God is not derived "from the analysis of man and the world's being"; ibid., 108: "all the prerequisites for knowing Yahweh do not lie in man and a pre-understanding to be found in him"; ibid., 109: "knowledge of God cannot be won by means of an analysis of the world's being and of its causer's being or an analysis of man's existence, nor can it be won by means of clarifying the world with a myth."

133. Ibid., 22.

134. Zimmerli, *Erkenntnis Gottes nach dem Buche Ezekiel* = "The Knowledge of God according to the Book of Ezekiel."

135. Zimmerli, "Das Wort des göttlichen Selbsterweises (Erweiswort), eine prophetische Gattung," = "The Word of Divine Self-manifestation (Proof-saying): A Prophetic

about God demonstrating himself" is a *Gattung* of prophetic speech that Zimmerli designates the "word of demonstration,"[136] i.e., the prophetic "word" to the effect that Yahweh will "demonstrate" himself to be God through historical occurrences that will take place. The basic instance of a "word of demonstration" is the prophet's speech in 1 Kgs 20:28: "And a man of God came near and said to the king of Israel, Thus says Yahweh, Because the Syrians have said, Yahweh is a god of the hills but he is not a god of the valleys, therefore I will give all this great multitude into your hand, and you shall know that 'I am Yahweh.'" Thus the "self-presentation formula," originally located in the priestly "service of the word" at a cultic shrine or in the temple, is embedded in the "cognition formula" that turns a prophet's prediction about history into a "word of demonstration of God," which is carried by the prophet out into the midst of life, there to vindicate its power in calling forth history.

Zimmerli understands his form critical research, i.e., his detection of the "self-presentation formula," the "cognition formula," and the "word of demonstration," in terms of a coordination of word and history. "The prophetic word of demonstration, where (with but few exceptions, in Ezekiel) the pure formula of self-presentation, 'I am Yahweh,' is used, is formulated in view of this occurrence in the worship service and understands itself as inwardly coordinated to it, even when it is spoken far from the shrine in the midst of battle (1 Kings 20). The truth of 'I am Yahweh' proclaimed back there in the congregation—the prophetic word now says—shows itself out here in the midst of the historic event, under the promissory word of the prophet (prophecy)."[137] Yet when the prophet's word points to "the historic proof for the truth of the claim that lives at the center in the worship service," i.e., "shows the truth and majesty of 'I am Yahweh,'"[138] then the role of the original proclamation "I am Yahweh" as full self-revelation might seem to some extent to be put in question. This relativizing of the word seems especially apparent when "the circle of people to whom the showing is to be visible cannot be limited to those directly addressed in the prophetic saying, but reaches far beyond,"[139] e.g.,

---

Genre"; quotation from *Gottes Offenbarung*, 124.

136. *Gottes Offenbarung*, 121.
137. Ibid., 126.
138. Ibid., 127–28.
139. Ibid., 128.

"all the trees of the field" (Ezek 17:24), "all flesh" (20:48), "all the inhabitants of Egypt" (29:6), "the nations" (36:23, 36; 37:28; 39:7, 23).[140] Here the structure of revelation seems to have shifted, contrary to Zimmerli's own intention, from a vindication of God's revelatory word by history into a revelation simply through historical occurrence itself.

It is in light of this research on Ezekiel and the "word of demonstration" that Rolf Rendtorff seeks to carry through the thesis that, for the Old Testament, God reveals himself primarily in history.[141] His positive presentation concerning revelation through history is prefaced with an analysis of such other Old Testament alternatives as might suggest revelation is to be separated from history. The Old Testament word that is most literally translatable as "revelation" can be safely ignored, since it is not a specifically theological term but is used primarily in nontheological contexts. In these cases even the Septuagint translation, *apokalyptein*, means simply "uncover."[142] Another verb, meaning "be seen," "appear," was originally used with cult etiologies, to legitimize a shrine as a place where a god was seen; but this verb is increasingly separated from such shrines and associated with promise and narration, i.e., it is historicized.[143]

---

140. Ibid., 131.

141. R. Rendtorff, "Die Offenbarungsvorstellungen im Alten Israel" = "The Concept of Revelation in Ancient Israel." Cf. the report and comment on Rendtorff by Gamper in Muschalek and Gamper, "Offenbarung in Geschichte," 186: "One can establish as the final outcome that knowledge of God is possible only on the basis of his historical action. (Is Zimmerli here correctly understood?)."

142. Zimmerli in his reply, "'Offenbarung' im Alten Testament," insists on 16, that such a formulation as Isa 22:14, "Uncovered is Yahweh Sabaoth in my ears," followed by an announcement of judgment in the form of an oath, is "not unimportant for determining the Old Testament's formulation of revelation." "The word of warning pressing forward to the occurrence, a word echoing in the ears of the prophet, is here said to be the place where God becomes revealed." Gamper in Muschalek and Gamper, "Offenbarung in Geschichte," 185, maintains that the secular and religious meanings are not as readily separable as Rendtorff would seem to assume.

143. Zimmerli, "'Offenbarung' im Alten Testament," 16-17, casts this development more in the direction of the shift from sight to audition. "As the really significant element there emerges the promissory announcement in word that points to coming occurrence. A further movement, e.g., away from word to pure occurrence, in which the word of promise in turn is devalued as something insignificant and preliminary, cannot be found in what has been treated thus far. A splitting of the word of promise and the occurrence it announces is in any case not suggested here." Similarly Günter Klein, "Offenbarung als Geschichte?" 68, argues that this development points to word rather than directly to history, in that the announcing of future deed is itself word, and in that Rendtorff himself, "Die Offenbarungsvorstellungen," 27 = "The Concept of Revelation," asserts

Another Old Testament concept that might come in question, the appearance of God's "glory," was originally located in the heavenly temple or its earthly equivalent (Isa 6:3), but was also historicized (Ps 97:6; Isa 40:5). Yet the priestly tradition does not share this location of the appearance of God's glory in historical occurrences, but rather regards the glory as "an entity of precise spatial dimensions, that comes down from heaven from time to time and in which Yahweh himself is present,"[144] either in connection with the cult,[145] or related to history—yet with a difference. "In distinction from the non-priestly tradition, 'seeing God's glory' does not here mean seeing his show of power directly; the glory appears rather in order to proclaim the imminent show of Yahweh's power."[146] This priestly understanding of God's glory as his appearance inaugurating[147] the cult or proclaiming what he is going to do is analogous to Zimmerli's understanding of the priestly "self-presentation formula" as God's self-revelation, or his emphasis on the revelatory role of the word even in the "word of demonstration" pointing to history. Yet Rendtorff regards the other view of God's glory, that it appears in "the obvious carrying out of

---

that attention is "not directed to a certain deed of the past," but rather assurance for the future is "attained from the *tradition* of Yahweh's saying acts" (italics by Klein), which is again word. (Rendtorff, however, also points to individual acts of the past, such as the Exodus.)

144. R. Rendtorff, "Die Offenbarungsvorstellungen," 29 = "The Concept of Revelation," 35

145. Ibid., 30–31 = ibid., 37–36. To be sure, even here Rendtorff discovers "an expressly historic function" of the glory, in that it institutes and thus legitimizes the cult. But is this not simply an instance of the original cultic etiological use of the term that was characteristic of its Canaanite origins?

146. Ibid., 30 = ibid., 35–36. It is unclear why Rendtorff adds: "Here the priestly alteration is especially evident. The glory has received such dignity that it remains in the background as the initiator of events, veiled in cloud." Is not this concept of God's glory rather a direct development of the original cultic context (cf. 29 = ibid., 35, where the "clouds" in Ps 97:2 are so understood), and more in agreement with the other aspect of the priestly use of the concept, in that the appearance limited to a cultic place becomes an appearance "only before the eyes of Israel" (31 = ibid., 37)?

147. R. Rendtorff (ibid., 30 = ibid., 37) seems to regard the role of God's glory in the cultic sense as "completed" once the cult is established, and rejects the view that there is "a self-revelation of God in the cult" (32 = ibid., 39). Although the Priestly Document, to which Rendtorff here makes reference, may not refer to God's glory continuing in the temple while the cult is in operation, this view would seem to be presupposed in priestly circles by Ezekiel.

his power" in the sight of "all flesh" (Isa 40:5) in history,[148] as the normative Old Testament position.

When Rendtorff then turns to Zimmerli's formulae, his presentation rapidly falls into the pattern of a criticism. Zimmerli had regarded "I am Yahweh" as a "formula of self-presentation," especially needed in the context of its polytheistic origin. "One previously unnamed comes forward out of his unknownness by making himself knowable and namable with his own name."[149] Rendtorff points out that this does not fit the *locus classicus* in the Old Testament, Exod 3:6, in that here God introduces himself to Moses as the God known to his fathers. "Obviously the reference back to the previous history of God with the fathers is the decisive element" in the formula, and it is coupled with a promise of events to come.[150] Hence Rendtorff argues that the brief version of the formula, consisting only of "I am Yahweh," is not the original form, as Zimmerli had assumed, but "a reduction of the expression to a formulation of extreme pregnancy."[151] To this Zimmerli replies that the short form occurs in prophetic oracles of the ninth century (1 Kgs 20:13, 28) and probably in the usage of the Yahwist, so that the argument of historical priority may be contested.[152] This form critical debate is an instance of the theological debate as to whether God's revelation is primarily in his word, with God being present[153] and thus revealing himself in the proclamation of the self-

---

148. Ibid., 29 = ibid., 34. Zimmerli in his reply, "'Offenbarung' im Alten Testament," 18, speaks rather of the "distinctive duplication" of God's glory in nature and history on the one hand and in the "verbal encounter" on the other and emphasizes that the latter is "something quite different from a merely human flow of words." In his "Postscript" to the 2nd ed. of *Offenbarung als Geschichte*, 132, Pannenberg refers to history as "a reality going beyond mere words." Thus the divergence is to a considerable extent over the meaning of the concept "word."

149. Zimmerli, *Gottes Offenbarung*, 11, cited by R. Rendtorff, "Die Offenbarungsvorstellungen," 33 = "The Concept of Revelation," 39.

150. R. Rendtorff, ibid., 33 = ibid., 39. Zimmerli does not think that this "logical contradiction" that "seems to result," alters the nature of the formula as one of self-presentation, "'Offenbarung' im Alten Testament," 20. E.g., in *Gottes Offenbarung*, 25, he says: "God presents himself as one already known by referring to what is already known or what has already happened."

151. R. Rendtorff, ibid., 34 = ibid., 40.

152. Zimmerli, "'Offenbarung' im Alten Testament," 20.

153. Zimmerli, ibid., emphasizes against Rendtorff that the formula presents (makes present) rather than represents (describes) God. In *Gottes Offenbarung*, 15, Zimmerli speaks of the "dissolution" of the formula of self-presentation "where the predication

presentation formula, or whether the revelation is primarily in history, to which the formula "I am Yahweh who . . ."¹⁵⁴ refers. Hence it is not surprising that at this point Pannenberg intervenes in the Old Testament debate to argue that since the early instances of the self-presentation formula to which Zimmerli appeals are all embedded in the cognition formula, they are to be regarded as abbreviations of the longer historical form of the self-presentation formula called for by Pannenberg's position.¹⁵⁵

Rendtorff focuses attention positively on one aspect of Zimmerli's presentation as "above all important": "The revelation of Yahweh is here not understood as if it were visible [only] to a certain group of people or as if there were special presuppositions for knowing it. All nations, 'all flesh,' the ends of the world see what happens, and it is intelligible to them all in its significance as Yahweh showing himself."¹⁵⁶ This emphasis leads Rendtorff to assume momentarily a position which they have

---

about the name Yahweh is put as an emphasized predicate before the whole formula of self-presentation and the name Yahweh is degraded to an attribute of the subject: 'Holy am I, Yahweh your God.'" Cf., also, 30. It is indicative of the different approaches that R. Rendtorff, "Die Offenbarungsvorstellungen," 33 = "The Concept of Revelation," and "Geschichte und Wort im Alten Testament," 628, states in criticism of Zimmerli that in some instances (e.g., Gen 26:24) the name Yahweh does not occur, even though such an exception cannot here be attributed to the Elohist, whereas Zimmerli, "'Offenbarung' im Alten Testament," 21, can appeal to the complete absence of a divine name in the "predicate" ("I am," Isa 48:12), to show that the formula is intended as one in which God presents himself rather than as one in which he characterizes himself or conveys information. Of course the reduction to "I am" is in form also a "dissolution" of the formula, Zimmerli, *Gottes Offenbarung*, 30.

154. Rendtorff is contesting the accuracy of Zimmerli's form critical analysis. E.g., he says of the use in sacral law, where the formula follows the legislation: "An understanding of the formula as one of 'self-presentation' is in any case excluded," "Die Offenbarungsvorstellungen," 35 = "The Concept of Revelation." In "Geschichte und Wort im Alten Testament," 628–29, he argues that the reference to history is constitutive of the formula as formula; in the royal psalms a predication in the third person ("Yahweh is king") seems to be the basic form. He does not accept Zimmerli's criticism that he had reduced the self-presentation formula to a neuter predication, since the formula in his view is insisting it is "Yahweh and no other who is spoken about," "Geschichte und Wort im Alten Testament," 628 n. 16. Perhaps by "neuter" Zimmerli had meant to refer to Rendtorff's focus upon something said about a person in distinction from his own focus upon the person presenting oneself.

155. *Grundzüge der Christologie*, 126 n. 29 = *Jesus—God and Man*, 128 n. 30. A somewhat parallel criticism is made by the systematician Jürgen Moltmann, *Theologie der Hoffnung*, 102–3 = *Theology of Hope*, 113–14.

156. *Offenbarung als Geschichte*, 38–39.

subsequently modified[157] when critics sensed it as the direction in which they were moving: the replacement of word with history, rather than an understanding of the two in their unity. "Especially in view of the nations that are to know Yahweh in his action from sunrise to sunset, a tying of revelation to the prophetic word seems to be from the very outset excluded."[158] In response to this Zimmerli comes nearest to an antithetic stance, which in general he has sought to avoid. "Where do these odd inferences come from, which quite obviously are not able to do justice to the Old Testament?"[159]

Rendtorff's idea of God's revelation in history apart from the word may well have come in large part from the Pannenberg group's antithetic relation to the theology of the word of God; but in this instance it would seem to be due as well to Zimmerli's presentation of Ezekiel.[160] In reply to Rendtorff, Zimmerli can say that in some instances (e.g., Ezekiel 25) the nations recognize Yahweh in history because of knowing about him in contacts with Israel. Yet Zimmerli concedes: "But alongside such sayings one may note that Ezekiel in his peculiar use of formulae, using obviously traditional phrases and expanding them greatly and using them in new contexts, supplies little express information as to how the name of Yahweh and his warning prediction come to the nations. That breaks through first in Second Isaiah, yet then with unmistakable clarity."[161] Second Isaiah defines Israel as "my witnesses" to the nations (43:10; 44:8). "An isolation of the occurrence effected by Yahweh from the word sent in advance is especially in Second Isaiah an exegetically untenable undertaking."[162] Just as Second Isaiah opens with the word of Yahweh that remains forever (40:8), it concludes with a concept of the

---

157. Especially in Rendtorff's reply to Zimmerli's article, Rendtorff begins by quoting Zimmerli to the effect that history is not to be separated from the word and saying that he agrees "completely," "Geschichte und Wort im Alten Testament," 622. Cf. below, 195.

158. "Die Offenbarungsvorstellungen," 40 = "The Concept of Revelation," 45-46.

159. Zimmerli, "'Offenbarung' im Alten Testament," 24.

160. Cf. above, 184-85, at notes 139, 140.

161. Zimmerli, "'Offenbarung' im Alten Testament," 24.

162. Ibid., 25. Here Moltmann, *Theologie der Hoffnung*, 104 = *Theology of Hope*, 115-16, shares Zimmerli's criticism. Cf. also Schweizer, cited above, 161, and Gamper in Muschalek and Gamper, "Offenbarung in Geschichte," 188. In reply Rendtorff points out, "Geschichte und Wort im Alten Testament," 628, in Zimmerli's words, that Israel witnesses to what God has done.

word effecting history that Zimmerli appropriates: "It shall not return to me empty, but it shall accomplish that which I purpose, and prosper in the thing for which I sent it" (55:11).

Zimmerli does not simply throw the Old Testament concept of the word over against that of history, but rather seeks to provide a definition of the Old Testament understanding of history in continuity with that of the word. Word is "itself occurrence that moves the world and history"; conversely "occurrence is actualized word, proclamation made good."[163] This means with regard to history: "It does not carry hidden within it a secret meaning that man can figure out by means of his own capacity to interpret. Rather God can make it become a living appeal to man by sending a spokesperson who names Yahweh's name upon this event."[164] This view of history is more precisely stated as follows: "This faith understands that the historic rescuing act over which Yahweh's name is proclaimed is an aimed occurrence, which is not intended to be understood in the connection of a historic whole, but rather to be heard today as a call under Yahweh's name, and is to be understood and responded to in reverent and believing obedience."[165] Rendtorff in turn denies one must choose between such alternatives. "Precisely in the prophets it is quite clearly discernible that their retrospective views of history and talk of Yahweh's plan, etc., are intended to prepare their contemporaries to recognize the imminent event as Yahweh's action."[166] Yet there do emerge different judgments as to which is primary for the Old Testament, with Rendtorff finding that prophets interpret all the better the further they have an overview of history—so that degrees of knowledge of God are related to the extent of history in one's vision, and complete knowledge possible only at the end of history—and Zimmerli finding the focal Old Testament emphasis to be that upon the importance of "proclaiming into the very hour," "calling for faith"[167]—so that one would not speak of degrees of knowledge, but rather of whether the word strikes home and produces faith.

163. Zimmerli, "'Offenbarung' im Alten Testament," 25. R. Rendtorff, "Geschichte und Wort im Alten Testament," 622, accepts Zimmerli's formulation.

164. Zimmerli, "'Offenbarung' im Alten Testament," 28–29.

165. Ibid., 29.

166. R. Rendtorff, "Geschichte und Wort im Alten Testament," 622–23, and esp. 640.

167. Zimmerli, "'Offenbarung' im Alten Testament," 29.

In view of Rendtorff's unwillingness to see in "I am Yahweh" a revelation of God in his name, Zimmerli senses "the degeneration of language and hence also of [the understanding of the role of] naming in our time."[168] Pannenberg had indeed in his introduction to *Revelation as History* drawn attention to antiquity's identification of the name with the being, as the context of the Barthian location of the revelation of the person in the disclosure of the name. "But the meaning of announcing the name in Exodus 3 is precisely not that from now on the Israelites know Yahweh's essence completely. The communication of Yahweh's name takes place—as 3:15 expressly says—for the purpose of being able to *call on* Yahweh with this name. An important event—Israel thus received the possibility of communion with Yahweh! But this is not self-revelation in the sense of full self-disclosing."[169] Thus the revealing of Yahweh's name is not for Pannenberg itself self-revelation, but is subordinate to the self-revelation to take place in history. When the revealing of God's name is put in the context of a "word of demonstration" of God in history to come (Exod 6:7), Rendtorff can emphasize the importance of the new event at the burning bush.

> Finally the concept of Yahweh showing himself is obviously sensed as inappropriate in general. . . . In Exod 6:3 one reads: "I let myself be seen by Abraham, Isaac and Jacob as God Almighty, but did not make myself known to them by my name Yahweh." Here knowing is set over against seeing, and there can be no doubt but that this takes place quite consciously in the careful terminology

---

168. Ibid., 23. Zimmerli's own presentation of the role of divine names in *Gottes Offenbarung*, 127–28, could itself have suggested to Rendtorff his position. For Zimmerli had contrasted the non-Israelite concept of name as the deity's power, where discovering the god's name means access to his power (e.g., in the Egyptian myth of Isis and Re), and where the glorification of the god consists in multiplying divine names (e.g., in the case of Marduk), with the Israelite view: "The whole display of the glory of the self-presentation in the name is awaited by Israel from Yahweh's historic action." R. Rendtorff, "Geschichte und Wort im Alten Testament," 643, 648, also points out that the potency of the divine word is a concept current in the ancient Near East, which would suggest that it is basically a mythological concept and not distinctive of Israel.

169. Pannenberg, *Offenbarung als Geschichte*, 13 = "Introduction," 9–10. Contrast Zimmerli, *Gottes Oftenbarung*, 17: "the full personal presentness of Yahweh is his word." Similarly Gamper in Muschalek and Gamper, "Offenbarung in Geschichte," 185, expresses his disagreement with Pannenberg's evaluation. Gerhard von Rad, *Theologie des Alten Testaments*, 1:182 = *Old Testament Theology*, 1:180, interprets the passage as a rejection of a "definition of Yahweh's essence in the sense of a philosophical statement about his being."

of the Priestly Document. Yahweh's being seen is relegated to a preliminary stage. With Moses something new begins: Yahweh gives himself to be known as *himself*.[170]

Zimmerli describes this, understandably enough, as a "beautiful observation"[171] on Rendtorff's part. But Rendtorff himself did not understand the priority of God's name in terms of the primacy of the word of God, but rather in terms of history (the "name" pointing ultimately to the Exodus) vs. theophany (which could however include a religious experience manifesting God's hypostatized name,[172] in distinction from historic occurrences from which God's name, i.e., might and deity, can be inferred). That is to say, he interprets the passage in line with Pannenberg's value structure.

An emerging focus upon the "history of the transmission of traditions" provides the possibility of transcending the alternative thinking that necessitated the question of the relative priority of prophetic word or historic occurrence. Indeed Rendtorff and Zimmerli seem both to wish to insist upon "event in the context of the history of the transmission of traditions."[173] This seems to function for Rendtorff as the integrating factor pulling together all the various kinds of history that come into question: the past history about which the stories tell, the contemporary history that molds the way the stories are told, and the history of the transmission itself as the central stream in Israel's cultural and intellectual history.[174] Here the model is the period prior to the amphictyony,

170. R. Rendtorff, "Die Offenbarungsvorstellungen," 25 = "The Concept of Revelation," 29–30.

171. Zimmerli, "'Offenbarung' im Alten Testament," 17. In *Gottes Offenbarung*, 44, the verbs for seeing and knowing had been described as "parallel" and "analogous."

172. Zimmerli, *Gottes Offenbarung*, 34, had called this "theophany." But he refers on 40 to the "further development within priestly literature, in which the element of epiphany recedes and the self-presentation formula is clearly to be located in the worship services oriented to the word," as the reemergence of a basic trait of the Yahweh cult. "Mowinckel's rejection of the *culte de la parole* [service of the word] cannot be maintained as sharply as he did." Cf. also, *Gottes Offenbarung*, 26.

173. R. Rendtorff, "Die Offenbarungsvorstellungen," 40 = "The Concept of Revelation," 46. Rendtorff quotes this formulation later, "Geschichte und Wort im Alten Testament," 622, to document his basic agreement with Zimmerli in this regard.

174. This was first suggested in an essay, "Hermeneutik des Alten Testaments als Frage nach der Geschichte," on which cf. my essay: Robinson, "The Historicality of Biblical Language," 130–31. Rendtorff has presented a more advanced statement in his essay, "Geschichte und Überlieferung."

which in the sense of political history is rather prehistoric, but where the decisive historic occurrences that can be discerned were precisely the development and merging of traditions, which is the basic thing the tribes were "doing" as they came together.

> On all sides it becomes clear that the origin and development of traditions is an essential component of Israel's history. Indeed the occurrences really effecting history are often to be found here, occurrences that determine Israel's history over and beyond the fluctuation in political conditions.[175]

> Hence with regard to the question as to God's action in Israel's history we will not rest content with the alternative between what critical historical research works out and the picture of history painted in the Old Testament. The history of Israel takes place in the external procedures that are customarily the object of the critical historical study of history *and* in the many inner procedures in many layers that we summarize in the concept of tradition. Only the total picture resulting from both shows in the full sense Israel's history.[176]

Rendtorff thus proposes to overcome the usual compartmentalization within Biblical studies into "History of Israel," "Introduction to the Old Testament," and "Theology of the Old Testament," under the uniting concept of the "history of the transmission of traditions."[177] And Pannenberg can say that "the history of the transmission of traditions" is "to be classed in general as the more profound concept of history."[178]

The understanding of the history of the transmission of traditions in the school of von Rad should hardly give consolation to the traditionalist, for the frequency of the mutations of the tradition is clearly emphasized in Volume 1 of his *Old Testament Theology*, which is devoted to *The*

---

175. R. Rendtorff, "Geschichte und Überlieferung," 88.
176. Ibid., 93-94.
177. Ibid., 94.
178. Pannenberg, "Kerygma und Geschichte," 139. Cf. the criticism by Moltmann, *Theologie der Hoffnung*, 101 = *Theology of Hope*, 112: "This occurrence of transmission, by means of which continuity is created in the fluctuations of history, cannot be taken as itself a deeper concept of history. The procedure of transmission in which one recalls history and has new historic experiences is only intelligible from what is transmitted; the promise, and the events' future it opens up."

Theology of Israel's Historical Traditions.[179] When correctly understood, the method of *Traditionsgeschichte* is as critical as is *Formgeschichte* (whose English translation "form criticism" is quite appropriate), even though both differ from the antecedent historical criticism in that the question as to the historicity of the events narrated in the tradition is for the most part bracketed (although there is indirect relevance to this issue). There is, however, something of a divergence of focus between *Traditionsgeschichte* and hermeneutic. In the former case the focus is upon a tradition, and the point being scored in any given narration of that tradition is investigated primarily as an influence in the forming of it. But it is not such a point that is followed up by this method, but rather the course of the given tradition, so that one traces continuity in the material used even where the points being scored stand in extreme discontinuity. The false prophets assuring Ahab victory at Ramoth-gilead (1 Kgs 22:10-12) are an instance of the holy war amphictyonic tradition in Israel.[180] Conversely hermeneutic has as its focus what happens when the language is used, the point being scored, so that it tends to be open to finding continuity where there is no continuity of tradition, from which results the problem of "anonymous Christianity."[181] This divergence of emphases can also be seen in the way in which those oriented to hermeneutic emphasize the verbal meaning of tradition, i.e., transmission, that aspect that can best be coordinated with the translational process taking place in the ongoing language event.[182]

---

179. *Theologie des Alten Testaments,* vol. 1 = *Old Testament Theology,* vol. 1.

180. Cf. R. Rendtorff, "Erwägungen zur Frühgeschichte des Prophetentums in Israel," 155-56: "In the context of our inquiry we may not without further ado take our point of departure in the answer that the prophets give, but must initially inquire again as to the tradition lying behind it. Obviously inquiring of Yahweh before an expedition is also rooted already in the tradition of holy war. . . . Obviously the difference between Micaiah the son of Imlah and the other prophets is not in terms of the tradition in which he stands. The contrast is rather in terms of the different evaluations of the war. . . . Of course one may not play down the contrast. The problem of 'false prophets' occurs here for the first time. But the debate is not concerning different forms of prophecy. Rather it receives its acuteness precisely due to the fact that both opposing prophets or groups of prophets are rooted in the same tradition, that of the amphictyony."

181. Cf., e.g., Ott, "Existentiale Interpretation und anonyme Christlichkeit," 367-79.

182. Gadamer, *Wahrheit und Methode,* 275 = *Truth and Method,* 290, uses the term *Überlieferungsgeschehen* (the "occurrence of transmission") to make this emphasis (compare Bultmann's shift from *Heilsgeschichte* to *Heilsgeschehen*). Cf. also, 355 (cited above, 135). Gerhard Ebeling, *Theologie und Verkündigung,* 14-15 (cited above, 128),

Rendtorff had completed his essay in *Revelation as History* with an explicit attempt to do justice to the fact that "the word has here an essential share in the occurrence of revelation."[183] Yet it was this brief discussion that had drawn the most criticism. Hence Rendtorff replied with an article, "History and Word in the Old Testament,"[184] which seeks more fully to explicate his position. He begins by pointing out that what he is denying is the necessity for the intervention of a prophet's word for an event to become revelatory, and that his rejection here of the term "word" does not involve a denial of the necessity for tradition.[185] Israelite narrators stood in a tradition, and so the conviction that Yahweh acts in history was "the presupposition on the basis of which it first became possible at all to speak meaningfully of history."[186] What is needed is not an inspired interpreter, such as an apocalyptic seer like Daniel. Instead, the Jewish tradition supplies the interpretation, which is now recognized to be a necessary presupposition. This presupposition is necessary for the nations as well as Israel—as indeed the Bible has functioned as a hermeneutical key within gentile Christianity. Although Rendtorff makes here no allusion to his previous statement, he seems to have given up what he initially regarded as "above all important," that the nations also know Yahweh from history and hence this knowledge "is not in need of special presuppositions."[187] Even though Zimmerli wishes to speak of this presupposition in Barthian vocabulary as the word, while Rendtorff speaks in terms of the history of the transmission of traditions, the area of disagreement would seem to have narrowed. Indeed Rendtorff moves

---

emphasizes the verbal element in the Latin noun *traditio* by setting it off against the term *traditum*, the unambiguous term for the substantial meaning, "what is transmitted." Cf. also, Ebeling's book, *Wort Gottes und Tradition*.

183. "Die Offenbarungsvorstellungen," 40 = "The Concept of Revelation."

184. "Geschichte und Wort im Alten Testament." It is in the form of a lecture, and hence only in the extended footnotes does he explicitly speak to his critics' points.

185. Ibid., 623.

186. Ibid., 635. Cf. also, 629: It is from the divine instruction and reassurance that "the occurrence is knowable as divine action." In "Geschichte und Überlieferung," p. 90, he says: "If we today seek to know God's action, how are we to establish where he acted if Israel's interpretation may not serve us as a guide line?" Cf. above, note 57.

187. R. Rendtorff, "Die Offenbarungsvorstellungen," 38–39 = "The Concept of Revelation," 45.

away from his original restriction of the term "word" to a prophet's proclamation, in which context he had denied it to be a necessary presupposition, and concludes by suggesting that the indispensable tradition can be so designated.[188]

Yet Rendtorff proceeds to draw the concept of tradition into a more functional relationship with a different concept, that of the divine plan for history. He draws attention to presentations (such as the histories of David's rise to power and of the struggle as to his successor, and the story of Joseph) in which the events are not correlated to a prophet's word,[189] but are understood in their theological meaning simply on the basis of the tradition. Here the connection between tradition and contemporary occurrence was mediated by the "insight" "that in every instance what Yahweh had willed and planned happens."

188. R. Rendtorff, "Geschichte und Wort im Alten Testament," 623, 649. Klein, "Offenbarung als Geschichte?," 68–70, argues that the various historical insights of Rendtorff point to an orientation in terms of word rather than history. The primary intention of the "cognition formula" is not to convey historical information about what Israel's opponents knew in encountering Israel, e.g., that Israel's God is the true God. Rather the formula functioned primarily within the subsequent life of Israel as a word of assurance. With regard to Old Testament statements about history, the question as to whether they refer to historical fact in distinction from themselves as an event of language often remains an open question. (Compare Christian Hartlich and Walter Sachs, *Der Ursprung des Mythosbegrifles in der modernen Bibelwissenschaft*, 157–58). Since the context of traditions is indispensable for a new occurrence to be revelatory, Klein concludes it is these traditions, i.e., word, that provide the revelatory dimension.

189. Pannenberg, "Heilsgeschehen und Geschichte," 221, in dependence on von Rad, had presented the situation differently: "In the beginning stands the promise to David by the prophet Nathan, the assurance of a continuation of the Davidic dynasty. Everything reported in what follows stands under the question: Who will be successor to the throne? How will the promise be fulfilled? Often it seems as if the promise will go unfulfilled. Finally with Solomon's enthronement the fulfillment is there." R. Rendtorff, "Geschichte und Wort im Alten Testament," 633–34 n. 27, suggests the reverse: "It is striking that both of the stories about prophets, 2 Sam. 7 and 12, are, to be sure, used in important positions, but that the authors do not suggest with a single word that the words of Nathan had had any significance for the course of the events." Probably Pannenberg has here interpreted the scope of the narrative better than has Rendtorff, who is seeking to carry through his thesis of the replacement of prophetic word with the divine plan. Rendtorff himself conceives of the sensitivity for a divine plan as due to tbe conviction that prophecy was inevitably fulfilled; thus the same assumption that led to the Davidic historiography can hardly be denied to have been implicit in the narration itself. Gerhard von Rad, *Theologie des Alten Testaments*, 1:314 = *Old Testament Theology*, 1:316, also draws an inverse inference from that initially characteristic of the Pannenberg circle: Since in such narratives Yahweh does not intervene in the form of the miraculous but acts only implicitly in all occurrence, his control of history "is fully hidden to the natural eye."

Attention to Yahweh's plan, which was carried out in the interrelations of occurrences, could have arisen precisely from the experience with Yahweh's word. If in Israel one experienced again and again that what had been announced by a word of Yahweh happened, then this could—one must almost say must—lead to the insight that in every instance what Yahweh had willed and planned happens. It was then no great step when in a different spiritual situation the inference was drawn that one is to speak of Yahweh's action and the realization of his plan even where no word of Yahweh expressly announcing this action had gone before. In any case one may not simply set up an antithesis between these different views.[190]

If thus tradition, by bringing individual instances of divine guidance together into a divine plan, can replace the prophet's word as the key to interpreting current events, it becomes questionable to Rendtorff whether the Old Testament concept of the word of God (that carried through what it says and does not return empty, Isa 55:10-11) is really to be identified with the individual prophet's word, and not rather with the divine plan.[191] Israelites knew that many specific predictions by prophets went unfulfilled; it was rather "the whole of the prophetic proclamations of doom that fulfilled themselves in Israel's fate.[192] In postexilic prophecy, words directed to specific concrete events "fade more and more into the background and finally disappear completely."[193] Thus both the individual prophet's word and even the individual event are subsumed under a "conception of history,"[194] a development that leads into apocalypticism, in terms of which the New Testament is to be understood.[195]

---

190. R. Rendtorff, "Geschichte und Wort im Alten Testament," 636.

191. Ibid., 644.

192. Ibid., 645.

193. Ibid.

194. Ibid., 648.

195. The argument to the effect that apocalypticism is a positive continuation of the Old Testament view of history (on which cf. also Koch, "Spätisraelitisches Geschichtsdenken"), and is the presupposition for the New Testament, is provided by Dietrich Rössler, *Gesetz und Geschichte*. For a criticism of Rössler, cf. Philipp Vielhauer, in "Apocalyptic Christianity," in *Neutestamentliche Apokryphen*, 3rd ed., 2:416-17 = *New Testament Apocrypha*, 2:594-95. The debate revolves largely around the extent to which the concept of two aeons is constitutive of apocalypticism.

We may conclude this section on the Old Testament by pointing out how the debate carried on primarily by Rendtorff and Zimmerli, while moving within the dimensions of technical Old Testament research, has at the same time been a debate within German theology as to the relation of history and word. Both sides maintain they advocate a unity of the two, and tend to reject as misunderstandings such criticisms as suggest they are advocating one at the expense of the other. Yet each side tends to approach this unity from one or the other term, and hence the degree of success attained by each approach is, in terms of an internal criticism, the extent to which each provides a theological conceptualization that does justice to that unity. For clarity's sake one may express the diverging emphases in terms of summaries that, while not including all the comprehensive statements from both sides or the potential developments of thought suggested above, yet do indicate the gravitational centers: Rendtorff has tended to locate the revelation primarily in history, in which the word is grounded and that in turn confirms the word so that knowledge of God takes place; or to define history as including the word in the form of the history of the transmission of traditions; or to see the valid claims of the word met in the form of an overarching plan of history. Zimmerli has tended to locate the revelation primarily in the (prophetic) word, which calls forth history and recalls history so that knowledge of God takes place; i.e., the occurrence of the word is itself the decisive historic event.

THE DEBATE IN CONTEMPORARY THEOLOGY

The discussion of the position of the Pannenberg circle broadened out into a general theological discussion with the appearance of the symposium, *Revelation as History,* consisting of papers presented at their semiannual meeting in October 1960.[196] In his introduction[197] Pannenberg points out that the Enlightenment destroyed the concept of revelation as involving revealed truths, but that Hegel redefined the term as the revelation of God's own person. Pannenberg argues that for this to be a complete revelation it must be God himself who reveals himself, so that it is from his role as complete revealer of God that the deity of Jesus is to be inferred. Now for Pannenberg the Bible does not have the concept of a direct self-revelation of God; e.g., appearances of God in the cult and in the prophetic word are divine manifestations but do not reveal God in his essence, except perhaps in the view of the Gnostic fringe of the New Testament (the Gospel of John). Rather one has "an indirect self-revelation [of God] in the mirror of his action in history."[198] "Indirect" does not refer to mediation by some third party. Indeed Pannenberg is concerned to emphasize that a prophet is not needed to add an interpretation to the event. Rather "indirect" means that the actual content of the revelatory experience, e.g., history, is not identical with what the experience is intended to reveal, namely, God himself, who is rather to be inferred indirectly from the historical event. Thus revelation is the inferential insight "that God is such a person as to do this and that."[199] To be sure this would seem to lead to an infinite number of revelations, since there are an infinite number of events. Yet this would be contrary to Pannenberg's concept that revelation, if it is to be the complete revelation of the one God, must be single. Hence it is only the *whole* of history in its unity and totality that reveals God, as was first recognized by Hegel, from whom Pannenberg derives his key term, universal history.

196. Pannenberg, ed., *Offenbarung als Geschichte* = *Revelation as History*, with an "Introduction" by Pannenberg, followed by four essays: R. Rendtorff, "Die Offenbarungsvorstellungen im alten Israel" = "The Concept of Revelation in Ancient Israel"; Wilckens, "Das Offenbarungsverständnis in der Geschichte des Urchristentums" = "The Understanding of Revelation within the History of Primitive Christianity."; Pannenberg, "Dogmatische Thesen zur Lehre von der Offenbarung" = "Dogmatic Theses on the Doctrine of Revelation"; and Trutz Rendtorff, "Das Offenbarungsproblem im Kirchenbegriff" = "The Problem of Revelation in the Concept of the Church." The second edition includes a "Postscript" by Pannenberg. The journal, *Kerygma und Dogma*, which published the symposium as a special supplement, has its center in Heidelberg, and represents by and large the tradition out of which the Pannenberg circle emerged.

197. Pannenberg, "Einleitung," 7-20.

198. Ibid., 15.

199. Ibid., 17.

After the approach of this symposium had been carried through for the Biblical material by Rendtorff and Wilckens, Pannenberg gives focus to the position with a series of "Dogmatic Theses on the Doctrine of Revelation":[200]

1. God's self-revelation, according to the Biblical witnesses, did not take place directly, e.g., as a theophany, but rather indirectly, through God's acts in history.

2. The revelation does not take place at the beginning, but rather at the end of revelatory history.

3. In distinction to special appearances of the deity, the revelation in history is open to everyone who has eyes to see. It has universal character.

4. The universal revelation of God's deity is not yet actualized in Israel's history, but rather first in what happened to Jesus of Nazareth, in that there the end of all occurrence took place proleptically.

5. The Christ event does not, as an isolated occurrence, reveal the deity of Israel's God, but only to the extent that it is a part of God's history with Israel.

6. The development of non-Jewish concepts of revelation in the gentile Christian churches brings to expression the universality of God's eschatological self-demonstration in what happened to Jesus.

7. The "word" is related to revelation as prediction, guidance, and report.

Pannenberg had worked out this position to some extent in terms of a criticism directed against the confessional Lutheran position, according to which God's "manifestation" in history was in need of supplementation by his "inspiration" in prophet, apostle, and Scripture. Hence it is not surprising that the leading contemporary advocate of that tradition, Paul Althaus, would, in spite of all appreciation for the anti-Bultmannian position of Pannenberg, argue that Pannenberg had gone too far in the opposite direction and had "missed" "the genuine nature of revelation."[201]

---

200. Pannenberg, "Dogmatische Thesen," 91–114. The theses quoted here stand in italics at the opening of each subsection commenting upon them.

201. "Offenbarung als Geschichte and Glaube," esp. 323.

He argues that faith is both knowledge and trust, and that such faith is effected by the work of the Holy Spirit. When Pannenberg says the revelation in history is visible to "uninhibited perception" and attributes its nonacceptance to man's reason being affected by sin, Althaus argues that this is "inadmissible anthropological rationalizing,"[202] since it is inherent in God's nature that his revelation should involve his hiddenness. Yet Althaus simply leaves the act of faith unintelligible.

Pannenberg's answer is entitled, "Insight and Faith."[203] He acknowledges that the relation between knowledge of revelation on the one hand and faith and the Holy Spirit on the other is the major problem in his proposal. And he agrees that faith is a gift of God, the only question being whether this is "through the mediation of a demonstrable knowledge of what happened to Jesus and of its significance," or whether the work of the Spirit is "just a subjective reassurance."[204] He also agrees that "faith" can be regarded as the overarching category that includes knowledge (Protestant orthodoxy's *notitia* plus *assensus*) and trust (*fiducia*). But he points out that this broader use of "faith" should not be permitted to obscure the question as to whether knowledge grounds trust or the reverse. He holds that if certainty concerning the contents of faith were grounded in man's decision to believe, then faith would ground itself, which would be "the corruption of the correct understanding of Christian faith."[205] "If [the gospel's] truth does not convince my judgment, then its acknowledgement does indeed become a matter of resolve, and thus we would arrive again at the ruinous consequence that faith grounds itself and thus destroys what is essential to it, which is to hang upon a truth outside itself."[206] And indeed when Althaus adds to the definition of "revelation as history" the phrase, ". . . and faith," one can sense that faith tends to become simply a human disposition blunting the rigor of critical rational reflection, an ideological prejudice one brings to the facts so as to be able to recognize them as revelatory. The Holy Spirit seems then a *deus ex machina*, or, as Pannenberg puts it, an *asylum ignorantiae*.[207]

202. Ibid., 327–28, citing Pannenberg, "Dogmatische Thesen," 101.
203. Pannenberg, "Einsicht and Glaube."
204. Ibid., 81.
205. Ibid., 83–84.
206. Ibid., 85.
207. Ibid., 90.

Pannenberg provides a more adequate focus for a modern interpretation of the work of the Spirit: "The Spirit is not added to the gospel as some supplement. Rather the proclaimed eschatological occurrence and, derived from it, the carrying out of the preaching of the gospel, is itself Spirit-filled. Hence the hearer receives a share in the Spirit in that he receives a share in the subject matter of the Gospel, in that he trusts in what he has heard."[208] The verification of the word takes the form of the verification of the history to which it witnesses. "The question as to whether the gospel that is proclaimed to me is true can only be answered from its content, by pointing to what it reports and the meaning inherent in the reported occurrence."[209] This leads to Pannenberg's historical demonstration, which for him includes not only the facts but also their saving meaning for the participants, as well as such nonpositivistic historical facts as the incarnation and resurrection of Jesus.

The only other alternative would seem to be "self-redemption by means of the so-called decision of faith," "frivolity and superstition," "arbitrary faith."[210] It is difficult to see how Althaus' position can be freed from such accusations. Yet the decision of faith can be understood other than as a self-saving work,[211] and as part of a program to free theology

---

208. Ibid., 85 n. 6.

209. Ibid., 86.

210. Ibid., 87–88. Similarly, in the "Postscript" to *Offenbarung ads Geschichte,* 144–45. Cf. Muschalek in Muschalek and Gamper, "Offenbarung in Geschichte," 194–95: "It is precisely because faith is effected by the Spirit that here too one must say that this 'contribution' of the will does not remove faith from its objectivity, but instead first fully gains access to it. When that is not recognized, then one of course has the impression that the participation of free decision in faith is to hide or replace its deficient objectivity and thus to make it suspect or unacceptable to the modern objectivistic age. In such a view it does indeed become an arbitrary act, so that one understands how Pannenberg can declare faith so understood to be 'self-salvation.'"

211. Cf. Bultmann's *Theologie des Neuen Testaments,* 3rd ed., 1:316–17 = *Theology of the New Testament,* 1:315–16: "As true obedience, 'faith' is freed from the suspicion of being an accomplishment, a 'work'. . . . As an aceomplishment it would not be obedience, since in an accomplishment the will does not surrender but asserts itself: in it, a merely formal renunciation takes place, in that the will lets the content of its accomplishment be dictated by an authority lying outside of itself, but precisely in so doing thinks it has a right to be proud of its accomplishment. 'Faith'—the radical renunciation of accomplishment, the obedient submission to the God-determined way of salvation, the taking over of the cross of Christ . . . —is the free deed of obedience in which the new self constitutes itself in place of the old. As this sort of decision, it is a deed in the true sense: In a true deed man actualizes his being as himself, while in a 'work' he stands side by

from arbitrary decisions.²¹² For demythologizing arose as an effort to overcome the impasse that results from the recognition that the mythological, though it is not accessible to historical verification, yet, as the conveyer of meaning, calls upon us to reach a nonarbitrary position toward it. When the mythologically formulated message is put in the form of an understanding of existence that confronts a person as a possibility for himself, it can become meaningful to him in the light that it sheds on his living. Thus in his concrete living the theoretical problem of pervasive relativism is overcome, though at the level of objective verification that problem remains.²¹³

---

side with what he does." Pannenberg's position (communicated in a letter) is that the decision of faith as understood by Bultmann is a work "to the extent that the authority of the word, the kerygma, is not 'demonstrable,' and becomes visible as God's authority only in carrying out the decision of faith itself." He then queries: "Does not the decision of faith here perhaps first make the word's authority into God's authority, or what is to be replied to this?" Something of a reply may be inferred from Bultmann's "Reply to Ernst Käsemann," in *Glauben und Verstehen*, 4:192: "There is no such thing as a decision without a cause—only the causes do not, as in nature, work with compelling necessity, but are rather the ingredients of decision."

212. Cf. Hartlich and Sachs, *Der Ursprung des Mythosbegriffes*, 1 and 163. "Every principal application of the concept of myth within exegesis brings with it of necessity a certain structure of problems. [Such an application] must begin with the distinction of the mythical form of conceptualization from that which it really intends—the 'content'; as [this application] is carried through, it confronts one with the problem of mythical clothing and (possible) historical factuality, as well as with the question as to the possible truth content of Biblical myths." "The clearer the insight was gained that for this kind of Biblical statements no preference can be claimed for one over another, from the point of view of the truth of [what they conveyed as] knowledge, the more urgent became the question as to whether they have truth and significance in some other sense than that of correspondence with some external objective reality." Cf. my essay: Robinson, "The Pre-History of Demythologization." Cf. also, Ott, "Existentiale Interpretation und anonyme Christlichkeit," esp. 367-70: "[Statements of faith] are not subject to verification or falsification by means of neutral disinterested observation. But if they can neither be verified nor falsified, then they are obviously statements without meaning, empty claims, a sort of declamation or interjection that need not concern us but floats unrelatedly above the realities that concern and determine us—unless another way to verify them can be found. For Bultmann, existentialistic interpretation is such a way.... If existentialist interpretation can show that in faith I attain a really new self-understanding, then it shows thereby that [the new self-understanding] really makes a difference..., i.e., that faith is not some irrelevant thing floating above reality.... For verification does not mean 'proof,' but rather clarification of where it relates to reality."

213. Cf. Klein, *Theologie des Wortes Gottes*, 35. Pannenberg's own position is not so far from such a view as the widely diverging emphases and terminologies might lead one to think. For he adds the significant clarification: "This is not intended to maintain

Pannenberg concludes his answer to Althaus with the observation "that God's revelation only comes to its goal when it effects faith and hence is revelation for someone."[214] It is this distinction between a revelation inherent in history on the one hand and that revelation becoming revelation to someone on the other that is in substance the point at which Lothar Steiger introduces his critique of Pannenberg's position.[215] He senses such a separation of the revelatory history in and of itself on the one hand and man's knowledge or appropriation of it on the other to be inherent in the structure of Pannenberg's programmatic essay, in its division into sections, "The Opening up of Reality as History by Means of the Biblical Revelation of God," and "God's History and Critical Historical Research." He also sees the separation in the sequence of Pannenberg's presentation in *Revelation as History,* where his "Introduction" and first two theses treat of revelatory history with "the problem of knowing and understanding it not yet touched," with the rest of the theses then devoted to that topic of appropriation.[216] Steiger argues that Hegel's problem of some "mediation" between history and the observer of history is not fully recognized; rather the facts are assumed to have some "inherent ontological quality" that "discharges as it were automatically their significance."[217]

---

that one could attain or maintain such knowledge in actual living without faith. That is a new question. The logic of faith and its psychology are to be distinguished. With regard to the logic of faith, what has been said applies, namely, that as *fiducia* it is grounded by knowledge (*notitia*). In the psychological experience both can be laid hold of in a single act. Trust can also emerge in the expectation that the knowledge already logically presupposed will only later be opened up, an anticipation of the result that is characteristic not only of the conduct of faith, but also of the process of knowledge [in general]: One anticipates conjecturally the result, but must then find this conjecture confirmed, verified. For believing trust to arise, the believer does not always himself have to test the knowledge [such trust] presupposes. That is the particular task of theology. Not every Christian need subject himself to this task. He can trust in the assumption that everything is all right with the ground of his trust. To be sure that presupposes an atmosphere of confidence in the Christian tradition that has more and more been lost in the course of the last centuries, not least of all because of the failure of theology. This atmosphere of confidence in what the pastor has to proclaim, to the extent that it is a matter of knowledge, must be rebuilt anew; and one might think that theology should devote all its strength to this task in full critical openness." "Einsicht and Glaube," 84–85. Similarly in the "Postscript" to *Offenbarung als Geschichte,* 145.

214. "Einsicht and Glaube," 90.
215. Steiger, "Offenbarungsgeschichte und theologische Vernunft."
216. Ibid., 93.
217. Ibid., 95.

For Pannenberg, when a person does not recognize that meaning, this is due to one's lack of intelligence, i.e., blindness. Steiger concludes: "The Pauline dialectic of wisdom and foolishness loses its eschatological background and is generalized and flattened into the relation of rationality and irrationality."[218]

Steiger's criticism to the effect that for Pannenberg theology becomes, without "difference" (i.e., undialectically), part of the history of ideas is put in terms of a theology of the word:

> [For Pannenberg] the facts speak only within the plan. The idealistic problem of revelation does not become Biblical simply by eliminating the mediation of thought. How then is the logic of the revelatory plan mediated? Pannenberg has no concept of the verbal nature of revelation, since he conceives of the facts entering into the conception of a plan of salvation as revelation and hence can make room for the word only as the reflex of these facts. On this level there occurs an invalid polemic against the word as revelation, [in arguing that] 'a revelation in need of supplementation in order to become revealed is not yet revelation.'[219] The word is no 'supplement' to the revelation at all! The word witnesses to the event *as* revelation, by saying and doing what an event is and signifies. This meaning of word has nothing at all to do with the Gnostic concept of word as a revelatory discourse.[220] Word is not the illumination of a content that a person could see. In the word it is a matter of the genuine indirectness of revelation, in that the genuine contingency of an occurrence is respected, which by its nature is not unambiguous, but rather is ambiguous.[221]

Actually, Pannenberg's own view, though cast in another category, is not as far from Steiger as the latter assumes. For Pannenberg holds that the mediation is provided by the process of transmission as a hermeneutical process.

A more congenial interpretation is that of Johannes Wirsching.[222] He senses that Pannenberg has challenged the current rejection of the

218. Ibid., 97. Much the same criticism is made by Ernst Fuchs, "Theologie oder Ideologie?," 258–59.

219. Pannenberg, "Einleitung," *Offenbarung als Geschichte,* 20 = "Introduction," to *Revelation as History.*

220. Steiger here alludes to Pannenberg, ibid., 14, 111.

221. "Theologie oder Ideologie?," 108–9.

222. Wirsching, "Ein neues theologisches System?," 601–9. Cf. Wirsching's own book, *Gott in der Geschichte.* The congenial reviews cited by Pannenberg in his "Postscript" to

concept of "systematic" theology, and finds precisely in this fact the positive significance of Pannenberg's proposal. Although he questions "whether theology may ever appropriate a ready-made thought pattern and its systematism as a *closed* unit," he thinks that a system that recasts the given terminology and is "open" to the future for revision (as he understands Pannenberg's to be) avoids the valid criticisms leveled against theological system-building.[223] And the advantage of systematic theology is that it can move beyond dogmatics, "the church's self-reflection on its own doctrine," to include "debate with Christian and non-Christian attacks," as "Polemics, Apologetics, the Philosophy of Religion," as well as to enter upon social action, as "Social Ethics." Thus Wirsching, though a pastor writing for pastors, welcomes the fact that Pannenberg's "system" represents what is "only to a certain extent a 'churchly' theology."[224] The broadening of the horizon to include problems that Dogmatics had tended to define as outside its scope, the desire not simply to witness but also to convince, are emphases that could help mark the difference between faith and superstition.

In an evaluation somewhat different from Steiger's, Wirsching approves of the concept of the Bible that "does not have to be constructed hermeneutically by means of preaching," i.e., that becomes normative by means of the Christ event without "any kind of hermeneutical operation separated from it." The "ontological autonomy" of the event itself "carries its case not only by means of the Biblical witnesses, but in some cases against them" and thus "speaks 'its own language, the language of facts.'"[225] This is appreciated as a return to Luther's emphasis upon the clarity of Scripture without ecclesiastical intervention, which occurs even in Protestantism in the form of "the (neo-Kantian) dominance of questions of understanding."[226] Of course "the theologian, especially the

---

Offenbarung als Geschichte, 134 n. 5, were not available to me, since they appeared in newspapers and magazines.

223. Wirsching, "Ein neues theologisches System?," 602.
224. All quotations ibid., 601.
225. Ibid., 604. Wirsching quotes Pannenberg, "Dogmatische Thesen," 100.
226. Ibid. Of course it hardly fits current German hermeneutic to describe it as an activity "separated" from the Christ event and to say that "only" Pannenberg really "takes seriously" Luther's emphasis on Scripture's clarity (ibid.). For this emphasis is the source of Ebeling's positive understanding of language at the basis of his bermeneutic. Cf. his essay, "Word of God and Hermeneutic." Apparently Wirsching sees the new hermeneutic primarily through Pannenberg's essay, "Hermeneutik und Universalgeschichte" =

one who works systematically, must show how this self-mediation of the Bible's contents is to be grasped conceptually and is able to illuminate the critical mind as true."[227] It is in this sense that Wirsching understands Pannenberg's analysis of the nature of the history of the transmission of traditions in correlation to a study of "historical" reason. The view that the facts interpret themselves fits the contingency of individual occurrences, their nonderivableness from some antecedently known principle. The facts are never so identical with any given interpretation that they could be inferred from or replaced by—that interpretation, but rather reassert themselves over against it as a new step in the history of the transmission of the traditions. Hence one does not have a pattern that one can project into the future. Continuity is visible actually only in retrospect, and whereas such a retrospective view of history can provide an anticipation for the future, such a prolepsis can be no more than that which is to be verified or corrected by subsequent contingent occurrences themselves.

This congenial interpretation of Pannenberg's intention is also accompanied by critical reservations. Wirsching refers to Pannenberg's system as "estheticism," in the original sense of the term: an "observing relation to reality," *visio intellectualis*.[228] The presupposition of Pannenberg's position is hence a "theoretical" relation to reality, rather than, e.g., one in terms of social action or of endurance, as indeed Pannenberg does distance himself from Ebeling's position by rejecting the ethical problem as the point of departure for theology.[229] Wirsching questions whether Pannenberg's theoretical approach does not actually endanger "the uniqueness of the Biblical witness," in that Pannenberg sees

> the "subsequently" intelligible "evidentness" of a step-by-step mediation of salvation at work, and notices too little that such an evidentness necessarily endangers the contingency of Biblical universalism. When all is said and done it is comparable to any esthetic ideological universalism, i.e., it is intelligible *also* in terms of the history of ideas and not only on the basis of its own distinc-

---

"Hermeneutics and Universal History."

227. Ibid.

228. Ibid., 606. The term "estheticism" seems poorly chosen, not only because it is not used in the sense one would most readily assume, but also because the "original" meaning is not unambiguously what Wirsching takes it to be. He does not seem to know that etymologically the term derives from a verb for hearing rather than for seeing.

229. "Die Krise des Ethischen und die Theologie."

tive occurrence. It has to involve some kind of logical evidentness. For the claim that it is "the sole appropriate view" of reality reveals after all a necessity such as can be justified only by rigorous logic.[230]

Furthermore the synthesis of Biblical and non-Biblical reality such as is evident in the fitting of the concept of resurrection to that of psychosomatic wholeness seems to Wirsching not to do justice to the "transforming power" of Christianity. "What then is really 'new' in the witnesses to the resurrection, if the significance inherent in them threatens to become an illustration for a truth that can also be discovered elsewhere?"[231] Wirsching is not willing to accept Pannenberg's view that it is merely "narrow-mindedness" not to assume that "accidental occurrences attain an almost rational transparency."[232] The subjection of the resurrection to "empirical confirmation" seems to put it "on a line with the given status of the world"; instead Pannenberg should have implemented his recognition that "all that is earthly must go through the cross," in terms of a "break, transformation and new creation."[233] Hence Wirsching senses that a reversal could take place. Rather than reason and the historian demonstrating the rationality of the Biblical witness, it could turn out that "Biblical investigations are able only to confirm what historical reason also bears in itself in outline without [the Bible]; in its depths the rationality of the Biblical picture of God comes to such conclusive consciousness that the Bible can only confirm but not contradict."[234] Thus, though his evaluation of Pannenberg's position is more penetrating and positive than some of the other articles treating it, Wirsching shares somewhat the same concern as do they. And in conclusion he expresses a further concern, which is more fully developed by William Hamilton in his contribution to *Theology as History*. In view of the emphasis upon *past* history as proleptic anticipation of future *end* of history, is not the *present* denied the significance that it theologically deserves? "Are *its*

---

230. Wirsching, "Ein neues theologisches System?," 606. He cites Pannenberg, "Heilsgeschehen und Geschichte," 287.
231. Wirsching, "Ein neues theologisches System?," 607
232. Ibid.
233. Ibid., citing Pannenberg, "Heilsgeschehen und Geschichte," 284 n. 66, and 237.
234. Ibid., 609.

questions, *its* needs, really picked up and treated seriously?" "Man must be met where he really is!"[235]

The sharpest and most extensive debate has been initiated by Günter Klein. His review article entitled "Revelation as History?"[236] analyzes individually each contribution in the symposium, *Revelation as History*. And this review was answered most fully among the critical articles treated by Pannenberg in his "Postscript" to the second edition of *Revelation as History*. Klein, in turn, presented an address answering Pannenberg at the meeting of Old Marburgers, in October, 1963. This address was subsequently expanded into a small book entitled *Theology of the Word of God and the Hypothesis of Universal History*, which appeared at the end of 1964.[237] It is this exchange that is now to be investigated.

In his review article, Klein first questions the approach outlined in Pannenberg's introduction to *Revelation as History*.[238] He wonders whether the concept of full divine self-revelation derived from German idealism but absent from the Bible can actually provide the appropriate category for approaching the Bible.[239] It presupposes the model of sight rather than hearing, and hence misses the dialectic of God's call, involving his unexposedness and hence calling forth the decision of faith or faithlessness rather than the theoretical judgment of comprehension or incomprehension. When Pannenberg advocates an "indirect" revelation in history, since God is "initially" not the content of the experience of history, Klein infers that the actual revelation takes place in man's *reflection* about history.

Ulrich Wilckens presents apocalypticism as the factor of continuity in primitive Christianity, from Judaism to Jesus and from Jesus to the church.[240] Jesus' conflict with Judaism is somewhat parallel to the clash within Judaism between "the apocalyptic understanding of the law,"

235. Ibid. Similarly Fuchs, "Theologie oder Ideologie?," 259–60.
236. Klein, "Offenbarung als Geschichte?"
237. Klein, *Theologie des Wortes Gottes und die Hypothese der Universalgeschichte*.
238. Pannenberg, *Offenbarung als Geschichte*, 7–20; Klein, "Offenbarung als Geschichte?" 65–68.
239. Pannenberg, in his "Postscript" to *Offenbarung als Geschichte*, 142 n. 24, replies to a similar criticism by Steiger to the effect that though the term self-revelation is not present, the substance is present in the biblical talk of the final revelation of God's "glory" and in the "word of demonstration." Cf. also Grobel's remarks, "Revelation," 163–66.
240. Wilckens, "Das Offenbarungsverstandnis in der Geschichte des Urchristentums"; Klein, "Offenbarung als Geschichte?," 71–77.

which Jesus himself as "eschatological place of salvation" incorporates,[241] and the Pharisaic view,[242] with Jesus' authority to instigate such a crisis perhaps beings based on some "inspirational visionary experience."[243] Thus a psychic occurrence in Jesus' life, together with an inevitable clash in the history of ideas, is in the case of Jesus the history that indirectly reveals God. Klein maintains, conversely, that it is Jesus' message as revelatory word event to which Jesus appeals for his authority. Since apocalypticism expected history to vindicate its conception, Jesus, in Wilckens'

241. Wilckens, "Das Offenbarungsverstandnis," 53 and 58 n. 39 = "The Understanding of Revelation"; Klein, "Offenbarung als Geschichte?," 72. Presupposed is Dietrich Rössler's dissertation, *Gesetz und Geschichte*. Pannenberg replies in his "Postscript" to *Offenbarung als Geschichte*, 141 n. 22, that Klein had not taken into consideration Wilckens' statement, "Das Offenbarungsverstandnis," 58 n. 39, that Jesus had a "distinctive eschatology." Cf. Wilckens' remarks in his review of August Strobel's *Die apokalyptische Sendung Jesu*, 671:

> Though it is true and worth emphasizing that Jesus can be correctly described only within the comparative religious horizon of the Jewish apocalyptic tradition, the picture of Jesus' distinctiveness the author works out is unconvincing.... The distinctiveness of Jesus does not at all consist merely in his sketching himself so to speak into the given framework of the traditional expectation of the end. Rather it is that, contrary to the soteriological structure of the traditional expectation, he proclaimed final salvation as God's gift to the wicked and hence bound it proleptically to their relationship to him.... The explicit opposition of Jesus to the Torah tradition and its advoeates is completely ignored by the author. Jesus is not, as the author maintains, simply an apocalypticist with remarkably heightened self-esteem. Most of the exegetes attacked by the author (especially Käsemann!) distance Jesus completely from apocalypticism (clearly incorrectly), primarily in view of this materially decisive opposition to the apocalyptic tradition. To this extent they are at least as basically eorrect over against the author as he over against them. Hence, it is not so 'simple,' but rather a thorny and at times puzzling historical problem, to understand Jesus (as in fact it must be done!) in the context of Jewish apocalypticism without making him an apocalypticist.

Wilckens would apparently free Jesus from the personality traits giving a pejorative overtone to the term "apocalyptist," even though he had initially (*Offenbarung als Geschichte*, 53) found in the "apocalyptic visionary" the nearest historical parallel to Jesus, and yet retain for Jesus enough of an apocalyptic ideology for Rössler's antithesis between its view of the law and that of Pharisaism to be applied to Jesus.

242. In the context of deriving Paul's ideological background from apocalypticism, Wilckens can also speak of a "Pharisaic apocalypticism," "Die Bekehrung des Paulus," 285. Cf. Klein, "Offenbarung als Geschichte?," 72 n. 14, and idem, *Theologie des Wortes Gottes*, 25 n. 22. Oscar Cullmann, *Heil als Geschichte*, 42, accepts W. D. Davies' rejection of a separation of Pharisaism and apocalypticism in his article "Apocalyptic and Pharisaism," and affirms that Rössler's thesis is "much too schematic," although adding "in a certain sense it is nonetheless a suggestive work."

243. Wilckens, "Das Offenbarungsverstandnis," 54 n. 31; Klein, "Offenbarung als Geschichte?," 73.

view, performed his miracles and brought things to a head in Jerusalem so that God would demonstrate the validity of his claim in what would happen,²⁴⁴ whereas Klein understands Jesus as rejecting such signs.²⁴⁵ Although Jesus expected the apocalyptic end of the world rather than an isolated instance of resurrection, the expectation of some confirmatory apocalyptic event provides for Wilckens the connection with the church's reference to the resurrection as such a confirmation. Wilckens had already presented a detailed argument to the effect that the connection of Paul's conversion with his rejection of the law indicated that he originated from an apocalyptic world of thought.²⁴⁶ And he had already carried this apocalyptic continuity through to the post-apostolic age with a monograph arguing that Luke had succeeded in replacing the imminent expectation that had failed, as well as the *Christus praesens,* understood as an "unmediated encounter with transcendence" of Gnostic implications, with a "historically mediated participation in a specific past." This "theological discovery of history as the 'comprehensive horizon of Christian theology'" makes of Luke—rather, than, e.g., the gnosticizing John—"undoubtedly the most important theologian of the post-apostolic age," and the canonical precursor of the Pannenberg circle.²⁴⁷

For the discussion of Lucan theology, Klein refers to Ernst Haenchen, whose commentary on Acts has made him one of the most influential interpreters of Lukan theology today. Haenchen points to the equivalent of the Pauline *Christus praesens* that is to be found in the Lucan concept of the miracle-working "name" of Jesus.

244. Wilckens, "Das Offenbarungsverstandnis," 60–61; Klein, "Offenbarung als Geschichte?," 74.

245. Klein, "Offenbarung als Geschichte?," 74. Pannenberg, *Grundzüge der Christologie,* 58–59 (= *Jesus, God and Man,* 63–64), develops a thesis of Jesus' positive stance toward signs.

246. Wilckens, "Die Bekehrung des Paulus." But cf. Wolfgang Schrage, "'Ekklesia' und 'Synagoge,'" esp. 198: "The source of Paul's antithesis to the law is not an apocalyptic system of coordinates that the pre-Christian Paul carried with him and into which he merely needed to sketch the new reality at his conversion; rather the source is the preaching of the 'Hellenists.'" Similarly, Klein, "Offenbarung als Geschichte?," 75 n. 21. Klein's essay "Römer 4 und die Idee der Heilsgeschichte," was in substance a criticism of Wilckens' view of Paul. Wilckens replied, "Zu Römer 3,21—4,25: Antwort an G. Klein," to which Klein in turn replied, "Exegetische Probleme in Römer 3,21—4,25: Antwort an U. Wilckens." Pannenberg holds that (apart from Jesus) Paul is the central figure of the New Testament.

247. Wilckens, *Die Missionsreden der Apostelgeschichte,* esp. 206–7, 218. Wilckens quotes the opening sentence of Pannenberg's programmatic essay discussed above.

> Luke—like all New Testament "authors"—is aware of this "transcendence" as the power that really determines everything, and not in the sense that God (one should rather speak of him than of "transcendence") directs every occurrence and hence lies behind every occurrence. Rather Luke is not afraid to report individual interventions of God in earthly occurrence. . . . One should not confuse the Lucan generation's massive conception of the resurrection with a "positive evaluation of history." Luke did not think that the salvation that the parousia "is expected to bring for the elect [is] in no sense different from the salvation that was already completely there in Jesus' earthly life." Even in Luke's view, there will be, after the parousia, no sick to be healed and no sinners to be converted. Perhaps the massiveness of some Lucan statements arouses a longing for a massive theology in which such uncertain things as a "direct encounter with transcendence" no longer occur.[248]

Klein's criticism of Pannenberg's theses[249] has its focus in the classification of Jesus' resurrection as history. "In the framework of this conception the Easter event loses of necessity its eschatological character and degenerates into a past phenomenon of the world."[250] Pannenberg in turn is able to deny this inference,[251] since for him history and apocalypticism do not stand in tension to each other. Hence he disagrees with the Bultmannian view that to call the eschatological event a historical event is paradoxical, and states instead that it is only a proleptic form of expression. His emphasis that Easter should be understood in its apocalyptic setting[252] seems to Klein to reflect an assumption that this setting is distinct (though not separable) from the fact, which can be conceived of in

---

248. Haenchen, *Die Apostelgeschichte*, 682–89, esp. 688–89 = *Acts of the Apostles*. For the longer quotation Haenchen cites Wilckens, *Die Missionsreden der Apostelgeschichte*, 215; the other allusions refer to quotations cited earlier by Haenchen. The other leading German Lucan specialist, Hans Conzelmann, was somewhat more blunt in rejecting the position of Pannenberg. Cf. his essay, "Randbemerkungen zur Lage im Neuen Testament," 228 n. 16. Klein's own contributions to Lucan research have in the background the debate with Pannenberg's position, esp. "Lukas 1,1–4 als theologisches Programm."

249. Pannenberg, *Offenbarung als Geschichte*, 91–114; Klein, "Offenbarung als Geschichte?," 77–84.

250. Ibid., 78.

251. In Pannenberg, "Postscript" to *Offenbarung als Geschichte*, 143.

252. Ibid., 140 n. 19.

and of itself.[253] Klein argues that this distinguishes the object of faith from the ground of faith, with the latter seeming to be the apocalyptic horizon in which that fact is capable of being understood as the revelation of God. As to the "ground of faith," Pannenberg refers to it as "knowledge" about the revelatory history. Yet such knowledge is "initially" hindered by "superficiality that in earthly affairs sees nothing at work . . . except human motivations."[254] Klein argues that this not only implies a rejection of current critical historical research, but also that it leaves unanswered the question as to how one moves from "superficiality" to "rationality." Recognition of the way Israel came to believe in God seems simply to be equated with recognition that Israel's God actually is. For descriptive statements cast in the mode of the history of religions are taken to be normative knowledge of God.

Trutz Rendtorff seeks in his essay[255] to overcome the current "emphasis on the *otherness* of the church over against the world," which has as its corollary "the basic distinction between the factual historical church . . . and the church of the word."[256] The historical demonstration that the church stems from Jesus is one with the vindication of the empirical church as the true church. Klein maintains that the distinction current in dialectic theology is not ontological, but hermeneutical, i.e., is intended to make clear that it is only as an act of faith that one can identify the empirical church as the true church. He fears that the identification of the historical demonstration of continuity back to Jesus with the vindication of the empirical church as the true church will lead to an "unconditional submission to institutional churchiness."[257]

Pannenberg begins his reply[258] to Klein by expressing surprise at the "tone" of some of the critical articles. "Who would have suspected that some advocates of the dominant theology of the word would be so

253. Pannenberg replies, ibid., 142, note 23, that Klein "bypasses our view that all occurrence strikes upon some context in the history of the transmission of traditions and can be expressed only in relation to this."

254. Pannenberg, "Dogmatische Thesen," 101, 103 = "Dogmatic Theses," 140, 142; Klein, "Offenbarung als Geschichte?," 81.

255. T. Rendtorff, "Das Offenbarungsproblem" = "The Problem of Revelation"; Klein, "Offenbarung als Geschichte?," 84–86.

256. T. Rendtorff, "Das Offenbarungsproblem," 116–17 = "The Problem of Revelation"; Klein, "Offenbarung als Geschichte?," 84.

257. Klein, "Offenbarung als Geschichte?," 86.

258. Pannenberg, "Postscript" to *Offenbarung als Geschichte*, 132–48.

uncertain of their position that they would have to avoid any divergent proposal by means of crude misrepresentations and worn-out tags?"²⁵⁹ It is to a considerable extent true that argumentation by gibe, innuendo, misunderstanding and inadequate representation has characterized the debate, which makes it at times difficult to sift out the points worthy of serious discussion. A considerable portion of Pannenberg's "Postscript" is devoted to correcting misunderstandings or misrepresentations that have simply been omitted here from the report of the critical essays. Yet there does emerge in the "Postscript" the beginning of a formulation of the Pannenbergian position that both addresses itself to the main line of the emerging criticism and understands itself as an alternative to the new hermeneutic (into which the Bultmannian side of the theology of the word has in part evolved), rather than primarily as an alternative to the various branches of the antecedent dialectic theology.

Pannenberg makes clear that he does not reject the concept of the word of God, but only "its isolated and generalized use as a theological principle."²⁶⁰ And he denies that the stance of observing from a distance involves disinterestedness; it can very well implement deep involvement in what is at stake. But rather than the historicness of existence being presupposed, the presupposition is rather "that human life always takes place already caught up in interconnections of traditions."²⁶¹ It is the history of the transmission of traditions that is "the unity of event and word (i.e., significance)."²⁶² The traditional context "mediates" the "original meaning," as well as "all knowledge about what happened (with regard to its factuality and with regard to its significance)," and to this extent is a kind of hermeneutic.²⁶³ He recognizes "the historical difference [between Biblical times and today] that is constitutive for the hermeneutical problem," but maintains "that the problems of hermeneutic have been taken up in the concept of universal history as the history of the transmission of traditions, i.e., [hermeneutic] is preserved as one aspect and also left behind as a whole."²⁶⁴

259. Ibid., 134.
260. Ibid., 136 n. 11.
261. Ibid., 137.
262. Ibid.
263. Ibid., 138.
264. Ibid., 139. The detailed presentation of this thesis, to which Pannenberg at this point alludes, is to be found in an essay significantly entitled, "Hermeneutik und

Pannenberg concludes his "Postscript" to *Revelation as History* with the expression of his hope that future discussion of his proposal might be more oriented to the material issues than had been the case thus far.[265] He proposes four questions, which are then accepted by Klein as the topics for the chapters of his response, *Theology of the Word of God and the Hypothesis of Universal History*.[266]

1. "The question of an alternative to the theology of the word."[267] Klein argues that Pannenberg does not in fact get beyond verbal revelation, since it is only the context of traditions that makes of an event revelation, and traditions are word—although to be sure a different model for language than "the happening word" of dialectic theology. The understanding of language as "mere words,"[268] in distinction from one oriented to the view that language "brings with it what it says," does call for complementation by history; but Klein argues that this is a deficient understanding of both language and history. He infers that the Pannenbergian position is obliged to "devaluate" the Biblical word. In the Old Testament this takes the form of pointing out that prophecies often go unfulfilled, to which Klein comments that the point of the prophetic word is misunderstood when it is taken primarily as prediction of future event rather than as present event of comfort or judgment.[269] The New Testament kerygma is in Klein's view "devaluated" by arguing as does Pannenberg that since it occurs in various forms it is always "left behind" by Jesus' eschatological history. Klein agrees fully that the kerygma is expressed in varying conceptualizations, but argues that there is continuity in the point coming to expression in them, upon which the attention of exegesis as material criticism should be focused.[270] Here one can sense the divergence of the two approaches, one hearing in Biblical language

---

Universalgeschichte" = "Hermeneutic and Universal History."

265. Pannenberg, "Postscript" to *Offenbarung als Geschichte*, 147–48.
266. Klein, *Theologie des Wortes Gottes und die Hypothese der Universalgeschichte*.
267. Ibid., 12–21.
268. Pannenberg, "Postscript," 132, cited by Klein, *Theologie des Wortes Gottes*, 12.
269. Pannenberg, "Postscript," 132–33; Klein, *Theologie des Wortes Gottes*, 13–15. Cf. the similar criticism of Pannenberg by Gerhard Sauter, *Zukunft und Verheissung*, 151 n. 5: "For [the Reformers] '*promissio*' is not one 'function' of the word of God among others (for example, as 'prediction,' [cf. Pannenberg's thesis 7]), but rather designates comprehensively the character of the life-giving divine word."
270. Klein, *Theologie des Wortes Gottes*, 21.

primarily a reference to fact, the other hearing it in primarily the scoring of a point.

2. "The understanding of the relation between the Old Testament, the New Testament and primitive Christianity itself, in terms of the history of the transmission of traditions."[271] Much as in the case of Bultmann's concept of a changing preunderstanding, Pannenberg in his way realizes that the context of traditions may be broken by what happens in history.[272] Yet Klein fears that the possibility of any real criticism of the traditional understanding is eliminated when criticism is "absorbed" as "only an aspect" in a broader context and when the "original meaning" of the "revelatory events" is said to be "mediated" "through the context of traditions."[273] The contingency of new stages in the transmission of traditions seems to be limited by Pannenberg's presupposition that such "steps" are "meaningful," and this in terms of "the understanding of history tending toward a comprehensive unity of meaning," with the history of the transmission of traditions providing the "continuity" between events.[274] From such statements the conventional model of the organic growth of tradition seems to Klein to emerge. Events that would eliminate tradition hardly fit into the coordinates of traditions in which history is here cast. And the contingency of events would seem to be endangered by the fact that although they are not subsumed under an *a priori* rational pattern or structure, still the given stage of the tradition at which they occur and in terms of which they must have their meaning does function to predetermine the scope of meaning they can be assumed to have. The predominance of tradition over event is also sensed when Pannenberg says that apart from Christianity, the "problem of Old Testament history" was unsolved "in fact" but not "in principle," from which Klein infers that this leaves the Christ event as only a "stimulant" for a "long since potentially complete solution" inherent in the history of the transmission of traditions.[275]

---

271. Ibid., 22–37.
272. Pannenberg, "Postscript," 137; Klein, *Theologie des Wortes Gottes*, 22.
273. Pannenberg, "Postscript," 138–39, cited by Klein, *Theologie des Wortes Gottes*, 22.
274. Pannenberg, "Postscript," 138 n. 16, and 133 n. 3, cited by Klein, *Theologie des Wortes Gottes*, 24.
275. Pannenberg, "Postscript," 139; Klein, *Theologie des Wortes Gottes*, 25.

Of course Klein is here drawing inferences from Pannenberg's approach that Pannenberg himself does not draw. And only in a secondary sense can such inferences, even if validly drawn, seriously challenge a theology that would prefer to reformulate its position than to be compelled to draw them. When, conversely, the right wing all too readily bypasses Pannenberg's comments that the relation to tradition may be that of a rupture, and simply takes satisfaction in the fact that intellectual history, often presented elsewhere in modern times in a strange and threatening way, is here cast into the familiar mold of the transmission of traditions, such an inference, neither necessary nor drawn by Pannenberg himself, cannot be made his responsibility.[276]

Klein's basic criticism of Pannenberg's approach in terms of the history of the transmission of traditions takes the form of the argument that such a conceptualization is not fully adequate to the subject matter itself. When Pannenberg emphasizes the "indissoluble connection of the Old Testament and late Israelite tradition on the one hand, and the ministry of Jesus and what happened to him on the other,"[277] Klein can agree with the truth in such a statement and yet senses that it is the converse of that structure that would most adequately fit the break with contemporary Judaism involved in Jesus' ministry and what happened to him. He formulates this criticism in the hermeneutical vocabulary of "the difference between language and the intention that calls forth the expression."[278] The (apocalyptic) form of the message and the message itself seem to him not carefully enough differentiated. Pannenberg argues that since the gospel of Jesus' resurrection arose in the context of Jewish apocalyptic expectations of the final resurrection, there is a "connection between that message and this expectation."[279] Klein argues that, materially speaking, one should only say that there was a connection between the form the message took and the apocalyptic expectation, i.e., he disagrees with Pannenberg's inference that we have to do here with "a relation that indeed may not be exchanged for just any other."[280] Pannenberg regards a person's deci-

---

276. On the role Pannenberg's position is playing in German conservative circles, cf. Heinz-Dieter Knigge, "Postbultmannian Hermeneutical Attempts," esp. 26 and 37 n. 37.

277. Pannenberg, "Postscript," 133, cited by Klein, *Theologie des Wortes Gottes*, 24.

278. Klein, *Theologie des Wortes Gottes*, 28–29.

279. Pannenberg, "Postscript," 140, cited by Klein, *Theologie des Wortes Gottes*, 30.

280. Pannenberg, "Postscript," 140 n. 19; Klein, *Theologie des Wortes Gottes*, 30. Klein regards such a view as "repristination," the "canonizing of the apocalyptic tradition,"

sion about the necessity of the apocalyptic sector of Jewish tradition as determinative for whether the person retains the Old Testament. Klein asks "why then [is there] not a corresponding evaluation of Qumran, average Hellenistic Judaism, Philo, the Therapeutae, gnosticizing Judaism, and Gnosticism influenced by Judaism," "to the extent that they have in some way affected primitive Christianity at one or the other layer of its conceptualizations, as many of them have?"[281]

3. "The proleptic character of Jesus' history and especially of his resurrection, is its significance for the concept of revelation."[282] Klein begins his evaluation by noting Pannenberg's remark that the concept of prolepsis is "all too much like a *deus ex machina*," unless, "on the basis of the prolepsis of the Christ event, the proleptic structure of beings as a whole and especially of intellectual acts becomes intelligible."[283] Klein senses a tension between this proleptic view of reality and the other view to the effect that the meaning of all that is preliminary will not only be revealed but will also be first decided by the final event.[284]

> The character of preliminariness, which hence pertains to all that is, is the very opposite of the proleptic quality that is to free the thing characterized by it of preliminariness and attribute to it "insurpassableness." By bringing together in his mind the proleptic character of the Christ event with the assumedly analogous nature of the whole of being, but then inexplicably declaring the latter to be preliminary, Pannenberg brings the "insurpassableness of the Christ event" that he has in view into the greatest of danger, and robs himself of whatever argument could be used against the objection that consequently the significance of the Christ event too will only be revealed and even only decided in the eschaton.[285]

Pannenberg emphasizes especially the proleptic nature of intellectual activity. For Klein, this prolepsis of the mind is simply what in hermeneutic

---

ibid., 31.

281. Pannenberg, "Postscript," 140; Klein, *Theologie des Wortes Gottes*, 34. Cf. conversely with regard to non-Jewish elements in Christian apocalypticism Hans Dieter Betz, "Zum Problem des religionsgeschichtlichen Verständnisses der Apokalyptik."

282. Klein, *Theologie des Wortes Gottes*, 38–53.

283. Pannenberg, "Postscript," 143; cited by Klein, *Theologie des Wortes Gottes*, 38.

284. Pannenberg, "Postscript," 142 n. 25; cited by Klein, *Theologie des Wortes Gottes*, 39.

285. Klein, *Theologie des Wortes Gottes*, 39, citing Pannenberg, "Postscript," 143.

is called the hermeneutical circle. If a prolepsis seems more intelligible in this area, it is because a prolepsis of the mind is an anticipation of something that already is, even if not already known, i.e., it is a subjective prolepsis, whereas the kind of prolepsis envisaged for the resurrection of Jesus would be an objective prolepsis, in which something that is not yet comes proleptically to be.[286] Klein argues that Pannenberg has not yet made the category of objective prolepsis an adequately clear concept for interpreting the resurrection of Jesus in relation to history.

Klein argues that the proleptic understanding of Jesus' resurrection as a special instance of the general future resurrection of the dead robs Jesus' resurrection of any decisive significance as itself achieving anything for mankind. He would prefer to think of Jesus' resurrection, rather than being the prolepsis of a future whose reality is in any case assured within the context of Jewish expectation, as the *basis* for the ultimate status of man, which would then be a "follow-up" of Jesus' resurrection.

4. "The dialectic of faith and knowledge in the light of the proleptic eschatological nature of the revelation in Christ."[287] Of course Klein maintains that to hold God to be the object of man's knowledge prior to the commitment of faith is to think of God as being at man's disposal and hence to make of God a thing of the world. But apart from this criticism characteristic of dialectic theology, Klein argues that there is an internal inconsistency in Pannenberg's insistence that knowledge of God is prior to faith and yet is not uninvolved.[288] The difference between the two po-

---

286. Klein, *Theologie des Wortes Gottes*, 40; cf. Gerhard Sauter, *Zukunft and Verheissung*, 266 n. 35: "Is there demonstrably a genuine connection between [the proleptic structure of beings in general and that of intellectual activity]? Hardly, in Pannenberg's terminology thus far. Here the apocalyptic structure of 'proleptic unveiling' ("Dogmatische Thesen," 107; cf. also 105 = "Dogmatic Theses," 146, 144), and what one could perhaps call the anticipation inherent in all knowledge—and hence for Pannenberg also inherent in faith ("Dogmatische Thesen," 102 n. 15, and 146 = "Dogmatic Theses," 157 n. 15)—stand alongside each other without mediation."

287. Klein, *Theologie des Wortes Gottes*, 54–71.

288. Ibid., 56–57; cf. Pannenberg, "Postscript," 136: "Every understanding reader of our work must after all see that precisely what is important for us is that the occurrence happening to men strike home to them. . . . Genuine knowledge takes place after all only where a person is completely 'with it,' so that he lets himself be laid claim upon by the subject matter in the act of knowledge—and indeed to the extent that the nature of the subject matter under consideration is able to lay a claim on man. . . . It is uncontested that a purely theoretical stance toward God and his revelatory action would be inappropriate, but this is true only because here the content of knowledge contains a claim upon

sitions would seem to be neither one of more or less involvement, nor one of more or less understanding as one gets involved, but rather of the nature of that understanding. For Klein, the fact that the gospel is "a claim upon the whole of one's life" suggests that a person should understand the orientation of one's life to God that one is carrying through in the act of faith when one makes that commitment, so that the act of faith is not arbitrary, but an understanding act. For Pannenberg, one's progressive approach toward demonstrated knowledge of the objective truth of the gospel story, to the effect that it happened and was divine action, implies a response commensurate to knowledge of God, which would be the act of religious commitment. In neither case does one come to the gospel equipped with faith as a special conditioning that makes it easier to respond; in neither case can real understanding fail to involve an implicit call for faith. In Klein's view one might, on understanding what is involved in orienting one's life in the light of the gospel, make a negative decision; in Pannenberg's view faith would more directly result as a consequence of demonstrated knowledge.

Pannenberg's distinction between a necessary logical priority of knowledge to faith but an unnecessary psychological priority seems to Klein to break down, since the necessity for the priority is argued psychologically. Klein describes the dilemma in which he sees Pannenberg as follows: "If preaching is assumed not to be able to say to the hearer that 'you must first make the leap into faith in order to be certain,' then [such preaching] would certainly have destroyed itself when it explains to [the hearer]: Before you make the leap into faith you must be certain—but possibly you will become aware of your certainty only after the leap."[289] In Pannenberg's view, on the other hand, one should reckon with degrees of probability in a progressive demonstration of the truth of the gospel, just as is characteristic of other areas of knowledge. The present state of one's knowledge would be adequate to make the act of faith the reasonable thing to do, in that one's present knowledge would lead one to anticipate an ultimate complete demonstration of the gospel's truth.

---

the whole of one's life, and hence true knowledge must perceive just this factor of being claimed, which points beyond 'mere' knowledge."

289. Klein, *Theologie des Wortes Gottes*, 58–59; the first quotation is from Pannenberg, in his explanation of Thesis 3, "Dogmatische Thesen," 101 = "Dogmatic Theses," 138.

Klein argues that Pannenberg's intention to ground faith outside itself, an intention shared by Klein, is not successfully carried through, in that faith is grounded in man's knowledge.

> For then the difference between the ground [knowledge] and what is grounded [faith] is no longer interpreted as the externality of the ground, but is rather reduced to the difference between two internal ways of human conduct; and this is no real distinction at all, since the grounding knowledge and the grounded faith are connected by an automatic mechanism, which reveals them to be two aspects of a single principle, namely self-assertion.[290]

The doctrine of the Holy Spirit seems on the one hand to have no real place, in that the path to faith is identical with the normal exercise of one's rational faculties. But on the other hand some "qualification" of that process is introduced, inconsistently, when Pannenberg affirms: "The elimination of such prejudices [as are in the common mind] can perhaps never be only a matter of rational argumentation.... To that extent some sort of illumination is needed in order that the truth, in itself clear and demonstrable, be also accepted by the individual person."[291] The result seems to Klein to be that faith has no certainty, in that it depends on an intellectual capacity largely absent today; lacking also is any implicit trust in the traditions that might replace such intellectual conviction. Hence the believer's assumption that the resurrection is not a hallucination is after all "a simple act of decision, which [Pannenberg] had otherwise so discredited."[292] Pannenberg however explains that

> it is not primarily the "modern world" that is to be brought to an acknowledgement of the truth of Christian claims with regard to history, but rather *the Christians themselves* who must live in an atmosphere of the reliability of the Christian message. There will always be a "world" that does not find the Christian message convincing. But the question is whether the Christians themselves can be validly convinced of the universal validity of this mes-

---

290. Klein, *Theologie des Wortes Gottes*, 66. Muschalek, "Offenbarung in Geschichte," 181, argues that such proven knowledge is not the objective of medieval theology, e.g., of Thomas, but is rather a Cartesian innovation.

291. Pannenberg, "Einsicht and Glaube," 89; cited by Klein, *Theologie des Wortes Gottes*, 67.

292. Klein, *Theologie des Wortes Gottes*, 69.

sage—and can also convince, to be sure not "the modern world," but indeed individual thinking persons.[293]

The most careful and important criticism to come from one who is also partly appreciative of the direction of Pannenberg's thought is that of Jürgen Moltmann, who was Pannenberg's colleague during the latter's three years on the faculty of the *Kirchliche Hochschule* in Wuppertal. Moltmann's *Theology of Hope*,[294] oriented to God's word of promise, is a more recent systematic theology to emerge from within the tradition of the theology of the word, and thus serves to bring to expression in discussion with Pannenberg not only the diverging formulations, but also the extent to which parallel developments are taking place.

Moltmann presents the Pannenbergian position as modeled after Greek more than Biblical thought.

> This theology of universal history obviously presents itself initially as an expansion and surpassing of Greek cosmic theology. In place of the cosmic proof of God that inferred from "reality as cosmos" a divine Arche or First Principle and thus demonstrated a cosmological monotheism, there emerges a theology of history that infers from the unity of "reality as history" the one God of history, by means of the same inferential procedure. The epistemological method remains the same, only in place of the closed cosmos that becomes theophany in the symmetry and harmony of the eternal return of the same, we have a cosmos open to the future with a teleological orientation. Thus "history" becomes the new category for "reality in its totality." In place of the metaphysical point of unity for the cosmos we have the eschatological point of direction and unity for history. Just as that metaphysical point of unity made the cosmos recognizable as indirect revelation of God, just so now the end of history makes history recognizable as indirect revelation of God.[295]

This comparison with Greek thought gradually moves into a contrast with the theology of the word, and the criticism implicit in Moltmann's presentation comes to the surface.

---

293. Quotation is from a letter of clarification.

294. *Theologie der Hoffnung* (1964; 2nd and 3rd ed., 1965). Quotation is from the 2nd ed.

295. Ibid., 68.

In the place of kerygmatic theology that experiences God in the event of the word of address, a theology of history would emerge that perceives God from the "language of facts." As in Greek cosmic theology the eternal being of God appears indirectly in the beings and can be inferred from them, just so God's being is here to be recognized in the having-been-ness of history. . . . In going beyond Greek cosmic theology, the basic insight of the Old Testament, that "history is the occurrence suspended between promise and fulfillment," which was the point of departure for Pannenberg and Rendtorff, has actually been given up in favor of a universal historical eschatology confirming itself in "reality as a whole." Such an eschatology achieves its eschatological character only from the fact that reality is not yet visible as a whole, since it has not yet reached its end. But in this position the Old Testament's God of promise is in danger of becoming a *Theos epiphanēs*, whose epiphany is presented by the whole of reality in its completion. . . . It remains unclear whether the place of a theophany in nature is merely taken over by the theophany in history, as nature open to the future, or whether the fundamentally other condition of the possibility of perceiving reality as history, namely on the basis of promise, is intended. This theology of history opposed to theology of the word remains exposed to Kant's criticism of theological metaphysics so long as it does not itself reflect critically on the condition of the possibility of perceiving reality as history in an eschatologically and theologically qualified sense.[296]

Moltmann does recognize that Pannenberg's understanding of the cosmos as in substance universal history reopens the question of the validity of the cosmological argument for the existence of God, in that Pannenberg argues that the unity of reality requires for its completion the existence of God. And Moltmann favors the hermeneutical inference that texts from the past are not to be made relevant to the present only by identifying their understanding of existence, but that "they are to be read with regard to their historical position and hour, their own historical connection backwards and forwards."[297] Moltmann agrees with Pannenberg's hermeneutical principle: "Only a conception of the course of history actually connecting then with today and its future horizon can provide the all-embracing horizon in which the limited present horizon

296. Ibid., 68–69.
297. Ibid., 254.

of the interpreter and the historical horizon of the text are fused."[298] But Moltmann observes: "Since this all-embracing historic connection within history can always be formulated only as a finite, preliminary, and hence surpassable perspective, it remains fragmentary in view of an open future."[299] That is to say, Moltmann finds at this point a missing link for a cosmological argument for the existence of God.

> Here is maintained the necessity for bringing "God" to expression in the whole of reality, and yet at the same time the impossibility is conceded of being able to grasp a still unterminated and hence historic reality as a "totality." So it would be better to give up the intentions of a cosmological proof of God. As long as this reality of the world and man in it is not yet "complete," and indeed its completeness is historically still at stake, no God can be proven from it. The "all-embracing historic connection" that connects then with today, the historical horizon with the present horizon of the future, is no connection of events related one to the other, but rather a connection of the history of commission and promise. The horizons do not "fuse" in the question of the connection of occurrences between today and then, but only in the question of the intended future then and today.[300]

Moltmann's presentation of Pannenberg's position moves into a more parallel structuring on the basis of the recognition of a second dimension in the Pannenbergian position, as the orientation of "history" to "the language of facts" is transcended by one in terms of the history of the transmission of traditions.

> The understanding of history as the history of the transmission of traditions no longer presents itself as an alternative to kerygmatic theology, as was the case with the expression "the language of facts," that after all could only be meant polemically. Rather the attempt is made to pull together what is becoming separated,

298. Pannenberg, "Hermeneutik and Universalgeschichte," 116 = "Hermeneutics and Universal History," cited by Moltmann, *Theologie der Hoffnung*, 255 = *Theology of Hope*, 277.

299. Moltmann, *Theologie der Hoffnung*, 255 = *Theology of Hope*, 277.

300. Ibid. Cf. Sauter, *Zukunft and Verheissung*, 191 n. 21: "[The agreement of such a universal-history interest with the intention of historicism] raises the question whether the prolepsis of the eschaton in Jesus' history is not primarily intended to ground anew what Troeltsch called the 'metaphysical faith' in the unity and totality of history. If this is the case, eschatology would again be weakened; for this unity and totality cannot be laid claim to as a hermeneutical principle for understanding past history."

namely "word," word event, interpretation, evaluation, etc., on the one hand, and "*factum*," facts and their interconnections on the other hand. . . . The modern separation of "factuality" and "significance" is thus eliminated in the understanding of history as the history of the transmission of traditions, in a way analogous to that in Gerhard Ebeling's "theology of the word event." If [in Ebeling's position] the events are done justice to in conjunction with the word in which they were originally proclaimed, then [in Pannenberg's position] the words and traditions are done justice to in conjunction with the historical occurrences. Yet the decisive question arises as to *how* the Cartesian and Kantian separation of reality from the perceiving of it is overcome. The intention of grasping the real occurrences in the original experiential and traditional connection in which they first came to expression can be implemented both hermeneutically as word event and in terms of universal history as event in the totality of historical reality.[301]

Moltmann emphasizes that modern historiography's criticism of the tradition must be done justice by both positions.

> Since the Enlightenment the historical criticism of the Christian traditions involves in ever increasing radicality a crisis of the traditions, if indeed one should not speak of a revolutionary break in traditions. Since this crisis and this criticism, "tradition" is no longer "a matter of course." The relation to history as tradition has become a reflective relation and has lost its immediacy. Hence if one wishes to understand "history as tradition," a new concept of "tradition" must be attained that takes up within it historical criticism and its consciousness of crisis with regard to history, without repudiating or nullifying it.[302]

Moltmann directs this criticism primarily to the Pannenbergian proof of the resurrection.

> The thesis that this occurrence of Jesus' resurrection must be basically verifiable "historically" would first have to transform the concept of the historical so that it admits resurrection by God and, in this resurrection, can make the announced end of history knowable. To call Jesus' resurrection historically verifiable presup-

---

301. Moltmann, *Theologie der Hoffnung*, 71 = *Theology of Hope*, 80–81. For an illustration of the extent to which the two new conceptualizations can be used in a parallel way in historieal research, cf. my essay "Kerygma and History in the New Testament."
302. Moltmann, *Theologie der Hoffnung*, 72 = *Theology of Hope*, 81.

poses a concept of history that is dominated by the expectation of a general resurrection of the dead as the end and completion of history. Thus there is a circle of understanding between the concept of history and resurrection.[303]

Apart from historiographical concerns, Moltmann has theological questions. He wonders if such an apocalyptic understanding of history suffices to give expression to the Easter event. For then the church would look forward less to Jesus than to its own resurrection, "the repetition of what already happened to Jesus, but not the future of the Resurrected." The gospel is not that we will be raised as he was, but that he is the resurrection and the life, "and that hence the believers find their future *in* him and not only *like* him." Moltmann's own position comes to expression in the criticism: "The apocalyptic, universal historical horizon for interpreting the whole of reality is secondary to the promissory and missionary horizon of this transformation of the world."[304]

Moltmann also thinks the apocalyptic understanding of history is responsible for a neglect of the theology of the cross, which is not just an interlude between Jewish apocalypticism and Christian eschatology but rather brands the latter as *eschatologia crucis*. "The contradiction of the cross also runs through the existence, the path and the theological thinking of the church in the world."[305] Moltmann favors the Pannenbergian openness to the world, which he also finds in Barth and Bonhoeffer's call to proclaim Christ's rule in the concrete everydayness of the world. But he questions whether Pannenberg has faced squarely the concrete reality of an eschatology in a world such as ours.

> The question remains whether [Pannenberg's] expression about "verifying the deity of the Biblical God on the totality of our time's experience of reality," is appropriate. For this task will turn out to be less a confirmation or surpassing than a conflict and a difference. The uncritical use of concepts such as "historical," "history," "facts," "tradition," "reason," etc., in a theological sense seems to show that the methodological, practical and ideological atheism of modern times is more nearly bypassed than taken seriously. If this atheism, as Hegel and Nietzsche most profoundly understood it, derives from a nihilistic perception of the "speculative

---

303. Ibid.
304. Ibid., 73.
305. Ibid.

Good Friday," i.e., "God is dead," then theology could actually be advocated only as a theology of resurrection over against this reality, over against this reason, and over against society structured in this way—and indeed as an eschatology of resurrection as the future of the Crucified.[306]

Concern for the problem of a ground for hope in the future in a world situation such as ours, a topic put in focus in Germany by the philosopher Ernst Bloch's two-volume work on *The Principle of Hope*,[307] together with the absence from Barth's *Church Dogmatics* of the concluding fifth volume on eschatology, may account for the fact that another young theologian in the Barthian tradition, Gerhard Sauter, has published a work rather similar to Moltmann's *Theology of Hope*, entitled *Future and Promise*.[308] And, like Moltmann, Sauter is in this regard rather comparable to Pannenberg himself, yet with many of the same reservations.

Sauter shares Moltmann's view[309] that apocalypticism is hardly a category from which to derive an understanding of history as revelation. "'History is reality in its totality'—but the apocalypticist means this, in spite of the divine 'world law,' in terms of world history as the history of the world that remains separated from God precisely in its totality. The end of history is the negation of [the world's] negativities: time not only as limited, but especially as corrupt time (cf. Rev 10:6); and the impotency of the world (4 Ezra 4:26f.)."[310] Furthermore, Sauter regards the view of Jesus as a prolepsis of the apocalyptic end, though related to apocalypticism's deterministic fixing of history before the beginning of time, as breaking down apocalypticism's understanding of revelation. "Admittedly the apocalyptic structure of revelation as a pre-temporal unveiling of the end has helped make 'what happened to Jesus Christ' intelligible as such a 'prolepsis.' Of course this took place at the cost of a reinterpretation of prolepsis, perhaps necessitated by the New Testament. Prolepsis cannot subject itself to the apocalyptic concept of revelation,

---

306. Ibid., 74.

307. Bloch, *Das Prinzip Hoffnung* = *The Principle of Hope*.

308. Sauter, *Zukunft und Verheissung* (1965). The book is a *Habilitationsschrift* presented under the Barthians Ernst Wolf and Otto Weber at the University of Göttingen in 1964. Sauter states (80) that his work was completed prior to seeing Moltmann's book.

309. Cf. above, 169 n. 83.

310. Sauter, *Zukunft und Verheissung*, 244 n. 49, citing Pannenberg, "Heilsgeschehen und Geschichte," 222 = "Redemptive Event and History," 319.

for it materially breaks through [that concept]."³¹¹ Sauter continues in terms of a quotation from Pannenberg:

> "For Jesus, the relation to the whole of reality is given through ... the eschatological character of his gospel, of his claim, and of what happened to him. For in that [history's] end, which happened in advance in the claim of Jesus and in what happened to him, comes into sight, history for the first time attains its completeness"—not at all! For this relation of sight to event destroys precisely the apocalyptic correlation between "complete" history and revelation! The "simultaneity" of completeness and the end remains a teleological, but not an eschatological axiom.³¹²

Sauter is also concerned to emphasize that a total view is inaccessible to finite man. "But the concept of 'universal history' lays claim to a totality of truth itself. The true is the universal! Yet this impulse may be appropriated only in view of the 'not yet' nature of our knowledge and [should] not permit completion to be reached ahead of time (1 Cor. 13:9f., 12)."³¹³ He recalls Barth's use of the term proleptic to refer to man's presumption ("no proleptic clutching after God's fulness"), to warn against a possible danger or misuse in the understanding of prolepsis.

> Anticipatory security, *securitas* as distorted hope, would take from prolepsis what grounds it—namely, its being God's own act. Man lays hold of promised future in proleptic security, even though it be merely that by pointing to the prolepsis of the end of the world he seeks to insure himself of its completeness and thus of the history of the promise. If, as with Pannenberg, "prolepsis" is to serve as a mobile teleological concept for the whole, this danger must be seen, precisely because it is an eschatologically suitable term.³¹⁴

The juxtaposition of the theology of history and the theology of the word comes to expression in Sauter's discussion of the history of the transmission of traditions, which he prefers to conceive of as the hermeneutical process through which a promise goes, as it is reinterpreted in the light of ongoing events, with the promise providing the basis in

---

311. Sauter, *Zukunft und Verheissung*, 256.
312. Ibid., 256 n. 12, citing Pannenberg, "Kerygma and Geschichte," 139 n. 19.
313. Sauter, *Zukunft und Verheissung*, 183–84.
314. Ibid., 265–66.

terms of which such events retrospectively come together into a course of divine acts that can be called a history.

> But can one then simply proceed to speak of historical *continuity*? This question, which prophetic reflection leaves completely open, must be posed over against the total claim of a "world as history." For this claim reckons with the continuum of a historical world in its unity and completeness.... If it is accurate that in prophecy "the future saving event is conceived of in analogy to the past [saving event]," then this "conception" is bound to the recall of the past and, to this extent, to the promissory tradition that helps set up the horizon for understanding. [Yet] is a promise [in fact] such a "concept," which, by referring to earlier divine action or at least to old announcements, would serve only to let what is coming be *known*?"[315]

Sauter would prefer to regard the promise as the active force calling forth history, rather than simply a commentary on it. Somewhat similarly, Sauter acknowledges the history of the transmission of traditions as a method, but prefers to think of promise rather than the transmission of traditions as what is basic to reality.

> The procedure of study, the investigation of prophetic texts for elements of tradition to permit conclusions about a context of tradition, can be confused with [the process in which] these texts themselves came to be. The method with its conclusions takes the place of the object, or at least is identified with it. The history of the transmission of traditions, as a process of eclectic and thus creative interpretation of what is transmitted—as can however be established only retrospectively in terms of its results, but not as it is taking place!—becomes [in such a view] the continuity presupposed by prophetic eschatology, and indeed by the promise itself. ... Hence, in such a concept in terms of the history of the transmission of traditions, "promise" can hardly "announce" anything other than the impetus of a tradition that is so saturated with contents that it cannot be exhausted by individual (quite unique and unrepeatable) situations.... Yet the interest in historical continuity as a pervasive "structure" of the promissory history will have to open itself to the question of whether it takes note of the mobility of prophetic reflection, which can project the future quite without the guideline of the past, and even outside the area of

---

315. Ibid., 208–9, citing Pannenberg, "Kerygma and Geschichte," 136.

play provided by growing experience. What has been remains too much in dialogue; it is subjected to reflection, or left to be forgotten. The breaks, turns, and new beginnings of the history to be investigated cannot be pointed out in terms of a given continuity; rather God's faithfulness "perseveres" in and in spite of all apparent discontinuity of the tradition.[316]

Hence Sauter is concerned for the openness of the future when the latter is projected upon the history of the transmission of traditions,[317] and prefers to think of the future in terms of God's promise, with *promissio* a favorite term of Luther's for designating the word of God.

The theology of Wolfhart Pannenberg is to some extent already known and discussed in America. He was a visiting professor at the University of Chicago during the Spring of 1963, and at that time lectured widely in the United States. *Christianity Today* has welcomed him as the way out of the "chaos in European theology."[318] And Daniel P. Fuller, then Dean of Fuller Theological Seminary, has become a stanch supporter of Pannenberg, and especially of his treatment of the resurrection, although Fuller would want to "adjust his system slightly" so as to include supernaturalism.[319] American Lutheranism, whose traditional conservatism has often made it more wary of contemporary German theology than its denominational and cultural affinities would otherwise indicate, has tended

---

316. Sauter, *Zukunft und Verheissung*, 210–11.

317. Ibid., 194.

318. The second installment in the series under that title, in the issue of Oct. 9, 1964, 19, concludes with a positive section entitled, interestingly enough, "The New Frontiers," which begins; "The formative theology of the foreseeable future is not likely to be Barth's, Brunner's, or Bultmann's, but rather an alternative to all three. The *Heilsgeschichte* school is calling for a fuller correlation of revelation and history. The traditional conservative scholars have long attacked dialectic theology in even wider dimensions. And a revolt against dialectic theology has been under way among several followers of Wolfhart Pannenberg of Mainz. . . ." Cf. in the same issue the article, "Revelation in History," 33: "In their insistence on objective historical revelation, traditional conservative scholars are now being joined by Heilsgeschichte scholars and the Pannenberg movement in a fresh probe of the problem of revelation and history." Similarly, Dec. 4, 1964, 13–14, in the editorial, "Basic Issues in Modern Theology: Revelation in History." Cf. also the republication of much of this same material under the editor's name, Carl F. H. Henry, "European Theology Today."

319. Fuller, "A New German Theological Movement," esp. 175; idem, "The Resurrection of Jesus and the Historical Method." Cf. also Fuller's Basel dissertation, *Easter Faith and History*, esp. 176–97, 237–38, 251–53.

to look with approval upon Pannenberg.³²⁰ Furthermore his criticism of modern historical method finds its congenial counterpart in Richard R. Niebuhr's study of *Resurrection and Historical Reason*, so that they have independently arrived at somewhat similar positions. And John B. Cobb Jr. has welcomed Pannenberg's radical break with dialectic theology and his concomitant openness to American theological trends that have stood in the Hegelian more than the Kantian tradition.³²¹ The publication of the English translations of Pannenberg's Christology,³²² his small volume on Anthropology,³²³ and his collected essays,³²⁴ together with a year as visiting professor at Harvard and Claremont in 1966-67, gave added impetus to the discussion of Pannenberg's theology in America. Thus the present essay is only a foretaste of a discussion that continued for some time.

---

320. The Lutheran journal *Dialogue* includes Pannenberg on its editorial board and has published articles by him: "The Crisis of the Scripture-Principle in Protestant Theology"; and "Did Jesus Really Rise from the Dead?" Cf. by its editor, Carl E. Braaten, "How New Is the New Hermeneutic?," in which his polemic against Volume 2 of the New Frontiers in Theology series (on which cf. my reply in the "Critic's Corner," ibid., pp. 277-82) is matched only by his enthusiasm for the theological position discussed in Volume 3. Cf. also the article by Robert L. Wilken, "Who is Wolfhart Pannenberg?"

321. Cobb, "A New Trio Arises in Europe," esp. 261-62.

322. *Jesus, God and Man* (1968; 2nd ed. 1977).

323. *What Is Man* (1970).

324. *Basic Questions in Theology*, 3 vols. (1970-73). See also *Theology and the Kingdom of God* (1969).

Bibliography 3

Althaus, Paul. "Offenbarung als Geschichte und Glaube: Bemerkungen zu Wolfhart Pannenbergs Begriff der Offenbarung." *TLZ* 87 (1962) 321–30.
Barth, Karl. *Die Auferstehung der Toten*. Munich: Kaiser, 1924.
———. "How My Mind Has Changed." *Christian Century* (July 4–11, 1984) 684. Reprinted from 1939.
———. *The Resurrection of the Dead*. Translated by H. J. Stenning. 1933. Reprinted, Eugene, OR: Wipf & Stock, 2003.
———. *Der Römerbrief*. 2nd ed. Zurich: Evangelischer Verlag, 1947. Translated as *The Epistle to the Romans*. Translated by Edwyn C. Hoskyns. London: Oxford University Press, 1933.
———. "Unerledigte Anfragen an die heutige Theologie." In *Die Theologie und die Kirche: Gesammelte Aufsätze II*, 1–25. Zurich: Evangelischer Verlag, 1928. Original publication 1920. Translated in *Theology and Church: Shorter Writings, 1920–28*, translated by Louise Pettibone Smith, 55–73. New York: Harper & Row, 1952.
Betz, Hans Dieter. "Zum Problem des religionsgeschichtlichen Verständnisses der Apokalyptik." *ZTK* 63 (1966) 391–409.
Bloch, Ernst. *The Principle of Hope*. Translated by Neville Plaice, Stephen Plaice, and Paul Knight. Studies in Contemporary German Social Thought. Cambridge: MIT Press, 1986.
———. *Das Prinzip Hoffnung*. Berlin: Aufbau-Verlag, 1954–59. 2nd ed., 1959.
Bohren, Rudolf. "Die Krise der Predigt als Frage an die Exegese." *EvTh* 22 (1962) 66–92.
Bonhoeffer, Dietrich. *Prisoner for God: Letters and Papers from Prison*. Translated by Reginald H. Fuller. New York: Macmillan, 1953. 2nd ed., 1954.
———. *Widerstand und Ergebung: Briefe und Aufzeichnungen aus der Haft*. Munich: Kaiser, 1951.
Bornkamm, Günther. *Geschichte und Glaube*. Gesammelte Aufsätze 3. BET 48. Munich: Kaiser, 1968.

———. "Geschichte und Glaube im Neuen Testament: Ein Beitrag zur Frage der 'historischen' Begründung theologischer Aussagen." *EvTh* 22 (1962) 1–15. Reprinted in *Geschichte und Glaube*, 9–24. Gesammelte Aufsätze 3. BET 48. Munich: Kaiser, 1968.

———. "Mythus und Evangelium: Zur Diskussion des Problems der Entmythologisierung der neutestamentlichen Verkündigung." In *Mythos und Evangelium*, 3–28. THE 26. Munich: Kaiser, 1951.

———. *Studien zu Antike und Urchristentum*. Gesammelte Aufsätze 2. BET 28. Munich: Kaiser, 1959.

———. "Die Theologie Rudolf Bultmanns in der neueren Diskussion: Zum Problem der Entmythologisierung und Hermeneutik." *ThR* 29 (1963) 33–141. Reprinted in *Geschichte und Glaube*, 173–275. Gesammelte Aufsätze 3. BET 48. Munich: Kaiser, 1968.

Bowen, Gilbert E. "Toward Understanding Bultmann." *McCormick Quarterly* 17.2 (1964) 26–39.

Braaten, Carl E. "How New Is the New Hermeneutic?" *ThTo* 22 (1965) 218–35.

Bultmann, Rudolf. *Essays Philosophical and Theological*. New York: Macmillan, 1955.

———. "General Truths and Christian Proclamation." In *History and Hermeneutic, JTC* 4 (1967) 153–62.

———. *Glauben und Verstehen*. Vol. 2. Tübingen: Mohr/Siebeck, 1952.

———. *Glauben und Verstehen*. Vol. 3. Tübingen: Mohr/Siebeck, 1960.

———. *Glauben und Verstehen*. Vol. 4. Tübingen: Mohr/Siebeck, 1965.

———. "History and Eschatology in the New Testament." *New Testament Studies* 1 (1954) 5–16.

———. "Ist die Apokalyptik die Mutter der christlichen Theologie?" In *Apophoreta: Festschrift für Ernst Haenchen zu seinem siebzigsten Geburtstag*, edited by Walter Eltester, 64–69. BZNW 30. Berlin: Töpelmann, 1964.

———. *The Presence of Eternity: History and Eschatology*. Gifford Lectures 1955. New York: Harper & Row, 1957.

———. *Primitive Christianity in Its Contemporary Setting*. Translated by Reginald H. Fuller. Living Age Books. New York: Meridian, 1956.

———. "Das Problem einer theologischen Exegese des Neuen Testaments." *Zwischen den Zeiten* 3 (1925) 334–57. Reprinted in *Anfänge der dialektischen Theologie*, edited by Jürgen Moltmann, 47–72. Vol. 2. Munich: Kaiser, 1963.

———. "The Problem of a Theological Exegesis of the New Testament." In *The Beginnings of Dialectic Theology*, edited by James M. Robinson, 1:236–56. Richmond, VA: John Knox, 1968.

———. *Theologie des Neuen Testaments*. Vol. 1. Tübingen: Mohr/Siebeck, 1948. 3rd ed., 1958.

———. *Theology of the New Testament*. 2 vols. Translated by Kendrick Grobel. New York: Scribner, 1951–55. Reprinted, Waco, TX: Baylor University Press, 2007.

———. *Das Urchristentum im Rahmen der antiken Religionen*. Zurich: Artemis, 1949.

———. "Zum Problem der Entmythologisierung." In *Kerygma und Mythos VI, 1. Entmythologisierung und existentiale Interpretation*. Theologische Forschung 30. Hamburg: Reich, 1963.

———. "Zur Interpretation des Johannesevangelium." *TLZ* 87 (1962) 1–8.

Campenhausen, Hans von. "Augustin und der Fall von Rom." In *Weltgeschichte und Gottesgericht*, 2–18. Lebendige Wissenschaft 1. Stuttgart: Kreuz, 1947. Reprinted in *Tradition und Leben: Kräfte der Kirchengeschichte: Aufsätze und Vorträge*, 253–71. Tübingen: Mohr/Siebeck, 1960.

———. "Augustine and the Fall of Rome." In *Tradition and Life in the Church: Essays and Lectures in Church History*. Translated by A. V. Littledale. Philadelphia: Fortress, 1968.

———. "Gottesgericht und Menschengerechtigkeit in der Geschichte." In *Vom neuen Geist der Universität: Dokumente, Reden und Vortrage 1945–46*, edited by K. H. Bauer, 64–73. Schriften der Universität Heidelberg 2. Berlin: Springer, 1947.

———. *Tradition and Life in the Church: Essays and Lectures in Church History*. Translated by A. V. Littledale. Philadelphia: Fortress, 1968.

Cobb, John B., Jr. "A New Trio Arises in Europe." *Christian Advocate* (July 2, 1964) 7–8. Reprinted in *New Theology* 2, edited by Martin E. Marty and Dean G. Peerman, 257–63. New York: Macmillan, 1965.

Conzelmann, Hans. "Randbemerkungen zur Lage im Neuen Testament." *EvTh* 22 (1962) 225–33.

Cullmann, Oscar. *Christus und die Zeit: Die urchristliche Zeit- und Geschichtsauffassung*. Zurich: Evangelischer Verlag, 1946.

———. *Christ and Time: The Primitive Christian Conception of Time and History*. Translated by Floyd V. Filson. Philadelphia: Westminster, 1950.

———. *Heil als Geschichte: Heilsgeschichtliche Existenz im Neuen Testament*. Tübingen: Mohr/Siebeck, 1965.

———. *Salvation in History*. Translated by Sidney G. Sowers. New York: Harper & Row, 1967.

Davies, W. D. "The Jewish Background of the Teaching of Jesus: Apocalyptic and Pharisaism." *ExpTim* 59 (1948) 233–37. Reprinted in *Christian Origins and Judaism*, 19–30. Philadelphia: Westminster, 1962.

Ebeling, Gerhard. *Theologie und Verkündigung*. Hermeneutische Untersuchungen zur Theologie 1. Tübingen: Mohr/Siebeck, 1962.

———. "Word of God and Hermeneutic." In *The New Hermeneutic*, edited by James M. Robinson and John B. Cobb Jr., 78–110. New Frontiers in Theology 2. New York: Harper & Row, 1964.

———. *Wort Gottes und Tradition: Studien zu einer Hermeneutik der Konfessionen*. Kirche und Konfession: Veröffentlichungen des Konfessionskundlichen Instituts des Evangelischen Bundes 7. Göttingen: Vandenhoeck & Ruprecht, 1964.

Elze, Martin. "Der Begriff des Dogmas in der Alten Kirche." *ZTK* 61 (1964) 421–38.

———. *Tatian und seine Theologie*. FKDG 9. Göttingen: Vandenhoeck & Ruprecht, 1960.

Fuchs, Ernst. "Christus das Ende der Geschichte" [review of Oscar Cullmann, *Christ and Time*]. *EvTh* 8 (1948–49) 447–61. Reprinted in *Zur Frage nach dem historischen Jesus: Gesammelte Aufsätze II*, 79–99. Tübingen: Mohr/Siebeck, 1960.

———. "Theologie oder Ideologie? Bemerkungen zu einem heilsgeschichtlichen Programm." *TLZ* 88 (1963) 257–60.

Fuller, Daniel P. *Easter Faith and History*. Grand Rapids: Eerdmans, 1965.

———. "A New German Theological Movement." *SJT* 19 (1966) 160–75.

———. "The Resurrection of Jesus and the Historical Method." *Journal of Bible and Religion* 34 (1966) 18–24.
Funk, Robert W. "The Hermeneutical Problem and Historical Criticism." In *The New Hermeneutic*, edited by James M. Robinson and John B. Cobb Jr., 167–80. New Frontiers in Theology 2. New York: Harper & Row, 1964.
Gadamer, Hans Georg. *Truth and Method*. Translation revised by Joel Weinsheimer and Donald G. Marshall. London: Continuum, 2004.
———. *Wahrheit und Methode: Grundzüge einer philosophischen Hermeneutik*. Tübingen: Mohr/Siebeck, 1960.
Geyer, Hans-Georg. "Geschichte als theologisches Problem: Bemerkungen zu W. Pannenbergs Geschichtstheologie." *EvTh* 22 (1962) 92–104.
Gogarten, Friedrich. "Between the Times." In *The Beginnings of Dialectical Theology*, edited by James M. Robinson, 1:277–82. Richmond, VA: John Knox, 1968.
———. "Vom heiligen Egoismus des Christen: Eine Antwort auf Jülichers Aufsatz: 'Ein moderner Paulusausleger.'" *CW* 34 (1920) 546–50. Reprinted in *Anfänge der dailektischen Theologie*, vol. 1, edited by Jürgen Moltmann, 99–105. ThBü. Munich: Kaiser, 1962.
———. "Holy Egoism of the Christian: An Answer to Jülicher's Essay: 'A Modern Interpreter of Paul.'" In *The Beginnings of Dialectical Theology*, edited by James M. Robinson, 1:82–87. Richmond, VA: John Knox, 1968.
———. "Theology and History." In *History and Hermeneutic*, *JTC* 4 (1967) 35–81.
———. "Zwischen den Zeiten." In *Anfänge der dialektischen Theology*, edited by Jürgen Moltmann, 1:95–101. ThBü 16. Munich: Kaiser, 1963. Originally published in *Die Christliche Welt* 34 (1920) 374–78.
Grass, Hans. *Ostergeschehen und Osterberichte*. Göttingen: Vandenhoeck & Ruprecht, 1956. 2nd ed., 1962.
Grobel, Kendrick. "Revelation and Resurrection." In *Theology as History*, edited by James M. Robinson and John B. Cobb Jr., 155–75. New Frontiers in Theology 3. New York: Harper & Row, 1967.
Haenchen, Ernst. *The Acts of the Apostles: A Commentary*. Translated by Bernard Noble and Gerald Shinn, under the supervision of Hugh Anderson, and revised by R. McL. Wilson. Philadelphia: Westminster, 1971.
———. *Die Apostelgeschichte*. 13th ed. KEKNT 3. Göttingen: Vandenhoeck & Ruprecht, 1961. 17th ed., 1977.
Hartlich, Christian, and Walter Sachs. *Der Ursprung des Mythosbegriffes in der modernen Bibelwissenschaft*. Tübingen: Mohr/Siebeck, 1952.
Henry, Carl F. H. "European Theology Today." *Faith and Thought: Journal of the Victoria Institute* 94 (1965) 9–91.
Holwerda, David E. *The Holy Spirit and Eschatology in the Gospel of John*. Kampen: Kok, 1959.
Kimmerle, Heinz. "Hermeneutical Theory or Ontological Hermeneutics." In *History and Hermeneutic*, *JTC* 4 (1967) 107–21.
———. "Hermeneutische Theorie oder ontologische Hermeneutik." *ZTK* 59 (1962) 114–30.
Klein, Günter. "Exegetische Probleme in Römer 3,21—4,25: Antwort an U. Wilckens," *EvTh* 24 (1964) 676–83.

---. "Lukas 1,1-4 als theologisches Programm." In *Zeit und Geschichte: Dankesgabe an Rudolf Bultmann zum 80. Geburtstag*, edited by Erich Dinkler, 193-216. Tubingen: Mohr/Siebeck, 1964.

---. "Offenbarung als Geschichte? Marginalien zu einem theologischen Program." *MPT* 51 (1962) 65-88.

---. "Römer 4 und die Idee der Heilsgeschichte." *EvTh* 23 (1963) 424-447.

---. *Theologie des Wortes Gottes und die Hypothese der Universalgeschichte: Zur Auseinandersetzung mit Wolfhart Pannenberg*. BET 37. Munich: Kaiser, 1964.

Knigge, Heinz-Dieter. "Postbultmannian Hermeneutical Attempts." *Perkins School of Theology Journal* 17 (1964) 26-37.

Koch, Klaus. *Die Priesterschrift von Exodus 25 bis Leviticus 16*. FRLANT 71. Göttingen: Vandenhoeck & Ruprecht, 1959.

---. "Spätisraelitisches Geschichtsdenken am Beispiel des Buches Daniel." *Historische Zeitschrift* 193 (1961) 1-32.

---. "Der Tod des Religionsstifters: Erwägungen über das Verhältnis Israels zur Geschichte der altorientalischen Religionen." *KD* 8 (1962) 100-123.

Körner, Johannes. *Eschatologie und Geschichte: Eine Untersuchung des Begriffes des Eschatologischen in der Theologie Rudolf Bultmanns*. Theologische Forschung: Wissensaftliche Beiträge zur kirchlich-evangelischen Lehre 13. Hamburg: Reich, 1957.

Kühn, Ulrich. "Das Problem der zureichenden dogmatischen Begründung der christlichen Auferstehungshoffnung." *KD* 9 (1963) 1-17.

Löwith, Karl. *Weltgeschichte und Heilsgeschehen*. Stuttgart: Kohlhammer, 1953.

---. *Meaning in History: The Theological Implications of the Philosophy of History*. Chicago: University of Chicago Press, 1949.

Marxsen, Willi. *Die Auferstehung Jesu als historisches and als theologisches Problem*. Gütersloh: Gütersloher, 1964; 2nd ed., 1965.

---. *The Resurrection of Jesus*. Translated by Margaret Kohl. Philadelphia: Fortress, 1970.

Moltmann, Jürgen, editor. *Anfänge der dialektischen Theology*. 2 vols. ThBü 16 and 17. Munich: Kaiser, 1962-1963.

---. "Exegese und Eschatologie der Geschichte." *EvTh* 22 (1962) 31-66.

---. *Theologie der Hoffnung: Untersuchungen zur Begründung und zu den Konsequenzen einer christlichen Eschatologie*. Munich: Kaiser, 1964. 2nd ed. and 3rd ed., 1965.

---. *Theology of Hope: On the Ground and the Implications of a Christian Eschatology*. Translated by James W. Leitch. 1967. Reprinted, Minneapolis: Fortress, 1998.

Muschalek, Georg, SJ, and Arnold Gamper, SJ. "Offenbarung als Geschichte." *ZKT* 86 (1964) 180-96.

Niebuhr, Richard R. *Resurrection and Historical Reason*. New York: Scribner, 1957.

Ott, Heinrich. "Existentiale Interpretation und anonyme Christlichkeit." In *Zeit und Geschichte: Dankesgabe an Rudolf Bultmann zum 80. Geburtstag*, edited by Erich Dinkler, 367-79. Tübingen: Mohr/Siebeck, 1964.

---. *Die Frage nach dem historischen Jesus und die Ontologie der Geschichte*. ThSt 62. Zurich: EVZ, 1960.

Pannenberg, Wolfhart. "The Crisis of the Scripture-Principle in Protestant Theology." *Dialogue* 2 (1963) 307–13.

———. "Did Jesus Really Rise from the Dead?" *Dialog* 4 (1965) 128–35.

———. "Dogmatic Theses on the Doctrine of Revelation." In *Revelation as History*, edited by Wolfhart Pannenberg, 123–58. Translated by David Granskou. New York: Macmillan, 1968.

———. "Dogmatische Thesen zur Lehre von der Offenbarung." In *Offenbarung als Geschichte* edited by Wolfhart Pannenberg, 91–114. Göttingen: Vandenhoeck & Ruprecht, 1961. 2nd ed., 1963.

———. "Einsicht and Glaube: Antwort an Paul Althaus." *TLZ* 88 (1963) 81–92.

———. "Exegese und Eschatologie der Geschichte." *EvTh* 22 (1962) 31–66.

———. "Focal Essay: The Revelation of God in Jesus of Nazareth." In *Theology as History*, edited by James M. Robinson and John B. Cobb Jr., 101–33. New Frontiers in Theology 3. New York: Harper & Row, 1967.

———. *Grundfragen systematischer Theologie: Gesammelte Schriften*. Göttingen: Vandenhoeck & Ruprecht, 1967.

———. *Grundzüge der Christologie*. Gütersloh: Mohn, 1964. Rev. ed., 1976.

———. "Heilsgeschehen und Geschichte." *KD* 5 (1959) 218–37; 259–88.

———. "Hermeneutics and Universal History." In *History and Hermeneutic*, *JTC* 4 (1967) 122–52.

———. "Hermeneutik und Universalgeschichte." *ZTK* 60 (1963) 90–121.

———. "Introduction." In *Revelation as History*, edited by Wolfhart Pannenberg, 1–21. Translated by David Granskou. New York: Macmillan, 1968.

———. *Jesus—God and Man*. Translated by Lewis L. Wilkins and Duane A. Priebe. Philadelphia: Westminster, 1968. 2nd ed., 1977.

———. "Kerygma und Geschichte." In *Studien zur Theologie der alttestamentlichen Überlieferungen*, edited by Rolf Rendtorff and Klaus Koch, 129–40. Neukirchen-Vluyn: Neukirchener, 1961.

———. "Die Krise des Ethischen and die Theologie." *TLZ* 87 (1962) 7–16.

———, editor. *Offenbarung als Geschichte*. Göttingen: Vandenhoeck & Ruprecht, 1961. 2nd ed., 1963.

———. "Postscript." In *Offenbarung als Geschichte*, 2nd ed., 132–48.

———. *Die Prädestinationslehre des Duns Skotus*. FKDG 4. Göttingen: Vandenhoeck & Ruprecht, 1954.

———. "Redemptive Event and History." In *Essays on Old Testament Hermeneutics*, edited by Claus Westermann and James Luther Mays, 314–35. Translated by Shirley Guthrie. Atlanta: John Knox, 1963.

———, editor. *Revelation as History*. Translated by David Granskou. New York: Macmillan, 1968.

———. *What Is Man? Contemporary Anthropology in Theological Perspective*. Translated by Duane A. Priebe. Philadelphia: Fortress, 1970.

Rad, Gerhard von. *Theologie des Alten Testaments*. 2 vols. Munich: Kaiser, 1957–60.

———. *Theology of the Old Testament*. 2 vols. Translated by D. M. G. Stalker. New York: Harper & Row, 1962–65.

Rendtorff, Rolf. "The Concept of Revelation in Ancient Israel." In *Revelation as History*, edited by Wolfhart Pannenberg, 23–53. Translated by David Granskou. New York: Macmillan, 1968.

———. "Erwägungen zur Frühgeschichte des Prophetentums in Israel." *ZTK* 59 (1962) 145–67.

———. "Geschichte und Überlieferung." In *Studien zur Theologie der alttestamentlichen Überlieferungen*, edited by Rolf Rendtorff and Klaus Koch, 81–94. Neukirchen: Neukirchener Verlag, 1961.

———. "Geschichte und Wort im Alten Testament." *EvTh* 22 (1962) 621–49.

———. *Die Gesetze in der Priesterschrift: Eine gattungsgeschichtliche Untersuchung.* FRLANT 62. Göttingen: Vandenhoeck & Ruprecht, 1954.

———. "Hermeneutik des Alten Testaments als Frage nach der Geschichte." *ZTK* 57 (1960) 27–40.

———. "Die Offenbarungsvorstellungen im Alten Israel." In *Offenbarung als Geschichte*, 21–41. Göttingen: Vandenhoeck & Ruprecht, 1961. 2nd ed., 1963.

———. "Reflections on the Early History of Prophecy in Israel." In *History and Hermeneutic*, JTC 4 (1967) 14–34.

Rendtorff, Trutz. "Das Offenbarungsproblem im Kirchenbegriff." In *Offenbarung als Geschichte*, edited by Wolfhart Pannenberg, 115–31. Göttingen: Vandenhoeck & Ruprecht, 1961. 2nd ed., 1963.

———. "The Problem of Revelation in the Concept of the Church." In *Revelation as History*, edited by Wolfhart Pannenberg, 159–81. Translated by David Granskou. New York: Macmillan, 1968.

———. *Die soziale Struktur der Gemeinde: Die kirchlichen Lebensformen in gesellschaftlichem Wandel der Gegenwart.* Studien zur evangelischen Sozialtheologie und Sozialethik 1. Hamburg: Furche, 1958.

Robinson, James M., editor. *The Beginnings of Dialectical Theology.* 2 vols. Translated by Keith R. Crim and Louis DeGrazia. Richmond: John Knox, 1968.

———. "Critic's Corner" [reply to Carl E. Braaten]. *TTo* 22 (1965) 277–82.

———. "For Theology and the Church." In *The Bultmann School of Biblical Interpretation: New Directions?* JTC 1 (1965) 1–19.

———. "The Historicality of Biblical Language." In *The Old Testament and Christian Faith: A Theological Discussion*, edited by Bernhard W. Anderson, 124–58. New York: Harper & Row, 1963.

———. "Kerygma and History in the New Testament." In *The Bible in Modern Scholarship*, edited by J. Philip Hyatt, 114–50. Nashville: Abingdon, 1965.

———. "The Pre-History of Demythologization." *Int* 20 (1966) 65–77.

Rössler, Dietrich. *Der "ganze" Mensch: Das Menschenbild der neueren Seelsorgelehre und des modernen medizinischen Denkens im Zusammenhang der allgemeinen Anthropologie.* Göttingen: Vandenhoeck & Ruprecht, 1962.

———. *Gesetz und Geschichte: Untersuchungen zur Theologie der jüdischen Apokalyptik und der pharisäischen Orthodoxie.* WMANT 3. Neukirchen-Vluyn: Neukirchener, 1960. 2nd ed., 1962.

Sauter, Gerhard. *Zukunft und Verheissung: Das Problem der Zukunft in der gegenwärtigen theologischen und philosophischen Diskussion.* Zurich: Theologischer Verlag, 1965.

Schempp, Paul. "Marginal Glosses on Barthianism." In *The Beginnings of Dialectical Theology*, edited by James M. Robinson, 1:191–200. Richmond, VA: John Knox, 1968.

———. "Randglossen zum Barthianismus." *EvTh* 6 (1928) 529–39. Reprinted in *Anfänge der dialektischen Theologie*, edited by Jürgen Moltmann, 2:303–13. ThBü 17. Munich: Kaiser, 1963.

Schrage, Wolfgang. "'Ekklesia' und 'Synagoge': Zum Ursprung des unchristlichen Kirchenbegriffes." *ZThK* 60 (1963) 178–202.

Schweizer, Eduard. "Some Trends in European New Testament Research of Today." *Chicago Theological Seminary Register* 54 (1963) 5–7.

Steiger, Lothar. "Offenbarungsgeschichte und theologische Vernunft: Zur Theologie W. Pannenbergs." *ZTK* 59 (1962) 88–113.

———. "Revelation-History and Theological Reason: A Critique of the Theology of Wolfhart Pannenberg." In *History and Hermeneutic, JTC* 4 (1967) 82–106.

Strobel, August. *Die apokalyptische Sendung Jesu: Gedanken zur Neuorientierung in der kerygmatischen Frage*. Rothenburg: Martin-Luther-Verlag, 1962.

Troeltsch, Ernst. *Gesammelte Schriften*. Vol. 2. Tübingen: Mohr/Siebeck, 1913.

Vielhauer, Philipp. "Apocalyptic Christianity." In *New Testament Apocrypha*, edited by Edgar Hennecke and Wilhelm Schneemelcher, 569–602. Translated by A. J. B. Higgins et al. Philadelphia: Westminster, 1963–66.

———. "Apokalyptisches Christentum." In *Neutestamentliche Apokryphen*, edited by Edgar Hennecke and Wilhelm Schneemelcher. 3rd ed. Tübingen: Mohr/Siebeck, 1964.

Wilckens, Ulrich. "Die Bekehrung des Paulus als religionsgeschichtliches Problem." *ZTK* 56 (1959) 273–93.

———. *Die Missionsreden der Apostelgeschichte: Form- und traditionsgeschichtliche Untersuchungen*. WMANT 5. Neukirchen-Vluyn: Neukirchener, 1961. 2nd ed., 1962.

———. "Das Offenbarungsverstandnis in der Geschichte des Urchristentums." In *Offenbarung als Geschichte*, edited by Wolfhart Pannenberg, 42–90. Göttingen: Vandenhoeck & Ruprecht, 1961. 2nd ed., 1963.

———. Review of *Die apokalyptische Sendung Jesu* by August Strobel in *TLZ* 89 (1964) 671.

———. "The Understanding of Revelation within the History of Primitive Christianity." *Revelation as History*, edited by Wolfhart Pannenberg, 55–121. Translated by David Granskou. New York: Macmillan, 1968.

———. *Weisheit und Torheit: Eine exegetisch-religionsgeschichtliche Untersuchung zu 1. Kor. 1 und 2*. BHT 26. Tübingen: Mohr/Siebeck, 1959.

———. "Zu Römer 3,21—4,25: Antwort an G. Klein." *EvTh* 24 (1964) 586–610.

Wilken, Robert L. "Who is Wolfhart Pannenberg?" *Dialog* 4 (1965) 140–42.

Wirsching, Johannes. "Ein neues theologisches System? Randbemerkungen zur Theologie W. Pannenbergs." *Deutsches Pfarrerblatt* 64 (1964) 601–9.

———. *Gott in der Geschichte: Studien zur theologiegeschichtlichen und systematischen Grundlegung der Theologie Martin Kählers*. Forschungen zur Geschichte und Lehre des Protestantismus, Reihe 10, 26. Munich: Kaiser, 1963

Zimmerli, Walther. *Erkenntnis Gottes nach dem Buche Ezekiel: Eine theologische Studie*. ATANT 27. Zürich; Zwingli, 1954. Reprinted in *Gottes Offenbarung*, 41–119.

———. *Gottes Offenbarung: Gesammelte Aufsätze zum Alten Testament*. ThBü 19. Munich: Kaiser, 1963. 2nd ed., 1969.

———. "Das Gotteswort des Ezechiel." *ZTK* 48 (1951) 249–62. Reprinted in idem, *Gottes Offenbarung*, 133–47.

———. *I am Yahweh*. Edited by Walter Brueggemann. Translated by Douglas W. Stott. Atlanta: John Knox, 1982.

———. "I am Yahweh." In idem, *I am Yahweh*, 1–28.

———. "Ich bin Jahwe." In *Geschichte und Altes Testament: Albrecht Alt zum 70. Geburtstag dargebracht*, edited by W. F. Albright, 179–209. BHT 16. Tübingen: Mohr/Siebeck, 1953. Reprinted in *Gottes Offenbarung*, 11–40.

———. "The Knowledge of God according to the Book of Ezekiel." In *I Am Yahweh*, 29–98.

——— "'Offenbarung' im Alten Testament: Ein Gespräch mit R. Rendtorff." *EvTh* 22 (1962) 15–31.

———. "The Word of Divine Self-manifestation (Proof-saying): A Prophetic Genre." In *I Am Yahweh*, 99–110.

———. "The Word of God in the Book of Ezekiel." In *History and Hermeneutic*, JTC 4 (1967) 1–13. Reprinted in idem, *The Fiery Throne: The Prophets and Old Testament Theology*, edited by K. C. Hanson, 96–106. FCBS. Minneapolis: Fortress, 2003.

———. "Das Wort des göttlichen Selbsterweises (Erweiswort): Eine prophetische Gattung." In *Mélanges Bibliques rédigés en l'Honneur de André Robert*, 154–64. Travaux de l'Institut Catholique de Paris 4. Paris: Bloud et Gay, 1957. Reprinted in *Gottes Offenbarung*, 120–32.

Index of Names

'Abd al Masīḥ, Yassah, 142
Albright, W. F., 145, 239
Althaus, Paul, 162, 179, 200, 201, 202, 204, 232, 236
Anderson, Bernhard W., 67, 238
Anselm of Canterbury, 38–39
Anz, Wilhelm, 4, 39
Aristotle, 21, 29, 57, 70
Ast, Friedrich, 77
Augustine, 99, 151–54
Bachmann, Ph., 93, 138
Barth, Karl, ix–x, 3, 12, 24, 26–27, 32–34, 44, 46, 54, 58, 64, 83, 87–97, 105, 115, 126, 138, 147, 149–51, 154, 158–63, 178–79, 182, 191, 195, 226–28, 230, 232
Bartsch, Hans Werner, 99, 138
Bauer, Walter, 79, 138
Baumgärtel, Friedrich, 85, 138
Beaufret, Jean, 1
Begrich, Joachim, 143
Behm, Johannes, 70, 93, 138
Berkhof, Louis, 82, 138
Bertram, M. Joachim Christoph, 139, 140
Betti, Emilio, 77, 136

Betz, Hans Dieter, 218, 232
Blackman, E. C., 75, 139
Blass, Friedrich, 79, 139
Bloch, Ernst, 227, 232
Boeckh, August, 80
Boisacq, Émile, 71, 139
Bonhoeffer, Dietrich, 51, 61, 64, 128, 140, 151, 226, 232
Bohren, Rudolf, 159–60, 232
Bornkamm, Günther, 102, 139, 151, 158, 159, 163–64, 232–33
Bourke, Myles M., 82, 139
Bowen, Gilbert E., 167, 172, 173, 233
Braaten, Carl E., 231, 233, 238
Braun, Herbert, 4, 62, 64, 164, 172
Brunner, Emil, ix, 230
Brunner, Peter, 154
Bultmann, Rudolf, ix–x, 3–4, 12–13, 19, 22, 24–27, 39–40, 44, 47, 51–56, 58–60, 64, 81, 86–90, 94–105, 114–19, 123–25, 128–30, 139, 147, 151, 153–54, 157–58, 160–61, 163–68, 171–73, 175, 179, 181, 183, 194, 200, 202–3, 212, 214, 216, 230, 233
Burnham, Sylvester, 82, 139
Campenhausen, Hans von, 151–54, 166–67, 172–73, 233–34

Index of Names

Cassirer, Ernst, 100, 139–40
Chafer, Rollin Thomas, 82, 140
Cobb, John B., Jr., x, 64, 67, 140, 141, 142, 144, 145, 146, 231, 234, 235
Colwell, Ernest Cadman, 79, 140
Conzelmann, Hans, 212, 234
Cross, Frank Moore, 140
Cullmann, Oscar, 104–5, 118, 140, 153–54, 162–63, 210, 234
Dannhauer, J. C., 76, 140
Davies, W. D., 210, 234
Debrunner, Albert, 79, 139
Denzinger, Heinrich, 82, 140
Descartes, René, 8, 15, 17, 21, 50–51, 58, 92–93, 221, 225
Dibelius, Martin, 81, 140
Diem, Hermann, 3, 9, 26, 62, 64, 103
Dillenberger, John, 118, 140
Dilthey, Wilhelm, 75, 85–87, 106–8, 114, 121, 129–31, 133–34, 136, 140
Dinkler, Erich, 235, 236
Dobschütz, Ernst von, 76, 83–84, 93, 140
Dungan, D. R., 82, 140
Dvoracek, J. A., 166
Ebeling, Gerhard, x, 4, 25, 37, 44–45, 55–56, 58, 61–65, 70–71, 73, 75, 77, 102, 103–5, 112, 117–19, 123–30, 133, 140–41, 162, 175–76, 183, 194–95, 206–7, 225, 234
Eidem, Erling, 84, 141
Elze, Martin, 155–56, 234
Ernesti, J. A., 76, 141
Eusebius, 72
Fascher, Erich, 86, 93, 141
Franz, Helmut, 4, 29, 34, 52, 55, 57–62, 65, 81, 109, 112–13, 141
Frick, Heinrich, 93, 141
Friedländer, Paul, 22, 65
Frör, Kurt, 104, 141, 145
Fuchs, Ernst, x, 3–4, 24, 37, 52, 55–60, 62, 65, 102–5, 109, 111–26,

Fuchs, Ernst (*continued*)
141–42, 151, 157, 163, 205, 209, 234
Fuller, Daniel P., 230, 234
Fuller, Reginald H., 64, 99, 232–33
Funk, Robert W., 79, 139, 142, 150, 235
Gadamer, Hans-Georg, 77, 85, 87, 91–92, 102, 106, 121, 124, 130–37, 142, 194, 235
Gamper, Arnold, SJ, 165, 185, 189, 191, 202, 236
Geyer, Hans-Georg, 159, 170, 235
Gilmour, S. Maclean, 104, 142, 145
Girgensohn, Karl, 93, 142
Gogarten, Friedrich, 3, 24, 65, 93, 118, 142, 149, 150, 151, 157, 165, 235
Gomperz, Heinrich, 86, 142
Grant, Frederick C., 142
Grant, Robert M., 75, 142
Grass, Hans, 141, 177, 235
Grobel, Kendrick, x, 64, 75, 139, 142, 209, 233
Guillaumont, Antoine, 73, 142
Gunkel, Hermann, 79–80, 85, 99, 100, 143
Güthling, Otto, 71, 144
Haenchen, Ernst, 39, 65, 211–12, 235
Hamilton, William, 128, 139, 208
Harnack, Adolf von, 90, 92–93, 138
Hartill, J. Edwin, 82, 143
Hartlich, Christian, 196, 203, 235
Harvey, Van A., 123, 143
Hebel, Johann Peter, 18
Heidegger, Martin, 1–63, 65–67, 76, 81, 87, 89–90, 92–93, 98, 106–13, 120, 125, 129–30, 133, 137, 143
Heimsoeth, Heinz, 85, 146
Heitsch, Ernst, 21–22, 67
Hennecke, Edgar, 238–39

Heinrici, Georg, 70, 78–81, 83, 85, 143
Henry, Carl F. H., 230, 235
Herrmann, Wilhelm, 90
Hippolytus of Rome, 73
Hofmann, J. Chr. K. von, 83, 143, 157
Hölderlin, Friedrich, 6, 10, 18, 38, 111
Holl, Karl, 125, 143
Holwerda, David E., 166
Husserl, Edmund, 107
Hyatt, J. Philip, 238
Jaspers, Karl, 27, 154
Jonas, Hans, 80, 88, 98–100, 129, 133–34, 143
Jülicher, Adolf, 93–95, 143
Jüngel, Eberhard, 4, 26, 33, 54–58, 62, 67, 103, 144
Kant, Immanuel , 5, 114, 130, 134, 136, 206, 223, 225, 231
Käsemann, Ernst, 105–6, 113, 144, 164, 166–67, 203, 210
Kierkegaard, Søren, 8, 26, 93, 100, 150, 157, 168
Kimmerle, Heinz, 76–77, 131–32, 134, 137, 144, 235
Klein, Günter, 148, 185–86, 196, 209–21, 235
Knigge, Heinz-Dieter, 217, 235
Koch, Klaus, 155–56, 197, 236–37
Koester, Helmut, 140
König, Eduard, 83, 144
Körner, Johannes, 163–65, 236
Kühn, Ulrich, 179, 236
Kümmel, Werner Georg, 142
Löwith, Karl, 3, 6, 9–13, 46, 67, 153–54, 236
Lücke, Friedrich, 76, 131, 145
Lütgert, Willi, 81, 85, 144
Luther, Martin, 58, 80, 91, 98, 125, 136, 152, 170, 206, 230
Macholz, Waldemar, 93, 144
Magnusson, Martin, 103, 144

Marxsen, Willi, 175–77, 180, 236
Mays, James Luther, 82, 144–46, 237
McNeill, John T., 75, 142
Menge, Hermann, 71, 144
Merz, Georg, 151
Meyer, A., 144
Mezger, Manfred, 103, 120–21, 144
Michalson, Carl, 60, 65, 67
Miskotte, Kornelis Heiko, 72, 103, 144
Moltmann, Jürgen, 159–60, 169–70, 188–89, 193, 222–27, 233, 235–36, 238
Muschalek, Georg, SJ, 165, 185, 189, 191, 202, 221, 236
Neske, Günther, 142
Niebuhr, Richard R., 231, 236
Nietzsche, Friedrich, 6–8, 21–22, 66, 226
Noller, Gerhard, 26, 67
Noth, Martin, 82, 144
Ogden, Schubert M., 61, 67, 123, 139, 143
Origen, 75, 100
Ott, Heinrich, x, 3–4, 12–13, 15, 19, 24–27, 29–40, 44–47, 51–60, 62, 67, 120, 161, 194, 203, 236
Otto, Rudolf, 37
Overbeck, Franz, 81, 144, 150
Pannenberg, Wolfhart, x, 82, 144–45, 147–48, 154–82, 187–89, 191–93, 196, 198–231, 236–37, 239
Papias, 72
Paul, 29, 51, 62, 70, 87–88, 91, 94–97, 119, 121, 151, 163–64, 174–75, 179, 205, 210–11
Pelagius, 99
Philo of Alexandria, 70, 75, 218
Photius, 72–73, 145
Plato, 1, 6, 21–22, 43, 70, 72, 76
Procksch, Otto, 93, 145
Pseudo-Demetrius of Phaleron, 70
Puech, Henri-Charles, 142

Quispel, Gilles, 142
Rad, Gerhard von, 82, 154, 158, 169, 191, 193, 196, 237
Ramm, Bernard L., 82, 145
Renan, Ernst, 83
Rendtorff, Rolf, 82, 148, 155–56, 161, 181–82, 185–200, 223, 237–38
Rendtorff, Trutz, 82, 156, 213, 238
Ritschl, Albrecht, 128
Robinson, James M., ix–x, 26, 32, 46, 61, 64, 67, 90, 104, 120, 140–42, 144–46, 149, 159, 164, 234–35, 238
Robinson, John A. T., 128
Rössler, Dietrich, 155–56, 163, 197, 210, 238
Rowley, H. H., 142
Sachs, Walter, 196, 203, 235
Sandmel, Samuel, 79–80, 145
Sartre, Jean-Paul, 1–2, 27, 67
Sauter, Gerhard, 169, 215, 219, 224, 227–30, 238
Schelling, Friedrich Wilhelm Joseph, 8
Schempp, Paul, 149, 238
Scherer, R., 52
Schleiermacher, Friedrich D. E., 76–77, 80–81, 85–86, 94, 106, 114, 121, 131–32, 145
Schlink, Edmund, 154
Schmidt, Karl Ludwig, 81, 145
Schmidt, Hans, 145
Schneemelcher, Wilhelm, 238–39
Schodde, George H., 82, 145
Schott, Andreas, SJ, 72, 145
Schrage, Wolfgang, 211, 238
Schrey, Heinz-Horst, 28, 52, 54, 61, 67
Schulz, Walter, 3–7, 9, 13, 26, 50, 61–62, 68
Schweitzer, Albert, 149
Schweizer, Eduard, 104, 145, 161, 189, 238
Seeberg, Erich, 93, 145
Seeberg, Reinhold, 93, 145
Senft, Christoph, 132, 145
Smalley, Beryl, 75, 146
Smith, R. Gregor, 128, 141
Socrates, 43, 108
Soden, Hans von, 153
Staiger, Emil, 7, 46, 65, 68, 81, 110, 129, 130, 146
Steiger, Lothar, 26, 68, 103, 146, 156, 170, 181, 204–6, 209, 238
Stendahl, Krister, 80, 88, 104, 146
Strobel, August, 156, 210, 238
Terrien, Samuel, 75, 142
Terry, Milton S., 81, 146
Theodore of Mopsuestia, 73
Theodoret of Cyrrhus, 73
Thurneysen, Eduard, 26, 68, 151
Till, Walter, 142
Torm, Frederik Emanuel, 79, 81, 84, 93, 103, 106, 113–14, 146
Trakl, Georg, 18
Traub, Friedrich, 93, 95, 146
Troeltsch, Ernst, 171
Uhsadel, Walter, 46, 68
Umberg, Johann Baptist, 82, 140
Vielhauer, Philipp, 197, 238–39
Wach, Joachim, 86, 146
Weber, Max, 85, 146
Weber, Otto, 227
Westermann, Claus, 82, 144–46, 237
Wilckens, Ulrich, 82, 155–56, 175–76, 199–200, 209–12, 239
Wilder, Amos N., 146
Wilken, Robert L., 156, 231, 239
Windelband, Wilhelm, 85, 146
Windisch, Hans, 93, 146
Wirsching, Johannes, 177, 205–8, 239
Wolf, Ernst, 159, 227
Wolff, Hans Walter, 82, 146
Wood, James D., 75, 146
Zimmerli, Walter, 82, 146, 159, 181–92, 195, 198, 239–40

Index of Scripture

OLD TESTAMENT

Genesis

Genesis	73

Exodus

3	191
3:6	187
3:14	34
4:16	70
6:3	191
6:7	191

2 Samuel

7	196
12	196

1 Kings

20	184
20:13	187
20:28	184, 187
22:10–12	194

Psalms

97:2	186
97:6	186

Isaiah

6:3	186
22:14	185
40:5	186, 187
40:8	189
43:10	189
44:8	189
48:12	188
55:10–11	197
55:11	190

Ezekiel

17:24	185
20:48	185
25	189
29:6	185
36:23	185
36:36	185
37:28	185
39:7	185
39:23	185

Index of Scripture

APOCRYPHA

Sirach

47:17	70

4 Ezra

4:26–27	227

NEW TESTAMENT

Matthew

1–2	83
1:23	71
28:16–20	175

Mark

5:41	71
15:22	71
15:34	71

Luke

24:27	72
24:32	72
24:45	72

John

1:38	71
1:41	71
1:42	71
9:7	71
13:34	122
20:6–7	121
20:19–23	175

Acts

4:36	71
8:35	72
9:36	71
10:40–42	175
13:8	71
14:12	70

Romans

7:24	116
10:4	151

1 Corinthians

1:20	29
1:22	29
9:1	175
12:10	69
12:30	70
13:1	69
13:9f.	228
13:12	228
14:5	70
14:13	70
14:26	69
14:27	70
14:28	70
15	96

Galatians

1:15	175

Hebrews

7:2	71

1 John

4:16	122

Revelation

10:6	227

Gospel of Thomas

	176
3	72–73

Index of Key Foreign Words and Phrases

GREEK

ἀλήθεια (*alētheia*), 21–22
ἀποκαλύπτειν (*apokalyptein*), 185
διαπορθμευον (*diaporthmeuon*), 72
διερμήνευσεν (*diermēneusen*), 72
ἐξήγησις (*exēgēsis*), 72
ἑρμᾶς (*hermas*), 71
ἑρμηνεία (*hermēneia*), 69–85
ἑρμηνεύειν (*hermēneuein*), 43, 45, 69, 71–72, 77, 107–8
ἑρμηνεύον (*hermēneuon*), 70, 72
ἑρμηνεύς (*hermēneus*), 70–71
ἑρμηνευτική τέχνη (*hērmeneutikē technē*), 76
ἔσχατον (*eschaton*), 169, 218, 224
ἰδεῖν (*idein*), 22
θεός (*theos*), 122
Θεός ἐπιφανής (*Theos epiphanēs*), 223
λόγος (*logos*), 21, 107, 118, 122
παρουσία (*parousia*), 120, 212
πνεῦμα Χριστοῦ (*pneuma Christou*), 96
ῥῆμα (*rhēma*), 49
φύσις (*physis*), 21, 47

LATIN

adaequatio rei ad intellectum, 17
analogia entis, 32–33
analogia fidei, 33
analogia operationis, 33
analogia proportionalitatis, 35
analogia relationis, 33
applicatio, 127
ars critica, 75
ars interpretandi, 76
assensus, 201
asylum ignorantiae, 201
Christus praesens, 211
civitas dei, 152
civitas terrena, 152
corpus juris, 75
energeia, 21
eschatologia cruces, 226
essentia, 1, 47
existentia, 1
explicatio, 127
expositio, 72
factum, 225
fatum, 20, 106
fiducia, 201, 204
in malam partem, 9

interpretari, 69
interpretatio, 72
litera, 96
locutio, 112
natura, 21
notitia, 201
praeteritum, 128
promissio, 215, 230
Qui non intelligit res, non potest ex verbis sensum elicere, 136
res, 49
securitas, 228
sero, 71
sermo, 71
traditio, 128, 195
traditum, 128, 195
universum, 169
verbum, 71

GERMAN

Anwesen, 17, 120
aufheben, 19
Auge, 48
Aussage, 87, 118
bauen, 49
bedingt, 50
die Bedingten, 50
bestellen, 23
brauchen, 41, 109
Dasein, 5, 8–9, 11–16, 19, 27–28, 36, 40–41, 43–44, 59, 87, 101, 107, 110–11, 134
destruieren, 6
Destruktion, 6
Ding, 49
dingen, 49
Einlass, 120
Entmythologisierung, 101
Entschlossenheit, 11
entsprechen, 33
Entsprechung, 33
Ereignis, 48
Erklärung, 85
Erweiswort, 181
Formgeschichte, 194
Gattungsgeschichte, 80
Geläut, 40
Geschichte, 20, 47
geschichtlich, 21
Geschick, 20
geschicklich, 20
Gestell, 23
gewesen, 17
heil, 29
Heilsereignis, 119
Heilsgeschehen, 119, 194
Heilsgeschichte, 118–19, 150, 153–54, 158, 162–63, 169, 194, 230
herstellen, 23
Historie, 47, 158
historisch, 172
Kehre, 9
Lichtungsgeschichte, 20
retten, 50
Ruf, 40
Sache, 49, 137
Sachkritik, 95–98, 114
Sage, 40
schicken, 20
Schlussgeschichte, 96–97
schonen, 50
schwören, 71
Seiendes, 28
Seiendheit, 16, 48
Sprache, 137
Sprachereignis, 116, 119
Sprechen, 116
Sprechereignis, 116
stellen, 23
Traditionsgeschichte, 194
Überlieferungsgeschehen, 133, 194
übersetzen, 45

Umkehr, 9
unbedingt, 50
Unbedingten, 50
das Ungedachte, 19
Unheil, 29
Urgeschichte, 158
Verschlossenheit, 11
Verstehen, 85
vorstellen, 15
Vorstellung, 15, 23
Wesen, 17
wohnen, 49
Wortgeschehen, 119, 133
Zeige, 40
zerstören, 6
Zerstörung, 6
das Zu-Denkende, 20

www.ingramcontent.com/pod-product-compliance
Lightning Source LLC
Chambersburg PA
CBHW031727230426
43669CB00007B/268